# THE MAVERICK GUIDE TO BERLIN

**mav-er-ick (mav'er-ik),** *n* 1. an unbranded steer. Hence [colloq.] 2. a person not labeled as belonging to any one faction, group, etc. who acts independently. 3. one who moves in a different direction than the rest of the herd—often a nonconformist. 4. a person using individual judgment, even when it runs against majority opinion.

## The Maverick Guide Series

The Maverick Guide to Australia
The Maverick Guide to Bali and Java
The Maverick Guide to Barcelona
The Maverick Guide to Berlin
The Maverick Guide to the Great Barrier Reef
The Maverick Guide to Hawaii
The Maverick Guide to Hong Kong, Macau, and South China
The Maverick Guide to Malaysia and Singapore
The Maverick Guide to New Zealand
The Maverick Guide to Oman
The Maverick Guide to Prague
The Maverick Guide to Scotland
The Maverick Guide to Thailand
The Maverick Guide to Vietnam, Laos, and Cambodia

# MAVERICK GUIDE TO
# BERLIN

## Jay Brunhouse

## 2ND EDITION

PELICAN PUBLISHING COMPANY
GRETNA 1999

First edition, January 1993
Second edition, July 1999

ISBN: 1-56554-314-9

*Information in this guidebook is based on authoritative data available at the time of printing. Prices and hours of operation of businesses listed are subject to change without notice. Readers are asked to take this into account when consulting this guide.*

*The street maps are courtesy of the Berlin Information Center, the Museum Island drawing is courtesy of the Staatliche Museum Berlin, and the graphic maps of Berlin 2000 were provided by Theres Weisappel, Büro für Gestaltung. You can reach her at Bülowstraße 90, D-10783 Berlin (Tel. 030-261-21-85, Fax 030-262-80-17).*

Manufactured in the United States of America
Published by Pelican Publishing Company, Inc.
1000 Burmaster, Gretna, Louisiana 70053

# Contents

# List of Maps

# Preface: Ich bin ein Berliner

Welcome to new Berlin! President John F. Kennedy, in front of the Schöneberg town hall, said, "There are some who say communism is the wave of the future. Let them come to Berlin. All free men, wherever they may live, are citizens of Berlin, and, there, as a free man I take pride in the words 'Ich bin ein Berliner.'"

Come to Berlin and experience the neon of Ku'damm, the reawakened Mitte, a flourishing new metropolis. These are exciting times. Berlin is driven, and change is on the march. There's electricity in the air. Watch Berlin grow and take flower before your very eyes. But hurry, the drama is unfolding at breakneck speed.

Now that Berlin is unified and the new seat of the German government, the city is building. A new metropolis has moved to Europe's center stage. The new changes surprise you, but not to worry. All Berlin's glitter and history and blemishes remain, revealing to you an agonized succession of war, defeat, and regeneration. It is impossible to ignore the struggles and conflicts of capitalism, communism, fascism, militarism, and Prussian imperialism that formed what you see in Berlin. It is precisely the power to evoke mixed and very strong reactions that makes Berlin such a fascinating place. What you see is history. What you feel is the future. Experience and see for yourself this dynamic phoenix of new Berlin.

Rejuvenation is the meat of Berlin. Street names and traffic directions, telephone numbers, postal (zip) codes and postage stamps, bus numbers and routes, locations of office buildings and ministries—all have changed. Museum collections are unified. Berlin planners can't tell you what more to expect next week.

The Wall is not down. It is gone, evaporated. Visitors buy jagged, sledge-hammered fragments (but no one authenticates them) on souvenir stands placed where the Cold War was most cryogenic. Construction crews drive bulldozers and steamrollers over grassy fields where mines were planted. The sharp break that divided democracy and communism like a razor's edge where lives and deaths were decided has become a trivial red line painted on the earth. Peaceful growth prevails, but the missing Wall is more than ever valued now that it has lost its ominous and repressive meaning.

You might see the change in the DDR as a *revolution*. Berliners call it a *Wende*, a "turning." For the first time since the Second World War, Germany became a full-fledged sovereign country and Berlin became whole again. You no longer feel like an extra in a John le Carré film. New, independent Germany finds its heart and muscle in Berlin. Eighteen percent of Berlin was destroyed during the War, but you see the city assuming the seat of the German government and building once again toward becoming a ("the") metropolis for the 21st century. Berlin is like a patient recovering from a near-fatal wound. It is healing, and its recovery is astonishing.

It was extraordinarily difficult for Berliners to understand why, after the reunification of East and West Germany, there should have been suddenly any discussion at all in Bonn about moving the parliament to Berlin, because from 1949 to 1989, for 40 years, the politicians had said over and over, "Germany is one country; Berlin is our capital; and the Reichstag is our parliament." It took Chancellor Helmut Kohl, in 1991, to say that not only is Berlin Germany's historic capital and its constitutional capital, but its "natural" capital.

Berlin is Europe's most happening city. The hub of the continent's most powerful country, it is crawling with architects, developers, restaurateurs, and entrepreneurs. All came for a piece of the future. Berlin will be the European capital of the next millennium. Along the Spree River you see Germany's legislative branch being installed in the Reichstag, the judicial branch setting up across the green platz, and the president taking tea in his Bellevue Palace. Both sides of the river are becoming a promenade with offices and housing for bureaucrats. On foot, you will be able to walk along the Spree from Palace to Parliament.

Berlin is layered with tumultuous history: militarism, Nazism, Cold War. You see it all in Berlin. Yet Berliners are survivors. Between curses Berliners have built magnificent palaces, created architectural styles, given the world its Golden '20s, and maintained a caustic wit. Berlin does not hide the stark results of Prussian militarism, fascistic terror, failed communism, '20s debauchery, '90s Szene, and unbridled optimism as it stretches toward new health as a born-again metropolis.

Come to the neon of the Ku'damm. Come to the dynamic Mitte. Come to the reborn East. Come to see how Berliners pulled a bright rabbit from a beat-up hat. Come to see new Berlin striding into the next century. In Berlin you no longer see the big picture of East-West relationships. You see a reborn metropolis reaching eagerly for the coming century with unbounded optimism.

# Acknowledgments

The author wishes to thank for their kind cooperation Hedy Wuerz, Bernd Buhmann, and Hanns Herger of Berlin Tourismus, Helga Brenner-Khan of the German National Tourist Office, Burkhard Baese and Kevin Kennedy of the Potsdam Tourist Office, Horst Peter Schaeffer of the Berlin Information Center, and Jim Freeman of Lufthansa German Airlines. He is particularly grateful to Theres Weisappel, the creative artist who provided the delightful graphic maps of Berlin 2000.

He appreciates the help and encouragement of Ursula Heming-Berejiani, Tom Bross, Benson Leung, Jan Nijboer, Armond Noble, and Nathan Sawyer. Flowery bouquets to expert editor Nina Kooij.

# BERLIN

# Introduction: Naund

In many cities you are content to look, shop, and eat, but Berlin challenges your mind. It is a place you explore with your head. You can approach Berlin on a number of levels. First of all you want to see the historically exciting landmarks of the Athens of the Spree—the Prussian architects created masterpieces. You want to experience the excitement of the rebuilding of the capital of Germany and the growth of the metropolis. You want to enjoy the truly great museums, theater, the beautiful parks, lakes, and swimming places. You want to discover the power centers and scars of Nazism and Stalinism. Perhaps you want to enjoy the nightlife or immerse yourself in the alternative scene. You want to be at home with the Berliners.

Nothing is more Berlinerisch than their phrase *Naund*, meaning "yes, I know, so what?" Laid-back is not an adjective that you apply to Berliners. West Berliners especially run on short fuses. They are outgoing, casual, fast, analytical, sly, skeptical, funny, permissive, enlightened, and tolerant. It's hard to surprise a person who has seen everything. Berliners are open. They welcome visitors. Surveys show that Germans are more likely to speak foreign languages than citizens of any other European Community country except the Netherlands. You will probably never meet a Berliner who doesn't speak workable English.

Berliners are notoriously law-abiding. They stand for minutes waiting for red lights to turn green, even if there are no cars in sight. In Berlin you can distinguish residents from tourists because tourists cross intersections as soon as it is safe, while Berliners wait for the light. Karl Marx is said to have asked, "How can you have a revolution if you can't get people to walk on the grass?" Similarly: "How can you storm the railroad station when the crowd first lines up to buy platform tickets?"

The Berliners are aloof. They're the leaders of Germany. They're making a new Berlin. They're proud of it and they show it. There is always something going on in Berlin. Berliners are so involved there's always a good turnout for anything and everything. The people of Berlin like to be outdoors. In warm weather they like to sit in outdoor cafés and drink beer, they like to go to parks and lie in the sun and drink beer, they like to swim in their rivers, lakes, and swimming pools and drink beer—they are fresh-air people who don't like to be inside.

Berlin is not expensive by European standards. Prices are the lowest among the five largest German cities and far lower than you will find in many large European cities. Prices always include taxes and tips in hotels and restaurants. Berliners' big worry is inflation—prices in East and West Berlin are creeping up to the rest of Germany.

For its size, Berlin is remarkably clean. Every morning you see crews in orange overalls sweeping the streets. And beware of the water-squirting trucks which rumble along thoroughfares, showering roads' shoulders, gutters, and pedestrians.

Berlin is one of the safest cities in Europe due to the law-abiding attitude, a 24-hour party cycle that keeps people on the streets at all times (some of the worst traffic jams are after midnight), and a reassuring police presence which effectively controls the beer-guzzling drunkenness, notorious drug scene, transient population, open prostitution, and gnawing homelessness. Rarely, purses are snatched, pockets are picked, and rooms are broken into.

Newspapers refer to the five Eastern states as "new federal states," but Berliners still use the phrases "East" and "West" to define their city. Indeed, Berliners still think of themselves as "Ossis"—East Berliners, or "Wessis"—West Berliners. At the time of the Wende, you could easily distinguish an Ossi from a Wessi, not from his or her clothing only, but because of their manner of behavior. According to Berlin Schnauze, that special kind of humor, when one Ossi asked another, "Nice day, isn't it?" the second replied, "Why are you interrogating me?" No more. Ossis and Wessi are becoming unified not only politically, but mentally.

In the heads of 99.9 percent of Berliners, "East" and "West" still exist. Most Berliners don't understand how the change affected them. You see and hear this everywhere. There was just too long a division. Almost everyone you meet was born after West Berlin was politically separated from the East.

East German Trabant automobiles have become museum items. Tourists pose for photos beside those still running. There was enormous demand for Volkswagens immediately following the Wende. Too bad. You could always distinguish Trabis by their noise, which warned pedestrians and kept down the number of accidents. "Too many cars in the West; too many parking spaces in the East." There are now so many cars in both sections that in both East and West certain neighborhoods require local resident stickers for parking.

When West Berlin was an island, Wessis flocked to cafés on weekends because it was too far to ride into the green suburbs. It was easier for East Berliners to flock to the many forests and lakes in their green surroundings, so they used weekend houses they called by the Russian name "Dacha." It took only weeks before restaurant owners in the West were planning to open Eastern branches and Eastern entrepreneurs were scouting promising new sites.

Property speculation shook areas of Berlin and Potsdam ruthlessly. The Scheunenviertel just north of Alexanderplatz became a prime development area. Friedrichstraße became lined with glass-and-steel commercial developments. Prices in Prenzlauer Berg skyrocketed. Potsdam property attracted politicians, lobbyists, and show business personalities and became the most expensive in the former DDR. Even the symbol of unification, the Brandenburg Gate, was elbowed by new construction on Pariser Platz.

Berlin lies in the valley of the northern German lowlands. The average altitude is 111 feet (34 meters). Even in the city center, there are few skyscrapers. The word Berlin has nothing to do with the Berlin Bear. It comes from a Slovakian word meaning "Built on a Marsh." Berlin spreads across an enormous potable water reservoir, which makes it very expensive and difficult to build heavy skyscrapers.

Although the size of Berlin is deceptive because of its lack of tall buildings, it is so huge that residents fill their gas tanks in the morning and they are empty by evening. The city stretches from the Wannsee, the lake bordering Potsdam in the west, to the Müggelsee in the southeast near Schönefeld Airport. Berlin will hold Munich, Frankfurt, Stuttgart, and half of Cologne. Its surface area of 341 square miles (883 square kilometers) barely trails New York City's 368. The city borders stretch 145 miles (234 kilometers) and the scope of its dimensions quickly becomes evident on the freeway circling Berlin. It is the third largest city in Europe after London and Paris. Such size leads to fragmentation of lifestyles. The working adjective for Berlin is: "diverse." Over 3.4 million live in the metropolitan area. Greater Berlin was formed in 1920 by consolidating 8 cities, 59 rural communities, and 27 housing developments into 23 self-administered districts, and forms both a city and a federal state. The districts vary greatly in size and each has a character of its own. All have their own town hall, market squares, shopping streets, and service industries. Spandau and Köpenick even have identifiable village atmospheres. Beginning in 1999, the 23 districts will be consolidated, "fused," into 12 by the time of year 2000, so already the political jockeying by the incumbents is in full swing.

Because Berlin is so large, it is a city of neighborhoods. Within Berlin there are no Berliners. Berliners think of themselves as Charlottenburgers, Kreuzbergers, Rixdorfers, or are from Schöneberg or Rudow. Some are former villages that were amalgamated into Greater Berlin but still keep their own identities, (in the case of Köpenick) dialect, and standard of living. Wannsee identifies with elegant villas, Prenzlauer Berg, tenements; Schöneberg has apartment houses. . . .

Before the Second World War about 4.5 million lived in Berlin. After the war the number fell to 2.8 million. Now it is back up to 3.5 million, of which about 12 percent are foreigners (including 10,000 Americans). By comparison Frankfurt/Main has 23 percent foreigners and Munich, 16 percent. With the influx of the federal government, Berlin's population surely will soar. Berlin has the most marriages and also the highest divorce rate (8.2 percent) in Germany. It has not only two television towers but the highest west of Moscow. There are 166 museums, palaces, and gardens worth visiting. Berlin has the most hospitals (113), the largest parliament (241), the most universities (3), the most high schools (17), the most college students (140,000), the most museums (88) visited by the most people (8,500,000 a year), the most police officers (one in 168), open-air swimming pools (35) and enclosed pools (45), the largest street network (3,040 miles—4,896 kilometers), automobiles (1,200,000), buses (2,119), open-air movie screens (8) and public and private theaters (32). Berlin is the most popular German tourist destination and one of the most frequented European convention sites, with a total of over 10 million visitors a year.

In a few locations you can see preserved remnants of the Wall, which was 10 to 13 feet (3.5 to 4 meters) high and 99 miles (160 kilometers) long, but now they are just memorials, relics of history, and do not figure into the life of forward-looking Berlin.

Forests and lakes cover 24 percent of the city area. By all means go into the suburbs to see that Berlin is really a green city, but you don't even have to go that far. The enormous, lovingly beautiful Tiergarten is smack in city center. All over Berlin there are green spaces and parks. The reason for this is that West Berlin was for so many years an island in the Communist ocean and residents had to build up their own recreation areas in the inner city. That is why Berliners have planted three forests, 60 city parks, and the most trees of any city on the European continent. Berlin has the most street trees as well; each of Berlin's 93,376 registered dogs (in 1996) has three street trees for his own.

Two names keep recurring: Carl Friedrich von Schinkel (1781-1841) and Peter Josef Lenné (1789-1866). Schinkel was an architect and painter. Whether you like his architecture or not (most Berliners consider him a genius; some visitors say he was without originality), he was responsible for all the neoclassical buildings of Berlin that give the city its Prussian feel. Structures such as the Schauspielhaus (Playhouse), Neue Wache (New

Police Station), and Schloßbrücke (Palace Bridge, currently called Liebknecht Bridge) owe their style to Schinkel. Lenné, on the other hand, was a landscape architect, and played a major role in keeping Berlin green. His laying out of Charlottenburg's gardens, the Grunewald, the Tiergarten, Peacock Island, the Glienicke Landscape Gardens, and the Landwehr Canal make Berlin still a comfortable city with quiet corners to escape hubbub. His masterpiece was the Royal Gardens of Sanssouci in Potsdam.

**Historical High (and Low) Lights in Berlin.** More than any other world city, Berlin has been formed by historical events. Or, looking at it in another way, more than any other city, events in Berlin have formed world history.

A look at history helps understand the city that always is buffeted by and buffets the world:

**1227:** First notice of the merchant city of Cölln on trade routes flourishing on the left bank of the Spree River.

**1251:** First notice of Berlin as a city, under the protection of Askanians.

**1307:** The two competitive cities are unified with the name Berlin.

**1447:** The elector of Brandenburg makes his residence in Berlin.

**1618:** Beginning of the Thirty Years War.

**1640:** Friedrich Wilhelm, the Great Elector, takes office near the end of the Thirty Years War.

**1647-48:** The Lustgarten and a path through Linden trees are laid out.

**1685:** Friedrich Wilhelm, the Great Elector, with the Potsdam Edict, guarantees religious freedom and welcomes French Huguenots to Berlin.

**1688:** Friedrich Wilhelm dies in Potsdam. Friedrich III takes the throne.

**1695:** Friedrich III builds Charlottenburg Palace for his wife.

**1701:** Elector Friedrich III crowns himself king of Prussia and calls himself King Friedrich I.

**1710:** The Berlin toll wall is constructed with 14 gates.

**1713:** Friedrich I dies. His successor is Friedrich Wilhelm I, the "Soldier King."

**1740:** Friedrich II ("the Great") takes the throne; invades and annexes Silesia.

**1745:** Friedrich II begins construction of Sanssouci Palace in Potsdam.

**1756:** Beginning of the Seven-Year War.

**1786:** Friedrich II ("Old Fritz") dies in Sanssouci Palace. His nephew, Friedrich Wilhelm II, takes the throne.

**1793:** Second partition of Poland between Prussia and Russia.

**1797:** Friedrich Wilhelm II dies in the Marble Palace in Potsdam; his son, Friedrich Wilhelm III, succeeds to crown.

**1806:** Napoleon invades Berlin.

**1815:** Vienna Congress; German Federation founded.

**1840:** Friedrich Wilhelm IV inherits the throne.

**1857:** Wilhelm I comes to the throne.

**1862:** Otto von Bismarck becomes Prussian prime minister.

**1866:** War with Austria.

**1870:** War with France.

**1871:** Bismarck collects the various kingdoms, duchies, principalities, and Hanseatic states of "Germany" and puts them under Prussian rule. The newly elected Reichstag meets in Berlin, making it the capital city of the German Empire. Wilhelm I of Prussia is crowned kaiser.

**1888:** Wilhelm II becomes kaiser of Germany and king of Prussia.

**1914:** First World War begins with Germany's whirlwind invasion of France.

**1918:** The First World War concludes with Armistice. Kaiser Wilhelm II abdicates. November Revolution and fighting between Social Democrats and Spartacists leads to proclamation of the Weimar Republic.

**1920:** Greater Berlin is established incorporating 23 administrative units.

**1923:** Hyperinflation racks Germany.

**1925:** Friedrich Ebert dies; World War I hero Field Marshal von Hindenburg is elected president.

**1933:** Germany elects Hitler; Reichstag burns; Hitler abolishes democracy; Oranienburg becomes site of the first concentration camp in Berlin area.

**1936:** Jesse Owens captures four gold medals at XI Olympic games.

**1938:** "Reichskristallnacht"—Nazis burn and plunder Jewish properties (November 9). Germany annexes Austria.

**1939:** Outbreak of the Second World War with German invasion of Poland.

**1941:** German army invades Russia; United States enters Second World War.

**1944:** Stauffenberg assassination attempt on Hitler.

**1945:** Allied armies enter Berlin and divide it into four sectors.

**1948:** Soviet Union blockades West Berlin, leading to 11-month-long Berlin airlift.

**1949:** DDR established.

**1953:** German workers revolt unsuccessfully against Stalinist government of East Germany (June 17).

**1961:** DDR builds Berlin Wall, dividing Berlin into East and West (August 13).

**1963:** President John F. Kennedy visits Berlin.

**1989:** Hundreds of thousands of East Berliners flood through the Wall into West Berlin, where the entire city celebrates (November 9). The Brandenburg Gate is opened (December 22).

**1990:** Half a million Germans celebrate the New Year at the Wall (January 1). Free elections in East Berlin give the SPD majority. A treaty between East and West Germany takes effect uniting their economies; all border controls in Berlin are removed (July 1). The former DDR is incorporated as five states in the Federal Republic (October 3). The Wall is totally removed. All-German elections give 44 percent to the CDU, and 11 percent to its ally, the FDP (December 2).

**1991:** The German parliament votes to move to Berlin (June 20). Friedrich the Great is reburied in Potsdam. Brandenburg Gate's 200th anniversary is celebrated. Mayor of unified Berlin moves into Red City Hall.

**1994:** Berlin City Council moves into former Prussian Legislative building in Kreuzberg.

**1997:** Federal chancellor opens Berlin office in Communist building.

**1998:** New German parliament is elected. Berlin voters favor the SPD, as does Germany nationwide (September).

**1998, December:** Workers complete remodeling of Reichstag building.

**1999, April 19:** Parliament celebrates its first session in Berlin and meets for the first time in its new plenary room.

**1999, May 23:** Parliament elects the new federal president in the new Reichstag building.

**1999, July & August:** Federal employees relocate to Berlin from Bonn.

**1999, mid-September:** Legislators begin regular sessions in the Reichstag building.

**2000, April:** Dorotheen-/Alsenblöcke offices open.

**2001:** Fusion of Berlin's 23 districts into 12.

**2001, May:** Workers complete construction of Luisenblock with library and archives.

**2001, summer:** Remaining federal employees relocate to Berlin from Bonn.

**2002, January 1:** Introduction of the new European currency, the Euro, completed.

# 1

# How to Get the Best from Berlin: Practical Tips

## Before You Leave

**German National Tourist Office.** The offices of the German National Tourist Office in the U.S. and Canada are your first source of information for Berlin. As soon as you think of traveling to Berlin, be sure to contact the office nearest you. Ask them for their packet of Berlin information together with information on your special interests. You will receive the current copy of the excellent *Berlin Magazine* which contains important basic information, a city map, and various interesting stories in English. Be sure to ask for a separate city map. They cost DM 1 in Berlin. Even when you travel beyond Berlin—to Potsdam—contact the German National Tourist Office.

German National Tourist Offices are located at 122 East 42 Street, 52nd Floor, New York, NY 10168-0072 (Tel. 212-661-7200, Fax 212-661-7174); 11766 Wilshire Blvd., Suite 750, Los Angeles, CA 90025 (Tel. 310-575-9799, Fax 310-575-1565); 175 Bloor St. East, North Tower, Suite 604, Toronto, Ont. M4W 3R8 (Tel. 416-968-1570, Fax 416-968-1986); and Nightingale House, 65 Curzon St., London W1Y 8NE (Tel. 495-00-81, Fax 495-61-29).

**Berlin Tourismus** is the marketing organization for Berlin. They publish *Berlin Magazine*, a Berlin city map; a hotel list; Berlin pur (hotel and special offers); a travel agent sales manual; plus information for bus tour operators and conference planners. With telephone prices so reasonable you can telephone Berlin Tourismus Marketing's **BMT Hotline** directly at (030) 25-00-25. From the U.S., don't forget to start with "011" for international access, then "49" for Germany, and drop the zero—and don't forget the time difference. They can book you the best-priced hotel accommodations, get tickets for your evening at the theater, and reveal the shortcuts into and through the capital.

There are many Berlin sites on the web. A good place for browsers to begin is *www.berlin.de/en/index.htm*.

Free **Railpass** information is available from DER Travel Services, 9501 W. Devon Street, Rosemont, IL 60018-4832 (Tel. 800-782-2424, Fax 800-282-7474, *http://www.dertravel.com*), and Rail Europe, 500 Mamaronech Avenue, Suite 314, Harrison, NY 10528 (Tel. 800-4-EURAIL, Fax 800-432-1329, *http://www.raileurope.com*). Ask for their free price/information brochure and InterCity Timetable.

**Visas, Passports, and Inoculations.** Americans, Canadians, New Zealanders, and Australians staying less than 90 days require only a valid passport to enter Germany. A visitor's card will suffice for British citizens. No visa or inoculations are required unless you are coming from an infected area. It usually takes about three to four weeks to obtain a U.S. passport. First-time U.S. passport applicants require 1) proof of citizenship, 2) two passport photographs, 3) proof of identity, 4) a fee of $60 ($55 when you apply by mail) for a ten-year passport for those over 16; $40 for a five-year passport for those under 16, and 5) an application form, which may be obtained from a passport agency, a post office, or a courthouse. Passport renewals cost $40.

**Youth Hostel Card.** The German Youth Hostel Association is a member of the International Youth Hostel Federation, of which American Youth Hostels (HI-AYH) is the American representative. You will need an AYH membership card to stay in German youth hostels. To join AYH, it's easiest to telephone 202-783-6161 with your Visa, MasterCard, or Discover. It's good to allow 10 to 14 mailing days for delivery. Express delivery is available for $7. You can also get memberships for other people. You just need to supply each individual's name, permanent U.S. address, daytime phone, and date of birth. By Internet, access *http://www.hiayh.org* and download the membership application. By fax, call 202-783-6161 and have a printed application mailed to you so you can fax it with a credit card number to 202-783-6171. You can order your membership by mail, but allow an extra 7 days. Mail your application form with a check to P. O. Box 37613, Washington, DC 20013 (Attn: Membership Department). In a hurry or don't want to use a credit card, purchase your membership at any of 500 sales agents around the country. To find the nearest location telephone 202-783-6161 or e-mail *hiayhserve@hiayh.org* (mention your city and state). Membership costs $10 for those under 18, $25 for adults, $35 for families, and $15 for those over 54 (credit cards accepted). AYH membership is valid worldwide.

Youth hostels in Berlin can be reserved up to six months in advance. Access *http://www.jugendherberge.de/reserv.html.*

**Driver's License.** You must carry a valid driver's license from your country of origin to drive in Berlin. International Driver's Licenses are not required.

**Passport Photos.** When you think you will need passport-sized photos for any reason, e.g., a student public transportation card, you can buy them from a machine in Berlin (four photos for DM 6). Compare this price with what you would pay before you leave.

## Getting There

### BY AIR

Until 1990, scheduled civil airline flights to Berlin from the West were restricted to Pan Am, Air France, and British Airways. Now you have a whole host of carriers from which to choose. With Tegel, Schönefeld, and Tempelhof airports, Berlin has three airports with a total annual capacity of 12.5 million passengers. They are administered by a joint holding company of Berlin and Brandenburg. More than 10 million passengers were processed in 1994 and 20 million are expected by the year 2000.

The first airport in Berlin was Tempelhof, but then came the Berlin Blockade (see Chapter 10), and a larger airport, Tegel, had to be built. Four bulldozers and 19,000 Berliners, 40 percent of them women, worked round the clock for 30 cents an hour plus a hot meal every shift. In just three months, they made Tegel Airport operational.

With the construction of the Wall, the East had to have its own airport, so Schönefeld was built. After the unification, Berlin has three airports: Tegel is used primarily for traffic from the West, Schönefeld primarily for traffic from the East, and Tempelhof for shorter range aircraft tolerating a shorter landing runway. With the expansion of Schönefeld Airport into Berlin-Brandenburg International Airport (BBI), it has been promised that Tempelhof will close, but Tempelhof lingers like perfume.

You want to arrive in Berlin as well rested and as economically as possible.

Airline fares are crazy, so you should search out bargains when they happen to be offered. Check the small advertisements in the major Sunday newspaper travel sections for the cheap fares offered by consolidators, the so-called bucket shops. Summer is the most expensive time to fly, but discounts begin to appear in the fall and last—off and on—until spring.

The ideal flight to Berlin is a nonstop flight, but unless you live in the New York area, you won't have that option. Code sharing between airlines, particularly between Lufthansa and United Airlines, makes it easier than ever for you to reach Berlin. Only Delta, which assumed Pan Am's preferred routings, and Lufthansa offer nonstop flights to Berlin—from New York/Kennedy, only. If you happen to live in the New York area you are in luck. All others have a stop or change of planes, somewhere, either in North America or Europe.

Lufthansa also has connecting flights to Berlin from all of its U.S. gateways via Frankfurt, Düsseldorf, or Munich. Because of this carrier's code-sharing agreement with United Airlines, when you check in at the United counter in your hometown, you receive also a boarding pass to your connecting Lufthansa flight(s). Similar arrangements exist between Northwest Airlines and KLM and other code-sharing airlines.

There are few international carriers that don't serve Berlin from their domestic hubs, but always check to see that the same terminal of the European airline's hub airport (London, Paris, Amsterdam, etc.) handles both your incoming flight and your departing flight for Berlin so you won't have to scurry long distances to connect.

**Phone numbers in the U.S.:** Listed below are the toll-free telephone numbers for the carriers serving Berlin Tegel Airport with connections from the U.S. SAS serves Tempelhof Airport.

| Air France | 1-800-237-2747 | (via Paris/CDG) |
| Alitalia | 1-800-223-5730 | (via Milan) |
| British Airways | 1-800-247-9297 | (via London) |
| Delta | 1-800-241-4141 | (via New York) |
| Finnair | 1-800-950-5000 | (via Helsinki) |
| Iberia | 1-800-772-4642 | (via Madrid) |
| KLM | 1-800-364-7747 | (via Amsterdam) |
| Lufthansa | 1-800-645-3880 | (see above) |
| SAS | 1-800-221-2350 | (via Copenhagen) |
| Swissair | 1-800-221-4750 | (via Zürich) |
| TAP Air Portugal | 1-800-221-7370 | (via Lisbon) |

Also serving Tegel airport are Aero Lloyd, Austrian Airlines, and Turkish Airlines.

**Tegel Airport.** Tegel Airport is not a mega-airport like Frankfurt's. It is constructed like a hexagonal doughnut with parking and taxi service in the middle. International pictographs are used (the same as in the train stations) so finding your way around is not difficult. On a good sunny weekend, people wait in line to watch airplanes taking off and landing from the viewing platform on top.

The Airport Service Center (open daily 5 A.M. to 10:30 P.M.) near gate "0," many bookstores, a barbershop, Berliner Bank tellers, Tel. 417-85-40 (open Mon.-Sat. 6 A.M. to 10 P.M., Sun. to 9 P.M.), and a first-aid office are located on the ground floor in the arrivals/departures areas. An ATM machine (*Geldautomat*) is located near gate 4; the processing for your duty-free refund takes place nearest gate 7 (you must do this before checking in for your flight). Also on the main floor is the Papillon Café (open 7 A.M. to 11 P.M.), which is the name of the cafeteria between gates 4 and 5. The less-expensive Libelle snack bar between gates 10 and 11 opens at 5:15 A.M. The beautiful, spacious Otto Lilienthal Restaurant offers views and eye-catching patisseries, cakes, and confections. On the third floor, you can snack at the Take Off Café.

Up the steps to the mezzanine level overlooking the ground floor, you find the first- and business class lounges of the many airlines, a post office (open Mon.-Fri. 7 A.M. to 9 P.M., Sat.-Sun. 8 A.M. to 8 P.M.). You can buy stamps for collections or use the stamp machines. They have a complete set of German telephone books.

**Schönefeld Airport.** While Tegel Airport is right near the center of Berlin, Schönefeld Airport, opened on October 6, 1960, with a 2.1-mile (3.8 kilometers) runway, is so far in the outskirts that it adds another unwanted leg to your long journey. Luckily, few travelers from the West will have occasion to use it, unless after visiting Berlin they continue to the East.

A list of airlines serving Schönefeld Airport includes Aeroflot (from Moscow), El Al (from Tel Aviv), Japan Airlines (from Tokyo via Frankfurt), and Singapore Airlines (from Singapore via Zürich) as well as most Balkan and Arabian airlines.

Schönefeld is served by GermanRail's regional "Airport Express" line RB24 train which will carry you with few stops to the center of Berlin— Ostbahnhof, Friedrichstraße, Alexanderplatz, and Zoo train stations. S-Bahn trains (see below) serve additional stops along the way and therefore take longer. Tickets for both regional and S-Bahn trains are sold at the airport. Rail passes are valid on both. Alternately, you may take bus 171 from the airport to U-Bhf Rudow to join the U-Bahn network—and this will be your fastest way to the southern part of Berlin, Kreuzberg, and Tempelhof. Your Berlin Transit Authority bus ticket will also put you aboard Berlin's U-Bahn system.

**Tempelhof Airport.** Tempelhof's shorter runways support only smaller aircraft, yet Tempelhof boasts service by Air France (from Paris), Crossair (from Switzerland), Luxair (from Luxembourg), Sabena (from Brussels) and SAS (from Copenhagen), plus many lesser-known and start-up European carriers.

**Airport Hotels.**

The **Novotel Berlin Airport** (Kurt-Schumacher-Damm 202, Tel. 4-10-60, Fax 41-06-700), across from the highway entrance to Tegel, is Berlin's airport hotel. Shuttle between airport and hotel free of charge. It is not especially close to the airport, but then downtown Berlin is not far either. US$102, single; US$120, double; breakfast buffet included.

**Hotel Carat** (Ollenhauerstraße 111, Tel. 41-09-70, Fax 41-09-74-44). Ten minutes from Tegel Airport by city-highway connection A111. US$67-125, single; US$83-172, double; breakfast buffet included.

**Hotel Econtel Airport Tegel** (Gotthardstraße 96, Tel. 49-88-40, Fax 49-88-4-555). Business-class hotel opened in 1995 close to airport. US$103-35, single; US$125-60, double; breakfast buffet included.

**Airport Transportation.**

*From Tegel:* Taxis are readily available outside your gate and prices to the center of Berlin compare favorably with charges at larger airports because Berlin's center is not far, but Tegel is one of the few international airports where city buses are actually convenient. You can take advantage of this service. Taxis will cost about DM 17 plus luggage surcharge from Tegel Airport to Bahnhof Zoo while a bus will cost adults DM 3.90 or less if you buy a day or multi-day card (see "Banking and Changing Money" section later in this chapter). It is quite convenient to use these city buses: Lines X9, 109, and 128.

Bus line X9 is an express route to Budapester Straße making stops only at Jakob-Kaiser-Platz (for line U7), Jungfernheide (for lines S45 and S46), and Zoo train station (for S-Bahn, long-distance trains, and lines U2 and U9).

Most visitors will use bus line 109: U-Bhf Jakob-Kaiser-Platz, S-Bhf Charlottenburg, U-Bhf Adenauerplatz, U-Bhf Kurfürstendamm, and Bahnhof Zoo. Buses on Line 109 make stops every few blocks, but Tegel is not far from Berlin's center, about 25 minutes, depending on traffic, and the buses are convenient to ride. They are usually single-deckers. Most people have luggage, but there is space, and the bus in not overwhelmed with luggage.

Bus line 128 gives an alternate way to join Berlin's far-reaching public transportation network via lines U6, U8, and U9 (see "How to Get Around" section later in this chapter). Boarding line U6 at U-Bhf Kurt-Schumacher-Platz may not be acceptable to those with heavy luggage because there is no escalator or elevator at U-Bhf Kurt-Schumacher-Platz—just two flights of stairs. Bus 128 then continues to U-Bhf Residenzstraße for line U8 and U-Bhf Osloer Straße for U8 and U9.

To buy your ticket for the airport bus use the orange automatic ticketing machine **Fahrausweise** by the bus stops. One-way fare is DM 3.90 for adults; DM 2.60 for ages 6 through 14, up to three children free. You won't yet be ready for a day pass (see below), but you may want to buy a seven-day pass (see below).

When your destination is the Zoo train station, and you are traveling with luggage, it is easiest just to board bus X9 or 109 and remain aboard until you arrive in front of the Zoo train station.

Along the way, however, there are certain stops where it is convenient for you to disembark and change to the U-Bahn system, especially at rush hour when your bus is standing bumper to bumper in traffic—but this involves schlepping your luggage. Your bus ticket is also valid for up to two hours on the S- and U-Bahn networks.

Jakob-Kaiser-Platz is your best place to change to the West Berlin U-Bahn system via Line 7 west to Spandau or southeast to Charlottenburg, Schöneberg, Kreuzberg, and Rudow.

When you make hotel reservations, at the Service Center in Tegel or before you leave home, ask for exact directions to your hotel by public transportation.

In reverse, going to the airport, you don't have to go to Zoo train station to board bus line X9 or 109, but you can use U-Bhf Jakob-Kaiser-Platz (line U7), Jungfernheide (U7), U-Bhf Kurt-Schumacher-Platz (U6), U-Bhf Residenzstraße (U8), or U-Bhf Osloer Straße (U8 and U9).

*From Schönefeld:* East Berlin's Schönefeld Airport lies so far from the core of Berlin and the hotels that a taxi ride becomes prohibitively expensive, but GermanRail's 1998 "Airport Express" regional trains take you easily to East Berlin's Ostbahnhof, Alexanderplatz, and Friedrichstraße train stations, and West Berlin's Zoo train station. Trains operate every 30 minutes between 4:30 A.M. and 11 P.M. You only require a DM 3.90 ticket. S-Bahn trains along the same line give you more stations to disembark, but of course take longer (see "How to Get Around").

When you arrive by air at Schönefeld, a shuttle bus takes you the 1,000 feet (300 meters) to the train station in about five minutes.

The Schönefeld train station is very large, with both S-Bahn and mainline connections built together. Ramps provide an easy way to cart luggage with wheels, but there is no escalator. A flower shop and fast-food fish snack outlet can be found here. The transverse hall is wide and very clean. For departures, the airplane profile leads from the bus via ramp or steps, with the sign "Zum Flughafen." Across the tracks you can see the sign

"Bahnhof Flughafen Berlin Schönefeld." You can use your S-Bahn ticket on the bus as well. Mainline trains to Dresden, Prague, Hamburg, and Vienna call in the mainline station. The S-Bahn line S9 takes you towards Westkreuz with stops at Ostbahnhof, Alexanderplatz, Friedrichstraße, and Zoo. Line S45 is an easy way to Jungferheide, Schöneberg, Bundesplatz (for U9), and the ICC Convention Center. Regional Express and Regional Bahn trains supplement the services to outlying villages. Buses and night buses complete the picture.

*From Tempelhof:* The airport closest to the center of town, you would think Tempelhof Airport would have the best connections. Wrong. There are bus services, to be sure (lines 104, 119, 184, and 341) that pull right up to the swinging doors to the airport, but the closest U-Bahn station (Platz der Luftbrücke, line U6) is a long walk with heavy luggage.

## BY TRAIN

Germany's Deutsche Bahn (DB) is the combination of the former Deutsche Bundesbahn (DB) of West Germany and Deutsche Reichsbahn (DR) of the East. The lines to Berlin were unified with astonishing speed and enormous outlays of money. InterCity Express (ICE), InterCity (IC), EuroCity (EC), and InterRegio (IR) trains take you to Berlin.

First- and second-generation ICE trains alternate departures every hour. The first generation ICE trains connect with the mainline ICE network via the new high-speed route to Hannover and continue to Munich via Frankfurt (Main). The second-generation trains continue from Hannover to Hamm, where they divide into two halves. One half carries you to Düsseldorf and the second to Bonn and Cologne (Köln) where you can connect with Thalys trains to Brussels and Paris. In addition there are daily departures of ICE trains to Hamburg and Dresden.

To price riding on top-of-the-line ICE trains, DB introduced a so-called "Loco-Price" concept whereby passengers' fares take into account the commercial benefits of the time saved in addition to distance traveled. As a rule of thumb, ICE fares are 10-20 percent higher than IC fares over the same route. These point-to-point prices do not affect railpass holders, who do not pay surcharges.

Reservations are not required on German trains, but if you desire, it is easy to make reservations in Germany (and you save money by not making them from the U.S.). DB charges a reservation fee of DM 3 to travelers who show their rail pass. You pay the same when you buy a ticket and reserve at the same time, but DM 9 if you buy a ticket and then come back later for a reservation.

GermanRail accepts Visa credit cards in 155 major train stations and waiters in BordRestaurants accept MasterCard (Eurocard), Visa, Diners Club, and traveler's checks in U.S. dollars, German Marks, and English pounds sterling.

**Arriving from the West.** Between Berlin and Hannover you ride DB's newest high-speed line. Leaving Hannover's Hauptbahnhof, your ICE first travels 48 miles to Wolfsburg over merely upgraded line. Leaving urban Hannover at Hannover Berliner Allee, your ICE reaches 100 mph over the ten-mile stretch to the outskirts of Lehrte. From Lehrte through Gifhorn to the outskirts of Wolfsburg, you peak at 124 mph. At last you enter the flat, 98-mile stretch across marshy country about 180 feet above sea level. You feel the acceleration as your ICE bursts to 155 mph.

Both ICE1 and second-generation ICE2 have the same white and red-striped livery and the same distinctive semi-continuous line of reflecting windows. Except that the ICE2 is shorter, the only obvious difference you see is that the new generation's front headlights rise much higher.

Now look closely at the train's front "bumper." Under some nose doors you can detect automatic couplers. These are what make ICE2 special. The new trains are designed so that two ICE2 "half-trains," each consisting of six carriages plus driving carriage, can split or combine to serve multiple destinations as GermanRail's new flexible timetable requires.

Past Rathenow be sure to take note of the expensive, high earthen embankments squeezing your line through a particularly marshy area. This marks the habitat of a colony of some 30 or so great bustards, one of the rarest birds in Europe.

You complete your trip in one hour, 45 minutes, which is considerably better than the four hours that former InterCity trains required with stops along the way.

In addition to ICE2 trains from Cologne via Hannover, you can ride ICE1 trains originating in Munich and boarding throughout western Germany. For the first time on June 2, 1991, travelers rode GermanRail's first-generation ICE trains in regular high-speed service on new track between Munich and Hamburg. These high-speed ICE trains made their first runnings to Berlin on May 23, 1993. They lock you into the integrated ICE network in West Germany, allowing you to reach Berlin from any city of size in Germany, Switzerland, or Austria in record time.

Following the tragedy of June, 1998, the 720 carriages of the ICE1 fleet were refitted with 2,880 new wheels. Experts pronounce them safe at any (high) speed.

By making the ICE slightly wider than conventional trains, GermanRail allowed travelers to ride more comfortably. Instead of 111.2 inches, the

width of GermanRail's early '90s InterCity carriages, GermanRail made
the ICE1 118.9 inches wide. A dining car with an atrium was introduced.
Ironically, this widening and lengthening subjected GermanRail to great
criticism within Germany when the German public realized that their
expensive ($30 million each) new domestic ICE1s were just that: domestic.
The 1996, second-generation ICE trains are shorter and lighter, but
remain wide and limited to domestic electrical supplies. When DB needs
high capacity, it couples two ICE2s, which are like half ICE1s, together with
their automatic coupler but separates the two halves quickly when called
for and sends them to different destinations.

ICE2's first assignment was to connect Berlin with Cologne. DB took a
full hour off the Hannover-Berlin transit time using ICE trains over the
high-speed line opened September 27, 1998.

Train tickets issued in Germany and destination signboards to Berlin
normally show the destination as "Berlin Stadtbahn." Don't try to find a
station of this name. Stadtbahn means "City Railroad," a fact that causes
some confusion among first-time visitors. Berlin Stadtbahn covers a number
of stations and such a ticket is valid to any of them—and connections by
S-Bahn if necessary.

After almost four years of reconstruction slowed to a snail's pace by the
need to defuse previously undiscovered bombs, rebuild unsuspectedly rotting
rail bridges, and endure catastrophic winters, in 1998 DB opened a rebuilt
length of the elevated route right through Berlin's heart (the so-called
Stadtbahn, or "city railroad,") for the use of mainline trains between East
and West Berlin. The new terminus for all of DB's high-speed ICE trains
became the Ostbahnhof which assumed its new name on the very day of the
opening of the rebuilt Stadtbahn. In addition to ICE trains, most InterCity
(IC) and InterRegio (IR) trains from West, North, and South Germany take
you to Ostbahnhof in East Berlin after discharging passengers at Bahnhof
Zoo in West Berlin. Trains from the opposite direction—from Warsaw,
Dresden, Prague, Cottbus, Budapest, and Görlitz—stop first at the Ostbahnhof before proceeding to Bahnhof Zoo. You can alight or board just
as easily in either half of the city. Bahnhof Zoo and Ostbahnhof now are
equally convenient and important, depending on which half of the city you
wish to visit.

Using locomotives built in Newcastle, England, the first railroad company
in Berlin opened its line to Potsdam, in 1838, from Berlin's first terminal,
the Potsdamer Bahnhof, along a route landscaped by Lenné. Until 1877
each new railroad company entering Berlin built its separate terminus. In
1882, the kaiser ordered 11 stations connected by an east-west line across
the city center on a still-standing, elevated brick viaduct and this is what we

know as the Stadtbahn today. From west to east, these stations were Charlottenburg, Savignyplatz, Zoologischer Garten, Tiergarten, Bellevue, Lehrter, Friedrichstraße, Borse (renamed Marx-Engels-Platz and now Hackescher Markt), Alexanderplatz, Jannowitzbrücke, and Ostbahnhof (which has had five names in 156 years, depending on which way the political winds were blowing).

**Arriving from Elsewhere.** Trains from the West make their first stops at Spandau and Zoo train stations but then continue to Ostbahnhof, the Eastern mainline station. Trains from the East—Poland—stop first at Ostbahnhof before terminating at Zoo. Ostbahnhof was substantially enlarged and rebuilt at the time of the joining of East and West Germany together. The timing was only coincidental. Naturally, the combined DB had to make further remodeling improvements. In 1998, when DB began using Ostbahnhof for mainline trains, only cosmetic changes had to be performed. There is no tourist office or post office, but Ostbahnhof has a Reisecentrum train information office, shops, fast food, and on the mezzanine a Reisebank (open 7 A.M. to 10 P.M., Mon.-Fri., 7 A.M. to 6 P.M. [to 8 P.M. during July and August] on Sat., and 8 A.M. to 4 P.M. [7 A.M. to 8 P.M. during July and August] on Sun.). The bank's ATM on the ground floor operates 24 hours.

Also on the mezzanine you will find the office of the **Historical S-Bahn Club**, Tel./Fax 29-72-02-46 (open Tue.-Thur. 5 P.M. to 8 P.M., and on the third Saturday, 10 A.M. to 2:30 P.M.). Next door is a bookstore specializing in German-language railfan books operated by the **German Railfan Club** ("Deutscher Bahnkunde-Verband" [DBV]).

Lichtenberg train station is a regional train station in the eastern part of the city. Lichtenberg's brick station building with a glass front has been enlarged. Near the front entrance you see the **Reisecentrum** ("Train Information") (open daily 5:15 A.M. to 11 P.M.). You can make all reservations and buy tickets. Train departures are printed on yellow posters; arrivals on white.

Upstairs you find a McDonald's restaurant (open 5 A.M. to 1 A.M.) and a Bistro Restaurant. The McDonald's is routine. The Bistro is dark and gloomy. No one is eating, just drinking beer and wine.

Shops selling take-away provisions are on the lower (train) level. Between the platforms and the station hall there is a ramp which makes it easy to pull luggage to and from trains. From Lichtenberg you will have to change to one of the frequent S-Bahn trains on platform A to reach the center or western part of Berlin. The U-Bahn line also runs to Alexanderplatz but makes many stops throughout the eastern part of Berlin. Your train ticket marked Berlin Stadtbahn is valid on the S-Bahn. There is an escalator up to S-Bahn platform A. Platforms A, B, and C are all open without covering, probably from damage during the War.

**Train Ticketing.** DB maintains ticketing offices in all mainline and regional stations such as Zoo, Friedrichstraße, Alexanderplatz, Lichtenberg, and Ostbahnhof.

For normal train trips when you are under 26, **Wasteels Reisen** (Pestalozzistraße 106, Tel. 312-4061) is the place to head. They sell young people round-trip and one-way tickets from Berlin to more than 100 destinations in West Germany and 4,000 destinations in Europe and North Africa at rock-bottom prices. Round-trip tickets are valid for two months while one-way tickets are valid for four days. You can make as many stopovers en route as you please within the time limits. Sample price: Berlin to Dresden, DM 19.

**Rail Passes.** No reservations are required in Germany, so with a rail pass, you need only board your train.

It's more convenient to buy Eurailpasses, Europasses, and GermanRail Passes from your travel agent at home before your departure. You have three months (not six) to begin using them. If you change your mind and want to buy one in Berlin, go to the **Bahnzentrum** in Bahnhof Zoo, Tel. 297-49-348, Fax 297-49-161 (open daily 5:15 A.M. to 11 P.M.).

Prices for these passes in Berlin are set at 10 percent above the list price you pay to your travel agent at home, and the dollar equivalent price is pegged, so that the price you pay in Marks will vary depending on the fluctuation of the dollar versus the Mark, but the dollar amount will always be 10 percent more than you would have paid at home.

*Eurailpasses:* These popular rail passes are valid for unlimited travel throughout Germany as well as in 16 other European countries (not Poland). When you travel extensively throughout Europe by train, they will save you time standing in lines to buy tickets. Bonuses include free steamer crossings north via Sassnitz to Trelleborg, Sweden (departing from Lichtenberg station), without going through Copenhagen, the Rhine River Cruise, and Europabuses along the scenic Romantic Road and Castle Highway routes.

First-class Eurailpasses are available for 15 and 21 consecutive days, one, two, and three consecutive months. A discounted, first-class Eurail Saverpass covers two or more traveling together and is available for the same durations.

Eurail Flexipasses cover any 10 days of travel, or any 15 days of travel of your choice within two months. Saver Flexipasses are the same, but less expensive for two people traveling together.

Travelers under 26 can travel on second-class Eurail Youthpasses for 15 or 21 days, one, two, or three months, or a Youth Flexipass for either 10 or 15 days of choice within two months.

*Europasses:* These best-selling rail passes are valid for unlimited travel in first-class throughout Germany as well as four other European countries (Italy, France, Switzerland, and Spain) with the option of purchasing two additional zones. An advantage of a Europass is that you purchase either five, six, eight, 10 or 15 days you plan to use it during any two-month period. Youthpasses are available for second-class travel for those under 26 on their first date of travel. A Europass Special discounted pass is available for two to five persons traveling together. Bonuses are the same as for Eurailpasses (above).

*GermanRail Flexipasses:* These are better buys than Eurailpasses or Europasses when you plan to do all your train travel solely in Germany. They are sold not only for first-class travel, but you can save money buying them for second class and for those under 26 as well. The discounted pass for two traveling together is called a Twinpass. Individual, Twin, and Youth passes are sold for your choice of exact number of days between five and ten days of travel within a month. Bonuses are the same as for Eurailpass and Europass, except that the ferry crossing to Sweden is excluded.

**GermanRail BahnCard**. In Germany you can buy a GermanRail BahnCard valid for half-fare travel on all regularly scheduled GermanRail trains throughout Germany. It is highly recommended and will pay for itself for those staying for extended periods and doing considerable train travel in Germany. It is valid for one year from date of validation.

The **BahnCard Classic**, costing about $133, is for persons aged 23-59. A first-class ("BahnCard First") card costs double. It will pay for itself in two round trips between Berlin and Hamburg or Berlin and Frankfurt.

There are six pricing variations for the basic BahnCard. BahnCards cost half for those over 60, for juniors aged 18-22, and for spouses of basic Bahn-Card holders. Teens (12-17) and children (4-11) pay about $33 and double for BahnCards First. In addition there is a family card.

In 1995 BahnCard also became, for those who asked for it, the "DB Citibank Visa BahnCard" which serves also as a Visa credit card with no Citibank service charge. Visitors who don't want a full Visa credit card can still buy the previous rail-only BahnCard or a DB Citibank Electron debit BahnCard which only allows the use of Visa ATMs.

Anyone under 23 and students under 27 can buy in Germany a "Tramper" ticket for 10 days of unlimited second-class travel in Germany within a month, but the period of use is limited to June 15 to October 15.

**Overnight Trains**. The new generation of high-tech, high-convenience, tilting, and double-decked sleeper trains provides you pampered service or even economic seats to Berlin. CityNightLine and InterCity Night trains are fresh air coming from the West. These trains have nudged aside the familiar, older generation of overnight trains that still carry seemingly endless strings of sit-up carriages, sleeping cars, sleeperettes, and couchettes between Berlin and Eastern Europe. Russian trains from Berlin to Moscow, Kiev, and St. Petersburg consist of Russian sleeping carriages.

The new overnight trains travel along the most appealing business routes, but they provide space for budget travelers using railpasses in new sleeperette seats and innovative couchette bunks costing $20-$36.

GermanRail's **InterCity Night (ICN)** trains are excellent.They actually consist of Spanish tilting carriages painted in GermanRail's InterCity Night blue livery with GermanRail embellishments. The trains tilt rounding curves and include a lavish dining room for first-class passengers and a Bistro for those less affluent.

In addition to carriages which contain deluxe sleeping compartments, you can ride in second-class carriages fitted with 1996-designed couchettes or a GermanRail first: sleeperette seats which recline deeply—the equivalent of business class in air travel. Caterers provide food service from a trolley. The luggage car also carries bicycles for a nominal charge.

ICN's first-class, air-conditioned cabins contain their own private shower, wash basin and toilet. You can book them either as a single or a double. The beds are aligned in the direction of travel. The compartments are locked by key cards. The trains are opened two hours before departure and need not be vacated until 8:30 A.M.

ICNs are your best choice for overnight travel between Berlin's Lichtenberg station and Munich Hauptbahnhof and between Berlin and Dortmund, Essen, Dusseldorf, Cologne, or Bonn. Railpasses holders pay less than half for cabins. You pay the equivalent of $3 for a sleeperette seat or couchette when you make your reservation in Germany.

Ride the **CityNightLine** train named "Berlin" between Berlin's Zoo station and Zürich, Switzerland. CityNightLine gives you three choices, all with breakfast included. When you choose "Luxury" category "A," you ride on the upper deck so that the additional panoramic windows expose the skyline; also, you have one or two wide beds, plus your own stall shower and private WC.

First-class railpass holders receive a discount of about one-third for the "A" accommodation. When you choose lower-cost, "Comfort" category "B" compartments, you have one or two beds, one above the other, and a wash basin. Stewards can connect two "B2" cabins together for four-person, family travel ("B4"). Railpass (including second-class, Eurail Youthpass) holders pay slightly over half.

Budget category "C" passengers sleep in reclining, giant-sized seats designed to give you a feeling of seclusion by incorporating a canopy containing a personal reading lamp. Deposit your backpack and luggage in the storage space above you or between the seats. Your small continental breakfast is served you on the fold-down table at your seat. Railpass holders, first or second class, pay $20, which is about 20 percent of the normal fare.

Until midnight, you can party in CityNightLine's "Thousand-Stars Bar" or you can dine in the small, white-tablecloth restaurant area of the lounge car.

## BY CAR

The corridors formerly required for driving to Berlin are no longer applicable. You can reach Berlin by any route you choose, but be aware of possible delays caused by the roadwork required to bring East German highways up to international standards.

## BY BUS

German long-distance coach drivers don't like their coaches to be called "buses." It's a matter of status with them. We'll call them "buses." Regular, usually daily, buses run between Berlin and more than 200 German and West European destinations. Operated by **Berlin Linien Bus** ("Berlin Lines"), they are equipped with reclining seats for sleeping, WC, wardrobe, attendant, and catering service. The bus fares are slightly cheaper than rail prices and there are reductions for passengers between 4 and 26 years and those over 60. Tickets can be purchased at all DER travel agencies, many other travel agents, and at the bus station in Berlin.

Deutsche Touring is Germany's participant in the Europabus system. Deutsche Touring's Europabuses leave Berlin for such destinations as Bosnia and Herzegovina, Bulgaria, Estonia, Greece, etc.

Buses depart and arrive at the **Zentral Omnibus Bahnhof (ZOB)** ("Central Bus Station"), located across from the broadcasting tower (see Chapter 5). The station has ticketing, waiting rooms, and for arrivals, a hotel reservations console similar to the one located in the Zoo train station except that here you speak to the hotel's reservations office through a speaker flush in the console and thus have to pay no telephone toll. The Hotel Ibis is directly adjacent. Use bus 104 or 149 to Messedamm stop.

## RIDE SHARING

In Berlin you may take advantage of a ride-sharing scheme coordinated by **Mitfahrzentrale** ("Ride-sharing Central") not only to and from other cities in Germany, but throughout Europe. Drivers and riders are put together by their offices, which are located in many U-Bahn stations throughout the city. When you have located a ride, you pay a fee to the Mitfahrzentrale and share the fuel costs with the driver (tell the agent at Mitfahrzentrale how much you can afford). Offices are generally open daily 8 A.M. to 9 P.M., Sun. 10 A.M. to 6 P.M., and have their own telephone numbers but Mitfahrzentrale Sputnik (riders Tel. 859-10-51; drivers Tel. 859-10-78) is mostly arranged by telephone.

Drop into U-Bhf Innsbruckerplatz (Schöneberg), U-Bhf Alexanderplatz (Mitte), U-Bhf Leopoldplatz (Genter Str. 7), U-Bhf Adenauerplatz (Sybelstraße 53), U-Bhf Rathaus Neukölln (Boddinstraße 3), U-Bhf Görlitzer Bhf (Manteuffelstraße 81), U-Bhf Yorckstraße (Yorckstraße 52), U-Bhf Hakenfelde (Spandau), Klausener Platz (Charlottenburg), U-Bhf Bismarckstraße (Charlottenburg), S-Bhf Savignyplatz, U-Bhf Walter-Schreiber-Platz (Friedenau), U-Bhf Leinestraße (Neukölln), U-Bhf Mehringdamm (Kreuzberg), U-Bhf Kottbusser Tor (Kreuzberg), U-Bhf Turmstraße (Moabit), or U-Bhf Pankstraße (Wedding), U-Bhf Zoo, Tel. 19-400 (open Mon.-Fri. 9 A.M. to 8 P.M., Sat.-Sun. 10 A.M. to 6 P.M.).

**Zweite Hand** maintains a telephonic *MitfahrBox*, which is a pay service. You dial according to your direction of travel. For questions on how it works and how much it costs, Tel. 53-43-28-37.

## HITCHHIKING

Hitchhiking in Germany is subject to all the same cautions as elsewhere.

## Berlin Information

You can hardly find anyone throughout the downtown area without a city map or at least a subway map.

**Berlin Tourist Office.** The agents in the offices of the Berlin Tourist Office operated by Berlin Tourismus GmbH are available to answer questions, provide all sorts of information and brochures, and most conveniently, make your hotel reservations for a DM 5 service charge. They are located in the Europa Center, Entrance Budapester Straße 45, Ground Floor (open Mon.-Sat. 8 A.M. to 10 P.M., Sundays 9 A.M. to 9 P.M.), and beside the Brandenburg Gate (open daily 9:30 A.M. to 6 P.M.), but no hotel reservations there.

Additional information points include the Dresdner Bank at Unter den Linden 17 (open Mon.-Fri. 8:30 A.M. to 2 P.M., plus 3:30 to 6 P.M. on Tue. and Thur.) and the Reisecenter ("Travel Center") on the ground floor of the KaDeWe department store on Wittenburgplatz (open Mon.-Fri. 8:30 A.M. to 8 P.M., Sat. 9 A.M. to 4 P.M.).

Directly on arrival, you can visit the **Airport Service Center** near gate "0" at Tegel Airport (open daily 5 A.M. to 10:30 P.M.). For hotel reservations they will charge you DM 5, but they will also check your luggage for you.

**Public Transportation Information.** For city transportation information, access *www.bvg.de* or drop by the compact **BVG kiosk on Hardenbergplatz** in front of Zoo station (open 8 A.M. to 10 P.M.). Personnel there are good at answering your how? and how much? questions and give you free public transportation maps as well as sell you tickets. The larger BVG customer service office at the top of the escalator at U-Bhf Turmstraße has a good selection of free and for-sale brochures, and you get to sit down. The S-Bahn Berlin GmbH company operates separate service centers in the Zoo, Friedrichstraße and Ostbahnhof train stations (open daily 9 A.M. to 6 P.M.).

**Euraide**, an American-run operation, has a neat office facing the post office in the rear of Zoo train station. Not only will ex-pats book your reservations and issue you train tickets in colloquial English, they will give you free information on getting where you want to go by train in Germany and guide you through the rail pass jungle (German Railpass, Eurailpass, Europass, and InterRailpass). Further they will help you with low-cost accommodations in Berlin and steer you onto the right *Berlin Walks* tours in English. They are open daily during the summer 8 A.M. to noon and 1 to 6 P.M. Check *http://www.euraide.com.*

**Airline Information.** Airlines no longer provide passengers with printed Berlin information. The main Berlin offices of the trans-Atlantic airlines serving Berlin Tegel are as given below:

| | | |
|---|---|---|
| Air France | Tegel Airport | Tel. 2-64-74-40 |
| Alitalia | Tauentzienstr. 16 | Tel. 21-01-81 |
| Austrian Airlines | Tauentzienstr. 16 | Tel. 2-18-50-24 |
| British Airways | Europa Center | Tel. 69-10-21 |
| Delta | Europa Center | Tel. 230-9400 |
| Finnair | Kurfürstendamm 209 | Tel. 885-41-31 |
| Iberia | Kurfürstendamm 207 | Tel. 882-74-77 |
| KLM | Tegel Airport | Tel. 4101-38-44 |
| Lufthansa | Kurfürstendamm 220 | Tel. 88-75-88 |
| SAS | Tempelhof Airport | Tel. 6951-2491-93 |
| Swissair | Tegel Airport | Tel. 4101-2615/16 |
| TAP Air Portugal | Europa Center | Tel. 261-16-87 |

**Women's Information.** The **Fraueninfothek Berlin**, Leibnitzstraße 57 (near Kurfürstendamm), Tel. 324-50-78 (open Tue.-Fri., 10 A.M. to 8 P.M.;

Sat. to 6 P.M.), provides free information for the visitor to orient herself and discover Berlin from a woman's perspective. They make hotel reservations, recommend counseling centers sensitive to women's issues, sponsor city bus tours, and organize exhibitions. **City Maps.** Simple maps of the city center appear in many brochures. The Berlin Tourist Offices (see above) sell one for only DM 1, but to find your way in the suburbs or even smaller streets in the city center you will need to buy a comprehensive map. There are at least three makers of Berlin maps. The most popular one is the Falk Berlin map with patented folds only an origami master can unravel. There are also maps from Rand McNally/Hallweg, and ADAC, the German Automobile Club.

## When to Visit

**Good Times.** The summer months of July and August are low season in Berlin because of a lag in business activity. It is an opportune time for a vacation traveler to come. December and January are also low season. Festivals and events with a special flavor can add to your enjoying Berlin. Some emphasize music, art, and theater in order to attract visitors interested in those events. Obtain details before you leave from the German National Tourist Office. The magazine *Berlin* showcases upcoming events. In Berlin visit the Tourist Offices and check the Berlin city magazines such as *Tip* and *Zitty*.

The Love Parade breaks the sound barrier around mid-July. The Berlin International Film Festival begins about the middle of February, the Berlin Drama Festival is in the first half of May, the Youth Drama Festival is in the last half of May, Bach Days occur on or around the first of July, Berlin Festival Weeks are in September, the JazzFest is in the second week of November, and the Festival of Young Authors is in late November. The **Weihnachtsmarkt** ("Christmas Market"), when the streets around Breitscheidplatz at the foot of the Memorial Church are closed to auto traffic (and there is virtually no parking space), begins on the first Sunday of December. Simultaneously in the East, the Lustgarten turns into a Santa's Toyland (open Mon.-Thur. noon to 8 P.M.; Fri.-Sun. 11 A.M. to 9 P.M.).

**Bad Times.** It is best to avoid visiting Berlin during major congresses (conventions), when hotels are packed tighter with delegates than sardine cans with little fish. Overloading occurs during the International Tourism Market at the beginning of March and the International Consumer Electronics Exhibition at the end of August/beginning of September during odd years (1999 and 2001). During the Berlin Marathon (end of September), hotels are almost completely sold out.

**Public Holidays.** Expect everything (except museums) to be closed on New Year's Day, Good Friday, Easter Monday, May Day (May 1), Ascension Day, Day of German Unity (June 17), Day of Prayer and National Repentance (third Wednesday in October), Christmas Eve, Christmas Day, and December 26.

**Climate.** One doesn't go to Berlin for the climate. Summers can be hotter than Cairo or there may be no summer at all. The warm days are splendid—outdoor cafés are packed until very late at night and the whole city seems intent on getting a suntan that will last the year. Winters seem never to end and fall comes earlier than you want. Summer features infrequent lightning and thundershowers but winter slugs you with frequent snow storms, bitter cold, and an inversion which brings polluted air from the south. Spring is always sweet with the renewal of the earth's cycle and fall can be grand with mists and changing colors, but summer's low-humidity, warm weather (July is the best month) and its long daylight hours lets you fully savor the excitement of Berlin.

|       | Avg. Temp. |       | Avg. Precipitation |          |
|-------|------------|-------|--------------------|----------|
| Jan.  | 29 F       | -1 C  | 2.2 in.            | 5.6 cm.  |
| Feb.  | 32 F       | 0 C   | 1.6 in.            | 4.1 cm.  |
| Mar.  | 41 F       | 4 C   | 1.2 in.            | 3.0 cm.  |
| Apr.  | 48 F       | 9 C   | 1.6 in.            | 4.1 cm.  |
| May   | 59 F       | 15 C  | 2.3 in.            | 5.8 cm.  |
| June  | 65 F       | 18 C  | 2.9 in.            | 7.4 cm.  |
| July  | 69 F       | 20 C  | 3.2 in.            | 8.1 cm.  |
| Aug.  | 68 F       | 20 C  | 2.7 in.            | 6.9 cm.  |
| Sept. | 60 F       | 16 C  | 2.2 in.            | 5.6 cm.  |
| Oct.  | 50 F       | 10 C  | 1.6 in.            | 4.1 cm.  |
| Nov.  | 40 F       | 4 C   | 2.4 in.            | 6.1 cm.  |
| Dec.  | 32 F       | 0 C   | 1.9 in.            | 4.8 cm.  |

These are averages. Temperatures can fluctuate widely from day to day.

## Where to Stay

Finding a place to stay in Berlin after you arrive is not difficult. There are locations that will help you make a reservation. If you arrive by air, use the transit authority's Service Center at Tegel Airport (open 5 A.M. to 10:30 P.M.). They charge a service fee of DM 5 to book a hotel. In addition they will check your luggage for DM 5.50 a day.

When you arrive by train at the Zoo train station, there is a console located on the mezzanine level that advertises mostly reasonably priced hotels, gives their locations, rates, telephone numbers and, by means of a red/green light signal, indicates their availability. A coin-operated telephone is located in the console (20 Pfennig minimum). Also on the mezzanine level is a private hotel reservations bureau that will book you a hotel for DM 5. Most reliably, a short walk of five minutes brings you to the tourist office a few blocks away in the Europa Center (open Mon.-Sat. 8 A.M. to 11 P.M., Sun. 9 A.M. to 9 P.M.). Tourist Office agents charge you DM 5 to find a place for you by telephone and to make your reservation. You pay the rest to the hotel or pension. The agent gives you a simple map to help you find the hotel he or she has located for you.

When you arrive by train at the Ostbahnhof, on the main floor you find a console similar to the one at Zoo station. Many of the hotels shown are in West Berlin. There is no tourist office nearby to help you.

**Hotels.** The crop of hotels in Berlin is among the best in Europe. Because Berlin is a business destination, hotels have more free space on weekends and often offer discounts Fridays to Mondays. You can find hotels to suit your every taste and budget. You will probably prefer to stay near the Kurfürstendamm in West Berlin where there is currently a hotel boom or near the historic section of the East. Your travel agent can book in advance most of the big hotels. The big names have toll-free numbers for you to use with their associated properties. These are indicated in this text. Prices quoted are from Berlin Tourismus' **1998/99 Hotels und Pensionen** converted at DM 1.8 per U.S. dollar, but you can usually beat them by shopping for discounts. Hotel prices quoted in dollars change daily according to the ever-fluctuating dollar/Mark exchange rate. To find today's dollar price you must multiply the dollar price quoted in this guide by the fraction $5x/9$, where x is the mark/dollar rate given in the financial pages of your local newspaper. You can expect yearly increases to account for inflation.

Smaller hotels and pensions can't afford the expense of an international reservations system—and many don't need it because of a high occupancy rate. From North America you can write them well in advance. Because of the steadily decreasing international telephone rates, it can be worth your while to telephone them directly.

First-time visitors should know that a few tricks are in order for using the showers in Berlin. Most showers use hose-squirters, which can cause great anxiety to those unfamiliar with them. The secret of not flooding the bathroom is to sacrifice modesty and go against nature. To avoid irrigating the room behind you, stand facing out of the bathtub. Also, pull up/out the chromium shower plunger *before* you turn on the water so that you don't have water pressure working against you.

Lovely bedding comforters called *Decke* are commonly used instead of blankets. During the summer you must crumple, billow, and fold them to keep at a comfortable temperature.

**Pensions.** The pension system is alive and in full flower in Berlin. Considerably less expensive than hotels, pensions offer convenient accommodations. They are usually small blocks of rooms located on the higher floors (with elevator) of a remodeled flat. They are run by families or, traditionally, an older lady. Because the doors are locked at night, guests keep their own keys and come and go as they please. Inferior pensions have iffy plumbing, often with facilities down the hall, stuffy ventilation, etc. Good ones are just as good as hotel facilities.

It is difficult to book pensions from North America because such small properties cannot afford an international booking system—and well-located ones are usually full, anyway, with walk-ins. You do best asking for one at the Tourist Office when you arrive.

**Rooms and Apartments.** Finding private rooms and apartments for longer stays during the summer is less difficult than you would expect, more because many Berliners going on long vacations are reluctant to leave their valued apartments vacant and inviting to burglars than for the money involved.

**Mitwohnzentrale** is similar to a rental agency. Its offices keep files of available apartments and rooms. Typically you explain your requirements to an agent who will connect you by telephone for you to speak personally with your potential landlord or lady. Mitwohnzentrale's cut is high, typically one percent of the yearly rental per month. This means that if you select an apartment renting for DM 500 per month (DM 6,000 per year), they take DM 60 per month, a hefty cut, which you pay directly to Mitwohnzentrale as soon as you sign a rental contract. New listings are usually placed in an office window for you to check from outside.

Their offices include **Erste Mitwohnzentrale**, Sybelstraße 53, Tel. 324-3031 (open Mon.-Fri. 10 A.M. to 8 P.M.; Sat.-Sun. 10 A.M. to 4 P.M.), **Agentur Wohnsitz**, Holsteinische Str. 55 (Wilmersdorf), Tel. 881-82-22, Fax 861-82-72 (open Mon.-Fri. 11 A.M. to 8 P.M.; Sat.-Sun. 11 A.M. to 2 P.M., use U-Bhf Blissestraße); **Mitwohnzentrale**, Yorckstraße 52 (Kreuzberg), Tel. 184-30, Fax 216-9401.

**ABC Agency**, Rheinsberger Straße 78, Tel. 44-37-67-0, Fax 44-37-67-49, *http://www.abc-hotelagentur.de*, arranges apartments and hotels for individual visitors and businesses in all sizes and price categories.

**Youth Hostels.** Hostels are inexpensive dormitory-style accommodations for travelers of all ages. They provide separate facilities for males and females, fully equipped self-service kitchens, dining areas, and common rooms for relaxing and socializing.

The **Deutsches Jugendherbergwerk (DJH)** ("German Youth Hostel Association"), Bismarckstraße 8, Postfach 1455, 32704 Detmold, Germany,

Tel. (05231) 9936-0, Fax (05231) 9936-66), has 15 regional associations and more than 750 hostels in Germany. Singles and small groups use three houses of the DJHin Berlin. For reservations contact **Zentralreservierung für Jugendherbergen** ("Central Reservations for Youth Hostels"), Tel. 262-30-24, Fax 262-95-29, or access *http://www.jugendherberge.de/reserv.html.*

**Youth Hostel "Ernst Reuter,"** (111 beds, 4-6 person rooms, DM 26/night) Helmsdorfer Damm 48-50 (Tel. 404-1610, Fax 404-59-72), is situated in the northern Berlin district of Reinickendorf a short walk from Lake Tegel where you may board a ship to start an interesting sightseeing tour of Berlin from the waterside. Use U-Bhf Alt-Tegel, S-Bhf Tegel or bus 125 to "Jugendherberge" stop, directly in front of the hostel.

**Youth Hostel Berlin**, (364 beds, 4-6 person rooms, family rooms, DM 32/night) Kluckstraße 3, Berlin (Tel. 261-1098, Fax 265-0383), is located in the center of Berlin near the Cultural Forum (see Chapter 6) in the Tiergarten district. Use U-Bhf Kurfürstenstraße and then walk five minutes or change to bus 129 and get off at "Gedenkstätte" stop right in front of the youth hostel.

**Youth Hostel am Wannsee**, (264 beds, 4-person rooms, family rooms, DM 32/night) Badeweg 1, corner of Kronprinzessinnenweg (Tel. 803-2035, Fax 803-5908), is located in the southwest corner of Berlin right on the Greater Wannsee Lake. Although it is only a 20-minute S-Bahn trip to the city center, the Grunewald green areas start right at your front doorstep and Potsdam is within easy reach by bus or S-Bahn. Use S-Bhf Nikolassee, then walk 10 minutes.

**Jugendgästehaus am Zoo**, at Hardenbergstraße 9a (Tel. 3-12-94-10), is a short walk toward the Technical University (and its inexpensive Mensa (cafeteria) from your likely arrival point, Bahnhof Zoo.

**Jugendgästehaus Nordufer**, Nordufer 28 (Tel. 4-51-70-30).

**Jugendgästehaus Tegel**, Ciecowstraße 161 (Tel. 4-33-30-46). Don't confuse the city quarter with the airport of the same name.

**Die Fabrik Hostel** (Kreuzberg), Schlesische Straße 18 (Tel. 611-7116, Fax 618-2974).

**Camping.** Here is a selection of four camping sites of the **Deutscher Campingclub (DCC)** Gleisbergstraße 11, Tel. 218-60-71/72, Fax 213-44-16. Contact them for more information. All sites are equipped with sanitary facilities and stores. Arrive before 6 P.M. if possible. Before then preference is given to those under 27 and families. No overnights after 10 P.M.

**Campingplatz Kladow**, Krampnitzer Weg 111-17, Tel. 365-2797, Fax 365-12-45. (Open all year, 6 A.M. to 1 P.M., and 3 to 10 P.M.) This is probably the best, in Spandau, near the former Wall. To get there use U-Bhf Ruhleben, change to bus 135 to Krampnitzer Weg, and walk about a mile.

**Campingplatz Dreilinden**, Albrechts-Teerofen, Tel. 805-1201. (Open April 1 to Sept. 30, 6 A.M. to 1 P.M. and 3 to 6 P.M.) Close to the border in the southwest of the city, take a #118 bus (direction: Kohlhasenbrück) from U-Bhf Oskar-Helene-Heim. This site is one and a half miles from the nearest bus stop. Free showers and a small restaurant.

**Campingplatz Kohlhasenbrück**, Neue Kreisstraße 36, Tel. 805-17-37. (Open April 1 to Sept. 30, 7 A.M. to 1 P.M. and 3 to 9 P.M.)In Zehlendorf (see Chapter 10).

**Camping am Krossinsee**, Wernsdorfer Straße 45, Tel. 675-86-87, Fax 675-91-50. (Open all year, 6 A.M. to 1 P.M. and 3 to 10 P.M.) In Köpenick (see Chapter 12).

## How to Get Around

In practice, most visitors find it most convenient to use the U-Bahn/S-Bahn/bus/streetcar system to get around. Bicycles are great—they make the city seem smaller—but few visitors bring them with them or even bother to rent them. Walking is tough because of the long distances.

But first a caution: Berlin is one of the few cities you will find where street numbers run in a circle. They start with "one," increase (very slowly) up one side of the street, and then continue to increase coming back the opposite side. Number 26 might be across the street from number 390. Few streets keep the same name for long distances. It will make your way easier when you check the signs you find on the street corners giving the numbers of the addresses in that block.

## TAXIS

Taxis are the easiest and yet not an exorbitantly expensive way of getting around the city. Several taxi companies supply vehicles by telephone: **Funk-Taxi-Berlin** (Tel. 26-10-26), **Spree Funk** (Tel. 44-33-22) (Prenzlauer Berg), or **Berlin-Taxi** (Tel. 813-26-23). You can also hail taxis on the street or board them at taxi stands (which are marked by the letter *T* or the whole word *Taxi*).

According to Berlin Schnauze, all taxi drivers in the East are former Stasi (they wrote themselves licenses when they saw the end of the regime). The good thing about this is that you only have to give them your name and they already know your address.

## PUBLIC TRANSPORTATION

Public transportation began in Berlin in 1847, when on January 1, the *Concessionirte Berliner Omnibus-Compagnie* began its first service over five routes with 120 horses. In Berlin you are able to ride **U-Bahn** ("Subway"), **S-Bahn** ("Rapid Transit"), and regional trains of the German Railroads through and across Berlin. In the West, you find also single- and double-decker buses, and, in the East, also streetcars.

One of the first things unified after the Wende was the Berlin transportation network. The separate transportation systems of the East and the West were placed under a single administration and ticketing became valid on both.

Most of the subway stops now have escalators and many have elevators. Forty-four of the 168 U-Bahn stations and 43 of the 154 S-Bahn stations have elevators (which are mainly used by parents pushing baby buggies, but are a boon for older and handicapped travelers). Too many visitors tote heavy suitcases up flights of stairs because they don't take the time to look for the signs indicating escalators or elevators. Unfortunately, many U-Bahn stations were puzzles because of the jungle of direction signs. Due to the intensity of enthusiastic planners, when a U-Bahn train made a stop, a visitor sometimes saw such a multitude of signs giving so many exit, transit, and subway-transfer directions that a neophyte couldn't figure out exactly where he or she was. Even Berliners from the East got confused in the West and vice-versa. Modern stations consolidate this information on simple station signs—sometimes suspended over the platforms—giving the station names and direction arrows with the names of the street exits, nearby attractions, and S- and U-Bahn connections. Make it a habit to always look at these directions when you step off your train. The station name is always painted on the wall beside the tracks (when there is a wall). Names displayed on backlit plastic panels often give the line number and direction of the line served by station. There are usually local street maps in stations to help you find your way in the neighborhood. Look at the information ("i") bulletin board.

In the 1930s, the city-wide Berlin S-Bahn network was a world model, but it was severely torn apart by the War. The building of the Berlin Wall in 1961 sealed its fate as a crosstown transportation system. Separate East and West Transportation Authorities diverged as they tended to the separate regional transportation patterns of their riders.

Reacting to the Berlin Wall, West Berliners boycotted the S-Bahn in their part of the city because by four-power treaty it was run by the East German Railroads (DR). References to the S-Bahn were deleted from signs at U-Bahn stations and bus stops. Only 5 percent of West Berliners used it for transportation. It became an issue in the Berlin 1981 elections. On January 9, 1984, operation of the S-Bahn in the West was purchased by West Berlin transit authorities and the number of travelers tripled from 50,000 to 150,000 daily.

At the Wende there were 239 miles (385 kilometers) of trains. The S-Bahn was split into 45 miles (72 kilometers) in the West; 107 miles (173 kilometers) in the East. The U-Bahn stretched 71 miles (114 kilometers) in the West; 16 miles (26 kilometers) in the East. Before the Wende it was only possible to interchange at the Friedrichstraße train station. In 1996, 721,000 passengers a day used 13 S-Bahn lines running on 186 miles (300 kilometers) of track to 147 S-Bahn stations. By the end of 1998 visitors could use 161 S-Bahn stations.

Now you can get almost anywhere in Berlin by using their excellent Bahn and Bus system. The transportation authority, BVG, operates the largest public transportation system in Germany. Anyone who has mastered getting around London or Paris will have no trouble in Berlin. By referring to the charts posted in all U- and S-Bahn stations, pasted to the walls of the trains themselves, available free from the BVG kiosk in front of station Zoo, and included in dozens of kinds of advertising material, you can move seamlessly (except for marching up and down stairs) from one line to another.

There are nine U-Bahn lines. Some long lines are good. They have frequent long trains which run every three or four minutes. Other short lines have short trains that run less frequently.

The direction that the trains travel is always indicated by the name of the end station. For example, consider line U7. It runs from far western Rathaus Spandau to Rudow deep in the East. If you want to go to one of the end stations you simply board a U7 train in the direction highlighted or sign-posted in the U7 station. More likely you'll board at an intermediate stop and want to go to a second intermediate station. Just check the chart. Say you want to board at Berliner Straße station and go to Hermannplatz. Hermannplatz is in the direction of Rudow, so you race off aboard that train. Suppose instead you want to go to Wittenau. Checking the chart, you see that Wittenau is the northern terminus for line U8. Line U7 does not go there. Again you see on your chart that Hermannplatz station is an interchange between U7 and U8, so that when you get to Hermannplatz you follow the signs to the platform for the U8 trains to Wittenau.

Wait. Back to your chart. You see that Berliner Straße is an interchange for line U9 as well as U7. You can take line U9 in the direction of Osloer Straße. At end station Osloer Straße change to U8 (direction Wittenau) and arrive there probably faster than when you used U7 and U8.

All the U-Bahn lines put together form an interwoven fabric so that by changing from line to line at interchange stations you can get anywhere in Berlin. Superimposed on this is the S-Bahn system which adds another dimension. You can change from U-Bahn to S-Bahn with the same ticket, but getting from one place in Berlin to another takes more time than you expect. Berlin is big, but you can get to your destination with just one transfer from a U-Bahn train to an S-Bahn train and then to a bus or street-car. Still, it takes a lot of time.

There really is no significant difference between U-Bahn and S-Bahn systems except that you must realize that they are separate networks with separate stations even though your chart says they have the same name. Many locations, in fact, have both U- and S-Bahn stations. You may have to go outside and walk a modest distance to get from one to another, but some stations are served only by S-Bahn trains.

GermanRail's use of RE and RB trains (see below) extends the S-Bahn network using the same tracks.

Suppose you now want to travel from Hermannplatz to Wannsee to go swimming. Check your chart. You can do it two ways. Both require changing from a U-Bahn station to an S-Bahn station. You can make your change from line U2 at Charlottenburg or from line U8 at Alexanderplatz. Both require significant walks.

**Tickets and Passes.** Berlin's public transportation has an amazingly simple ticketing system. Buses, streetcars, U-Bahn, S-Bahn, and regional trains within Berlin all share the same tickets.

Tickets are checked so seldom on the U- and S-Bahn trains that you are almost on an honor system in Berlin. The penalty for riding without a ticket is DM 100, plus major hassling by guards and police.

You may buy your BVG tickets from agents at windows during the day when they are staffed, but it is more convenient to buy them from machines. To operate the machines, you first select the type of ticket you desire by pressing the indicated button. The fare required is then displayed. Drop the necessary coins into a slot or feed 10-, 20- or 50-Mark bills through the roller. Change is returned with your ticket.

Single-ride and seven-day tickets are always available from the blue machines at the entrances of all stations and bus stops, including those at the Tegel Airport. Day tickets are dispensed by some, but not all machines. The Welcome (three-day) Card is available at U- and S-Bahn ticket counters, tourist offices, the Service Office at Tegel Airport and many hotels. A single two-hour ticket (*Fahrschein*) is delivered already time-stamped. Insert all others for time-stamping into one of the orange automatic date/time/location validators at platform entrances.

Actually, Berlin is divided into three tariff zones: A, B, and C. In practice, you forget all this and buy a Day Card, a Welcome (three-day) Card, or a Seven-Day Ticket for zones AB. Rarely will you travel into zone C. The day cards are remarkably cheap compared to single tickets.

Zone A covers everything you probably want to see, and includes all of the main train stations. Zone B gets you to the two outer airports, Tegel and Schönefeld. You can get as far as Potsdam in zone C.

With any ticket, you can take, without extra charge, up to three children under seven years with you. Bicycles are allowed on U-Bahn trains from 9 A.M. to 2 P.M., after 5:30 P.M., and all day Saturdays, Sundays, and holidays. There is a fare for bicycles, but buyers of some of the multi-day cards below take their bicycles without additional charge.

A *Kurzstrecke* ("short-distance") is the cheapest and least useful ticket. It costs DM 2.50. It covers only three stations by U- or S-Bahn or six stops with a regular bus or streetcar. Express buses count the stops bypassed toward your total allowed. A *Langstrecke* ("long-distance") ticket costs DM 3.90. It is valid for up to two hours in two zones so that you can change trains or buses in any direction, even run an errand and return to your starting point. A *Ganzstrecke* ("network") ticket costs DM 4.20 and is valid for two hours in all three zones.

A *Tageskarte* ("Day Card") costing DM 7.80, valid until 3 A.M. the following day, is a bargain. With your three children you can also take along a bicycle, a baby buggy, and a dog. If you want to add a third zone, add DM 0.70.

The so-called *Berlin Potsdam WelcomeCard* is valid for 72 hours, covers all zones, three children, bicycle, baby buggy, happy pooch, and museum discounts and costs DM 29.

Included with your Welcome Card is a booklet allowing you sightseeing discounts (DM 5 off BBS, Berolina, BVB, Severin und Kühn, and Tempelhofer Reisen) (see "City Tours," below); discounts on guided tours of art:berlin, Kulturbüro Berlin, StattReisen Berlin, Berlin Walks, Exklusiv Tourismus in Potsdam, and Urania (Potsdam); boat trip discounts (25 percent off BWTS; Stern- und Kreisschiffahrt, Reederei Bruno Winkler, Havel Dampfschiffahrt, and Weiße Flotte; (see "River and Lake Steamers," below); 25 percent off Berlin by bike, City-Rad Potsdam, and the Velotaxis; half off almost all museums in Berlin and Potsdam; discounts on attractions such as the Botanical Garden, Butterfly House in the Britzer Garden, the Berlin Casino, the Spree Park, Zoos in the East and West, the Zeiss Planetarium, and the Babelsberg Studio Tour; you receive 25 percent off productions at Deutsche Oper, Deutsche Theater, Friedrichstadtpalast, House of Cultures of the World, Hebbel Theater, Konzerthaus am Gendarmenmarkt, Komische Oper, Maxim Gorki Theater, Renaissance Theater,

Schaubühne am Lehniner Platz, Staatsoper Unter den Linden, Theater am Kurfürstendamm and Komödie, Theater Tribüne, Theater des Westens, Vaganten Bühne, Volksbühne, Magic Theater Igor Jedlin, Hans Otto Theater, and Potsdamer Hofkonzerte; 30 percent off shows at the Berliner Ensemble, La vie en rose, and Wintergarden. A discount of 35 percent applies to the Brandenburgische Philharmonie.

Note that these discounts duplicate some of those granted by the Culture Card, so you may not want to have both cards at the same time.

Best transportation value of all is the *7-Tage-Karte* ("7-day ticket") valid up to midnight on the seventh calendar day. Loan it to your companion when you aren't using it. For zones AB or BC, it costs DM 40; for zones BC, DM 42. Adding a third zone ups its cost to DM 48.

A *Familienpaß*, introduced in 1999, allows both parents to take all their children to and from sporting and cultural evens for DM 10. Those visiting Berlin for extended periods can take advantage of a month- or year-*Umweltkarte* ("Environmental Ticket"), either standard or premium (so you can take your bicycle with you). Environmental tickets start at DM 99/month. Less expensive month- and year-*Schülertickets* and *Ausbildung-stickets* apply to those taking courses of study in Berlin or Brandenburg. Month- and year-*Seniorenkarten* apply to those over 65 with certification from German authorities. Take your passport and one passport photo to BVG-Kundenzentrum (open Mon.-Fri. 8 A.M. to 6 P.M., Sat. 7 A.M. to 2 P.M.), at the top of the escalator at U-Bhf Turmstraße. Those applying for student rates should also take their student I.D. The large, yellow BVG card is valid for six months, but each month you must affix a new stamp available from any ticket counter.

**S-Bahn.** The term S-Bahn used for Berlin's suburban electric railroad system is an abbreviation of *Schnellbahn*, and not of *Stadtbahn*. It's not true that all S-Bahn trains are old and rickety and run on square wheels. Some of those dating from 1927 might seem that way, but the 10-year-old ET480 and the beautiful 1998 ET481 trains coast into the stations with doors that open with a press of the button instead of having to tear them apart like Hercules breaking chains.

Berlin's "Great Electrification" program of 1928 brought the fastest and most modern local transportation to Berlin. On June 11, 1928, electric trains rolled over the Stadtbahn. Most lines were electrified by 1930, with 1,013 electric trains replacing the steam trains. Transit time between Ostbahnhof and Charlottenburg decreased from 31 minutes by steam to 22 minutes by electric S-Bahn in 1928. At the turn of the millennium, it is still 22 minutes. The badge was a white *S* on a green background in 1928. It is still used today. Further lines were electrified in 1933 and a north-south connection across the city, mainly in a tunnel, was completed in 1939. Several lines were interrupted by bombing raids in 1943, but most were repaired until the Red Army brought the system to a halt in April 1945. In order to keep the Soviets from using the tunnels, they were flooded.

**Regional trains.** DB provides regional train service as a supplement to the S-Bahn trains and take you into Berlin's suburbs. Five Regional Express (RE) lines run through Berlin's heart. Board these lines, in addition to Zoo and Ostbahnhof, at Alexanderplatz and Friedrichstraße stations which DB converted to regional train stations. A transportation ticket or pass covering zone C will cover the entire local network, although only zone B coverage is required to Potsdam. Regional train departure times from Zoo station are shown on the mechanical departures board in the main hall. Trains on RE lines 4 and 5 run to the outlying East Berlin airport of Schönefeld in only 31 minutes from Zoo. Understandably, DB calls these trains *AirportExpress* trains, but at the same time understands that travelers from the west usually arrive at Tegel Airport where buses take them the short distance into town.

You can reach 110 stations in the surrounding state of Brandenburg from the capital city without changing trains and without change you can travel all the way from Magdeburg to Cottbus via Berlin's stations. You will need separate tickets for those cities outside the Berlin metropolitan district.

**Regional Express** (RE) trains provide services up to 100 mph on trips averaging up to 31 miles at a minimum of two-hourly frequency. Look for the new, red double-decked RE trains. DB inherited a fleet of double-decked trains from the former East German Railroads (RB) when East German voters elected to merge with West Germany. They were the pride of the RB, but were downright uncomfortable to ride. Luckily they have been mostly replaced by DB's new, red, double-decked regional trains which are a pleasure to ride. Seating is comfortable. The air-conditioning purrs, there are pull-down sunscreens and so much head room in the upper deck that there is even room overhead for your luggage. On the lower deck, you can use the space provided for bicycles and baby carriages. It's a fine regional train and on Berlin's improved tracks, runs smooth as Schultheiß beer on tap.

**Regional Bahn** (RB) trains are locomotive hauled, but are shorter trains. They are slower and cost less to ride. They cover local services with an average length of 18.5 miles, speeds of up to 62 mph, and at least two-hourly frequency. They contain space for bicycles. Traveling in either a RE or RB train, although far short of riding in an ICE, is faster and more comfortable than traveling aboard an S-Bahn, but the trains call at far fewer stations.

**U-Bahn.** The Berlin U-Bahn network is one of the longest in the world.

The first lines were opened in 1902 and included an elevated line on viaduct now part of Line U1. The initial system was completed in 1930, and construction did not start again until 1953. Since then, several lines have been newly built or extended in West Berlin, and all of the lines in the West were modernized and therefore have been more efficient than the older S-Bahn lines. For visitors, the U-Bahn network in the West is centered on Zoo station, but you may change between U-Bahn trains at any of the many hubs throughout the city. Use the maps posted in the trains. In the East, Alexanderplatz and Friedrichstraße are often used for changing.

**Buses.** The transportation authority and almost no one else celebrated the 150th anniversary of buses in Berlin in 1997, not because the new double-decked, single-decked, and articulated ones aren't any good, because they are, but because Berliners take their far-reaching, on-time, and reliable bus network for granted. You can ride 157 bus lines stopping at 6,698 bus stops (one near you) over 2,350 miles (3,782 kilometers). West Berlin is one of the few places in the world outside the British Isles where a large number of the buses are double-decked. Bus lines were renumbered in 1991 from two to three digits to make them uniform throughout the city and eliminate duplication between East and West. Only night buses with the prefix "N" and express buses with the prefix "X" have fewer. Streetcars in the East hold to two digits.

Given the time, you see more while traveling by bus than U-Bahn, and in fact many routes save you time by not requiring you to make U-Bahn changes. Once you get to know where you are and where you are going, you can begin to use the Berlin bus system to your best advantage. On glassed-in bus-stop walls and in most U-Bahn stations you find large Berlin maps showing the bus routes. Once you get used to this back-up network, you will prefer using it for selected trips.

Bus stops are marked by a green *H* (for *Haltestelle*) on a yellow background. The newer ones have vertical, plastic picket signs with each of the regularly scheduled and night buses indicated. Older ones have attached metal tags with green numbers on yellow indicating regularly scheduled buses.The tan-on-orange As, Bs, and Cs indicate the tariff zone of the stop. A useful feature is that precise departure times for each route are posted at every stop, and are generally observed. Buses keep closely to the posted timetables. The timetables also list the names of the stops the buses serve to help you determine which line to take. Those stops are usually so well indicated that you can generally read their names from inside the bus.

The buses themselves are outstanding. The comfortable Mannesman double-deckers are rarely so full that you can't sit in front upstairs and watch Berlin unfold before you. You enter the front and pay the driver if you don't already have a valid, already validated ticket. The front steps to the upper level can be considered "up only," and rear steps, "down only." There is no standing allowed upstairs.

The 1997 Mannesman double-deckers have *three* side doors with the stairs in the far back. This makes it convenient for those holding tickets to enter the back doors while those needing to buy tickets from the driver are forming a line at the front door. However, after 8 P.M. the driver locks the back doors and snarls at anyone trying to use them. You must enter the front door. Bummer.

**Streetcars.** Streetcars fill out the transportation network in the East the same way that buses do in the West. They are an effective way of getting to places located between S- and U-Bahn stations. They are very much a force in East Berlin where you can ride 26 lines over 217 miles (361 kilometers). In May 1998, the Berlin Transport Authority retired the last of the original streetcars that the communist East German government had purchased in 1976 for use in East Berlin. The driver on the final ceremony was the same now-veteran driver that had piloted the streetcar's inaugural run in 1976. These articulated vehicles were built by Tatra in Czechoslovakia and are referred to as the *Tatra-Bahnen*. In May 1997, the last of the 663 *alte Dame* ("old lady") Tatra-Bahnen that were built subsequent to 1976 (until 1991) were overhauled to make the yellow "Oldies" more comfortable, safer, and quieter. Workers equipped them with new seats, leaf doors, and electronic safety devices. The Czech-built streetcars run with lightning speed and great efficiency past the cars on the now auto-clogged boulevards of East Berlin and connect where necessary with West Berlin's double-decked bus network.

Electric streetcar history began in Berlin in 1879 when Dr. Werner von Siemens introduced the first electric streetcar at a trade show. The world's first electric streetcar went into service in Berlin on May 16, 1881. The line, about 1.2 miles (2 kilometers) long, ran from today's Lichterfelde-Ost station to the Kadettenanstalt. The 26 passengers (14 standing and 12 sitting) in the 16.4-foot (5 meters) by 6.6-foot (2 meters) streetcar sped through the city streets at 12 mph (20 km/hr). After 1896 electrification gradually replaced horses and the last horse-drawn streetcar was withdrawn on December 14, 1902. Streetcar traffic in West Berlin expired on October 2, 1967, when Line 55 ran for the last time to Zoo station. In the East, well-maintained and clean electric streetcars continued racing down the median strips getting you from Prenzlauer Berg to Köpenick. Look for the streetcar stops marked with *H* emblems. BVG tickets and passes are accepted.

**Night Buses and Steetcars.** Most subway and regular streetcar and bus lines stop running about 1-1:30 A.M. and don't start again until 4-5 A.M.

(except Lines U12 and U9, which run 24 hours during the weekends). During this downtime the night bus system in the West and the night streetcar system in the East provide excellent half-hourly service from about 1 A.M. to 4 A.M. You can still get to your bed during the wee hours, no matter where you are staying, but it requires learning alternate networks.

First, find out what night bus or streetcar serves your residence. Just look for the night bus tag at your bus stop. Night buses are indicated by the letter *N*. On the older, metal signs, the "N" precedes the yellow numbers on tags with green backgrounds. In the west, go to Zoo station where many originate. When you get the system down, it often takes less time to get home via night bus than by connecting U-Bahn lines during the day. There is very light traffic. Night bus and streetcar maps are posted at only a few locations, but obtain a free *Nachtliniennetz* map at the BVG information office in front of Zoo station.

Your regular transportation ticket covers the 67 night lines which spread from 32 hubs from Spandau to Köpenick. The largest concentration is from Zoo station with service at least every half-hour; more often on weekends and on the Ku'damm, Tauentzienstraße, and Mehringdamm lines. The *Nachtliniennetz* map gives you the exact departure times and routes.

## AUTO RENTAL

For seeing and getting around Berlin, driving an automobile is a problem. You don't have to be crazy to drive in Berlin. You have to be prepared for terminal gridlock, construction delays, and detours that aren't on the map. These contribute to the fact that driving an automobile in Berlin is safer than anywhere else in Germany, based on 1997 traffic fatality figures. Parking downtown is almost as difficult as driving. Parking on 11 streets in the heart and historic centers of Berlin is reserved for residents displaying an appropriate sticker on their car.

Only when you are traveling to an out-of-the-way village in the surroundings should you not consider using public transportation (city public transportation stretches from Potsdam to Schönefeld Airport). In this case, however, traffic fatality figures show a 12-fold increase.

If you decide to buck the system, car rentals are available at Tegel Airport from the following: Hertz, Avis, National, Europcar, Westfehling, and Sixt/Budget. To reach their collective office building at Tegel, exit the main airport building and descend the well-marked escalator. It's about a five-minute walk in the open air. Automobiles rented in Berlin may be driven to any West European country, except that Mercedes models are not allowed in Italy. Only Opels, Fords, Fiats, and Renaults may be driven into Poland, the Czech Republic, Slovakia, Slovenia, Hungary, and Romania. Entry is not allowed into the other Eastern and Baltic countries, including Greece and Finland. **Avis** (Budapester Straße 41, Tel. 2-61-18-81), **Hertz** (Budapester Straße 39, Tel. 2-61-10-53), and **Europcar** (Kurfürstendamm 101-104, Tel. 2-35-06-40) pickup and drop-off garages are located in the street behind the Europa Center, convenient to the Holiday Inn Crowne Plaza and Palace hotels. The Westfehling office is at Quitzowstraße 33 in the East (Tel. 396-4031).

**ADAC**, the German Automobile Club which offers emergency road service similarly to AAA in the United States, also offers automobile rentals for club members through Sixt in 10 offices including Tegel (Tel. 4-12-20-20). ADAC's office is at Bundesallee 29/30 (mobile Tel. 0-180-5-10-11-12, Fax 0-180-5-30-29-28).

## BICYCLES

Berlin is an excellent city for riding bicycles with a well-organized bicycle path network totalling 480 miles (800 kilometers) in length. The heavy big-city traffic is not too friendly to bicyclists, yet its congestion is the best reason to ride your bike. Bicycling is faster. You see more. Many bicycle paths are well marked. On a survey of 41 German cities with populations over 200,000, West Berlin ranked 14th (Münster was first) and East Berlin ranked 28th. Berlin is so flat you will immediately notice the few hilly sections in Prenzlauer Berg and Kreuzberg and complain about the lack of marked bicycle lanes only in a few areas, but pedestrians are generally aware of the ting-a-ling sound of bicycle bells.

Letting you take your bicycle on U-Bahn, S-Bahn, and regional trains makes bicycling Berlin much easier. Note that during weekdays you can only take your bicycle aboard during the very early morning, between 9 A.M. and 2 P.M., and from 5:30 P.M. until the last train. When you take your bike, you have to buy it a ticket unless you have a card such as the seven-day card.

You can use the S-Bahn or regional train to travel to S-Bhf Wannsee and then over the Havelchausee to a lovely beach. Or you can take an S-Bahn train to S-Bhf Bernau or S-Bhf Königswusterhausen deep in Berlin's surroundings and begin a bicycle tour through the green.

Each weekend you can join *Fahrrad-Stadtrundfahrten* ("bicycle trip around the city"), bicycle excursions in the countryside, or an extended bicycle tour through Brandenburg, Mecklenburg-Vorpommern, or Poland. Every Saturday at 10 A.M. from April to October, "Berlin by bike" leaves from Hackesche Höfe, Rosenthaler Straße 40/41, Tel. 28-38-48-48, Fax 28-38-88-77. Cost: DM 20 for a two-hour tour. A further nine bike tours focusing on themes ranging from women to architecture to train stations leaves from this depot on various dates.

GermanRail has bicycle rental stations in the Zoo train station (Tel. 297-49-319) and Lichtenberg train station (Tel. 297-121-43). You can rent rebuilt bicycles (with deposit of either your passport or money) for DM 3 per day at **bikecity**, Waldener Straße 2-4, Tel. 39-73-910 (Tiergarten) (open 7 A.M. to 9 P.M.). Use U-Bhf Turmstraße. Their other eight loan stations are located

• at Schloßplatz at the former Staatsratsgebäude (Mitte), use U-Bhf Hausvogteiplatz, U-Bhf Französische Straße, or bus 100;

• Pohlstaße in the parking lot by Möbel Hübner (furniture) (Tiergarten) (open 7 A.M. to 9 P.M.), use U-Bhf Kurfürstenstraße;

• Hansaplatz (Tiergarten) (open 7 A.M. to 9 P.M.) use U-Bhf Hansaplatz;

• Jugendcafé Glatz-T, Chausseestraße 8, Tel. 3088-4423 (Mitte) (open 9 A.M. to 9 P.M.), use U-Bhf Oranienburger Tor or S-Bhf Oranienburger Straße;

• Bildungsmarkt, Marzahner Chausee 36, Tel. 540-0116 (Marzahn) (open Mon.-Fri. 8 A.M. to 4 P.M.), use S-Bhf Springpfuhl;

• Bistro des Kulturhauses, Mauerstraße 8, Tel. 333-4022 (Spandau) (open Mon.-Sat. 9 A.M. to 9 P.M.), use U-Bhf Rathaus Spandau;

• SPOK, Nordendstraße 56, Tel. 477-1034 (Pankow) (open 9 A.M. to 9 P.M.), use S-Bhf Pankow, then streetcar 52 or 53;

• Bildungsmarkt, Vulkanstraße 13, Tel. 550-9303 (Lichtenberg) (open Mon.-Fri. 8 A.M. to 4 P.M.), use streetcar 6, 7, 8, 17, or 18.

Other bicycle rental agencies include:

• **Fahrradstation Kreuzberg**, Möckernstraße 92, Tel. 216-9177 (Kreuzberg), use U-Bhf Möckernbrücke;

• **Radsport Sonntag**, Uhlandstraße 98, Tel. 873-6562 (Wilmersdorf), use U-Bhf Uhlandstraße;

• **Rikscha Mobil-Taxidienst**, Rosenthaler Straße 40-41, Tel. 2859-9895 (Mitte). You can ride along or pedal yourself.

In-line skates? Visit **strawberry**, Emser Straße 45, Tel. 881-3096 (Wilmersdorf) (open Mon.-Fri. 10 A.M. to 6:30 P.M., Thur. to 8:30 P.M., Sat. to 2 P.M.)

## RICKSHAWS

No you are not seeing things. No you are not in the Orient. In 1997, Berlin introduced Germany's first bicycle-rickshaw taxis. Thirty **Velotaxis** are available to take you over four set routes of nearly two miles each. You can board at an end station or hail one en route, just as a four-wheeled taxi. The driver will pedal up to two passengers with light luggage. The four routes are 1) Kurfürstendamm (Adenauerplatz to Wittenbergplatz), 2) Tiergarten (Zoo to the Brandenburg Gate), 3) Unter den Linden (Brandenburg Gate to Alexanderplatz), and 4) along Oranienburger Straße in the Scheunenviertel. Route 4 began in 1998 with new-model, lighter-weight Velotaxis. When you ride Velotaxi, you can pat yourself on the back for being environmentally conscious. They are relaxing and fun, and the fares aren't bad. You pay DM 2 per person for 0.6 mile or DM 5 for 2 miles. A half-hour tour costs DM 15. The velotaxis are rented by 148 self-employed chauffeurs for DM 5 a day. The pedalers consist of 51 percent students, one-fifth women, and a quarter of previously unemployed. Two-thirds of the passengers are German. It may not be long before authorities do away with all gasoline-powered vehicles on Unter den Linden. Bicycle taxis run 1-7 P.M., April to October.

## How to See Berlin

Visitors flock to Berlin from all over Europe for sightseeing and nightlife. You meet Italians, Dutch, and Scandinavians everywhere. Poles come in buses only for shopping and return with boxes filled with purchased and bartered goods.

**Public Transportation**. Buses, streetcars, S-Bahn, and U-Bahn trains (when they run above ground) provide an inexpensive way to see Berlin. The big yellow double-decker buses are your best bet because you have good views from the "lounge" on top, and you get closer to sights worth seeing so that you can get out to visit them. Stops are announced, but there are no sightseeing announcements and you should travel with guidebook handy for reference.

**City Tours.** You can make city tours in conventional, air-conditioned buses with excellent rapid-fire narration in English and German, you can take a bicycle taxi or a walking tour, or you can choose a sightseeing trip in a white-painted antique open-air vehicle driven by a person wearing a helmet reminding you of the Red Baron. If you want to learn about the things that make Berlin special, choose a standard or walking tour. If you want a lark, and the weather is good, choose a bicycle taxi or the Red Baron.

The major sightseeing bus companies have assembled starting points up and down Kurfürstendamm, depending on the state of construction nearby. They all have similar names and initials and all offer a similar selection of two city sightseeing itineraries and excursions to Potsdam, Dresden, and the

Spreewald. They all provide glossy brochures with small maps and a listing of sights.

Four of the leading tour bus companies cooperate on the "City-Circle" sightseeing scheme, which is a clever plan whereby for one price you can get on and off buses which circle Berlin on a half-hourly schedule. The transportation authority, BVG, offers a similar "Top-Tour-Berlin" scheme. The tours are "auto guided" in seven languages. You get on and off wherever you please as often as you like. A full day's ticket, starting at 10 A.M., costs DM 35. A half-day's ticket, from 2:30 to 6 P.M. costs DM 20. Last complete roundtrip departure from Kurfürstendamm in front of the Café Kranzler or Alexanderplatz is at 4 P.M. Stops are: Kurfürstendamm/Aschinger Beer Salon, Lützowplatz/Bauhaus-Archiv, Trebbiner Straße/German Technical Museum, Potsdamer Platz/Cultural Forum, Gendarmenmarkt, Mohrenstraße/Planet Hollywood, Friedrichstraße/Galeries Lafayette, Unter den Linden/German Historical Museum, Karl-Liebknecht-Straße/Berlin Cathedral, Alexanderplatz/TV Tower, Spandauer Straße/Nikolai Quarter, Hackescher Markt/Hackesche Höfe, Friedrichstraße/Antique Market, Brandenburg Gate/Tourist Office, John-Foster-Dulles-Allee/House of World Cultures, Luisenplatz/Charlottenburg Palace, Fasanenstraße, Wittenburgplatz/KaDeWe. Keep in mind you can do all this on your own with a day ticket and this guide book. You won't have the audio commentary but you will have more time to visit sites that interest you.

When you take the City Circle Tour you have the possibility of leaving the bus at the Berlin Cathedral and walking five minutes to the Nikolai Quarter. There you can change to a roundtrip aboard a ship of the Stern & Kreis Shipping Company for an additional DM 13.50 per person. Departures from Spree Landing at the Nikolai Quarter are at 11:15 A.M. and 12:45, 2:15, and 3:45 P.M. daily from April to November. Later or earlier you might want to bring your ice skates.

The morning, three-and-a-half-hour "Super" Berlin tour takes you past the Memorial Church into Kreuzberg, past the Anhalter Station remains, the Prussian Parliament and Martin Gropius Building, past Potsdamer Platz, up Friedrichstraße to the Gendarmenmarkt, into the Nikolai Quarter, past the Red City Hall to Alexanderplatz and the TV Tower, back past the Berlin Cathedral down Unter den Linden through the Brandenburg Gate to the Reichstag Building, through the Tiergarten to Charlottenburg Palace, the Olympic Stadium and then back on Kurfürstendamm. A good three and a half hours. Two photo stops included.

The afternoon, four-hour "Mega" Berlin tour deletes some of the outer sights, but takes you to the Cultural Forum and includes a one-hour stop so that you can visit the Pergamon Museum on Museum Island. One hour is not long enough to see Museum Island, but it is better than nothing. It is better to take the three-and-a-half-hour "Super" Berlin tour and go to Museum Island on your own and take your time. If you can't do this, by all means take the "Mega" Berlin tour with its one-hour opportunity to visit the Pergamon Museum.

A four-hour tour of Potsdam/Sanssouci is a good way to see Potsdam in a short time. You visit the summer residence of Friedrich the Great. The trip to Dresden (11 hours) consumes too much time on the Autobahnen. You will be happier overnighting in this worthy city. Trips to the Spreewald (forest) (seven hours) appeal mostly to German visitors although the tour is also in English.

The closest sightseeing departure point to the Memorial Church, Kurfürstendamm 225 (U-Bhf Kurfürstendamm), is BVB, **Bus-Verkehr-Berlin** (Tel. 88-59-88-0, *http://www.bvb.net*), across from the Kranzler Café.

Second down the line, on the corner of Meinekestraße at Kurfürstendamm across from the Hotel am Zoo, is the **Berolina Sightseeing Company**, Meinekestraße 3 (Tel. 8856-8030, Fax 882-41-28).

Past the Lufthansa office at Kurfürstendamm 220, on the third corner, Fasanenstraße, across from the Kempinski Hotel (U-Bhf Uhlandstraße), you finally come to **Severin + Kühn**, Kurfürstendamm 216 (Tel. 880-41-90, Fax 882-56-18).

The coaches of a fourth excellent tour company, BBS, **Berliner Bären Stadtrundfahrt** (Tel. 351-952-70, Fax 351-952-90) depart from Rankestraße, which is just around the corner from Kurfürstendamm directly across from the Memorial Church. Their East Berlin departure point is on Alexanderplatz at the Forum Hotel. The **Stadtrundfahrtbüro Berlin** buses depart from the Memorial Church. Tickets are available in the Europa Center, 15th floor (Tel. 261-20-01, Fax 261-20-22).

**Tempelhofer Reisen**, (Friedrich-Wilhelm-Straße 57-59, Tel. 752-40-57, Fax 751-70-35) also offers a Berlin by Night and two different nightclub tours on Saturday nights. Their pickup points are Kurfürstendamm 231 in front of the Wertheim/Hertie department store, Tauentzien 16-17 across from the Europa Center, Under den Linden 14 on the corner of Friedrichstraße, and the Brandenburg Gate.

The transportation authority, **BVG** (Tel. 256-247-40), operates *Berlin vom Bus und Schiff* ("Berlin by Bus and Ship") combination trip on Thursdays through Sundays every hour and a half starting at 10:30 A.M. from the Neue Wache on Unter den Linden. For DM 25 you ride in open-air historical Zille buses (authentic reproductions of the Robert Kaufman vehicles from between 1916 and 1924), with the driver dressed to reflect the "Golden '20s" of Berlin. These tours are not narrated (but provide a printed sightseeing guide), so they are more fun for those already familiar with Berlin. At the Nikolai Quarter you transfer to the historic steamship *Kaiser-Friedrich* for an hour to complete your trip.

**Walking tours.** There are by now about two dozen tour organizers, including associations as well as private enterprises. The tours through the Scheunenviertel (Chapter 4), covering Jewish history around the synagogue on Oranienburger Straße, became a part of the standard program long ago. Next to these classics, you can find a palette of specific themes: discover Berlin, Nazi Berlin, ecological Berlin, woman's Berlin, gay and lesbian Berlin, particular districts, literature, film, theater, architecture, city planning, even fashion. The guides are often academics with intensive knowledge of the area, and most of them are enthusiastic. They have to be. No one is ever going to get rich running city theme tours. Most of the tours take between 90 minutes and three hours. The charges range from DM 5 to DM 18, with discounts for seniors and students. You usually don't have to reserve them in advance, just show up with good walking shoes and a public transportation ticket. Identify your guide at the meeting point by his or her badge.

On three walking tours, you receive a reduction using a Welcome Card. These are:

**Berlin Walks**, Harbigstraße 26, Tel./Fax 301-9194 (at 10 A.M. and 2:30 P.M.), lead you through Berlin in the English language: Discover Berlin, Infamous Third Reich Sites, and Jewish Life in Berlin. Meeting point: outside Zoo Station main entrance at top of taxi stand. You can get details and book at the Euraide office in Bahnhof Zoo.

**Kulturbüro**, Greifenhagener Straße 62, Tel. 444-09-36, offers extensive "city seductions" on theater history, literature, architecture, art, history, fashion, districts, cemeteries, also outside the city to Grunewald, Babelsberg, and Sommerswalde.

**StattReisen Berlin**, Malplaquetstraße 5 (Wedding), Tel. 455-30-28, Fax 45-80-00-03 (Mon.-Fri. 10 A.M. to 4 P.M.), offers an extensive program in English, Russian, or French: history, literature, film, theater, Fascism, Jewish Berlin, a stroll along the Wall, Pankow, and Tempelhof.

## Banking and Changing Money

The unit of currency in Germany is the Deutsche Mark (DM), which often is called simply the "Mark." Its international designation is "DEM." One Mark is divided into 100 Pfennig (pf.). Coins include 1, 2, 5, 10, and 50 pf., and DM 1, 2, 5, and 10. You seldom have occasion to use the one- and two-Pfennig coins. Introduction of the much-discussed European currency, the "euro," is already upon us. Germany is one of its staunchest supporters. On January 1, 1999, the rate at which national currencies such as the deutsche Mark convert to the Euro was fixed, but the only difference you see is that exchange bureaus now post currency values twice—against the DM and the euro. There is no difference in rates between bureaus. The only difference is the fees or commissions they charge, and these charges are indicated on your receipt. Finally, on January 1, 2002, euro coins will fill your pockets and euro notes will flow from your billfold and the changeover to the euro will be complete—although for six months the Deutsche Mark also will circulate in Berlin and cash handling operations and equipment will be chaotic. On July 1, 2002, *Auf Wiedersehen, deutsche Mark.*

The exchange rate with the U.S. dollar however can vary substantially. When the dollar is "strong," you receive more Marks per dollar than before.

You want to use plastic whenever possible in the major hotels and restaurants to get the bank exchange rate (which is higher than you will receive by changing cash or traveler's checks), but their use otherwise is limited to a few book- and music stores, so you will have to rely primarily on cash from ATMs or traveler's checks in Berlin.

**Banks.** Banks are generally open Mon.-Fri. 9 A.M. to 1 P.M. and 2 to 6 P.M., except Wed. afternoon and at 5 P.M., on Fri. The **ReiseBank** in the Zoo train station (connected to the German Railroad), holds longer hours. It is open daily 7:30 A.M. to 10 P.M. The **Berliner Bank** at Tegel Airport is open Mon.-Sat. 6 A.M. to 10 P.M., Sun. to 9 P.M.

Banks in Berlin accept all kinds of traveler's checks, in dollars, Marks, pounds sterling, and yen. They also level a service charge to cover their overhead and cheer their shareholders.

Buyers of dollar-denominated American Express traveler's checks may have their traveler's checks cashed without a service charge at an **American Express office**. American Express has two offices: one in the West and one in the East. In the West, visit Bayreuther Straße 37, Tel. 214-9830 (open Mon.-Fri. 9 A.M. to 6 P.M., Sat. 10 A.M. to 1 P.M.). Use U-Bhf Wittenburgplatz. In the East, use the office at Friedrichstraße 172, Tel. 201-7400 (open Mon.-Fri. 9 A.M. to 6 P.M., Sat. 10 A.M. to 1 P.M.). Use U-Bhf Französische Straße.

Thomas Cook office is at Friedrichstraße 56, on the corner of Leipziger-straße (open Mon.-Fri. 9:30 A.M. to 6 P.M.). Tel. 2016-5916.

Watch out for nonbank exchange bureaus masquerading as banks in the Zoo area. They give lower exchange rates.

Berlin's banks are iffy regarding electronic money transfer methods. The *Geldautomaten* ("ATMs, automatic teller machines") in Berlin may or may not be programmed to honor U.S.-issued Visa, MasterCard, or any of

the bank teller systems such as Star or PLUS. It depends upon the relationship between the Berlin bank and your card-issuing bank. The tellers at
most banks will grant you cash advances on your credit cards, but you must
shop around to find them. Branches of the **Berliner Bank** will issue cash
against American-issued Visa cards; the **Sparkasse** in the heart of Berlin
and its dozens of branches throughout the city will take American-issued
MasterCards. You will receive the favorable bank exchange rates but your
bank at home may slap on a sizable service charge.

Using an international bank such as Citibank, which has a dozen or
more offices and *Geldautomaten* in Berlin allows you to deposit U.S. dollars
in your account before you leave and in Berlin draw it out in DM without
service charge at a more favorable exchange rate than you would get with
traveler's checks. Presenting your plastic also relieves you of the service
charge for cashing traveler's checks.

American Express guarantees personal checks for holders of American
Express cards, but does not give cash advances, such as German banks give
holders of Visa and MasterCards.

## Shopping

According to a 1998 study by the Swiss Corporate Research Group,
Berlin is Germany's most expensive large city, but cheap by comparison
with other European and world metropolises. Costs in Berlin are half those
in Hong Kong. Berlin is #58 in the rank of world cities. Düsseldorf is #62.
München (Munich) is two places back. Frankfurt/Main is #66 and Hamburg
#71. One doesn't shop in Berlin to save money, but to find specialty items
one can't find at home at any price. If it exists, you can find it in Berlin.
Prices include 14 percent **Mehrwertsteur (MWS)** ("value-added tax"),
which you can arrange to be refunded on substantial purchases taken out
of Germany/Europe.

Cute items to bring home include stuffed toys (especially bears, the
city's mascot). The German word for traditional stuffed bears is **Teddys**.
Kitchen gadgets are flashy. Bedding (especially feather-filled comforters) is
beautiful. Model trains, tin soldiers, original art, and porcelain are popular.

Most shops are open Mon.-Fri. from 9 or 10 A.M. to 6 or 8 P.M. and close
earlier on Sat. to 2 P.M. All shops are closed on Sunday. Some 60 shops and
grocery stores in the East, including Prenzlauer Berg and the Historical
Center, that were open before the Wende have an exemption from the law
and may remain open late.

You can perhaps best experience Berlin's *Herz mit Schnauze* ("a big heart
and a big mouth") during shopping through Berlin's various markets. No

matter how many new shopping centers spring up, the traditional markets have endured over the decades and have become increasingly popular with the opening of the Wall. More than 70 weekly markets, 9 market halls, and 10 flea markets make Berlin one of the most market-happy cities in Europe. No other place affords as much insight into the Berliner's true character.

During the first two weeks of August the major stores of Berlin normally have a summer sale, reducing prices as much as 80 percent (according to their advertisements).

**Tax Free.** You can save up to 10 percent VAT (value-added tax) by following these rules:

1. Articles should be purchased in shops displaying the Tax Free sign.
2. Ask for the Tax Free certificate in the shops.
3. Certificates must be stamped by the German Customs Authority prior to your departure to a non-European Union country. When departing from Tegel Airport, have them stamped before checking in. If you are going to another European Union country, you must have them stamped at your final European Union departure.
4. On presentation of your checks, you can receive cash at any of over 3,000 dispensing points at borders, airports, or on board ship in Europe. Alternately, the Tax Free shopping check can be mailed in the envelope listing the reimbursement points so they it can be cashed in by check or credit card.

Tegel Airport is one of the easiest for you to claim your refund. Things couldn't be simpler. Ask for directions at the information counter there. When you depart the European Union via a different European airport, allow enough time because you may well have to wait in a long line.

## Restaurants and Cafés

Berlin overflows with cafés indoors and out. It has more than 2,000 restaurants, serving a variety of menus in all price ranges. Twenty of Berlin's restaurants rank in Germany's "best" 515, making it the best restaurant city in Germany. Munich places 18 and Hamburg 17. Prices always include tax and service charge unless specifically noted, but are unique in another way. They don't tip according to percent. They tip by "feel." They feel that tipping is a reward for perfect service. It is customary always to leave the small (less than one Mark) coins from your change or (more commonly) to tell the waiter how much you are paying. For example, if the bill were to be DM 6.60, you would say, "Seven."

German food is an endangered species in Berlin. It is hard to find a

Berlin specialty unless you like **Eisbein** (pig's knuckles), **Kassler Rippchen** (smoked and pickled pork chops), which trace their origin to Friedrich the Great's imposition of compulsory salt purchase and Berliners had to scrounge for uses for the mineral. **Aal** (eel) is another item almost no one in Berlin eats anymore. When you see the East Prussian specialty, **Königsberger Klopse** (meatballs), on the menu think of it as the nickname for the fountain in front of the Europa Center. The blending of cultures and Berlin's position as a world city produced more international restaurants than German ones. The trend is toward south-of-the-Alps restaurants, soya and lemon grass. Berliners returning after sun holidays have taken to pasta, cappuccino, and espresso. You find Greek, Turkish, Argentine, and Chinese restaurants in every other block in West Berlin. The best and most historic are listed in this guide by city section, but wherever you are, you will never have to search long for a café or restaurant.

Except in the most exclusive restaurants, it is not uncommon for strangers to share tables, so don't be surprised if a new face points to a chair at your table and asks: *"Ist das frei?"* ("Is anyone sitting there?") You can do the same.

Berliners say you should eat like a kaiser at breakfast, like a king at lunch, and like a beggar at dinner. Berlin's cooking has traditionally been very working-class and few restaurants of any quality serve traditional Berlin fare. **Kassler Rippenspeer**, the Kassel spare rib, has nothing to do with the city of Kassel, but was created by the late master butcher Cassel, a Berliner. "Hamburgers" in Berlin used to be called **Bulletten** and were introduced by the Huguenots, but now Berliners have taken to the American word. **Berliners** are jelly donuts, **Doner Kebab** (meat on a skewer) was introduced by the Turks, and a **Molle** is a beer.

You can get an inexpensive sandwich on every other street corner. Berlin **Wurst** (sausages), which are not a specialty, compare poorly with sausages in other German cities. A steamed Bockwurst, Bratwurst, or Ketwurst comes with a shabby slice of white bread. A Currywurst shows its ethnic heritage.

Particularly popular in Berlin (especially in cafés after work) is **Eiskaffe**, which consists of strong Berlin coffee with one or two scoops of vanilla ice cream floated on top, sometimes sprinkled with chocolate chips and served in a goblet or a tall glass with a straw.

## Living It Up

In Berlin, "Culture" is a code word for "Living it up." Berlin's **KulturCard** covers discounts of 15-50 percent on jazz clubs, events of the "scene," open-air musical performances, festivals, movies, theater, opera, dance, musicals, cabarets and concerts as well as churches and museums. Plus you receive discounts on sightseeing buses. When you are in Berlin long enough to get your money's worth, at DM 19, the Culture Card is a real deal. The card is valid mid-June to early September. You can hardly miss an opportunity to buy one. It is available at tourist offices in the Europa Center and Brandenburg Gate, at Tegel Airport, at the Dresdner Bank on Unter den Linden, at all branches of the Deutsche Bank in Berlin and surroundings, at KaDeWe department store, at the ticketing offices of the Berlin S-Bahn, at many hotels, cultural attractions, newspaper kiosks, and souvenir shops.

The three-day **Welcome Card** preempts the Culture Card for 72 hours, because it offers even better deals on museums, attractions, theaters, opera, boat trips and tours for the length of the card's validity. At DM 29, including travel on all S- and U-Bahnen, buses and streetcars, this is more than a real deal. This is a no-brainer.

**Bars (Kneipen).** *Kneipe* is a German word that you can loosely translate as "pub." Berlin is very famous for its Kneipen. They say that on every corner you find five Kneipen.

Berlin is a beer city and Schultheiss has captured most of the market. *Weißbier* ("wheat beer") is always the favorite. Dark beer comes in second. Alcohol-free beer is growing in popularity. The Berliner Bügerbräu brewery has introduced *Rotkehlchen* according to an old recipe. Making up a small portion of Berliners' consumption, you can find special beers with flavors of cherry, raspberry, pear, and chili in Szene Kneipen. The Berlin specialty is to add extracts to make *Berliner Weiße mit Schuß*, or *Weißbier mit Schußfarbstoff*, which is wheat beer colored red with a raspberry syrup or green with an elixir from *Waldmeister* ("woodruff," a European flower). The colorings only slightly modify the taste. It is often served in a wide glass with a flat bottom. Berliner *Molle mit Korn* is a lager beer with a shot of north-German Schnapps. In the East a shot of vodka is a political statement.

The green beer that catches your eye, Berliner Kindl Weiß, is *Alcohol-frei*, like Klausthaler. It comes in green and red.

**Discos.** Discos abound, and everyone has their own favorite. Before midnight the crowd is mostly in their teens. Then the disk jockeys change, the music becomes harder, and an older crowd arrives. The walls of discos throb until 5-6 A.M. on weekends.

**Movies.** Berlin is a moviegoing city. One or more movie theaters showing American, German, French, Italian, and other foreign films are located in almost every block in the Kurfürstendamm area. Every neighborhood has more. Consult the local newspaper or events magazine for details. Open-air movies are popular in Berlin during the summer. The *Waldbühne* in Charlottenburg is the largest in Europe of this kind, but you will find others, including seats at the *Zitadelle* in Spandau. The courtyards of *Künstlerhau Bethanien* in Kreuzberg and the *Podewil* in the historic district also display movies on outdoor screens. Take your popcorn and picnic basket.

**Theater.** Berlin is a lively theater town. You find three opera houses in Berlin (the Ossis rebuilt the beautiful one on Unter den Linden; the Wessis built the **Deutsche Oper Berlin** in Charlottenburg; and finally there is the **Komische Oper**). Berlin's 32 legitimate theaters offer something for everyone from serious dramas to comedies. Many of the most interesting are spotlighted in the Current Program available from German National Tourist Offices and Berlin Tourist Offices. Most are usually closed between the middle of July and the middle of August or the first of September, so theatergoers should time their visits around those dark days.

Most plays are spoken in the German language. Tickets are often sold out very early for many theater, concert, and opera performances, but try especially for tickets to the **West Berlin Philharmonic**, the **Unter den Linden Staatsoper**, and the **Schauspielhaus** on the Gendarmenmarkt. They will make more memorable your visit to Berlin.

Tickets for theaters and concerts can be obtained directly from the theater box offices or at advance sales offices. At the latter, a service charge is added to the price of the ticket. You can reserve tickets before you leave through the Berlin Hotline or via several internet providers such as the Koka Concert Ticket Office at *http://www.icf.de/koka36*.

At the German opera and state theaters, students with identification can buy tickets at half-price a half-hour before the performance (assuming there are still tickets available).

Similarly, you can buy tickets at half-price after 4 P.M. for rock-pop, musical, theater, cabaret, football games, and the Olympic stadium from Hekticket in the West at Kantstraße 54, Tel. 313-45-54 (use S-Bhf Savignyplatz or U-Bhf Wilmersdorfer Straße) and Kurfürstendamm 14, Tel. 242-6709 (use U-Bhf Kurfürstendamm) and in the East at Rathausstraße 1, Tel. 242-67-09 (use S- and U-Bhf Alexanderplatz); and "Karten . . . von Heute" at Friedrichstraße 35, entrance at Kneifzange (use U-Bhf Friedrichstraße).

In Charlottenburg, buy your tickets at the Kant-Kasse, Krumme Straße 55, Tel. 313-4554; Theaterkarten-Service Laur, Hardenbergstraße 6, Tel. 312-70-41; or the Technical University Theaterkasse, Hardenbergstraße 34, Tel. 313-8017 (open Mon.-Fri. 10 A.M. to 6 P.M., Sat. to 1 P.M.); Theater Kasse City-Center, Kurfürstendamm 207-208, Tel. 881-78-87; or Theaterkasse Schöneberg, Akazierstraße 2, Tel. 781-21-06.

In the neighborhoods, visit Tele Card, Birkbuschstraße 14 (Steglitz), Tel. 834-40-73; Konzertkasse Lichtenrade, Bahnhofstraße 24, Tel.

744-70-02; Theaterkasse Reinickendorf, Residenzstraße 133, Tel. 495-51-14; or TK im Märkischen Zentrum (Reinickendorf), Senftenberger R. 1-3, Tel. 415-28-76.

In Potsdam, use Info-Laden & Ticket-Service in the Dutch Quarter, Tel. (0331) 270-91-50.

**Museums.** Visitors can spend weeks in Berlin's 88 museums, but most are closed on Mondays. Here are some of the exceptions: Bauhaus Archiv, Brücke Museum, German Historical Museum, and Käthe Kollwitz Museum are open Mondays. Admission is free on the first Sunday of the month.

The *Staatliche Museen zu Berlin* ("State Museums of Berlin") makes an offer whereby you can visit as many of their museums (and they have the cream of the Prussian collections) as you possibly can in one day with just a day card costing DM 8. Because their museums' single admissions cost DM 4, it will pay you to buy a day card and chase from museum to museum until they close. Covered are those on Museum Island (Pergamon Museum, Altes Museum); in Charlottenburg (Egyptian Museum, Gallery of the Romanticists, Berggruen Collection); in the Cultural Forum (New National Gallery, Arts & Crafts Museum, Music Instrument Museum, Engraving Museum, Art Library); in Dahlem (Indian Art Museum) and more (Hamburger Bahnhof, Schinkel Museum, Köpenick Arts & Crafts Museum). If you wish to visit the same museum during a three-day period, buy the three-day tourist ticket (**3-Tages-Touristenkarte**) costing CM 15. You can buy them at the tourist offices.

The Culture Card has provision for discounts on the Bröhan Museum, the Georg Kolbe Museum, the House of Cultures of the World, the Käthe Kollwitz Museum, and the Checkpoint Charlie Museum. The Welcome Card mentioned above (see "Public Transportation") provides discounts on nearly every museum.

## Electricity, Temperature, and Time

Like most of Europe, Berlin operates on the metric system, degrees Celsius, 220 volts, and a television system incompatible with that in North America.

If you must bring anything electrical, it should have an adapter switch for 220 volts and you'll need a plug adapter with prongs that push into the sockets, but battery power is your best bet because all size batteries are readily available in supermarkets and specialty shops. Audiotapes, especially in battery-powered units with earplugs, work just fine.

Converting degrees Celsius to degrees Fahrenheit is a snap. You multiply degrees Celsius by two, subtract 10 percent, and add 32. If it's 20 degrees, multiplying by two makes 40, less 10 percent is 36, plus 32 is 68 degrees

Fahrenheit. Anything cooler than 20 degrees C might require a sweater. If it's 32 degrees C, times two is 64, less 6 is 58, plus 32 makes 90 degrees Fahrenheit. Time for the beach.

It is not unusual to express time using the 24-hour clock, but Berliners are no more punctual than Americans and if you adapt to the 24-hour life, breakfast is eaten in the afternoon. Berlin lies on a latitude with the Aleutian Islands so the sun goes to bed late in the summer, but rises exceedingly early.

Young people seldom carry an umbrella in Berlin because it gets windy when it rains, but then, too, when it is warm they don't mind getting drenched to the skin in a sudden summer thundershower.

## Health

Air pollution is not of major proportions during the summer in Berlin, but hay fever sufferers may be troubled. They should bring their medications. Air pollution from the burning of brown coal and the weather patterns blowing chemical industry effluent from the south is noticeable in the winter, when white snow doesn't stay white very long. Tap water, while not great tasting, is perfectly drinkable but some Berliners prefer bottled water, and most Berliners prefer beer. Swimming in rivers and lakes is safe unless marked.

## Sports

The DDR built two large and very complete **Recreational Centers** with swimming and nearly every activity that could interest anyone. One center is in Friedrichshain (see Chapter 4), the other in Köpenick (Chapter 12). You can find very inexpensive **Sportjungendclubs (SJC)** ("Youth Sport Clubs") in 10 districts: Hohenschönhausen, Köpenick, Kreuzberg, Lichtenberg, Marzahn, Pankow Buch, Prenzlauer Berg, Reinickendorf, Treptow, and Wedding. These sports centers for youth offer billiards, skateboarding, table tennis, basketball, and gymnasium as well as aerobic and dance classes. They organize weekend trips and bicycle tours. A day card costs DM 6; a six-month admission costs DM 300. Saunas charge DM 15 for three hours. For more information Tel. 300-02-160.

**Swimming** is far and away the most popular sport in Berlin. In many districts (addresses are listed by city section) there are dozens of lake and river beaches that swarm with hundreds of thousands of visitors on sunny summer days. The several traditionally nude beaches don't raise eyebrows. In winter there are well-equipped indoor pools.

**Beach Volleyball** is played on the outdoor beaches such as the Wannsee.

For information on organized tournaments contact the Volleyballverband Berlin, Tel. 300-061-82.

**Bungee Jumping** and Super-Swing. Certain events are arranged. For more information contact Super-Swing Freizeitanlagen, Tel. (0172) 311-00-31.

**Golf.** In many countries, there are public golf courses where anyone can play a round for an admission fee. In Germany, golf is the kind of sport where only club members are allowed to play. Twelve golf courses in and around Berlin relax this policy during the summer and open their doors to the public. For an admission fee of DM 60-120, the public may play a round during the week from Monday to Friday. Some 30,000 so-called Golf-Flights have been made available. For more information and bookings, Tel. 25-00-25.

**Ice/Roller skating** For DM 4 to 7 per hour, you use the rinks in Charlottenburg, Neukölln, Steglitz, Wedding, and Wilmersdorf. Skate-boarders tend to congregate on the Matthäikirchplatz in the Cultural Forum (Chapter 6), by the fountain next to the Memorial Church (Chapter 3), on the Spittelmarkt, and in the tunnel of the ICC (Chapter 5). **Ice skating** is popular in the **Eissporthalle** in Charlottenburg.

Spectator sports include **Fußball** ("soccer"). The soccer club Hertha BSC has aroused excitement, recently advancing to the *Erste Bundesliga* ("First Division"). The "Grand Old Dame" of Berlin soccer is once again giving Germany's finest teams a run for their money and regularly drawing upwards of 50,000 fans to the Olympic Stadium—more than the Munich or Dortmund clubs.

A few kilometers away, the **Basketball** players of Alba Berlin are also keeping fans on the edge of their seats. Berliners have always loved a success story, and in 1995 the "Albatrosses" transformed Berlin into a bastion of basketball when they unexpectedly won the Kovac Cup.

**Tennis** is largely confined to private clubs with limited access. **Freizeitpark Tegel** (Tel. 434-6666) has courts. The Ladies German Open is held in May at the **Tennisclub Rot-Weiß** (Tel. 8-26-22-07; tickets 25-00-25). Every year the world's best female tennis athletes compete on the courts in Grunewald. Nine of the top 10 came in 1997.

**Racing** includes the **ADAC-Avus automobile races** in May, the **ADAC motorcycle races** in September, and **trotter racing** at **Trabrennbahn Mariendorf** (Mariendorferdamm 222, Tel. 741-20-65), **Trabrennbahn Karlshorst** (Hermann-Duncker-Straße 129, Tel. 509-08-91), and **thorough-bred racing** at **Galopprennbahn Hoppegarten** (Goethestraße 1, Dahlwitz Hoppegarten, Tel. 559-61-02), which is outside of Berlin in Dahlwitz (use

S-Bhf Hoppegarten). The **International Horse Show** is usually held in November. The six-day **bicycle race** in October is held in the Max Schmeling Stadium.

**Fishing** is permitted with a license. Apply to **Fischereiamt** (Havelchaussee 149-51, Tel. 305-2047).

## Telephones, Faxes, E-Mails, and Post Office

If, in your fantasy, you have ever wanted to telephone from a neon-pink telephone, you have your wish in Berlin. Deutsche Telekom's new marketing strategy has provided a pink motif to their telephone booths up to and including pink headsets.

Deutsche Telekom, the former monopoly, is still the Goliath of telephones in Germany. About 9,000 operators handle 500 million directory assistance calls per year. For Telekom directory assistance press "11-833" for numbers within Germany or "11-834" for international numbers. Prices continue to decrease with improved technology and competition. The other telephone carriers are Telegate, Arcor, Otelo, and Viag-Intercom. For Telegate directory assistance, select "11-880."

The mail and telephone services in Germany used to be administered together, so you will normally find telephone access in post offices which you can easily identify from the posthorn symbol.

Post offices of course are spread throughout the city, but some are open extended hours. The post office in Bahnhof Zoo is open Mon.-Sat. 6 A.M. to midnight; Sun. from 8 A.M. The post office on the upper floor of Tegel Airport is open Mon.-Fri. 7 A.M. to 9 P.M., Sat.-Sun. 8 A.M. to 8 P.M. You can also buy stamps from the yellow-enamel machines near some mailboxes.

Berlin, like the rest of Europe, is divided into numerous five-digit *Postleitzahlen* ("Zip Codes"). You should use these to expedite delivery of your letter. Some yellow drop boxes are segregated according to the zip code of your addressee. You will normally use "*andere*" ("other").

Window #7 inside the Zoo post office offers **stamps for collectors** (open Mon.-Fri. 8 A.M. to 6 P.M., Sat. 8 A.M. to 1 P.M.).

Letters in all Europe (including Germany) cost DM 1.10. Delivery by the fastest method, air or surface, is promised. Surface letters to the rest of the world cost DM 2. Airmail costs DM 3 for letters less than 20 grams. Heavier letters cost increasingly more. Postcards cost DM 1 in Germany and Europe; DM 2 elsewhere (by air).

Berlin's telephone system is the most modern in Europe because they started from scratch installing the latest telephone technology in the former DDR. The area code for Berlin is 030, for Potsdam 0331. Drop the zero if you dial from abroad using the "49" country prefix. Don't be put off by the fact that telephone numbers have different numbers of digits. There is no standard length.

You find two kinds of pay phones, coin and *Kartentelefon* which take telephone cards only, no coins. The card phones feature a LCD readout either in English, French, or German. To display instructions in English you press a white button to select language. Twenty seconds before the telephone card is used up, the credit indicator lamp will flash and the signal will sound. To continue the call, press the green button, and exchange the telephone card.

Telephone cards are available at post offices in two sizes: DM 12 for 60 *Einheiten* ("pulse units"), or DM 50 for 260 *Einheiten*. This means DM 0.2 per *Einheit* for the 60 *Einheiten* capacity, or DM 0.19 per *Einheit* for the 260 *Einheiten* capacity, a five percent savings. You can't get money back for an unused portion of a telephone card, but you might be able to sell it to a friend.

You will be much better off buying a telephone card at your very first opportunity. You won't need to worry about carrying coins for the pay phones (normal coin phones require three 10-Pfennig coins to function), but the real advantage of buying a telephone card is that you usually won't have to wait as long because phone booths taking telephone cards are far more common than those taking coins.

The post office at Bahnhof Zoo provides a row of some 12 telephone booths that are open 24 hours and a complete set of German telephone books. Some of the telephones accept coins, most require telephone cards, and one accepts a bank credit card. The fax machine is accessed from inside the post office so you can only use it during the hours when the post office is open. For collect (reverse charge) calls to the U.S., dial 01300010; for the U.K., dial 0130800044.

Most post offices are able to send faxes. You will also find occasional fax/telephone booths where you can send a fax using your telephone card.

For e-mail, repair to one of Berlin's avant-garde cyber cafés, order a beverage, and settle in before you access the World Wide Web and the mysteries of German-language keyboards. Good luck.

**Internet-Café Hai Täck** ("High Tech"), Brünnhildestraße 8, Tel. 85-96-1413, Fax 85-96-1415, *www.haitaeck.de* (open 11 A.M. to 1 A.M..) has 11 Internet stations, e-mail service, and AOL access. Use U- or S-Bhf Bundesplatz.

**Alpha Internet Café Galerie**, Dunckerstraße 72 (Prenzlauer Berg), Tel. 4-47-90-67 (open 3 P.M. to midnight) also has MS Office, Netscape, printers, and scanners.

**Website Café**, Joachimstraler Straße 41, Tel. 886-796-30, Fax 886-782-67, is Berlin's largest cyber café with 33 machines upstairs through a futuristic bar. Use U- or S-Zoo.

**Amerika Gedenk-Bibliothek** ("Library"), Blücherplatz 1, Tel. 90-22-61-05.
**Cyberb@r KaDeWe**, in KaDeWe department store, Tauentzienstraße 21, Tel. 2-12-10. Use U-Bhf Wittenburgplatz.
**Cyberb@r Zoo**, Joachimstaler Straße 5-6, Tel. 88-02-40, www.mem.de/cyberbar/home.htm. Use U- or S-Bhf Zoo.
**Loginn**, Rosenthaler Straße 71, Tel. 28-59-81-17.
**Netz-Werk**, Sonntagsstraße 6, Tel. 29-49-06-54.
**Pro-Markt KuDamm**, Kurfürstendamm 207-208, Tel. 88-67-90-89.

## Television and Radio

The unification of the Germanys caused serious problems combining television and radio programming. West Germany was structured so that each state had its own television channel, but East Germany had only one, the official East German network connected with the East German Post Office (which handled the technical matters and transmission and owned the cameras, etc.). Formerly there were two morning programs televised for children with the same name, one from West Berlin, and one from Adlershof. Although the characters were the same, the programs were different. Schoolteachers in the East could determine (and report) which families watched Western television by asking their young pupils, "What was the story this morning?"

There are now some 57 television channels available in Berlin, and more to come. They include 13 by antenna, 41 on cable (70 by late summer 1999), and 3 by satellite. Cable includes Ted Turner's CNN, SuperChannel, NBC, Eurosport, and MTV. Many broadcast 24 hours. The newspapers print complete guides and *Tip, the Berlin Magazine* (DM 4), http://www.tip-berlin.de includes a two-week pullout TV guide. American videotapes are incompatible and cannot be played on German sets and Berlin videos cannot be viewed back home.

Figure about a hundred radio frequencies including antenna, cable and satellite. Voice of America and the private company, Dornier Medien, provide German-American broadcasting in the tradition of Armed Forces Radio at 87.9 Star FM.

## Learning the German Language

There are several schools in Berlin which specialize in teaching the German language to foreigners. The **Goethe-Institut** is as close to an authority on the German language as exists in Germany. Its Berlin building on Friedrichstraße is surprisingly close to Checkpoint Charlie (Friedrichstraße 209, D-10969 Berlin, Tel. 2-59-06-3, Fax 2-59-06-400).

## Lost and Found

The lost and found (Fundbüro) office for the Berlin Transit Authority (BVG) is located at Fraunhoferstraße 33-36, 9th floor, room 119F, Tel. 256-23-040 (open Mon.-Thur. 9 A.M. to 6 P.M.; Fri. 9 A.M. to 2 P.M.).

Central Lost and Found (Zentrales Fundbüro) is at Platz der Luftbrücke 6 in Tempelhof, Tel. 6995.

GermanRail Lost and Found (Fundbüro der Deutschen Bahn) is at Mittelstraße 20, Tel. 297-29-612, Fax 297-29-625 (open Mon., Wed., Thur. 10 A.M. to 4 P.M.; Tue. to 6 P.M.; Fri. 8 A.M. to noon).

Lost or stolen Eurailpasses can be replaced, providing you present a police report of the theft or loss, at the Reisezentrum in the main hall of Bahnhof Zoo.

# 2

# Getting to Know
# Berlin

Berlin is a big city—big enough for two cities. You can spend months here and never see everything important. Yet, the most interesting sights are concentrated in the two centers of the city so that you can skim the cream conveniently in a day or two. If you have limited time, make an agenda of what you want to see. Allow plenty of time to get around. Below, we nominate Berlin's top 10 things of interest and suggest ways for you to see them.

## Getting Your Bearings

Berlin's inner city was 70 percent destroyed by bombing and the Red Army invasion, but the suburbs and the residential neighborhoods were largely spared. Kurfürstendamm was lightly damaged because it was not of strategic importance except for the Zoo train station. Ku'damm has lost some of its attraction as the heavily damaged Unter den Linden and Friedrichstraße have been rebuilt from cellar to skylight and become Berlin's second center. When the final touches are put on the rebuilt Potsdamer Platz, it will become another focal point—but Ku'damm will

remain famous because it always has been Berlin's street of entertainment—
although not a high-class shopping, business, or political center.

Because the division caused West Berlin to scurry to provide new cultural
attractions and to house the art treasures stored in the West, unified Berlin
still has duplicates of many things cultural: philharmonic halls, libraries,
national galleries, opera houses, Egyptian museums, sculpture collections,
etc. Only a small fraction of the sightseeing attractions of Berlin reside in
the West—west of the famous former Berlin Wall and west of the Spree
River. These include Charlottenburg Palace and museums, the Reichstag
and other government buildings, the Victory Column, Bellevue Palace, the
Berlin and Jewish Museums, the Technical Museum, and the remaining
Dahlem collections. The East has more. Everyone will want to visit the
Brandenburg Gate, Pariser Platz, Unter den Linden, Museum Island,
Alexanderplatz, the Nikolai Quarter, and Potsdamer Platz's Info-Box.
Some will want to visit the beautiful green Berlin lakes and forests, East
and West; some will want to explore the tragic remains of the ugly Hitler
years near the center; and some have already left for the alternative scenes
in Kreuzberg (West) and Prenzlauer Berg (East).

One of the curious things you will notice throughout East and West Berlin
are the 2,065 **Pumpen** ("water pumps") painted green, blue, or orange. In
the West, all 1,577 pumps work. That is, one for every 1,366 residents. In
the East, 488 pumps give water—or one for every 2,637 residents. The
much-loved pumps date from the turn of the century. They were designed
to supply water from the underground water table to the citizens. Some of
the older ones are under protection as national monuments—and still
work, which you can discover for yourself by pumping the handle. Those
with water you can drink are marked: *Trinkwasser*. Be careful of those
marked *Kein Trinkwasser*. Water quality is checked in the neighborhoods
near schools, parks, and clinics. They were the neighborhoods' main
source of water after the War when all the water pipes were broken. Now
they are used mostly for washing automobiles, but are much cherished by
their neighborhoods for sentimental reasons and for possible use in the
case of a catastrophe.

Berlin is more or less bisected by the Spree River, which meets the Havel
River in Berlin's western reaches. The Dahme River flows into the Spree in
Köpenick in the East. In the West, an arm of the Spree called the
Landwehr Canal was artificially constructed by Peter Josef Lenné in the
middle of the last century to link the upper and lower Spree River and
form an island containing Berlin's most important museums and Marx-
Engels Square.

Knowledgeable travelers find it easiest to orient themselves by picking
an easily identifiable feature and keying their city-seeing to it. That doesn't

work in Berlin. Berlin is too big for that. It is so spread out that there are many focuses and you can assimilate it best by breaking it down into three parcels. In the West, choose the Memorial Church for your orientation. In the East, the television tower on Alexanderplatz is your prominent landmark. Between, fix on the Brandenburg Gate.

It's equally interesting to stay in the West, as close to Ku'damm as possible, or in the East, among the historic buildings, and use the public transportation system to fill your agenda, but that still takes time. The S-Bahn connections are time-consuming, but you will need to use these trains to get between East and West and into the outer districts. Automobile driving is awkward because construction forces detours that aren't on your map and in any event the connecting streets are still insufficient for the traffic. The best way around town is by bicycle, which explains why the bicycle courier business is such an outrageous success.

## Berlin's Top 10 Sights

There are precious, exciting, and overwhelming places to visit in Berlin that every visitor will enjoy seeing. Making a list is subjective. Berliners say, "What you see is what you know." Your favorites will undoubtedly differ, but this is a starter list:

**1. Brandenburg Gate and Reichstag.** These is the focus of Berlin as a metropolis. Their histories are fascinating; their importance is undeniable.
**2. Pergamon Museum.** A candidate for the world's greatest museum, the sheer size and grandeur of its exhibits are without peer.
**3. Gendarmenmarkt.** Possibly Europe's most beautiful square, the ensemble of the French and German churches and Carl Friedrich von Schinkel's theater make a staggeringly beautiful photograph.
**4. Charlottenburg.** The combination of the palace's beautifully restored chambers and its gracious gardens makes a happy visit.
**5. Potsdam.** A visit to see the magnificent buildings and gardens is not to be missed.
**6. Breitscheidplatz/Ku'damm.** There is always a party on the Breitscheidplatz. Europa Center has everything. The Memorial Church is well worth a few minutes. A stroll along Kurfürstendamm reveals Berlin's Western center.
**7. Cultural Forum.** The magnificent collection in the new Gemäldegalerie makes this site irresistible.
**8. Alexanderplatz.** Despite Western efforts to tame the square, you need to see it to get a feeling for the direction of the DDR before the Wende. The Red Rathaus and the Nikolai Quarter are well worth visiting.
**9. Green Berlin.** The beautiful green corners of Berlin—the Grunewald,

Wannsee, Nikolassee, the Tiergarten, the Müggelsee—make Berlin livable and separate it from other great historic cities. You may mistake Wannsee, the lake within essentially flat Berlin, as an Alpine lake, and you won't be alone.

**10. Save some free time** to see Jewish Berlin or the sites of Nazi terrorism or find a spot to indulge the whim of your choice. From Berlin's list of special museums at least one will attract you, whether for postage stamps, Prussian locomotives, or paleontology. Check the alternative scene. Go to the beach.

## Berlin in One to Four Days

Seeing Berlin will depend on how much time you have allotted to visit this exciting city. There is a bare minimum of things a visitor simply must see to be satisfied. When you have only a short time you will have to pack them into a fast whirl. Guided sightseeing tours are regimented and more expensive than seeing the sights on your own, but they are the most time-efficient.

You will preferably schedule more than four days in Berlin to give you more time so you can do more things on your own, more leisurely, on foot, and get to know the beautiful green side of Berlin. How to spend the evenings, nights, and wee hours pretty much depends on your taste. Berlin is your oyster 24 hours a day. You can visit the theater or opera, have a fine dinner, linger at an outdoor café, or go to a raunchy bar or alternative party in Prenzlauer Berg and disco till dawn.

**Day 1:** Choose a Berlin tour which includes a visit to the Pergamon Museum. Evening on Ku'damm.

**Day 2:** Ride Bus 100 from Zoo to the Reichstag, walk to the Brandenburg Gate, along Unter den Linden, continue to Alexanderplatz, and visit the Nikolai Quarter.

**Day 3:** Choose a day excursion to Potsdam.

**Day 4:** In the morning choose a half-day Green Berlin tour or a half-day boat trip on the Spree River. Visit Charlottenburg Palace in the afternoon.

## Berlin in Four Hours on Your Own

So you really don't like sightseeing? You are here on business or to party all night and sleep all day. Still, your friends and your mother are going to ask you what you saw and you have to have photos and some kind of story. Good news: You can "do" Berlin in four hours with nine stops on a single DM 7.80 public transportation day ticket. Put a wide-angle lens on your camera.

1. Start at the Tourist Information Center at Breitscheidplatz (Europa Center). Photograph the Memorial Church and the Earth-ball fountain behind you. Walk down Taunentzienstraße to photograph KaDeWe. You won't have time to snack in the food department on the sixth floor. At Wittenburgplatz, buy and be sure to validate an *AB Tagesticket* and board U-Bahn line U2 direction Vinetastraße.

2. Get off at Potsdamer Platz subway station. Photograph the red building on stilts called the Info-Box. It contains information about Europe's largest construction site which you could view from the observation platform if you had time, which you don't.

3. Back down to the next subway stop, Stadtmitte. Walk quickly to the Gendarmenmarkt, one of Europe's most handsome squares. This is worth a good two to three photos. Back to Friedrichstraße (west) and walk north past Galeries Lafayette.

4. At Unter den Linden, walk west to photograph the Brandenburg Gate and Pariser Platz. Board bus 100 back up the boulevard to Opernpalais stop. Here photograph the Opera House, the Royal Library, St. Hedwig's Church, Humboldt University, the statue of Friedrich the Great, and the Neue Wache.

5. Continue walking east. Detour to the Pergamon Museum on Museum Island. Photograph its impressive entrance. Tell everyone you saw the Pergamon Altar (it's old) but that cameras were not allowed inside.

6. Back on Unter den Linden, pass the Dom (cathedral), which you photograph, cross the Schloß Bridge to the park with the Marx-Engels monument (photograph) to the Red Rathaus (photograph) and the Nikolai Quarter where you can photograph the 1237 Nikolai Church.

7. Retrace your step to the television tower on Alexanderplatz. You can photograph it side by side with the tower of the St. Mary's Church, but you won't have time to take the high-speed elevator to the revolving restaurant.

8. Continue into the 1998-reopened Alexanderplatz regional train station and use your ticket to board an S-Bahn one station west to Hackescher Markt where you cross for a peek and a photograph of Hackesche Höfe before continuing down Oranienburger Straße to the glittering New Synagogue. Luckily you brought your wide-angle lens.

9. Take the subway from Oranienburger Straße station back to Unter den Linden station, still on the same ticket. Board bus 100 heading west toward Zoo station. Sit on the top level so you can photograph through the bus window the Reichstag building, the House of World Cultures, Bellevue Palace, and the Victory Column. At Zoo station you are back where you started and should be happy with your four-hour, multi-roll trip.

## From the Zoo to Prenzl with Bus 100

This is the best ticket in town: two hours for DM 3.90. It is so good it is known as the *Hunderter*. The Berlin Public Transit Authority runs double-decker buses over a core route between East and West that not only gets you from center to center but reveals en-route jewels that you might otherwise overlook. This bus, which costs only the same as a regular bus, is much more popular than the sightseeing buses standing around the Kurfürstendamm area which cost much more. You may board the bus at any of the bus stops with the green-on-yellow "100" tags, but if you're smart, you'll be first aboard at the well-marked starting point on Hardenburgplatz in front of the Zoo station. You can scurry up the stairs and claim the deluxe front row seats before all the seats are taken. You are not allowed to stand on the upper level of the bus.

You can get off at any stop to see any of the sights close-up, and that's an advantage, because your bus runs past so many places of interest. Bus 100 also provides a practical way to just get yourself between East and West.

This bus is probably the most popular with tourists, both German-speaking and from abroad. Many come equipped with fold-out city maps, but be sure to pick up the free Bus 100 brochure at the information kiosk in front of the Zoo station or either of the tourist offices.

Bus 100 departs past U-Bhf Zoo and immediately swings around the corner face to face with the symbol of West Berlin, the Kaiser Wilhelm Memorial Church. Zipping down the underpass emerging at Europa Center on the right you pass the main Berlin Tourist Office, British Airways, and the Palace Hotel. On the left you see the blue Panoramic Theater globe and the famous Elephant Gates in front of the Zoo. Your first stop is at **Europa Center (Breitscheidplatz)**, where you can also board.

Bus 100 continues down Budapester Straße and then Kurfürstenstraße, stopping at Bayreuther Straße. It passes the Hotel Sylter Hof and turns left at the Paris arc. At Lützowplatz off to the right you can see the green park and Grand Hotel Esplanade. Get off here to visit the Moorish-white Bauhaus Archives. The bus then crosses the Landwehr Canal, actually passes the Bauhaus Archives, which looks like a subway station, and the Church of the Latter Day Saints. On the left you see the *Tiergarten Dreieck* ("Tiergarten Triangle") with the embassy of Mexico facing the street and the beautiful complex of five Nordic embassies occupying the corner of Tiergartenstraße.

Crossing Tiergartenstraße you enter the Tiergarten Park, where straight ahead you see the Victory Column at the center of the Big Star traffic circle. From the Big Star the bus turns onto Spreeweg, with the stop marked

**Großer Stern.** Get off here to climb the Victory Monument or stroll through the Tiergarten Park to the Brandenburg Gate. Continuing down Spreeweg, you first see the President's Egg to the left through the trees and then, at your next stop, Schloß Bellevue, palace of the federal president.

Bus 100 turns right on John-Foster-Dulles-Allee. Straight ahead you see the Pregnant Oyster with bronze sculpture by Thomas Moore. Disembark here for a cruise on the River Spree. You might hear the chiming of bells floating from the 138-foot carillon tower clad with shiny, black Norwegian Labrador granite. Soon ahead you see the Reichstag with its transparent new dome. This is the only bus that serves the Reichstag, but depending on the state of construction, Bus 100 continues past what used to be the Wall and past the Brandenburg Gate and Pariser Platz to Unter den Linden. Get off here to walk to the Brandenburg Gate where they are selling souvenirs and snacks.

Down Unter den Linden, you run past the various storefronts, hotels, the Guggenheim Museum and restored Prussian buildings. You can disembark at **Opernpalais** stop as you pass Bebelplatz on the right, the German National Opera, and tourists drinking coffee or Berliners drinking beer outdoors at the Opera Café. Now Bus 100 crosses the ornate Schloß Bridge over the Spree River. On the left you see the SAS Radisson Hotel Berlin and stop at **Alexanderplatz**, with the Red Rathaus directly across the square.

Past Spandauerstraße, St. Mary's Church, at the foot of the television tower, your bus crosses under the S-Bahn/mainline railroad tracks, stopping at bus stop **U- und S-Bhf Alexanderplatz**. Those interested in visiting the wicked Prenzlauer Berg should stay aboard.

## Across Berlin by Bus 119—Airlift Memorial to Grunewald

Bus 119 crisscrosses through the West. Like Bus 100, you see a cross section of the city for a small price, but this view is more contemporary.

Bus 119's western terminus is Hagenplatz in Grunewald, a place to visit for a tasting of Green Berlin. Its eastern terminus is the Airlift Memorial on Platz der Luftbrücke in Kreuzberg. Between, you pass along Kurfürstendamm, see Wolf Vostell's Cadillacs, the Schaubühne ("theater") at Lehniner Platz, and pass Wittenbergplatz, Nollendorfplatz, Potsdamer Straße, and Kreuzberg Straße, which offer good starting points for various explorations from the Wannsee to Victoria Park.

You don't board at Zoo station. When you want to take the bus westward to Grunewald or Hagenplatz, a good place to board is at the Europa Center, but a better place to board is in front of the Kranzler Café, at U-Bhf Kurfürstendamm on the north side of the street, a few steps from Hotel am Zoo.

Be sure the 119 bus that you board is marked *Hagenplatz*, if that is your destination. Not all No. 119 buses run the entire distance, which forces you to make an inconvenient change. Traveling southeast, board at Bleibtreustraße or Uhlandstraße or another of the marked stops on the south side of Ku'damm.

## West Berlin Round Trip by Bus

The following route takes you past some of the more interesting sights in West Berlin. It begins and returns from Kurfürstendamm.

At the Memorial Church board Line 129 going westward on Kurfürstendamm. You travel past Adenauerplatz, Lehniner Platz (to the left is the Schaubühne, Berlin's famous theater), to Henriettenplatz. Here you change to Line 104 (direction: Taupitzer Straße) and ride southeastward, at first along Westfälischen Straße through the well-to-do Wilmersdorf district. You pass Rathaus Wilmersdorf at Fehrbelliner Platz and continue across Brandenburgische Straße, Berliner Straße, and Badensche Straße toward Rathaus Schöneberg on John-F.-Kennedy-Platz. Turning right you see on the right the front of the town hall where John F. Kennedy made his "Ich bin ein Berliner" speech.

At Hauptstraße bus station, change to Line 148 (direction: Philharmonie) and ride farther northwest. Hauptstraße, a treelined promenade, and its extension, Potsdamer Straße, are parts of the old road that used to connect Potsdam with the center of Berlin. On the left opposite is the village church, built in the 18th century. You continue across Kaiser-Wilhelm-Platz and then through Schöneberg to Grunewaldstraße. From here the street is named Potsdamer Straße. On the left are the Kings' Colonnades in the Heinrich von Kleist Park and the former seat of the Four Power Commission. The treaty governing Berlin was signed here in 1971. At the Pallasstraße intersection a former sports stadium stood where mass rallies were held during Nazi times. The six-day bicycle races held here were transferred to the Deutschlandhalle, until it closed in 1997. The following part of Potsdamer Straße is a shopping street and home of the editorial offices of newspapers, magazines, and radio.

At Potsdamer Brücke station, leave the bus and cross by foot Potsdamer bridge over the Landwehr Canal. At the National Gallery get back on Bus Line 129 (direction: Roseneck). In front you see the Cultural Forum, which includes the National Library, the Chamber Music Hall, the Handicrafts Museum, the Music Instruments Museum, and the new Paintings Gallery. Only a few hundred feet beyond lies Potsdamer Platz. The ride west leads you first along the Landwehr Canal past the Shell House, with its steplike facade built between 1930 and 1932 now being restored. Looking down Stauffenbergstraße you see the German Resistance Memorial. A wide curve takes you past the white Bauhaus Archives to Kleiststraße, with the Urania on your left, to Wittenbergplatz, with the historic U-Bahn station in the middle of the square. Past KaDeWe department store on the left, you continue back down Tauentzienstraße to the Europa Center, where your trip ends.

## Cross City by S-Bahn

You see almost nothing from U-Bahn trains except at the ends of a few lines where they run above ground, but by spending a few hours on the S-Bahn trains running elevated across the city you can gain a valid impression for greater Berlin. S-Bahn trains take you great distances. Line S-3 can take you from Potsdam diagonally through Berlin to Erkner on the eastern border, 35 miles (57 kilometers) in 86 minutes averaging 25 mph (40 km/hr).

For a worthwhile roundtrip, board the S-Bahn at Zoo station (direction: Potsdam). You pass through Savignyplatz (with Ben Wargin's mural *World Tree*) to Charlottenburg and Westkreuz. From the Westkreuz station, you can easily reach the ICC and Radio Tower by foot (see Chapter 5). Your S-Bahn train runs parallel to the Avus (Chapter 11) beside Grunewald colony, founded at the end of the last century. From Nikolassee you pass station Wannsee.

At the station at the end of the S-Bahn line, Potsdam Stadt, you can catch a glimpse of the dome of the Peter and Paul church and make a pleasant stroll leading to Sanssouci (see Chapter 13).

Now you must return to Wannsee station to change lines. It's worth breaking your trip here for a short walk to the Großer Wannsee where the piers for the Wannsee Fleet are located. Passenger ships cruise regularly from here to Spandau/Tegel, to Peacock Island (see Chapter 11) as far as Werder via Potsdam. At Wannsee station a quick change lets you return via S-Bahn line S1 to Berlin (direction: Oranienburg). Passing through Nikolassee and Schlachtensee, you pass Mexikoplatz, the Botanical Gardens, arrive in Steglitz (see Chapter 10), and then continue farther along the path of the former city wall. After Yorckstraße, in the heart of Kreuzburg (Chapter 8), the big S-Bahn tunnel carries you under the Landwehr Canal and the Spree River to Anhalter Bahnhof station (Chapter 7). The next stop, Potsdamer Platz, gives you a chance to visit the Info-Box nearby (Chapter 4).

Still aboard S1, you continue through Friedrichstraße station across the

Scheunenviertel (Chapter 4) into Prenzlauer Berg (Chapter 9). You could continue to the end of the line at Oranienburg, but to save time, change at Bornholmer Straße to S-Bahn line S8 (direction: Grünau) which winds you through Eastern districts to Ostkreuz. You could continue farther through the East to Grünau, but again time is short, so you disembark here, change to a west-bound S-Bahn line (there are four) and begin your return trip via Alexanderplatz. From Alexanderplatz S-Bahn platform you have excellent views of the square and the television tower.

Past Friedrichstraße station, this route takes you across the Museum Island, between the museums (you can use either the Hackesher Markt or Friedrichstraße S-Bahn stations to visit the museums). You cross through Lehrter Bahnhof, where you see the construction of the new north-south tunnel, the Tiergarten, and back to your starting point, Zoo station.

During the final stretch, visitors point and say, "*Oh!* That's where the Wall was, look how everything has changed!" as they look out of the train window. Berliners snicker to themselves. It is very difficult to pick out on your own the place where the Wall stood. Ask another passenger to show it to you. The traces have been obliterated.

If you choose to take the S-Bahn through the East, you can ride as far as Schönefeld Airport or visit Köpenick (Chapter 12). It really is a long, not very fruitful trip along the way, but you pass along sections of the old city wall which were rebuilt into the S-Bahn ring, and see the difference in the outer communities which were incorporated into Berlin only in 1920. Each of them retains a special character, sometimes almost that of a village located around the community town hall with special industries that were never integrated into Berlin-wide schemes.

## Bike Berlin

Set off with your passport, DM 3, and a smile on the orange U-Bahn line 9 for U-Bhf Turmstraße and then to **bikecity**, Waldenserstraße 2-4, or you can pick up the bicycle route from one of their other locations. The city map you bought from the tourist office for DM 1 will be helpful. From bikecity pedal westward along Waldenserstraße through Moabit industry architecture. Turn left on Waldstraße to Gotzkowskybrücke, but before you reach the bridge angle left and not straight ahead. By the Gotzkowsky-brücke you find on your left Universal Hall, known for its weekend nightlife. Passing underneath on Levetzowstraße, the freight car you see is a memorial for the deportation of 55,699 Jews, 1941-45. Now pedal underneath the S-Bahn and then straight ahead toward Großer Stern. On the left you pass the Hansaplatz. The Grips Theater for children is at the U-Bahn station. Farther along Altonaer Straße you can't miss the Victory Column. You can climb almost to Golden Else except in winter.

Großer Stern is noted as the center of the annual Love Parade. Swing left into Spreeweg, past the new President's Egg and Schloß Bellevue. Next right on John-Foster-Dulles-Allee past the Pregnant Oyster where you can drop into the cafeteria for a snack or soak your legs in the fountain in front.

Straight ahead is the Reichstag. You can take a break either left or right in the Tiergarten, either to rest, jog, or toss a frisbee or football. Turn right on Entlastungsstraße and continue through traffic to the Cultural Forum where you can spin past or explore the Matthias Church, the New National Gallery, or the newly located Paintings Gallery. You will perhaps return another day to spend more time.

Continuing straight ahead along Potsdamer Straße takes you past Kumpelnest, a hangout on Lützowstraße and the Wintergarden Theater. The bicycle path is constantly crisscrossed by pedestrians. After many Imbiß stalls, boutiques, and shops, turn right on Winterfeldtstraße for one block and then to Maaßenstraße where you can lock up your bike and explore the center of the Schöneberg scene. Around the Winterfeldtplatz are many "in" cafés, designer shops, and second-hand shops.

Back to the saddle, at the end of Goltzstraße turn left on Grunewaldstraße toward Kleistpark. Watch out for the autos. Berlin drivers don't may much attention to bicyclists. Crossing Hauptstraße, angle right on Langenscheidtstraße and back onto the bicycle path. Past Monumentenbrücke turn left into Kreuzbergstraße to Victoria Park.

Past Victoria Park, left on Mehringdamm and the elevated bicycle path. Straight ahead leads into Wilhelmstraße. At Kochstraße you want to make a right for one block to Checkpoint Charlie and then circle back via Niederkirchenerstraße past Göring's Air Force Ministry building, the flags of the Berlin City Council building, and the Martin-Gropius-Building. Bicycle past the Topographie des Terrors exhibition and then head north through construction on Stresemannstraße to Potsdamer Platz and the fire-red Info-Box. Continue across to Ebertstraße which will sneak you into Pariser Platz and the Brandenburg Gate. Pull a right and cruise at your leisure down Unter den Linden past the Prussian buildings and Humboldt University on your left where students are selling books in front.

At Alexanderplatz you can lock your bike and take the elevator to the observation platform. Your quickest return to U-Bhf Turmstraße from U-Bhf Alexanderplatz is via line U8 to U-Bhf Osloer Straße, changing to U9 to U-Bhf Turmstraße. If you wish to cycle, cross via Dircksenstraße (drop in at the Hackescher Höfe) to Oranienburger Straße past the New Synagogue, up Friedrichstraße to Invalidenstraße. Turn left and pedal past the Hamburger Bahnhof's Contemporary Art Museum to Alt-Moabit to Turmstraße. A good day.

**Bikecity** (Rosentahaler Straße 40-41, in den Hackeschen Höfen, Mitte, Tel. 28-59-98-95). Open Mon.-Fri., 10 A.M. to 7 P.M.; Sat., 10 A.M. to 4 P.M. Use S-Bhf Hackescher Markt.

**Bikecity** (Gipsstraße 7, Mitte, Tel. 216-91-77). Open Mon.-Fri., 10 A.M. to 6:30 P.M.; Sat., 10 A.M. to 2 P.M. Use U-Bhf Weinmeisterstraße.

**Bikecity** (Schloßplatz 1, Mitte, Tel. 216-06-66-2). Open 7 A.M. to 9 P.M. Use U- or S-Bhf Alexanderplatz.

**Fahrradstation** (Möckernstraße 92, Kreuzberg, Tel. 216-91-77). Open Mon.-Fri., 10 A.M. to 6 P.M.; Sat., 10 A.M. to 2 P.M. Use U-Bhf Möckernbrücke.

## Seeing Berlin by Steamer

"The Spree keeps on flowing through Berlin," the song which Marlene Dietrich sang in the '20s can be heard coming out of the loudspeaker. It told Berliners about the beautiful aspects of their city and encouraged those without "a cent to their name" to simply stay at home for their holidays.

Berlin was built in the 12th century on low-lying land crisscrossed by streams and rivers. Successive electors, kings, and kaisers dug canals to reclaim the land and improve commerce. Berlin now has 62 lakes and 127 canals and waterways with more than 1,000 bridges over them—more than Venice.

Cruising the rivers and lakes is a way to travel in a natural way following the development of Berlin from district to district and seeing the lakes and beaches of the outlying areas. This has only become possible with the reunification of the two Berlins. At one time the Spree River comprised part of the Wall.

Cruising up- and downstream gives you a new perspective on Berlin and allows you to see much in a short time. From water level you can appreciate the interconnection between important historic buildings and realize the stimulus of river traffic on the growth of Berlin. You come so close to some historic buildings that you can reach out and touch them. Passing through the historic center you rise and descend in locks dating from the Middle Ages.

The Spree is as squalid a river as you will find, but when it widens into the Havel and forms the Wannsee it reminds you of an Alpine lake. From the water's edge at Cecilienhof in Potsdam, where swans swim gracefully along the banks and bathers get a full-body tan, idlers wave to the passing boats.

You see the beautiful historic buildings in Berlin Mitte—you were never ever better able to do this. The problem with seeing historic buildings from the river is that you want to get out and visit them. The list of things you see includes a muster of Berlin's famous sights. Boats pass beneath the Mühlendamm Bridge into the beginnings of Berlin and its ancient rival city, Cölln, past the Nikolai Quarter, under the Schloßbrücke decorated with Schinkel's neoclassical sculptures, under Liebknecht Bridge, around Museum Island, and under the Friedrichstraße Bridge. They use the landing in back of the former Congress Hall and cruise past Charlottenburg Palace, where there is another landing. You can use steamers to the landing at Potsdam (to see Sanssouci), to Köpenick (for the town hall and palace), to Treptower Park (for the Soviet Memorial), and to Charlottenburg (for the palace). On the river you see prewar wooden sailboats, mahogany immaculately maintained, Fiberglas and plastic cruisers, commercial barges, and nude beaches. You have a good selection of landing sites and available tours:

**Stern und Kreis Schiffahrt** (Puschkinallee 16-17, Tel. 53-63-60-0, Fax 53-63-60-99, *http://www.sternundkreis.de*) has a selection of 25 casual cruises winding their ways in and around Berlin. They support some 16 boats, ranging from the 10-year-old 400-passenger *Havel Queen* and *Havelstern* to three 84-passenger boats of the *Raubvogel* ("Bird of Prey") class. S&K's journeys take you through Berlin's historic city center over the Landwehrkanal and Spree, from Spandau Lindenufer or Wannsee, from Tegel and the Greenwich Promenade, and on the Spree. They take you almost anywhere you fancy that is accessible by boat over almost 100 miles (160 kilometers) from distant Werder (past Potsdam) to Spandau, Potsdam, Tegel, Köpenick, (lake) Müggelsee, (lake) Möllensee, and the (lake) Wannsee.

S&K's excursions alternate according to the day of the week and offer you a wide choice of departure points, so you should ask for information/free brochure either at their office or at the Berlin Tourist Office.

The S&K people have worked a deal with the Berlin Transit Authority (BVG) for a 24-hour card valid on both company's vehicles throughout the entire area. Buy it from subway ticketing offices April until October.

Steamer landings are about a five-minute walk from S-Bhf Wannsee, about seven minutes to Lindenufer from U-Bhf Rathaus Spandau, and about 10 minutes to Greenwich Promenade from U-Bhf Tegel. Landings are near U- and S-Bhf Jannowitzbrücke, S-Bhf Treptower Park, S-Bhf Grünau, U- and S-Bhf Friedrichstraße, S-Bhf Friedrichshagen, behind Charlottenburg Palace and the House of Cultures of the World.

**Reederei Bruno Winkler** (Mierendorffstraße 16, Tel. 349-95-95, Fax 391-80-49) takes passengers aboard the new "City-liner" *Charlottenburg* from the Schloßbrücke by Charlottenburg Palace for a three-hour sightseeing trip with expert guide past Berlin's sights. Walkmans with headphones are available for a fee to narrate your city tour on the Spree and Landwehr Canal. Other Winkler ships depart from Bridge 3, Tegel (use U-Bhf Tegel), and the Spandau-Lindenufer (U-Bhf Rathaus Spandau) for the Wannsee and Pheasant Island. You can buy your tickets in the tourist offices.

**Reederei Riedel** (Planufer 78, Tel. 6-91-37-82, Fax 6-94-21-91) schedules narrated, three-and-a-half-hour city tours on the Spree and Landwehrkanal departing at 10 to 10:45 A.M. and 2:30 to 2:45 P.M. from the Hansabrücke, Märkisches Ufer, and Kottbusser Brücke. At the pier in back of the House of World Cultures there are departures six times daily. Longer trips take you to the Wannsee and Neu Helgoland.

**Reederei Hartmut Triebler** (Tel. 371-16-71, Fax 372-88-31) sends their MS *Roland von Berlin* (150 seats) and MS *Berolina* (400 seats) around Potsdam and through canals west of Berlin. You can board them conveniently at Spandau, Tegel, and Wannsee.

## Red-lining the Wall

Everyone wants to see the **Wall**. It's usually a first-time visitor's first request. Sadly for visitors—or happily for Berliners—there isn't much left of the Wall to see, but you can find preserved segments here and there thanks to the world interest in the Wall. To mollify visitors, the Berlin Tourist Office has arranged for a bright red line to be placed in the asphalt, cobblestones, or whatever surface along the path where the Wall once stood. It took longer to lay a three-inch-wide red stripe than it did to put up the Wall. In some places motorists misread the meaning of the red stripe, swerving and suddenly changing lanes to the amazement of the traffic police and the danger of other drivers. In some places the red stripe is an engraved copper strip which seems much more appropriate.

• Your first stop should be the former Checkpoint Charlie border crossing (Chapter 7) and, when you like, a visit to the popular Checkpoint Charlie Museum of the Wall.

• On the border with the Western Berlin district of Wedding, at the corner of Gartenstraße and Bernauerstraße in Mitte, opposite the Nordbahnhof ("North Train Station") where only S-Bahn trains run, you see the **Gedenkstätte Berliner Mauer** ("Berlin Wall Memorial") which was opened on August 13, 1998 (see Chapter 6). Use S-Bhf Nordbahnhof, bus 245 or bus 328.

• Segments of the Wall, a watch tower, and the original Checkpoint Charlie shack are on display in the l998 **Alliiertemuseum** ("Allied Museum") in Zehlendorf (see Chapter 10).

• You can see about 800 feet (250 meters) of the Wall on Niederkirch-nerstraße across from the former Nazi Air Force Ministry (also Chapter 7).

• Some graffiti-covered segments are located below Potsdamer Platz's Info-Box.

• Relics of the Wall remain at the three-quarter mile (1.2 kilometers) **East Side Gallery** on Mühlenstraße at Oberbaumbrĕcke on the west bank of the Spree in Friedrichshain. It claims to be the world's largest open-air art gallery because 118 artists from 21 different countries came to exercise their artistic talent and judgement on various Wall segments. Use U-Bhf or S-Bhf Warshauer Straße, bus 123.

• You can see the last remaining watch tower on Schlesische Straße in Kreuzberg (Chapter 8).

• You can visit the most authentic standing remnants of the Wall border-ing the Friedrich-Ludwig-Jahn Park in Prenzlauer Berg (Chapter 9) in the shadow of the new Max Schmeling Sports Arena. Use U-Bhf Eberswalder Straße, bus 120 or tram 20.

• Finally, selected segments are used for decoration outside the Checkpoint Charlie Museum, inside the Europa Center, at the entrance to the Sender Freies Berlin radio skyscraper, and next to a Trabi automobile at a flea market on Bernauerstraße across from the Nordbahnhof. It was on Bernauerstraße that East met West to begin the official demolition of the Wall. It went so fast it made their official heads spin.

# WESTERN HEART OF BERLIN

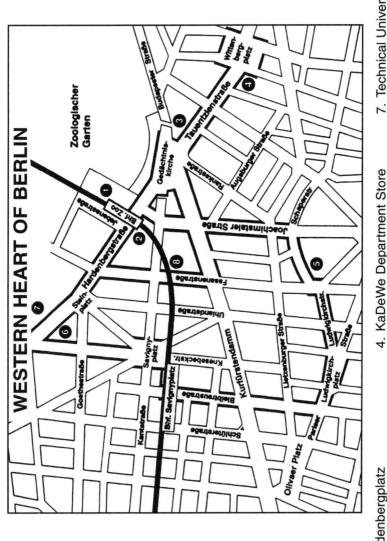

1. Hardenbergplatz
2. U-Bahn Station Zoo
3. Europa Center Tourist Office
4. KaDeWe Department Store
5. Freie Volksbühne
6. Renaissance Theater
7. Technical University
8. Jewish Community Center

# 3

# Western Heart of the City

## 1. Orientation

The Western Heart of modern Berlin is the neon-light area of the district of Charlottenburg comprising the Kurfürstendamm and its beckoning side streets; the Kaiser-Wilhelm-Gedächtniskirche, Breitscheidplatz, Europa Center, and Tauentzienstraße extending into Schöneberg district past Wittenbergplatz to Nollendorfplatz; the Zoo train station; and Hardenbergstraße extending up to the university and Ernst-Reuter-Platz. You won't find a more lively area in Europe.

The Kaiser-Wilhelm-Gedächtniskirche ("Kaiser William Memorial Church"), which many call the "Memorial Church," is your landmark. The Kurfürstendamm ("Boulevard of the Electors"), which everyone calls "Ku'damm," is your pleasure.

Because of the former isolation of the East, this is where you begin your visit to Berlin. The West is for entertainment, eating, and sleeping; the East is for history.

At the foot of the Memorial Church on the Breitscheidplatz, you find the hoopla center: street musicians, artists, magicians. It's a great show you won't want to miss, but this carnival is not what you came to Berlin to see.

On another direction, north from Zoo train station is Hardenbergstraße. This is quieter (although "quiet" is not an adjective we associate with Berlin). It is a student area with Mensa (see "Restaurants and Cafés" below), bookstores, restaurants, and of course the university buildings.

## 2. The Hotel Scene

The center of the city is a treasure chest of excellent hotels, pensions, and rooms to let distributed in Schöneberg, Tiergarten, Wilmersdorf, and Charlottenburg. You can see the surge of construction bringing a hotel boom to the Kurfürstendamm area. A new hotel is springing up on the corner of Kant- and Wilmersdorfer Straße. The new 70-room Domicil Hotel will open in summer 1999. A four-star hotel will open in the renovated hotel Kudamm-Eck structure where asbestos was removed. A super-luxury hotel with a 185-foot (56 meters) tower will open on the corner of Augsburger and Joachimstaler Straße. The corner of Kurfürstendamm and Knesebeckstraße will sport the Hollywood Media Hotel. The Zoofenster Hotel will open in year 2000 at Ku'damm 193-194. Most of the better ones can be booked by toll-free telephone from the United States before departure. The smaller ones and pensions must be booked by long-distance telephone, letter, fax, by the Berlin hotline, or in person in Berlin. All can be reserved at the Service Center at Tegel Airport and at the Berlin Tourist Office in the Europa Center. Train and bus arrivals may use the reservations consoles located in the stations. Prices quoted are rack rates; discounts are frequently available for those booking in advance.

## LARGE HOTELS

**Hotel Ambassador** (Bayreuther Straße 42, Schöneberg, Tel. 219-02-0, Fax 219-02-380, *http://www.utell.com*). A quiet hotel on a side street near Wittenbergplatz and KaDeWe. US$94-128, single; US$107-39, double; breakfast buffet included. In the U.S., Tel. Utell at 800-207-6900.

**Askiener Hof** (Kurfürstendamm 53, Charlottenburg, Tel. 8-81-80-83, Fax 8-81-72-01). Farther out, but still in the center of things. Guests praise the rooms with beautiful furnishings, modern baths, and elegant breakfast room. US$103-17, single; US$133-56, double; including breakfast buffet.

**Hotel Berlin** (Lützowplatz 17, Tiergarten, Tel. 26-05-0, Fax 26-05-27-16, *http://www.utell.com*) is one of those that the architects now regret designing. It shows its age even though it was designed in the post-War era, located just off Kurfürstenstraße, which is not to be confused with Kurfürstendamm.

Fronts on pleasant park. US$103-217, single; US$130-250, double; including breakfast buffet. Ask about their three-day, two-night packages. In the U.S., Tel. Utell at 800-207-6900 or Golden Tulip at 800-344-1212.

**Berlin Excelsior Hotel** (Hardenbergstraße 14, Charlottenburg, Tel. 31-55-0, Fax 31-55-10-02, *http://www.utell.com*) is a busy modern hotel convenient to the Technical University area. US$103-86, single; US$130-215, double; breakfast buffet included. In the U.S., Tel. Utell at 800-207-6900 or Golden Tulip at 800-344-1212.

**Berlin Mark** (Meinekestraße 18, Charlottenburg, Tel. 88002-0, Fax 8-80-02-804, *http://www.utell.com*) is an economy hotel off Ku'damm. US$81-153, single; US$109-85, double; breakfast included. In the U.S., Tel. Utell at 800-207-6900 or Golden Tulip at 800-344-1212.

**Hotel Berliner Hof** (Tauentzienstraße 8, Charlottenburg, Tel. 25-49-50, Fax 2-62-30-65). In the same block as the Europa Center. US$109-25, single; US$133-56, double; breakfast included.

**Berlin Plaza Hotel** (Knesebeckstraße 63, Tel. 88413-0, Fax 2-14-12-00, *http://www.utell.com*) is off on a side street a half-block away from one of the Burger King outlets on Kurfürstendamm. US$81-153, single; US$110-85, double; breakfast buffet included. In the U.S., Tel. Utell at 800-207-6900 or Golden Tulip at 800-344-1212.

**Bleibtreu Hotel** (Bleibtreustraße 31, Charlottenburg, Tel. 884-74-0, Fax 8-84-25-450). This new and modern hotel with specially designed Italian furnishings was constructed according to strict ecological guidelines and with natural materials. US$130-92, single; US$152-214, double; breakfast US$14 extra. In the U.S., Tel. Steigenberger Reservations, 1-800-223-5652.

**Hotel Boulevard am Kurfürstendamm** (Kurfürstendamm 12, Charlottenburg, Tel. 884-25-0, Fax 884-25-450). Wonderful view on Ku'damm and the Memorial Church. US$100-28, single; US$128-78, double; including breakfast. Use U-Bhf Kurfürstendamm. In the U.S., call Best Western, Tel. 1-800-528-1234.

**Hotel Brandenburger Hof** (Eislebener Straße 14, Wilmersdorf, Tel. 214-05-0, Fax 214-05-100, *http://www.berlin.de/graphics/tourismus*). Turn-of-the-century Relais & Chateau mansion in quiet surroundings two blocks south from the Memorial Church with spacious conservatory, piano bar, and gourmet restaurant *Die Quadriga*. US$153-220, single; US$183-247, double, breakfast included. Use U-Bhf Augsburgerstraße. In the U.S., Tel. Relais & Chateau.

**Hotel Consul** (Knesebeckstraße 8-9, Tel. 31-01-6, *http://www.utell.com*) is a simple hotel without restaurant that is very convenient to the schools and universities on Hardenbergstraße. It is 10 minutes from Ku'damm and the

Zoo station. US$66-93, single; US$97-149, double; breakfast buffet included. Use U-Bhf Theodor-Heuss-Platz. In the U.S., Tel. Utell at 800-207-6900 or Golden Tulip at 800-344-1212.

**Hotel Frühling am Zoö** (Kurfürstendamm 17, Charlottenburg, Tel. 8-81-80-83, Fax 8-81-64-83) is right in the heart of street activity. The Kranzler is across the street. Zoo Station and the Memorial Church are a block away. US$78-122, single; US$94-156, double; breakfast buffet included. A Comfort Hotel. Use U-Bhf Uhlandstraße. In the U.S., Tel. Choice Hotels at 800-424-4777.

The **Hotel Hamburg** (Landgrafenstraße 4, Tiergarten, Tel. 264-77-0, Fax 262-93-94, *http://www.utell.com*). This plain hotel in the Tiergarten is adequate for tour groups. Despite small rooms and a slow elevator, it is perfectly acceptable for American visitors. A Ringhotel, it has a nice bar and reading room. US$110-43, single; US$122-78, double; breakfast buffet included. Use U-Bhf Wittenburgplatz. In the U.S., Tel. Utell at 800-207-6900.

**Hotel Hardenberg** (Joachimsthaler Straße 39-40, Tel. 8-82-30-71, Fax 8-81-51-70, *http://www.utell.com*) is a traditional hotel. Some of the rooms have balconies with geraniums growing from flower boxes. US$92-103, single; US$108-30, double; breakfast buffet included. In the U.S., Tel. Utell at 800-207-6900.

The **Holiday Inn Crowne Plaza** (Nürnberger Straße 65, Schöneberg, Tel. 210-07-0, Fax 213-20-09, *http://www.crowneplaza.com*) is located in an enviable location behind the Europa Center across from Avis and Hertz car pickup/return and down the street from InterRent/Europcar. It sets a talked-about breakfast buffet. US$161-222, single; US$189-250, double; US$16, breakfast buffet. In the U.S., Tel. Holiday Inn Crowne Plaza at 800-2CROWNE.

**Holiday Inn Garden Court Berlin-Kurfürstendam** (Bleibtreustraße 25, Tel. 88-09-30, Fax 8-80-93-939, *http://www.holiday-inn.com*). Nicely located just south of Kurfürstendamm. US$125-59, single; US$158-94, double; breakfast included. In the U.S., Tel. Holiday Inn at 800-465-4329.

**Hotel Inter-Continental Berlin** (Budapester Straße 2-3, Tel. 2-60-20, Fax 26-02-807-60, *http://www.interconti.com/interconti*). The "Interconti" in the Tiergarten District is known to Berliners as the "checkerboard" because of its appearance from afar. The Schweizerhof Hotel at Budapster Straße 21-29, formerly under the same management, was reopened in May 1999. Consider that the Inter-Continental has 441 rooms, 70 suites, 3 restaurants, 2 bars, room service, etc. US$192-275, single; US$220-303, double; US$18, breakfast buffet. Ask for special rates during the summer and on weekends. In the U.S., Tel. Inter-Continental at 800-442-7375.

**Kempinski Hotel Bristol** (Kurfürstendamm 27, Tel. 884-34-0, Fax 883-60-75, *http://www.kempinski.com*). To the left of the Fasanenstraße entrance and six feet above ground, you can see the plaque that emphasizes that the owners of the hotel were forced to sell their business in 1937 because they were Jews, and that they were "killed, or able to flee." The family spent the War years in London, returned to Berlin after 1945, and opened their Ku'damm restaurant and hotel in 1952. This Ku'damm classic still has the number-one name; always called "the Kempinski." Berliner Schnauze claims the Kempi was so exclusive that even the bellhops tipped each other. Momentum has swung to Kempinski's *Adlon* in East Berlin (see Chapter 4) and the extravagant *Schloßhotel Vier Jahreszeiten* in Wilmersdorf (Chapter 10). US$201-84, single; US$252-335, double; breakfast included. Use U-Bhf Kurfürstendamm. In the U.S., contact Kempinski Tel. 800-426-3135 or Leading Hotels at 800-223-6800.

**Hotel Kronprinz** (Kronprinzendamm 1, Wilmersdorf, Tel. 89-60-30, Fax 8-93-12-15) is established in a Gründerzeit house from 1894. It rebuilt in 1984, keeping the same architecture. US$70-103, single; US$92-139, double; breakfast buffet included. Located near outer Kurfürstendamm near the Halensee.

**Hotel Kurfürstendamm am Adenauerplatz** (Kurfürstendamm 68, Charlottenburg, Tel. 8-84-63-0, Fax 8-82-55-28). Near Adenauerplatz but still in the high-rent district. No restaurant. US$100, single; US$150, double; breakfast buffet included. Use U-Bhf Adenauerplatz. Good connections to airport bus.

**Hotel Mondial** (Kurfürstendamm 47, Tel. 884-11-0, Fax 884-11-150) is oak-finished modern with attention to detail that does not sacrifice comfort. Because it fronts on Ku'damm close to Bleibtreustraße, street rooms have double windows, but open for ventilation. A good choice. US$94-211, single; US$122-250, double; breakfast buffet included. Use U-Bhf Uhlandstraße.

Convenient to the car rental garages is the elegant **Hotel Palace** (Budapester Straße 42, Charlottenburg, Tel. 25497-0, Fax 2-62-65-77, *http://www.utell.com*), which is right "in" the Europa Center next to the gambling casino. Car hops wait for you to drive through their front traffic loop. US$156-257, single; US$183-294, double; breakfast buffet US$16 extra. In the U.S., Tel. Utell at 800-207-6900.

**Hotel President** (An der Urania 16-18, Schöneberg, Tel. 21-90-30, Fax 2-14-12-00) is a modern, chic hotel not far from Wittenburgplatz. US$130-65, single; US$155-96, double; breakfast buffet included. In the U.S., call Best Western, Tel. 1-800-528-1234.

**Hotel Prinzregent** (Prinzregentenstraße 47, Wilmersdorf, Tel. 853-80-51, Fax 8-54-76-37) is directly across from the Zoo train station. No restaurant. US$67, single; US$94, double; breakfast buffet included.

**Hotel Savigny** (Brandenburgische Straße 21, Wilmersdorf, Tel. 881-30-01, Fax 882-55-19). Out-of-the-way hotel in Wilmersdorf with single and double rooms. US$39-72, single; US$67-106, double; including breakfast. Use U-Bhf Adenauerplatz.

**Savoy Hotel** (Fasanenstraße 9-10, Charlottenburg, Tel. 311-03-0, Fax 311-03-333) has just that kind of old-fashioned, very nice ambience that North Americans expect from a European hotel dating from 1930. It is not modern, but well appointed with classic furniture. It attracts a knowledgeable, repeat European clientele. Excellent location. US$130-75, single; US$175-220, double; breakfast US$16 extra. In the U.S., Tel. Steigenberger Reservations, 1-800-223-5652.

**Scandotel Castor Berlin** (Fuggerstraße 8, Schöneberg, Tel. 21-30-30, Fax 21-30-3-160, *http://www.utell.com*). US$94-127, single; US$103-47, double; breakfast buffet included. Weekend Special: US$83, single; US$97, double. Five minutes by foot from KaDeWe department store. Use U-Bhf Wittenburgplatz or U-Bhf Augsburger Straße. In the U.S., Tel. Utell at 800-207-6900.

**Hotel Steigenberger** (Los-Angeles-Platz 1, Charlottenburg, Tel. 21-27-0, Fax 21-27-702). A monolithic hotel with 386 rooms and suites nestled behind trees on a beautiful, quiet site only one block from Kurfürstendamm and the Kaiser-Wilhelm-Gedächtniskirche. Bathrooms contain second telephones, tubs, and radio connections to the main room. On the second floor, guests swim in a circular pool, have a massage, and visit the sauna or solarium. US$161-253, single; US$189-280, double; breakfast US$16 extra. Use U-Bhf Kurfürstendamm. In the U.S., Tel. Steigenberger Reservations, 1-800-223-5652.

**Sylter Hof** (Kurfürstenstraße 114-116, Tel. 2120-0, Fax 214-28-26) is a medium-sized, modern hotel with 81 single rooms and 45 double rooms beautifully located five walking minutes to Zoo train station and Memorial Church. US$75-92, single; US$103-128, double; US$14, breakfast buffet.

## SMALL HOTELS AND PENSIONS

The trend in Berlin is toward small, fine pension accommodations.

**Herberge Große** (Kantstraße 71, 4th floor, Tel./Fax 324-81-38, e-mail *HerbergeNGrosseBerlin@t-online.de*). Single, double, and three-bedded rooms from US$40 to US$80 per room. Breakfast US$7 extra. Welcomes backpackers. Use S-Bhf Charlottenburg or U-Bhf Wilmersdorferstraße.

**Hotel-Pension Funk** (Fasanenstraße 69, Tel. 8-82-71-93, Fax 8-83-33-29). This was the home of Danish actress Asta Nielsen from 1931-37 before she was hurried to leave by Adolph Hitler. Converted to a pension after the

Second World War, many of the furnishings of the 1895 house date from her stay. Twenty-four beds; no restaurant. US$36-61, single; US$56-89, double; breakfast buffet included.

**Hotel Avantgarde** (Kurfürstendamm 15, Tel. 8-82-64-66, Fax 8-81-98-77, *http://www.utell.com*). Fifty beds on Ku'damm. US$128-39, single; US$161-94, double; breakfast buffet included. In the U.S., Tel. Utell at 800-207-6900.

**Hotel-Pension Modena** (Wielandstraße 26, Charlottenburg, Tel. 8-85-70-10, Fax 8-81-52-94). Thirty beds near Savignyplatz. US$36-61, single; US$44-78, double; breakfast included. Use S-Savignyplatz.

**Pension Niebuhr** (Niebuhrstaße 74, Charlottenburg, Tel. 3-24-95-95, Fax 3-24-80-21). Twenty-one beds near Savignyplatz. US$53-78, single; US$67-94, double; including breakfast. Use S-Bhf Savignyplatz.

**Hotel Remter** (Marburger Straße 17, Tel. 24-50-88-0, Fax 2-13-86-12) is located down an alley off the Tauentzienstraße so that this 61-bed hotel is in a good location. US$70-92, single; US$80-122, double; breakfast buffet included. Use U-Bhf Kurfürstendamm.

**Hotel-Pension Rheingold** (Xantener Straße 9, Wilmersdorf, Tel. 8-83-10-40, Fax 8-82-20-06). One block from outer Kurfürstendamm, 29 beds. US$48-72, single; US$78-103, double; breakfast buffet included. Use U-Bhf Adenauerplatz.

**Pension Villa Depêche II** (Lübecker Straße 24, Tiergarten, Tel. 3-96-30-13, Fax 39-03-41-47). Thirty beds two subway stops from U-Bhf Zoo. US$36-61, single; US$44-78, double; breakfast from US$3. Use U-Bhf Turmstraße.

## 3. Restaurants and Cafés

Many of the best restaurants are in this part of town. The Europa Center, for starters, has worthwhile restaurants: facing on Breitscheidplatz is the Mövenpick, the Swiss company, which advertises Swiss hospitality and service; on the bottom level the Alt-Nürnberg features Bavarian specialties; in the interior there's Daitokai; off to the side you can drink at the Irish Pub; and if you want to venture into the Palace Hotel, you can dine well at Restaurant First Floor.

**Mövenpick**, Tel. 264-76-30, the Swiss conglomerate has spread like oil on the European waters into ice cream, hotels, health food restaurants, and supermarket specialties. The bit of Switzerland in the Europa Center brings with it decor from various cantons of Switzerland, especially the Engadine in Canton Graubünden. Moderately priced, you dine in bright surroundings. Specialties change monthly. The *Geschnätzltes mit Rösti* here is just like that served in Zürich. It also serves Sunday brunch from 8 A.M. to noon.

The kitsch decor in the moderately priced **Alt-Nürnberg**, Tel. 261-43-97, is designed to look like Bavaria. It features butcher-block tables and gemütlich benches and decor. The house specialty is the *Nürnberger Rostbratwurst*, with either wine sauerkraut or potato salad, just like those served in the Wurst houses in Nürnberg (Nuremberg). Service personnel speak with a Brandenburg accent.

**Daitokai**, Tel. 261-80-99 (open Tue.-Sun. noon to 3 P.M. and 6 P.M. to midnight), is literally a beautiful restaurant with specialties flown from Japan. How does raw fish go with German beer? Expensive.

The moderately priced **Irish Pub**, Tel. 2-62-16-34 (open Mon.-Thur. 11:30 A.M. to 3 A.M., Fri.-Sat. until 4 A.M., Sun. from 10:30 A.M.), is a strong, hearty dose of Ireland: you enter and there is nothing but the longest bar east of Dublin which stretches to the end of the long room and then wraps around. The main service here is dark Guinness ale, toast sandwiches, and live music every evening.

**First Floor im Hotel Palace**, Europa Center, Tel. 25-02-10-20 (open Mon.-Fri. from noon to 3 P.M. and 6 P.M. to 11:30 P.M., Sat. 6 to 11:30 P.M.). Very German, very gourmet, and very expensive food. Michelin star. Reservations recommended.

If you can't find a free table outdoors on the Breitscheidplatz in front of the Europa Center (moderately priced) you can walk across the street to similarly priced **Eierschale 2**, Rankstraße 1, Tel. 882-53-05 (open Sun.-Thur. 8 A.M. to 2 A.M., Fri.-Sat. to 4 A.M.), in the shade (or vice versa). Eierschale (which means "Eggshell") features live music nightly and is good with live music for breakfast on Sundays.

For years the signature red-and-white awnings of the sidewalk **Café Kranzler**, Kurfürstendamm 18-19, Tel. 8-82-69-11, Fax 8-83-27-37 (open 8 A.M. to midnight), were the Cold War symbol of free West Berlin and a favorite scene for postcards. By year 2000, Chicago architect Helmut Jahn will have torn away the awnings and sent the Kranzler packing to the first floor of the corner location. "It wasn't the most beautiful café, but you had to have *been* there." Jahn's *Neue Kranzler Eck* ("New Kranzler Corner") will present a new look on the Kurfürstendamm site, established in 1931. Kranzler's mother location on Unter den Linden/Friedrichstraße was Germany's oldest coffeehouse, established in 1834. About 100 years ago, Kranzler hired the first female waiters and opened the first separate rooms for smokers. The resulting scandal rocked Berlin. Use U-Bhf Uhlandstraße.

Across the street, the similarly expensive **Café Möhring** at the corner of Kurfürstendamm and Uhlandstraße, is in big trouble because of escalating rent. Despite slashing its staff, the Möhring may not be around much longer. Open daily 7 A.M. to midnight, facing the Memorial Church in an imperial building, the Möhring was formerly the Hofkonditorei Schilling. The epitome of elegant Berlin cafés, Möhring features every sort of beautiful-looking and good-tasting cake and fancy confection. Gray-haired and well-dressed clientele gather here to talk of the good old days. Use U-Bhf Uhlandstraße.

**Hard Rock Café**, Meinekestraße 21, Tel. 88-46-20, 884-62-88 (open noon to 2 A.M.). "Love all—serve all." The Hard Rock serves the largest Hamburger in Berlin. Use U-Bhf Kurfürstendamm.

**Paris Bar**, Kantstraße 152, Tel. 313-80-52 (open noon to 2 A.M.), expensive, near Savignyplatz, has very good food. Steak a la minute, stuffed rabbit, and beef Bourgignon are popular. One of the most attractive restaurants in Berlin, with black and white checked floors, Warhol pictures on the wall, and arrogant waiters, it has been for years *the* French bistro, attracting artists, writers, and intellectuals. "See and be seen," is the motto. The list of VIPs of the film world that come here regularly would fill the entrance hall of the train station. They nearly outnumber the tourists that come to gawk at them. Reservations recommended.

**Florian**, Grolmanstraße 52, Tel. 313-91-84, Fax 3-12-39-75 (open 6 P.M. to 3 A.M.), is more modern than the Paris Bar, but colder. Volker Schöndorf and Wim Wenders are seen here. Excellent, but expensive, southern German and French cuisine. Open for dinner and late snacks only. Reservations recommended. Use U-Bhf Ernst-Reuter-Platz or S-Bhf Savignyplatz.

**Diener**, Grolmanstraße 47, Tel. 881-53-29 (6 P.M. until late), near Savignyplatz is a moderately priced German Kneipe with simple Berlin cooking. Behind the nicotine-yellow curtains, you find lots of sauerkraut and sausages. Old Berliners still come here because it is off the tourist track. Founded by champion German boxer Franz Diener, it used to be a boxer's hangout, so the wood-paneled walls are covered with photographs of German boxing stars. The decor hasn't changed since the 1930s. No reservations. Use U-Bhf Uhlandstraße.

**Café im Literaturhaus**, Fasanenstraße 23, Tel. 882-54-14 (open 9:30 A.M. to 1 A.M.). In summer you can sit beside a fountain in one of Berlin's most beautiful gardens in incredible peace in one of Berlin's best cafés. Someone always reads from his or her works on Monday evenings at 9 P.M. It is relatively expensive. Use U-Bhf Uhlandstraße.

**Café Zillemarkt**, Bleibtreustraße 48a, Tel. 881-40-70 (open 8 A.M. to midnight—breakfast until 6 P.M.), is one of many shabby but atmospheric pleasant inexpensive little bars in the area off Kurfürstendamm. You can say that this is "typical Berlin." Zillemarkt is located in a former antique shop serving breakfast, coffee, and dinner and featuring billiards. Try the stuffed cabbage. Young crowd.

**Bleibtreu**, Bleibtreustraße 45, Tel. 881-47-56 (open 9:30 a.m to 1 A.M.). Here *Nachtschwärmer* ("night people") find their *Zweites Frühstück* ("late breakfast") until 3:30 P.M. or bountiful breakfast buffet on Saturdays and Sundays.

The **Schwarzes Café**, Kantstraße 148, Tel. 3-13-80-38, Fax 3-15-29-54 (open 24 hours with breakfast round the clock from Wednesday at 11 A.M. to Monday at 3 A.M., open Tue. from noon), is said to have been the hangout of anarchists. The whole left ideology has collapsed, so things are quiet—and inexpensive—at the moment, but the cappuccino machine works round the clock and the classic café, now an institution, is still atmospheric and filled with a feeling of intrigue. The designer toilettes are a real experience. The summer patio is gorgeous. The clientele never changes. It is always young.

**Café Savigny**, Grolmanstraße 53, Tel. 312-81-95 (open 10 A.M. to 2 A.M.), has good breakfasts, intellectual clientele, and cachet. Next door, **Tucci**, Grolmanstraße 52, Tel. 313-93-35 (open noon to 1 A.M.), features excellent pasta dishes. Both are modestly priced.

**Ottenthal**, Kantstraße 153, Tel. 313-3162 (open Mon.-Sat. 10 A.M. to 2 A.M., Sun. from 4 P.M.), serves south-of-the-border Austrian food in extraordinary Berlin. Use U-Bhf Uhlandstraße.

**Marjellchen**, Mommsenstraße 9, Tel. 883-26-76 (open 5 P.M. to midnight), has cooking like mothers, provided your mother is from East Prussia. If you only have heard about original Königsberger Klöpse (meatballs) from friends, go here. Use S-Bhf Savignyplatz.

**Arc**, Fasanenstraße 81a, Tel. 313-2625 (open 9 A.M. to 2 A.M.), is one of the youngest flowers of the Berlin scene located beneath the S-Bahn and mainline train overpass. You can find an honest, business lunch. By night, expect a Kneipe flavor.

**Ristorante Biscotti**, Pestallozistraße 88, Tel. 312-3937 (open 6 P.M. to 12:30 A.M.), is an Italian restaurant for those with plump wallets. Use U-Bhf Deutsche Oper or U-Bhf Wilmersdorfer Straße.

**Park-Restaurant im Steigenberger-Hotel**, Los-Angeles-Platz 1, Tel. 212-7755 (open Tue.-Sat. from 6 P.M.), serves healthy, light food on the air-conditioned first floor.

On Wittenbergplatz, **KaDeWe** has an excellent restaurant on the fifth floor with attractive decor.

**Café Einstein**, Kurfürstenstraße 58, Tel. 261-50-96 (open daily 10 A.M. to 2 A.M.), is one of Berlin's institutions with moderately priced breakfasts until 2 P.M.. It successfully transplants a Viennese Kaffeehaus atmosphere into the Western Heart of Berlin. Patrons lounge in the plush, Jugendstil decor and read international newspapers clamped on poles. The yuppie clientele prefers the outdoor patio in back. From U-Bhf Nollendorfplatz walk one block up Einemstraße to Kurfürstenstraße 55 (upstairs).

The cheapest place to eat is probably the student **Mensa**, Hardenbergstraße 34. The students call it the "grease pit," but they go there nevertheless for the price. The cafeteria can be fearsomely crowded and serves some items whose origins defy identification. The cafeteria, for students only, is open 11:15 A.M. to 2:30 P.M., school days only. Plastic meal cards are sold, but there is also a *Barkasse* ("cash cashier"). A more expensive (but still cheap), limited cafeteria to the right on the ground floor is open to all (open 8 A.M. to 4 P.M. and 4:30 to 8 P.M. on school days). On the third floor a smaller, limited cafeteria offers more comfort and is open to all. Food quality ranges from pretty good to marginally edible. Use S- or U-Bhf Zoo.

The **Café Hardenberg**, Hardenbergstraße 10, Tel. 312-33-30 (open 9 A.M. to 1 A.M.), across the street is popular to overflowing with students who get fed up with the hassle of the Mensa. Reasonably-priced breakfast. Use S- or U-Bhf Zoo.

# 4. Sightseeing

## MEMORIAL CHURCH

The neoromantic **Kaiser-Wilhelm-Gedächtniskirche** ("Emperor William Memorial Church"), Breitscheidplatz (Tel. 218-50-23) is your first orientation point to fix upon in West Berlin. Because it's so close to the strategic Zoo train station it was nearly destroyed during the Second World War.

Berliners are always ready with a nickname, so as soon as the shower of bombs and the echoing of artillery died down at the end of the War, they named the ruins of formerly the highest church tower in Berlin (370 feet/113 meters), "Hollow Tooth," because there was nothing else remaining.

The church, named after Kaiser Wilhelm I, who had died seven years earlier, was personally dedicated by his grandson, Kaiser Wilhelm II, on September 1, 1895. It cost 6.5 million gold Marks, an astronomical sum at the time, and was designed by the royal Prussian architect, Franz Schwechten.

Only a massive campaign by Berlin magazines prevented the ruins from being razed, and by 1961, on the same day the new Coventry cathedral was consecrated in England, there appeared an ensemble of church ruins designed by Professor Egon Eiermann. Berlin Schnauze immediately called the new freestanding 170-foot (52 meters) modern bell tower (with six bells), the "Lipstick." The squat, new octagonal church building, was variously dubbed the "Compact" or the "Egg Carton," or even more cynically, with reference to the nearby *Kaufhaus des Westens* (KaDeWe department store), some called it the *Taufhaus des Westens* ("Baptism House").

The new church's 20,000 windows of glass blocks were created by Gabriel Loire and made in Chartres, France. They give it a strangely surreal atmosphere glowing within by day and radiating blue outside by night. Inside the modern pillbox church, organ concerts and religious services are held, illuminated by the blue glow from the translucent bricks and the golden Christ, but in 1998, the bell tower fell silent. Rust. It remains silent until the parishioners or a good angel can scrape together money for the repairs. The church is open 9 A.M. to 7 P.M. English-language services are held Sundays at 9 A.M., June to August.

On January 7, 1987, the entrance of the former church was reopened as a **Memorial Hall** (open Mon.-Sat. 10 A.M. to 4 P.M.). It is a place for observation against war and destruction and a call for preservation in Jesus Christ. Inside there are guided tours on Thur.-Fri. at 1:15, 3, and 4:30 P.M. including information about the construction, history, and reconstruction of the church. Meet in front of the hall. It is worth seeing just for the mosaic ceiling over the small hall that is just as beautiful as the original church once was. Most of the exhibits are identified in the German language only, but it is a very visual exhibit including a cross made of building nails from the 14th-century Gothic Cathedral of Coventry, which was destroyed together with Coventry's inner city by a German air attack in November 1940.

On the **Breitscheidplatz**, between the Memorial Church and the Europa Center, there is a wonderful water fountain centered around an almost 60-foot (18 meters) diameter, 33-foot (10 meters) high hemisphere of polished reddish granite. Berlin artist Joachim Schmettau intended it to be called *Weltenbrunnen* ("Globe Fountain"), symbolizing the split nature of the Earth, but Berliners call it the **Wasserklops**. "Klops" is the "meatball" usually found in the Berlin goulash that comes from Königsberg (now Kaliningrad). Try not to laugh when you see it on the menu.

Clever and original figures (one shows artist Schmettau at work with welding torch and goggles) play within the fountain and from a distance, while about 106,000 gallons (400,000 liters) of water flow over the fragmented sphere Mon.-Thur. 10 A.M. to midnight from March 30 to October 31, and until 1 A.M. on weekends.

The site of the legendary Romanische Café, the pre-war barn of a café where Berlin's Expressionist painters, chess players, and intellectuals sat among up to 1,000 customers on Breitscheidplatz, is now a gathering point for acrobatic skateboard artists and the homeless, who use the long rows of benches facing the Memorial Church. You can have your hair done in cornrows, have your portrait sketched, listen to street musicians, and buy souvenirs and pieces of junk. On the Breitscheidplatz is a monument to a smaller ginkgo surrounded by a fence. Leaves from Japanese ginkgo trees are supposed to bring luck. The brass plaque adjacent to the tree carries a quote from Goethe: "This tree from the east honors my garden and gives secret meaning. . . ." This particular ginkgo tree doesn't look too lucky to have been planted in the midst of a boozers' gathering place.

The building topped with the giant three-pointed Mercedes star, constantly revolving and neon-lit, is the 1963-5 **Europa Center**, 282 feet (86 meters) high with 22 floors and more than 100 attractions. Inside you shop and eat in more than 74 shops and 20 restaurants, visit eight entertainment centers, rent autos from two companies, trod supermarket aisles, gamble in an exclusive casino, and pick up information from airline offices and the Berlin Tourist Office. It was built on the site of the famous Romanische Café, which was destroyed by the War.

The centerpiece of the Europa Center is the **"Uhr der fließenden Zeit,"** the hypnotic "time-flows" clock, designed by the French physicist Bernard Gitton to indicate time to the minute by use of a labyrinth of chemistry-laboratory-looking glass tubes filled with a fluorescent liquid. By some baffling means, one of 30 flattened glass balls fills every two minutes and 12 spherical balls fill every hour to indicate the time of day. Crowds gather to watch the gushing, astonishing changes of the hours. Berliners say that time doesn't "fly" here: it flows.

On the ground floor there is another hypnotic water sculpture called the *Lotus Stream*. Stainless steel lotus cups fill with water via tubes concealed in their metal stems, tip from the water's weight, shower into other lotus cups, etc.

Inside the Tauentzienstraße entrance you find, sheathed from post-Wende graffiti, an excellent segment of the **Wall** together with several memorial plaques. This is one of the best saved segments you will find anywhere. It is located so conveniently that it saves you a bus trip into Berlin's hinterlands.

In front of the entrance to the Berlin Tourist Office (where there is inlaid in the tiles a tribute to Berlin's 750th anniversary) you see the fascinating **Mengenlehre Uhr** ("Set Theory Clock") created by Dieter Binninger in 1975. There are two upper rows of four lights each. The upper two rows tell the hour. The lights in the top row stand for five hours each, those in the second row indicate single hours. Remember this is a 24-hour clock. If two lights in the top row and two in the second row are lit, it is 12 noon, not midnight. The lights in the third row indicate five minutes each and the bottom row tells the minute. Suppose the first light in each row were lit; it would be five hours plus one hour plus five minutes plus one minute, or 6:06 A.M. When three lights in each row are lit, it is 15 hours plus three hours plus 15 minutes plus three minutes or 18:18 (6:18 P.M.). You can buy miniatures in the souvenir shops.

## KURFÜRSTENDAMM

Kurfürstendamm is 2.2 miles (3.5 kilometers) long and 170 feet (52 meters) wide, but length and width are not the measure or meaning of Kurfürstendamm. Kurfürstendamm is a street of coffeehouses and people. It is a street of the people, not of nobility or the military. Bismarck wanted Berlin to have an avenue like Paris' Champs Elysées, but lacked the Place de la Concorde anchoring one end and Kaiser Wilhelm Memorial Church could hardly compare with the Arc de Triomphe.

Its roots go back to the 14th century, when Ku'damm was a muddy hunting path for the Prince Electors (*Kurfürsten*) connecting Grunewald hunting lodge with the former Berlin City Palace on Schloßplatz. Where the route from the city to the Grunewald passed over marshy ground that bogged down carriage wheels and horses' hooves, Joachim II had a long causeway of logs—a *Damm*—laid down. It became known as the Kurfürstendamm. It was the idea of Otto von Bismarck, the first German chancellor, to make it the first shopping and amusement avenue. In 1871, during a visit to Paris, he fell in love with boulevard Champs-Elysées and determined to build in Berlin as well such a beautiful lane with richly decorated facades, cupolas, columns, and corners. He ordered that all buildings had to have exactly four stories. The facades were decorated with beautiful stucco. In front of the houses English gardens were laid out. Corner houses were required to have a dome on top. Unfortunately only 48 of the 250 former "imperial buildings" survived World War II, but these 48 reveal something of the earlier magnificence of Kurfürstendamm.

After the Russian Revolution of 1917, Berlin became the center for Russians in exile as 300,000 Russian elite fled, sometimes spending three weeks in a freight car, finding peace at Zoo train station. They formed a Russian colony and called Charlottenburg, "Charlottengrad," and Kurfürstendamm, "Kurfürsten-Prospekt." The ateliers and writer's cafés around the Zoo station and Kaiser-Wilhelm-Kirche buzzed; world-famous canvases were created by the painters Wassily Kandinsky and Alexander Archipenko. Marc Chagall and Kasimir Malewitsch discovered their genius. Boris Pasternak, Lew Lunz, and Ossip Mandelstam in Berlin gave literature a new impulse. Often Berlin, so near to Russia, was merely a first step toward Paris or America.

During the Golden '20s, Germany became the cultural center of Europe and Kurfürstendamm became the cultural center of Berlin. Artists like Ernest Lübitsch, Fritz Lang, Carl Mayer, Georg-Wilhelm Papst, actors like Marlene Dietrich and Emil Jennings, theatrical geniuses like Bertholt Brecht and Max Rheinhardt, and writers like Erich Kästner, Thomas Mann, Heinrich Mann, Kurt Tucholsky, and Maxim Gorki sat together in the coffee shops exchanging their new ideas and learning new philosophies. Albert Einstein came from Switzerland to take a large fifth-floor apartment on Haberlandstraße from 1927 to 1933. The writer Thomas Wolfe called Kurfürstendamm, "The longest coffee shop in the world."

Unfortunately Kurfürstendamm is no longer an exclusive boulevard. Very expensive rents are forcing the smaller shops away. Berliners blame the McDonald's and Burger King outlets for inflating rents, paying $12 per square foot where formerly rents were about $1.60 per square foot. They say that the sum Mercedes Benz paid for their Kurfürstendamm showroom is astronomical.

Although Berlin has always been an international city, the Ku'damm was very, very German. There were no French or English or Japanese or Burger King restaurants. Before Burger King no company was allowed to spill over onto the wide Kurfürstendamm sidewalks. There was a big fuss when the two Burger King outlets took this valuable space.

Now Berliners call Kurfürstendamm the "pizza, pop, and porno promenade," because many of the traditional and exclusive shops have moved into the side streets to make way for erotic museums, fast-food restaurants, and souvenir kiosks that can afford the rental of DM 300 per square meter. That is why you can find more interesting shopping, coffee shops, and restaurants in the side streets off Kurfürstendamm than on Kurfürstendamm itself.

The streetlights along Kurfürstendamm are imitations of the originals that were taken down during World War II in order to transform them into cannons. In 1987, they were installed here at a total cost of DM 4.5 million, so each of the 146 lamps cost DM 27,600.

Many businesses carried the name *West*, such as the Kaffeehaus of the West, the Department Store of the West (KaDeWe), and the Theater of the West. West of course had nothing to do with the political situation after the Second World War.

Throughout the Western Heart of Berlin you see fragments of modern art scattered around. In 1987, Sen. Volker Hassemer for Berlin's 750th anniversary contributed eight sculptures—crazy gifts for a birthday present. At the intersection of Bleibtreustraße and Ku'damm, you see the bow-and-arrow arch known as "Communication."

## OFF KU'DAMM

What would the Ku'damm be, even with all its successful veneer, without its side streets? Turn-of-the-century buildings surprise you with their charming facades and stairways. Businesses and restaurants are more chic, more original, and more exquisite than on Ku'damm. Look especially at Meinekestraße, with some of the best remaining turn-of-the-century townhouses; Bleibtreustraße (named for the painter Georg Bleibtreu (1812-92), but its translation, meaning "remain faithful," is contrary to the spirit of the area, especially where it meets Savignyplatz with streetwalkers roaming at night); and the part of Fasanenstraße (*Fasanen* meaning "pheasant") between Ku'damm and Lietzenburger Straße. Altogether there are 13 landmarked buildings on Bleibtreustraße. The building with the restored facade on the corner of Mommsenstaße was built in 1905; the corner building at Bleibtreustraße 15-17 was built at the beginning of the century using English architecture.

The Off-Ku'damm district continues on the side streets on both sides of the Ku'damm from the Memorial Church to Leibnitzstraße (about one-third of Ku'damm's two-mile length). You find cafés, Kneipen, boutiques, antique stores, and large and small hotels and pensions.

On Fasanenstraße between Ku'damm and Lietzenburger Straße you find the so-called **Wintergarten-Ensemble** at #23, #24, and #25. House #24, a two-family villa, was built at the same time as the settling of the area in 1871. The villa next door, #23, the actual Wintergarten, was built in 1889 for a captain named Hildebrandt. It's now the **Literaturhaus Berlin** (Tel. 882-6252), with a large bookshop, art gallery, and one of Berlin's best cafés. Someone always reads from his or her work on Monday evenings. Two years later, architect Hans Grisebach, later architect of U-Bhf Schlesisches Tor, built a delightful residence and atelier called Villa Grisebach, a Jugendstil palace housing the worthwhile **Galerie Pels-Leusden**. Address #24 was donated by Pels-Leusden to the city of Berlin for the Käthe-Kollwitz-Museum.

Follow the sign on Ku'damm pointing to the **Käthe-Kollwitz-Museum** at Fasanenstraße 24 (Tel. 882-5210, open Wed.-Mon. 11 A.M. to 6 P.M., admission DM 6). The house is not Kollwitz's (see Chapter 11); the collection was given to Berlin in 1986 by Hans Pels-Leusden. Through three floors you see an overview of the artist's work from her first drawing (*Self Portrait on the Balcony*), 1892, leading through her woodcuts of hunger, disease, and death, to her last lithograph. It is the largest Kollwitz collection in Europe. The famous socialist and feminist fled to Dresden in 1943 to escape the bombing of the Second World War. She died a few days before the War ended in 1945. The Nazis banned her exhibitions in 1936. Exhibitions of other artists are also held. Use U-Bhf Uhlandstraße.

The **Jüdisches Gemeindehaus** ("Jewish Community House"), Fasanen-straße 79-80 (Tel. 80-02-80), is another chilling reminder of the devastation of the Nazi period. The modern, 1957-59, cultural center for Berlin's 6,000 Jews was built on the foundations of the splendid Byzantine synagogue that stood here until the Nazis burned it to the ground on *Kristallnacht*, November 9, 1938. It served Charlottenburg's Jewish community of over 20,000 in the 1920s. The new building's entrance is constructed from Byzantine fragments of the former synagogue's portal. Richard Hess's modern bronze sculpture in front has an inscription attributed to Moses.

It was inevitable that Berlin Schnauze should call Fasanenstraße's 1997 **Ludwig Erhard Haus**, the "Armadillo." Take a look at it. British architect Nicholas Grimshaw's 128-foot (39 meters) high building has the look and hide of the desert animal. This business building was completed on the hundredth anniversary of its namesake's birth. You almost need to be a chief financial officer to enter. It is home to the Berlin Stock Exchange, the Berlin Chamber of Industry and Commerce, and the Association of Berlin Merchants and Industrialists among many others.

## ZOO TRAIN STATION

For the 750th anniversary of Berlin in 1987, **Bahnhof Zoo**, which handles both mainline on elevated platforms and S-Bahn trains and U-Bahn trains in an underneath annex, was remodeled with DM 40 million. The structure was cleaned, relighted, and modernized stage by stage. Escalators and a travel center were installed. The police cleaned out the homeless, the prostitutes, the alcoholics, and the drug dealers. It's a constant fight to keep them away; however, but generally the police and their police dogs prevail.

Because Zoo train station is the center of the Zoo complex, you can't fail to find any possible service or shop in the station itself or nearby. In the station itself you find a bookstore, snack opportunities of every sort, lockers, and a do-it-yourself hotel reservations information board.

The agent in the service center in the middle of the hall is available to answer quick questions only. The **Reisezentrum** is the place to go for reservations and ticket purchases where you stand in lines which move v e r y slowly. For first-class ticket holders, including holders of Eurailpasses, Europasses, and first-class GermanRail Passes, a special counter is open.

The toilets are called "McClean" and the troop of ladies responsible for the cleaning tries to live up to its reputation. To use them you will pay DM 1.50, except that men using only the urinals pay DM 1 and children relieve themselves without charge. Sooner or later in Berlin, probably sooner, you will be confronted by one of Berlin's take-no-prisoners *Toilettenfrauen* ("toilet women") who will demand 50 Pfennig or a Mark. Grin and bear it. It's their profession and they should be paid handsomely for working in such disgusting surroundings. It's also cheaper than in some neighboring countries.

On the mezzanine look for the hotel reservations display of some 42 hotels with an accompanying map showing their locations. Inserts show pictures of the hotels, their prices for single and double rooms, what services they offer, and other details. Adjacent is a cluster of buttons which are either red or green depending on whether they are full or have rooms available. Using this information you can choose one suiting your location and financial requirements and call the telephone number shown in the insert rather than walk over to the tourist office and stand in line and pay their DM 5 service fee. The attached coin telephone takes three 10-Pfennig coins.

Lockers in back of the station require DM 2 for 24 hours. Luggage carts standing on the platform require you to insert either a DM 1 or DM 2 coin to release them. There are elevators in back that you will have to search for. You get your coin back when you return your cart to a stand, but of course you can't make any money by inserting a one-Mark coin and hoping for a two-Mark coin to be returned.

Maria and Josef moved into the new DM 32 million *Hippo-haus* in September, 1997. Across from the Zoo train station you find the main entrance to the **Zoologische Garten** ("Zoo"), Hardenbergplatz 8, Tel. 254-01-0 (open daily 9 A.M. to sunset, admission DM 13). It isn't the zoo's size or number of animals that interests Berliners. It's the giant panda named Bao Bao. In 1981 the Chinese government gave to Chancellor Helmut Schmidt a male panda named "Bao Bao" (meaning "Luck") and a female, "Tian Tian" ("Darling"). When Tian Tian died in spring 1984, from an unidentified infection, there was great mourning in Berlin. Zoo officials have been trying to inseminate the new female companion, "Yan Yan," with Bao Bao's seed, and Berliners have avidly been following Yan Yan's hormone level, but so far Yan Yan's body chemistry has been uncooperative.

Trends change in the souvenir business. Ever since the zoo acquired Bao Bao, the traditional little brown Berlin bears with sashes and tiny Prussian crowns that fill the shelves of the souvenir shops have been fading from fashion. More and more customers, both in department stores and souvenir shops, are buying panda bears (which are called, in German, **Teddys**). Nevertheless the Berlin Tourist Office continues to buy 15,000 to 20,000 logo bears a year for advertising and promotions.

The zoo was founded in 1844, the first in Germany. The gardens were laid out by landscape architect Lenné. The first animals came from the royal menagerie located on Peacock Island (see Chapter 13), a personal gift from the king. At that time the grounds were not "in" Berlin, but "by" Berlin, that is, wide from the gates of the city. Now in the Western Heart of the city, the zoo's location is unusual and very fortuitous. It gained its reputation before the War when the animals were kept in sections according to the countries from which they came. Out of 10,000 animals the Berlin Zoo claims more species (2,000) than any other zoo. The bird house, with a volume of almost 500,000 cubic feet (14,000 cubic meters) and a surface of 35,000 square feet (3,300 square meters), is the largest in Europe. The range for Berlin's wild cats is the world's largest.

Because of the former division of the city, Berlin has a second zoo, the **Tierpark** in Friedrichsfelde. It was laid out in 1955, one of the largest in the world. It has 7,500 animals of 1,000 different kinds, so it doesn't rank with the West Berlin zoo but it contains the largest polar bear collection in the world as well as the largest deer collection (19 different kinds). The lion sculptures in front of the **Alfred-Brehm-Haus** were sculpted by Reinhold Begas, Berlin's most important 19th-century sculptor. Before the War they stood before the former Berlin City Palace (Chapter 4).

At the end of 1996, West Berlin's zookeepers counted 1,439 mammals, 2,325 birds, and 387 reptiles. The Tiergarten in the East claimed 1,700 mammals, 2,607 birds, and 637 reptiles. They have yet to find anyone dumb enough to try to count the number of fish, amphibians, and invertebrates. About 60 percent of the 3.7 million visitors in 1997 visited the zoo in the west.

The two elephants from Dresden forming the Budapesterstraße entrance to the West Berlin zoo are among the most photographed in the West. Berliners like to think it is because the **Elefanten-Tor** ("Elephant Gate") contains exact reproductions of the 13-foot-high (4 meters), 27-ton stone jumbos that had stood before the main entrance to the zoo since 1899, when they were created by architects Zaar and Wahl, but more likely it is because Japanese tourists think that photos of the 33 foot (10 meters) long Asian pagoda arch made out of several kinds of woods, green ceramic, and copper sheet that soars high above them will be a hit back home.

Ten million Marks from Lotto proceeds were sent to Dresden in 1985 to recreate from old photos the elephant portal that was lost during the War. Two new monumental Indian elephants were chipped and polished of Elbe River sandstone and shipped across the former German-German border in 52 pieces by specialists from their East German workshop.

One usually doesn't have time to visit aquariums abroad, but worth noting is the Berlin **Aquarium** (Hardenbergplatz 8, admission, DM 7; combined Zoo/Aquarium admission, DM 11), located in the recently modernized 1913 building next to the Elephant Gate. Curious fish swim behind inch-and-a-half-thick glass on the ground floor while more than 40 crocodiles, alligators, snakes, and turtles prowl through the tropical hall on the first floor up. On the top floor you'll find the **Insektarium**.

Across the street you can't miss the new, rounded sandstone building, home of the **GrundkreditBank**. Within are shops, a café, and a **Kunstforum** ("Art Forum"), Budapester Straße 35, Tel. 269-80 (open 10 A.M. to 8 P.M.), sometimes used by the Berlin Museum/Märkisches Museum for exhibitions such as the history of the Brandenburg Gate. Use bus 100.

The **Staatliche Kunsthall** ("State Art Gallery") in the colonnades of Budapesterstraße, opposite the Europa Center and the Memorial Church, is also sometimes used for exhibitions.

Next to the zoo and across from the casino in the Europa Center (Budapester Str. 38, Tel. 262-80-04, admission DM 10) you can't miss the 1989 eyesore. It's a huge, blue globe comprising **Panorama**, the 360-degree *Kino* ("Movie House") with wraparound projection on a 62 foot (19 meters) diameter screen. With hour-long showings beginning on the hour, it's a novel way to see *Destination Berlin*, through the eye of an aerial camera with music by Tangerine Dream, but not nearly as enjoyable as seeing the live show going on around you outside.

## HARDENBERGSTRASSE

Hardenbergstraße runs north toward the university and the Ernst-Reuter-Platz from the back exit of Zoo Bahnhof. Along this street you may have occasion to visit the student Mensa for cheap food, eat or drink at student-oriented outdoor cafés, shop at Berlin's best bookshop, visit the Amerika-Haus, or attend the Theater des Westens.

Walking north under the Zoo station overpass on the west side of Hardenbergstraße, the American flag flying over the two-story cubical building across from the back of the Zoo train station signifies the **Amerika-Haus** (Hardenbergstraße 22-24, Tel. 819-7661), which is a leftover from the Cold War era. Inside the 1991-remodeled building, the U.S. Information Center provides a library, exhibit, lecture rooms, and information to further American-German friendship. A shield against thrown stones was strung up during the Vietnam War. The **Amerika-Gedenkbibliothek** ("American Memorial Library") in Kreuzberg, Am Blücherplatz, (open Tue.-Sat. 11 A.M. to 8 P.M., Mon. from 4 P.M.) remembering the blockade winter of 1948-9, is the number one German library in terms of books checked out. Use U-Bhf Hallesches Tor.

On the northwest corner of Steinplatz you find the **Mahnmal für die Opfer des Stalinismus** ("Memorial to the Victims of Stalinism"), a simple stone from the destroyed synagogue on Fasanenstraße embossed with the

# HARDENBERGSTRASSE AND SAVIGNYPLATZ

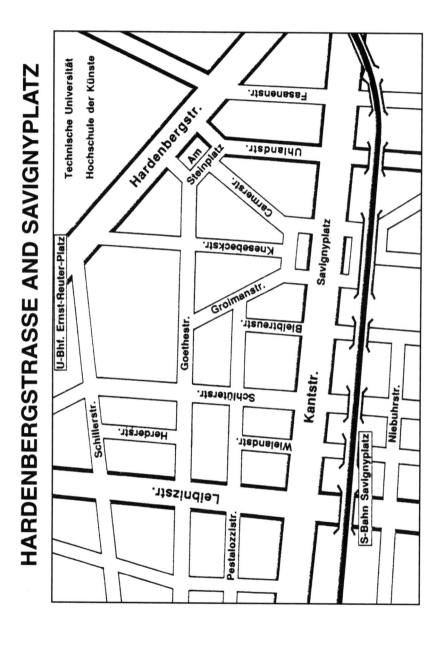

letters *KZ (Konzentrationslager)*. From Steinplatz northward, the University
Quarter begins. On the west you find cafés and one of the best bookstores in
Berlin, **Kiepert**. On the east you find the student **Mensa** and the **Technische
Universität**, which occupies a nicely landscaped and attractively designed
modern green building.

## SAVIGNYPLATZ

One block north of Ku'damm on either Knesebeckstraße or Grolmanstraße you come to the elevated Savignyplatz S-Bahn station and, on
the other side, the green **Savignyplatz**, named for Prussian statesman
Friedrich Carl von Savigny (1779-1861). In 1882 Berlin's first train crossed
through the city on the elevated Stadtbahn, and in 1882, the first stores
opened below the elevated Stadtbahn. Stores have come and gone. With
the restoration sparked by the 750th anniversary of Berlin in 1987, they
have come again once more. Below the station, on the alley known
as S-Bahn-Bögen, you hear the loudspeakers broadcasting Pavarotti and you
find a colorful collection of bookshops, architectural and art galleries, cafés,
and pubs such as XII Apostoli, an Italian restaurant with Mediterranean flair
and chairs in the street. Nearly opposite is the architect forum with models
and sketches of modern buildings. In the Café Aedes you hear discussions
about the world of tomorrow. A few yards farther, you hear the rumble of
trains passing overhead. Between Knesebeckstraße and Grolmanstraße, bei
Arno has been selling stylish lamps for over 70 years. During the Second
World War everything was in shambles. Now designer lamps illuminate
Savignyplatz, touched only slightly by the touristic presence of Ku'damm not
far away. This is typical Berlin with an intellectual flair below the run-down
S-Bahn station.

While you are in the Savignyplatz S-Bahn station, take some moments to
look at the astonishing artwork (not graffiti) including Ben Wargin's *World
Tree* mural on the adjacent wall to the north. Environmental concerns are
graphically presented.

## WITTENBERGPLATZ

The section down Tauentzienstraße south from the Europa Center is
one of the most modern shopping streets in Berlin. In prewar years it was
primarily known for shoes, and you can still find large shops selling
shoes: men's, women's, and sports. On an island in the middle of the
street you pass an interesting **sculpture** by German artists Brigitte and
Martin Denninghoff for the 1987 anniversary called *Berlin, Berlin* or *The*

*Gate*, consisting of two agonizing, chrome-nickel tubes, reaching one toward another, symbolizing the political situation of the divided city. Now of course its significance has been bypassed by events, but it still provides an excellent place to photograph the Memorial Church through the arch formed by the tubes.

The square and the adjacent street were named for Count Gen. Tauentzien von Wittenberg (1760-1824). White-painted benches surround the green, and fountains cascade down to men and women reclining in the sun. The owners of the cafés nearby set out tables under cigarette-advertising umbrellas, serving coffee and tea, breakfasts, pizza, etc. Before the War, Adolf's brother, Alois Hitler, established here a *Bierstube* frequented by Nazi officials.

The U-Bahn station is flanked by two not-quite-symmetric mushroom-shaped fountains from Waldemar Grzimek. The 3.2 tons of stainless steel on the south side blend well into the feeling of the square, but even more delightful is the fountain on the north showing happily bathing and smirking figures.

On the west corner of the U-Bahn island, there is a simple matter-of-fact signpost with a chilling message: "Places of horrors that no one should forget: Auschwitz, Stuthof, Maidanek, Treblinka, Theresienstadt, Buchenwald, Dachau, Sachsenhausen, Ravensbrück, Bergen-Belsan."

U-Bhf Wittenbergplatz is one of the oldest stations of Berlin, opened in 1902. The Jugendstil ("Art Nouveau") building itself was opened in 1913. You find a flower stand and a minibistro selling croissants, sandwiches, and an assortment of pastries as well as coffee, tea, and soft drinks. The walls are decorated with posters current when the station was built. You see period posters for ADAC, the German Automobile Club; the Beckstein piano factory; and the Opel Motorcar Company, 1919. Behind the flower shop you can read: On February 18, 1902, the first electrical elevated and underground railroads in Berlin began running between Strahlauer Tor and Potsdamer Platz. Construction of the railroad by Siemens and Halske was begun on December 10, 1896. In the opening year service was extended to Warschauer Brücke and Knie. The rail fleet consisted of 56 powered cars and 27 trailers.

The stairs and escalators are always busy here with 50,000 daily commuters rushing up and down to jump aboard or change among the subway lines serving the station: Line U1 to Dahlem, branch line U15 to Uhlandstraße, and line U2, one of Berlin's most important.

The **KaDeWe (Kaufhaus des Westens)**, "Department Store of the West," is so big and so famous that the flag-decorated store facing Wittenbergplatz transcends just being a department store; it is a tourist attraction.

# TAUENTZIENSTRASSE AND WITTENBERGPLATZ

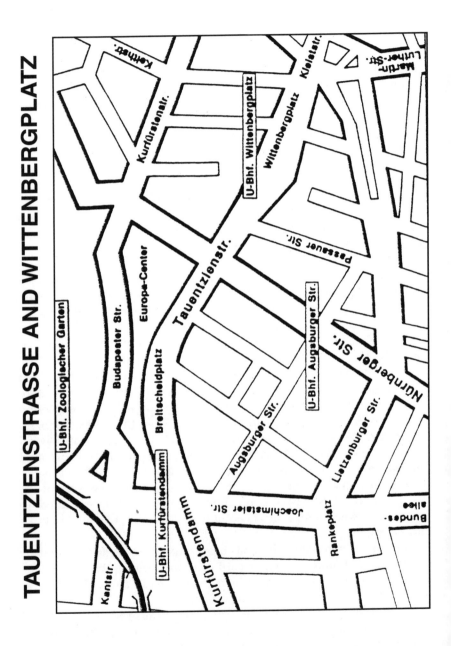

Opened in 1906 and at that time the most elegant in all of Berlin, it has six floors, but its main claim to fame is the giant delicatessen on the top floor because that, it argues, is the largest one in Europe (maybe not). You can choose from 1,700 kinds of cheese, 1,000 varieties of sausages, dozens of concoctions you will only find in Germany, and hard-to-find specialties imported from the Eastern European countries. The fifth floor contains a restaurant.

Admittedly KaDeWe is the largest department store in Germany and the third largest in Europe (after Galeries Lafayette in Paris and Harrods in London), but realistically the sprawling postwar shopping malls of North America make it look like a mom and pop store. Mall of America in Bloomington, Minnesota, has 2.6 million square feet of store area.

KaDeWe reopened after the War in 1950 and as a symbol of a consumption society became a showpiece as the capitalists defended Berlin against communism.

KaDeWe belongs to the Hertie company. "Hertie" comes from Hermann Tietz, the father of the Berlin department store. Tietz was imprisoned by the Nazis. The Nazis—this is hard to imagine—changed the name of Kaufhaus Tietz to "Hertie." The name "Hertie" is therefore a Nazi contraction of Hermann Tietz, a Jewish name. Tietz is buried in Weißensee cemetery (see Chapter 7).

KaDeWe acquired its name because it was built, 85 years ago, west of the Tiergarten hunting forest to cater to the residents of Charlottenburg, also to the west of the Tiergarten, a very upscale quarter, so that the wealthy residents wouldn't have to travel far to do their shopping.

## NOLLENDORFPLATZ

What was once West Berlin's last streetcar ran on the elevated tracks between the top of Nollendorfplatz U-Bahn station and Potsdamer Straße. The station has been rejuvenated since the Wende and is an essential U-Bhf stop on cross-city U-Bahn lines 1 and 2. Across the road the adjacent **Metropol Theater**, Berlin's famous legitimate theater of the 1920s, and now Berlin's prestige disco, is a landmark late at night.

Readers of *Berlin Stories* and *Mr. Norris Changes Trains*, as well as viewers of the films *Cabaret* and *I Am a Camera*, will be curious to see the plaque commemorating the Berlin **residence of Christopher Isherwood** at Nollendorfstraße 17. When he came to Berlin he was 24 years old and determined, he wrote later, "to unchain his desires and hurl reason and sanity into prison." Berlin in the '20s seemed the perfect place to do it. Nollendorfstraße does not connect to Nollendorfplatz, so you must walk one block west along

Maaßenstraße to see the bronze commemorative plaque marking his former apartment and the dormer windows and wooden balconies from which Isherwood observed the neighborhood. Isherwood's Sally Bowles was based on Jean Ross, an English would-be singer and actress. At one point she managed to land a walk-on part in a Max Reinhardt production where she was one of pairs of lovers carried onstage in litters. She boasted that she had romance on stage with her partner, in full view of the audience, at every single performance. Isherwood sneaked into several performances, armed with high-power binoculars, but was never able to verify her claim.

## AN DER URANIA

The black **Curve of 124.5 Degrees** steel-tube configuration by artist Bernard Venet at the intersection of Kleiststraße and An der Urania duplicates the angle between Berlin and Paris. It was the gift of the prime minister of France, Jacques Cherac, to the people of Berlin on the occasion of the Tour de France held in Berlin in 1987. In summer skateboarders sometimes use it for practice.

On the south side of An der Urania, you see the **Urania**, the oldest adult education school of Germany, founded in 1888 by the industrialist Werner von Siemens and the astronomer Max Wilhelm Meyer as a place where ordinary Berliners could continue their education.

Next to it is the **Post- und Fernmeldemuseum** ("Postal Museum"), An der Urania 15, Tel. 750-16-890, Fax 750-16-810 (open Tue.-Sun. 9 A.M. to 5 P.M., admission free), with a postal coach standing outside in a glass case. This small museum relates the story of Prussian postal delivery, with documents, costumes, and models from the past 300 years to the most modern technology, including some astonishingly intricate 19th-century telephones and telex machines.

Stamp collectors find a bonanza here. The exhibit includes all German stamps—more than 10,000—ranging from the black, one-Kreuzer Bavarian stamp of 1849, through Prussian, Nazi, and Cold War times, including West Berlin, the DDR, and associated regions. While the Postal Museum in the East (Chapter 4) is being renovated, they are allowing a semi-permanent exhibition here of pivotal collections they have selected as well as changing special exhibitions.

## 5. Sports

One look at the reddened eyes and dissipated demeanor of the customers of the *Lokals* on and off the Ku'damm, and you can tell the center of town is not a healthy place for athletes, who use the facilities in the greener parts of Berlin.

## 6. Shopping

You can begin your shopping at the famous KaDeWe on Wittenbergplatz and continue all the way to Halensee Bridge. The "shopping mile" on Tauentzienstraße and Kurfürstendamm is actually 2.2 miles (3.5 kilometers) long. The main shopping streets and many side streets to the right and left offer something for everyone: small boutiques, exclusive shops, and large department stores offering everything from ripped jeans to elegant designer dresses.

The Western Heart of West Berlin contains all the luxury shopping that you have seen in the fashion magazines ever since the Wall was built. Along Ku'damm, fashionable men's stores are between Bleibtreustraße and Olivaer Platz. The paradise for women's apparel extends from Wittenbergplatz to Fasanenstraße: **Gucci**, Fasanenstraße 73, Tel. 885-63-00 (open Mon.-Fri. 10 A.M. to 7 P.M., Sat. to 4 P.M.), **Versace**, Ku'damm 185, Tel. 885-74-60 (open Mon.-Wed. 10 A.M. to 7 P.M., Thur.-Fri. to 8 P.M., Sat. to 4 P.M.), **Yves Saint Laurent** (at Ku'damm 52), **Jil Sander**, Ku'damm 185, Tel. 886-70-20 (open Mon.-Fri. 10 A.M. to 7 P.M., Sat. to 4 P.M.), **Chanel**, Berlin designers **Veronica Pohle, Mossina, and Mareysey** (Ku'damm 109-192). **Baccarat**, Ku'damm 42, Tel. 881-69-69 (open Mon.-Fri. 10 A.M. to 7 P.M., Sat. to 4 P.M.) has fine crystal and objects for home. **Bleibgrün**, Bleibtreustraße 27, Tel. 885-00-80 (open Mon.-Fri. 10:30 A.M. to 6:30 P.M., Sat. to 4 P.M.), offers unusual fashion and spectacular shoes.

Facing Ku'damm are busy shopping malls with countless shops selling everything from airline tickets to next year's fashions now. The **Europa Center** is the largest, but just as busy are the **Ku'damm Karree** and **Gloria Passage**. The 1998 **Benetton** on Ku'damm is the third largest in the world (after London and Milan) in the former Gloria Palast movie house. Be sure to note the historic facade, stairs and floors which were preserved. **Warner Bros. Studio Store**, Tauentzienstraße 9, Tel. 254-54-401 (open Mon.-Sat. 10 A.M. to 8 P.M.) next to the Europa Center, gives you Bugs Bunny, Tweety, and Road Runner cuff links. Use U-Bhf Zoo. Tauentzienstraße was known for its shoe shops.

**KaDeWe**, Tauentzienstraße 21-24, Tel. 2121-0 (open Mon.-Fri. 9:30 A.M. to 8 P.M., Sat. 9 A.M. to 4 P.M.), at Wittenbergplatz, is justly famous for its food delicacies, but you will also find a good collection of English-language books and a fine toy department. Just as complete are the **Wertheim, Hertie,** and **Karlstadt** American-style department stores.

**Kaufhaus Schrill**, Bleibtreustraße 46, Tel. 882-40-48 (open Mon.-Fri. 11 A.M. to 7 P.M., Sat. to 4 P.M.), sells eccentric accessories including ties decorated with movie stars, dollar bills, gorillas, and much, much more. The "garish department store" is a classic for curiosities.

Those attracted to antiques and bric-a-brac will find a veritable paradise in Berlin. Many interesting shops are located on Eisenacher Straße/Motzstraße and the vicinity, Keithstraße, Ludwigkirchplatz, and Fasanenstraße. One of the best known is the **Zille Yard** on Fasanenstraße, named after artist Heinrich Zille, who described in his drawings the *Milljöh* ("milieu") of life in the backyards of Berlin's tenement blocks. On Bleibtreustraße you find **Medici** for lovely things old and new, **Astoria** for art-déco, and **Depot** for everyday accessories. Between Bleibtreu-, Pestalozzi-, and Momsenstraße a number of antique dealers specialize in Art Deco.

**Willi Müller Antique,** Kantstraße 150, made millions after the War selling antiques to Americans. He still takes credit cards. **Bethmann-Hollweg,** Fasanenstraße 26, specializes in wrought-iron work. **Siedel und Sohn,** Fasanenstraße 70, features baroque and Biedermeier. **Bogart's,** Schlüterstraße 34, is good for Art Deco. **Krishke,** Schlüterstraße 49, sells beautiful jewelry.

Forget your budget. You can purchase exquisite porcelain, figurines, cameos and glassware in the exhibition and sales rooms of the 1763 historical undertaking, **Königliche Porzellanmanufaktur** ("Royal Porcelain Factory"), Kurfürstenstraße 26a (open Mon.-Fri. 10 A.M. to 7 P.M., Sat. to 4 P.M.).

**Galerie Pels-Leusden,** Fasanenstraße 25, next to the Käthe-Kollwitz-Museum, specializes in early 20th-century art. He always has top exhibitions.

The **Zinnfigurenkabinett** ("Tin Soldier Cabinet"), Knesebeckstraße 88, has 30,000 models for sale or for home casting.

## 7. Nightlife and Entertainment

The Western Heart of Berlin offers everything in nighttime entertainment from theater, to cabaret, artistic haunts, disco dancing, opera, jazz, beer gardens, movies, gambling in the casino, and classic Eartha Kitt at midnight in the Theater des Westens singing "I Want to Be Evil." The *Szene* is around Savignyplatz where academics and better-paid Berliners frequent the cafés and restaurants between Leibnitz- and Fasanenstraße. It's a good place to live with expensive boutiques and barbers.

# THEATERS AND JAZZ

**Theater des Westens,** Kantstraße 12, Tel. 88-22-888, Fax 319-03-188, *http://www.theater-des-westens.de*, is a spark of light from old Berlin. Inside and out you see Bernhard Sehring's architecture surviving from 1896. The interior furnishings make it the most beautiful and representative theater in Berlin, but they were touched up a few years ago with the latest musical theater equipment and yielded such treats as Horst Buchholz in *Cabaret, My Fair Lady, Sweet Charity,* and others. Use U- or S-Bhf Zoo.

**Komödie** and the **Theater am Kurfürstendamm**, Kurfürstendamm 206-9, Tel. 4702-1010, Fax 881-84-77, were built by famous theater designer Oskar Kaufmann for director Max Reinhardt 1921-23. After renovations in 1986 and 1989, they are among the most pleasant in Berlin. Their parallel red-and-chrome marquees stand separated a few doors on Ku'damm. They present contemporary comedy and drama in German. Use U-Bhf Uhlandstraße, bus 109 or 119.

**Schaubühne am Lehniner Platz**, Kurfürstendamm 153, Tel. 89-00-23, looks like a stranded ship. It took a turn in 1997 when it released its 30-member-strong repertory company founded in 1962. The building, designed by Erich Mendelson as the *Universum-Kino* in 1927-28, survived the War and was reconstructed and turned into a theater by Jürgen Sawade in 1976-81. You see clever productions of Ibsen, Chekhov, etc., with original settings. Use U-Bhf Adenauerplatz or S-Bhf Charlottenburg.

The **Freie Volksbühne** ("Open People's Stage") harks back to the creative stage of the Golden '20s in the Scheunenviertel of East Berlin, but because of the political division of Berlin after the War, a new Freie Volksbühne was founded and moved into their own house at Schaperstraße 24 (Wilmersdorf), Tel. 884-20-884, Fax 884-20-888, *http://www.shakespeare.de*. Use U-Bhf Spichernstraße.

The **Renaissance Theater Berlin**, Hardenbergstraße 6, Tel. 312-42-02, Fax 3-12-63-69. Opened in 1902; converted by Oskar Kaufmann into a "jewel among theaters" in 1926. Its intimate interior dating from this time is a unique example of the magnificent interior decor of the theaters in the '20s. The theater specializes in German drama. Use U-Bhf Ernst-Reuter-Platz or S-Bhf Zoo.

**Vagante Bühne**, Kantstraße 12a, Tel. 312-45-29, presents classics and modern, serious works. Use U-Bhf Kurfürstendamm.

**Bar Jeder Vernunft**, Schaperstraße 24 (Wilmersdorf), is hidden by trees and difficult to locate. Depending on your attitude, the theater either resembles an Arabian bordello or a tattered Art Nouveau tent. Theater boxes are lined in red velvet, but most seats are folding chairs. After the show is over, stay and party to live music. Use U-Bhf Spichernstraße.

**Kabarett "die Wühlmäuse"** ("Cabaret the Field Mice"), Nürnberger Straße 33 (Wilmersdorf), has perfected a program of political and satirical cabaret. Since 1986, nearly all of the great cabaret artists have appeared here. Use U-Bhf Augsburger Straße.

**Quasimodo**, Kantstraße 12a, Tel. 312-8086, Fax 312-2439, *http://www.quasimodo.de*, the big-name jazz, blues, folk, funk, soul *Lokal*, features well-known international stars next to the Theater des Westens. Use U- or S-Bhf Zoologisher Garten.

## DISCOS AND HANGOUTS

The **Metropol**, Nollendorfplatz 5, Tel. 216-41-22. "Discotheques nowadays have to offer something special," according to the disko-boss. He stresses erotic. There's room for 1500, but no fewer than 350 dance every morning from 1 A.M. on the stage in this 8,600 square foot (800 square meters) Babylonian-Egyptian complex to funky and soul music. Techno is *verboten*. Admission costs DM 25. Use U-Bhf Nollendorfplatz.

Renovated in 1990 and with an expanded entertainment concept, **Quartier** (Tel. 262-90-16), the club at Potsdamer Str. 96, has five bars. On weekends it's "Dance All Nite," Fridays with "Heatwave" and Saturdays in the "Party Zone." DJs mix discs, but jazz is increasingly featured.

The **Big Eden**, Kurfürstendamm 202, Tel. 3-23-20-16, a disco with pool tables and pinball machines, was the hottest thing during the Cold War. You found party-goers like Jane Mansfield, Klaus Kinski, the Rolling Stones, Roman Polanski, and Telly Savalas. Now it seems to attract mostly short-time tourists and Berliners who want to meet them. The goon at the door won't let you in if you look drunk or disorderly. Open Sun.-Thur. 7 P.M. to 4 A.M., Fri.-Sat. to 7 A.M. Use U-Bhf Uhlandstraße.

**Aschinger Gasthaubrauerei** am Ku'damm 26, Tel. 882-55-58, Fax 881-69-67, you can drink one meter (three and one-fourth feet) of house-brewed beer lined up mug to mug for DM 28. Between Kempinski and Café Kranzler. When you are near, come to this lively atmosphere with a few friends. Open 9 A.M. to 2 A.M.; breakfast 9 A.M. to noon.

**City-Loretta**, Lietzenburger Straße 89 (corner Knesebeck Straße), is Berlin's largest beer garden, with 5,000 seats, spare ribs, Chinese, Mexican food. Use U-Bhf Uhlandstraße or S-Bhf Savignyplatz.

# MOVIES

Berlin is a movie town. It was in Berlin, in 1895, that the Skladanowsky brothers invented their first, rattling projector. On the day Marlene Dietrich left Berlin for her first job in Hollywood, the *Blue Angel* opened in the **Gloria Palast**. Kevin Costner danced with wolves on the 21- by 46-foot (6.4 by 14 meters) screen, James Bond battled Gert Fröbe's Goldfinger for 12 weeks under the eyes of 140,637 Berliners, and in 1957, the Trapp family brought 90,000 Wessis to tears. The **Zoo-Palast**, Kurfürstendamm 225/226, has been named one of Berlin's landmarked buildings. It was built in 1895, transformed during Berlin's toughest year (1948) into *Kino im Kindl* *("KiKi"),* and remodeled in 1951 to become one of Berlin's largest movie houses. Home to the Berlin Film Festival since then, it has been transformed into a tasteful multiplex which shows the latest Hollywood releases on nine screens. The large theater, with its splendid architecture, gives you additional thrills with a laser show. The 1998-polished **Marmorhaus**, ("Marble House") on Ku'damm invites you in to while away the hours in four theaters or admire the completely refurbished lobby. You have no problem finding a movie theater anywhere in Berlin, and especially in the Ku'damm area where there are movie palaces on every block showing American, French, Italian, British, and German films. The **Hollywood**, which caters to the more demanding Ku'damm crowd, has added a second (smaller) theater.

# CASINO

The **Spielbank Berlin** in the Europa Center (enter outside near the hotel), Tel. 250-08-90 (open 3 P.M. to 3 A.M.—5 A.M. for baccarat), is Berlin's elegant casino for gambling with a ritzy touch. Ties are required of men. Minimum bet is DM 5; limit DM 5,000. Someone walked off with 1.9 million Marks in a single day in 1988. Play French and American roulette, blackjack (DM 10 minimum), baccarat (DM 50 stake), and American slots. Bring your passport as well as a full wallet; the Berlin Tax Authority takes 90 percent of the casino's earnings. Use U-Bhf Kurfürstendamm.

**PARISERPLATZ TO ALEXANDERPLATZ**

# 4

# Berlin's Historical Center

## 1. Orientation

East of the Brandenburg Gate, Berlin opens into a district rich with architectural gems dating from Prussian times and ill-flavored with Prussian militarism. The Wall is not only down, it is *gone*. There are great eyefulls here. You can stroll leisurely past the structures, squares, and streets that made Berlin famous before the War: the Brandenburg Gate, Unter den Linden, Friedrichstraße, Gendarmenmarkt, Museum Island, and Alexanderplatz. The city section is named, "Mitte." You find 90 percent of Berlin's historical buildings at home here.

After first enjoying the restored Prussian buildings and monuments of Schinkel and others, move farther to see the streets and sections that were restored as showpieces for tourists for Berlin's 750th anniversary in 1987. First, see the Nikolai Quarter surrounding the oldest church in Berlin and then the "representative" streets (which are not representative at all) of the Scheunenviertel and nearby Prenzlauer Berg.

## 2. The Hotel Scene

Twenty-two percent of Berlin's hotel space is in the East and most of that is in the historical district. Treuhandanstalt, the German privatization office, was entrusted with selling the 34 Interhotels built by the former DDR. These included eight in Berlin: the Grand Hotel on the corner of Friedrichstraße and Unter den Linden, the new Dom Hotel on Gendarmenmarkt, the Palasthotel next to the Berlin Cathedral, the Hotel Metropol next to Friedrichstraße train station, the Hotel Stadt Berlin on Alexanderplatz, the Hotel Berolina on Karl-Marx-Allee, the Hotel Unter den Linden on the corner of Friedrichstraße, and the Hotel Krone near the Platz der Akademie.

## LARGE HOTELS

The US$250 million **Hotel Adlon Kempinski** (Pariser Platz, Unter den Linden 77, Tel. 226-10, Fax 22-61-22-22) was fully booked on its opening in 1997, and no wonder, no other Berlin hotel has the history and prestige and, at its opening on Pariser Platz, the publicity. Its 337 rooms including two presidential suites, the fitness room and the American bar were ready for the opening. US$233-328, single; US$272-367, double; US$20, breakfast buffet extra. Weekend special US$231, single; US$297, double. In the U.S., call Kempinski, Tel. 800-426-3135.

**Hotel Albrechtshof** (Albrechtstraße 8, Tel. 308-86-0, Fax 308-86-100) is located in a historic building in the mini-theater district across the Spree from Friedrichstraße train station. US$110-80, single; US$135-205, double; US$20, breakfast buffet included. Use S- or U-Bhf Friedrichstraße.

**Alexander Plaza Berlin - Mercure Hotel** (Rosenstraße 1, Tel. 2-41-50-67, Fax 2-42-38-04) is your entree to the Scheunenviertel. Mercure Hotels have a very good reputation in Germany. US$110-65, single; US$140-95, double; US$20, breakfast buffet included.

**art'otel ermelerhaus berlin** (Wallstraße 70-73, Tel. 240-62-0, Fax 240-62-222), opened in 1997, is similar to a gallery. The ultramodern, five-story location overlooking the Spree is dedicated to the artist Georg Baselitz, whose aim was to liberate painting from form and content. This led him to presenting his subjects upside down, which gave the impression that the paintings were hanging upside down. His works are presented in the public areas and rooms of the hotel. Connected to the Ermelerhaus (see text), the hotel provides a restaurant on land and a beer garden on an old barge on the Spree. In the U.S., contact Design Hotel, Tel. 800-337-4685.

The 36-room, landmarked **East Side Hotel** (Mühlenstraße 6, Friedrich-shain, Tel. 293-83-3, Fax 293-83-555) dates back to 1870 when the quiet neighborhood of artisans and gardeners began to slowly turn into a working-class haven of workshops and factories. Reopened in 1996, those rooms facing south open upon a beautiful view of the Spree with the **East Side Gallery**—a part of the former Wall that is now also a protected landmark. US$77-92, single; US$104-31, double; breakfast buffet included. Weekend special: US$55, single; US$83, double. Use S- or U-Bhf Warschauer Straße.

The blue-gray 475-foot (145 meters) skyscraper you see on Alexanderplatz is the second tallest building in East Berlin. **Hotel Forum** (Alexanderplatz, Tel. 23-89-0, Fax 23-89-45-42, *http://www.interconti.com/interconti*), built in 1970, the former DDR mass-tourism hotel accommodates 1,540 guests with an entrance right on the television-tower square. US$110-60, single; US$160-85, double; breakfast buffet included. Use S- or U-Bhf Alexander-platz or bus 100. In the U.S., contact Inter-Continental Hotels, Tel. 800-327-0200.

**Four Seasons Hotel Berlin** (Charlottenstraße 49, Tel. 203-38, Fax 20-33-60-09, *http://www.fshr.com*). Total immersion luxury hotel nestled in a fashionable complex. Enjoy the modern and preserved architecture around a quiet courtyard. Rooms have a view of the Gendarmenmarkt. In the U.S., Tel. Four Seasons at 800-332-3442. Use U-Bhf Stadtmitte.

Built from 1985 to 1987 on former "coffeehouse corner" at Unter den Linden and Friedrichstraße, the **Grand Hotel** (Friedrichstraße 158-64, Tel. 20-27-0, Fax 20-27-34-19) was first touted as the best hotel in both Berlins. After the Wende it was feared that it was not commercially viable and passed through several ownerships to the Westin Group in 1997. The exterior is not beautiful. It was designed by an East German architect. But the graceful interior was designed by Japanese. US$180-265, single; US$211-94, double; US$16, breakfast buffet extra. In the U.S., Tel. Westin at 1-800-937-8461.

Opened on October 19, 1998, as part of the Daimler-Benz project on Potsdamer platz, **Grand Hyatt Hotel** (Marlene-Dietrich-Platz 2, Tel. 2553-1234, Fax 2553-1235, *www.hyatt.com*) was the first Grand Hyatt in Europe. It offers every luxury you would expect in a spanking new, five-star hotel plus spectacular views from its rooftop fitness center. Designed by Spanish architect Jose Rafael Moneo, the exterior features deep arcades and a red sandstone facade. US$156-211 per room, breakfast buffet extra. In the U.S., call Hyatt, Tel. 800-233-1234.

The **Berlin Hilton**, formerly the *Dom Hotel* (Mohrenstraße 30, Tel. 20-23-0, Fax 23-42-69, *http://www.Travelweb.com/hiltonint.html*) in back of the German Church on the Gendarmenmarkt, is very Hiltony in an excellent location. Remodeling of the lobby was completed in December 1998. By year 2000, the US$17 million complete modernization will be finished. US$190-235, single; US$210-65, double; US$18, breakfast. In the U.S., Tel. 1-800-HILTONS.

**Maritim proArte Hotel** (Friedrichstraße 151, Tel. 203-35, Fax 2033-4209, *http://www.maritim-hotels.de*), in a sublime location for a modern property, a few steps away from Friedrichstraße Regional Train Station and fewer steps from Unter den Linden, is the DDR's prized **Hotel Metropol** embellished, brightened, and transformed by French designer Philippe Starck, who was also responsible for Manhattan's Paramount and Royalton hotels. US$132-255, single; US$147-286, double, depending on season. Breakfast US$16 extra. Weekend prices are far more reasonable and include breakfast.

A recommended hotel on the Alexanderplatz is the **Radisson SAS Hotel Berlin** (Karl-Liebknecht-Straße 5, Tel. 2-38-28, Fax 23-82-75-90, *http://www.radisson.com*), with its location directly across from the cathedral and a few minutes walk to the Nikolai Quarter and Museum Island. It was designed by a Swede and built by Japanese in 1979. It has gilded windows which give it a striking exterior appearance. Its 540 rooms are modern, comfortable, and air-conditioned, which is a plus in July and August. US$156-206, single; US$172-228, double; US$15, breakfast buffet extra. In the U.S., Tel. Radisson at 800-333-3333.

**Hotel Unter den Linden** (Unter den Linden 14, Tel. 23-81-1-0, *http://www.utell.com*), with 324 rooms, is an impersonal former-DDR hotel directly opposite the Grand Hotel along the best-known theater mile. It's in a great location, but needs work. US$80-122, single; US$105-50, double; breakfast buffet included. In the U.S., Tel. Utell at 800-207-6900.

## SMALL HOTELS AND PENSIONS

**Hotel-Pension Aacron** (Friedrichstraße 124, Tel. 2-82-93-52, Fax 2-80-80-57), 100 beds. US$19-44, single; US$28-64, double; no breakfast.

**Hotel am Scheunenviertel** (Oranienburger Straße 38, Tel. 2-82-21-25, Fax 2-82-11-15), 32 beds, no restaurant. US$50-72, single; US$56-89, double; no breakfast.

**Pension Clairchen** (Claire-Waldoff-Straße 2, Tel. 20-23-42-21, Fax 20-23-46-45), eight beds. US$65, single; US$88, double; including breakfast.

**Hotel Gendarm** (Charlottenstraße 60, Tel. 204-4180, Fax 208-2482) is a 52-bed hotel without dining room, which makes for a good deal. The corner rooms face the Gendarmenmarkt, which is one of the great views to wake up to. US$78-89, single; US$83-94, double; breakfast buffet included.

**Hotel-Pension Kastanienhof** (Kantanienallee 65, Tel. 44-30-50, Fax

44-30-5-111), 66 beds, no restaurant. US$72-89, single; US$89-100, double; including breakfast buffet.

**Hotel Luisehof** (Köpenicker Straße 92, Tel. 2-41-59-06, Fax 2-79-29-83), 46 beds. US$117-61, single; US$139-200, double; including breakfast buffet.

**Hotel Märkischer Hof** (Linienstraße 133, Tel. 2-82-71-55, Fax 2-82-43-31), 40 beds, no restaurant. US$67-80, single; US$75-110, double; including breakfast buffet.

**Hotel-Pension Merkur** (Torstraße 156, Tel. 2-82-95-23, Fax 2-82-77-65). US$42-61, single; US$70-83, double; including breakfast.

## 3. Restaurants and Cafés

The pace of change of restaurants in the East since the fall of the Wall has astonished even the most particular gourmet. During the Cold War, West Berliners stayed within the city on weekends and spent long hours in flourishing sidewalk cafés while Ossis took to bicycles and Trabis and went to the woods nearby in order to escape East Berlin restaurants that were staffed by rude personnel who didn't care for their job or their customers. In turn, customers of the Eastern restaurants resented having to stand in long lines outside while they could see empty tables inside. Now free-market entrepreneurs have made your choice of restaurants and cafés in the East rival that in the West. Who wouldn't prefer to dine in historic surroundings?

In the former Prinzessinnen Palais you find four different restaurants. At the busy ground-floor **Opera Café**, Unter den Linden 5, Tel. 20-26-83 (open 9 a.m. to midnight) you can help yourself to the opulent breakfast buffet that lets you choose from over 50 kinds of astonishingly tiny pastries. The Linden-front terrace lets you enjoy a sunny Berlin afternoon in a garden shaded by stately trees while sipping a Berliner brew or relaxing with a cup of coffee or your buffet choice of soft drinks, croissants, and pastries. The historical **Opernschänke**, in 1920's style, serves old-fashioned Berlin cuisine. Every Sunday from 11 A.M. to 2 P.M., you can join the jazz brunch with live music. At #5 drop into the **Fridericus im Opernpalais**, Tel. 20-26-83 (open noon to midnight), a beautifully decorated country-house style restaurant with Prussian and fish specialties. The masterpiece upstairs restaurant in the white Opera Palace building at #6 Unter den Linden, **Königin Luise im Opernpalais**, Tel. 20-26-84 (open Tue.-Sat. for dinner only), serves excellent German cuisine in a lavishly restored rococo interior. Use U-Bhf Hausvogteiplatz or bus 100.

After the blooming of new restaurants in East Berlin, the new culinary center of Berlin has established itself at the Gendarmenmarkt. The first house of the beautiful square is named **Vau** (Tel. 202-9730). In the Four

Seasons Hotel, find **Seasons** (Tel. 20-33-8). **Lutter & Wegner** (Tel. 202-95-40) and **Borchardt** (Tel. 203-97-10) add to the attraction.

There are several pleasant outdoor beer garden/dining halls you find while strolling through the restored Nikolai Quarter. The DDR restored the **Café Zum Nußbaum**, Am Nußbaum 3, Tel. 242-30-95 (open noon to 2 A.M.) to its historical *Gemütlichkeit.* The original Nußbaum dates from 1571, making it the oldest restaurant in the city. Inside you find not more than four old, dark wooden tables and several more tables to stand at by the windows. It's a nice stop for a Krug (mug) of beer or a plate of filling food. **Reinhard's** is campy and fun. The atmosphere is bistro (rich, dark woodwork and caramel-colored walls), the crowd boisterous, and the menu ranges from salads and pastas to schnitze.

Moved from Ku'damm to the Nikolai Quarter, **Fofi's Estiatorio**, Rathausstraße 25, Tel. 242-3435 (open from noon), is a *Schickeria* (with the accent on "chic") restaurant. When you prefer expensive Greek food, and want to be seen, come here. Everyone who wants to see someone or wants to be seen goes to Fofi's. The Ku'damm site was such a quintessential Berlin hot spot that John Le Carré supposedly used it as a setting in *Little Drummer Girl.* Outdoor tables and interior walls are covered with modern art; reservations are essential. "Mother" Fofi greets everyone warmly. Open daily 7:30 P.M. to 3 A.M.

In the Hackesche Höfen you find restaurant **Hackescher Hof**, Rosenthaler Straße 40-41, Tel. 282-52-93 (open 7 A.M.) which tempts you with international, upper-class food and drink with equivalent prices. You feel lucky to be able to drop by for a coffee break in front of the large, glass show window. Reservations are recommended for evening meals.

Also in the Hachesche Höfen **Oxymoron Restaurant** serves breakfast until 4 P.M. or try **Modellhut**, Tel. 283-55-11, **Schwarzenraben** ("Black Raven"), Tel. 28-39-16-98, or **Aedes**, Tel. 282-21-03 (open 10 A.M.), a chic little café designed by a Dutch architect. Berliners visit as well as tourists for the Viennese coffeehouse atmosphere. You can dine quietly or take a cake & coffee break. Use S-Bhf Hackescher Markt or U-Bhf Weinmeisterstraße.

Along Unter den Linden, at #42 opposite the Komische Oper, you find a new location of **Einstein**, the "in" café of West Berlin. It is a perfect place to pause and fantasize you are on the Unter den Linden of the '20s. Tel. 204-36-32, Fax 204-36-35. Use U-Bhf Französische Straße.

**Zur Letzten Instanz**, Waisenstraße. 14-16, Tel. 242-55-28, Fax 242-68-91, (open Mon.-Sat. noon to 1 A.M., Sun. to 11 P.M.). Established as a public house as early as 1621. Built against the ruins of the medieval city wall. It is a meeting place for artists, notable figures, and all who appreciate Berlin ribaldry. It is a good place to meet people. Use U-Bhf Klosterstraße.

As mentioned above, across from the Gendarmenmarkt, consider **Lutter & Wegner**, corner Charlottenstraße/Taubenstraße, Tel. 202-95-40 (open from 6 P.M.). After the location was destroyed during the Second World War, the restaurant rose from the ashes and moved to brighten the Savignyplatz scene in the West. The wine cellar, the *Lutter Keller*, had been since 1811 a favorite meeting point for writers and artists, including Karl Marx and Friedrich Engels, Count E. T. A. Hoffmann, Carl Maria von Weber, and Heinrich Heine. Early in May 1997, Lutter & Wegner returned only two doors from its original location (which had been occupied by the Vier Jahreszeiten hotel) facing the rear of the Konzerthaus on the Gendarmenmarkt. In the evening, when your feet are cold and the shopping bags heavy, nothing calls so insistently as a glass of wine, or even two, at the Lutter & Wegner Wine Bar. Use U-Bhf Stadtmitte.

**Borchardt**, Französische Straße 47 (am Gendarmenmarkt), Tel. 203-97-10 (open 11:30 A.M. to 1 P.M.). Borchardt originally served as a meeting place for the exiled Huguenots in Prussia. Then August Friedrich Wilhelm Borchardt opened a grocery in 1853. The space, which was being used as a stock room, was restored to its original form and reopened in 1992. It instantly became the most talked about new restaurant in the East. Waiters serve French cuisine in the bright, chic location near the Gendarmenmarkt. Use U-Bhf Französische Straße.

**Maxwell**, Bergstraße 22, Tel. 280-7121 (open noon to 1 A.M.) has moved East from Wilmersdorf into the middle of a former brewery. The perch would do credit to a more expensive restaurant. Reservations are recommended. Use U-Bhf Rosenthaler Platz.

**Brazil**, Gormannstraße 22, Tel. 28-59-90 (open Mon.-Fri. 6 P.M. to 2 A.M., Sat.-Sun. from 10 A.M.) is one of the best restaurants in one of Berlin's most exciting areas. During the summer you can sit in an oasis in a back courtyard. It's not expensive, which helps explain why it is always full. Use U-Bhf Rosenthaler Platz.

**Las Cucarachas**, Oranienburger Straße 38, Tel. 282-2044 (open Mon.-Fri. noon to 1 A.M., Sat.-Sun. from 10 A.M.). Mexican and vegetarian food is served stylishly in one of East Berlin's booming districts. Use S-Bhf Oranienburger Straße.

**Oren**, Oranienburger Straße. 28, Tel. 282-82-28 (open 10 A.M. to 1 A.M.) next to the New Synagogue and Jewish Center, has great bagels. Great bagels are hard to find in Berlin. The Jewish owned restaurant serves Kosher food, vegetarian and fish, in simple black and white surroundings. There's always something happening, but the prices aren't lowest. Use U-Oranienburger Tor or S-Oranienburger Straße.

**Beth Café**, Tucholskystraße 40, Tel. 281-31-35 (open Tue.-Sun. 1 to 10 P.M.,

Mon. to 8 P.M.), "the Jewish café in the middle of town" in the Scheunenviertel, has kosher food and a lovely courtyard. Use S-Bhf Oranienburger Straße.

**Bar-Celona**, Hannoversche Straße 2, Tel. 282-9153 (open daily from 11 A.M.). In the long, thin, humorously decorated room, you eat some of the best Spanish food in Berlin. It features classic tapas, tortillas, and authentic paella. Use U-Bhf Zinnowitzer Straße.

**Blue Gout**, Anklamer Straße 38 (second back courtyard), Tel. 448-5840 (open Sun.-Fri. noon to 1 A.M., Sat. from 6 P.M.). In the second back courtyard of a former weaving establishment, you wouldn't expect such good service, excellent Italian cuisine, and substantial prices. Between U-Bhf Bernauer Str. and S-Bhf Rosenthaler Platz.

**Im Eimer**, Rosenthaler Straße 68, Tel. 282-20-74 (open Fri.-Sat. from 11 P.M.), is in an underground, psychedelic house in the Scheunenviertel.

**Silberstein**, Oranienburger Straße 27 (open 6 P.M. until late), is another "in" place which is part of Scheunenviertel night life, a meeting place for painters and sculptors whose works are on show.

**Planet Hollywood**, Friedrichstraße 68, Tel. 20-94-58-20, Fax 20-94-58-01 (open Sun.-Thur. 11:30 A.M. to 1 A.M., Fri.-Sat. to 2 A.M.). There's a place that's out of this world (near Checkpoint Charlie) where the always-smiling waiters and waitresses may have been cloned. See! Marlene Dietrich's feather boa from *Shangai Express*. The Baby-Back-Ribs are good. Use U-Bhf Stadtmitte.

**Osvaldo**, Schiffbauerdamm 8, Tel. 282-39-65 (open 4 P.M. to 2 A.M.). Don't even think about going to the Berliner Ensemble Theater without thinking about good dining at Osvaldo around the corner. The meals are prepared by an Italian cook according to southern German recipes. Use U- or S-Bhf Friedrichstraße.

**Cantamaggio**, Alte Schönhauser Straße 4, Tel. 283-18-95 (open 6 P.M. to 2 A.M.). Drop by this Mediterranean cantina after an evening at the Volksbühne. It's the way Berliners imagine it. The menus are hand-written. Use U-Weinmeisterstraße.

The **Turmstuben**, Gendarmenmarkt 5, Tel. 229-93-13 (open noon to 1 A.M.) inside the French Church is worth your visit for the view. Use U-Bhf Stadtmitte.

**Möve**, Palais am Festungsgraben, Tel. 201-20-29 (open Mon.-Fri. 5 P.M. to midnight, Sat.-Sun. from 3 P.M.), is located between Humboldt University and the Zeughaus off Unter den Linden behind the Neue Wache. The former government building before the War subsequently became the House of German-Soviet Friendship, but it is the terrace under the chestnut trees that beckons you for a laid-back summer evening.

# 4. Sightseeing

## BRANDENBURG GATE

At the end of Unter den Linden, the **Brandenburger Tor** ("Brandenburg Gate") with the restored Quadriga atop has become the symbol of Berlin's reunification.

The Gate has always been Berlin's dramatic statement, bound together snugly with Prussian and German history. After World War II, it was considered the symbol of the division of Germany. After the Wende, it became the symbol of German unity.

When Unter den Linden was extended in 1734 to the present Pariser Platz, a first Brandenburg Gate was built as part of the early wall that ringed Berlin when it was a walled city. The first high wall was not built for defense, but for taxation. All goods that passed through the wall into the city were taxed. Serendipitously, it effectively kept Prussian army conscripts from deserting.

In 1802, after 15 years' work under the direction of an architect from Breslau, Karl Gotthard Langhans, the number of gates was increased to 14. A few were elaborate. The Rosenthal and Potsdam gates were lavishly ornamented. Oranienburg Gate was built like a Roman triumphal arch, crowned with an obelisk. Hamburg Gate was decorated by two pyramids. In 1860, the city walls were pulled down for the last time. The gates simply became names on the map, with the exception of by far the grandest gate of them all, the enlarged gateway completed at the western end of the Linden. Its design was not simply a baroque victory arch, but based on the Acropolis in Athens with six Silesian sandstone Doric columns. At the entrance to the Acropolis is the Propylea; the Propylea was the entrance to the cultural capital of ancient Greece. Langhans' inspiration was that the Brandenburg Gate should be the entrance to the Holy Prussian Empire. The broad, 18-foot (5.5 meters) central opening was reserved for the use of royal coaches. Other riders and coaches had to use the narrower passages. The gate was supported with two wings that were originally a guard house and a duty house. Its construction began with the tearing down of the old gate in 1788.

The present Gate was opened on August 6, 1791, without speeches, hurrahs, fireworks, or the presence of King Friedrich II, who was with Prussian troops in Mainz. In 1991, Berliners celebrated its 200th anniversary. It is 215 feet (65.5 meters) wide, 36 feet (11 meters) thick, and 85 feet (26 meters) high (including the Quadriga). The Berlin Tourist Office has occupied the house in the south wing.

When the Gate was opened, decoration hadn't yet been completed. By 1795, Johann Gottfried Schadow (1764-1850) had added reliefs showing the saga of Hercules on the walls and on the arch, statues of Mars and Minerva in the niches, and most important, the five-ton Quadriga above the Gate.

After Napoleon's victories over Prussian troops at Jena and Auerstedt, King Friedrich Wilhelm III fled with his wife Luise to East Prussia. On October 17, 1806, Berlin's acting governor posted the famous sign: "The king has lost a battle. Order is now the citizen's first duty." On October 23, the first French division entered Berlin. On October 27, Napoleon I, at the head of his royal guard, rode through the Brandenburg Gate with fireworks and music. The local newspaper reported, "The thunder of cannon and the pealing of bells preceded the arrival. A countless throng welcomed his royal majesty with the friendliest greetings." Berliners were fed up with Prussian militarism and curious to see French enlisted soldiers as they slouched into Berlin, some smoking pipes.

History continued to storm through the Gate for 200 years. It is a miracle that the Gate survived at all. Victory parades marked Prussian triumphs over Denmark (1864), Austria (1866), and France (1870-71) which resulted in the formation of the German Reich and Bismarck, flanked by Moltke and Roon, rode through the Gate. Visitors such as Britain's King Edward VII and Russian Czar Nicholas II rode through the Gate. At the end of the First World War, Kaiser Wilhelm II abdicated on November 10, 1918 and was driven in a Daimler-Landaule through the Gate to board the imperial train to the Dutch frontier. In the Netherlands he went to the estate of Count Godard Bentinck and asked for a cup of tea ("strong English tea") and shelter. It was a tradition of the Knights of the Order of St. John that one gave sanctuary to a brother.

On January 30, 1933, when Hitler took power and became Reichs Chancellor, Joseph Goebbels organized a nighttime candlelight victory parade through the Brandenburg Gate to the former Reichs Chancellery. "A river of fire flowed past the French Embassy," the French ambassador wrote. On June 12, 1987, President Ronald Reagan approached the Gate from the West with a speech that was dated the instant his writer wrote it: "Mr. General Secretary, if you want peace, Mr. Gorbachev, open this Gate. Mr. Gorbachev, tear down this Wall."

Before the War the Gate was really a passage between East and West portions of Berlin. After the removal of the Wall and the rebuilding of the area the problem was: should street traffic be permitted to travel through the Gate or not? Preservationists said no; city planners said yes—if street traffic were routed around the Gate, then it would create an undesirable island. The compromise, argued in Berlin and on the floor of the Bonn parliament, was a standoff. Only buses, taxis, and bicycles may use the gate. Private vehicles must drive around the Gate.

The best way to the Brandenburg Gate is by bus 100 to Reichstag south side or S-Bhf Unter den Linden. Reach S-Bhf Unter den Linden by changing at S-Bhf Friedrichstraße or U-Bhf Yorckstraße.

When the Brandenburg Gate was constructed, the patina-green **Quadriga** goddess figure represented Irene, the Greek goddess for peace, in a Roman chariot pulled by four horses. She held a long staff with a wreath and a graceful, peaceful Roman eagle at the tip.

During his occupation of Berlin, Napoleon, in order to tweak the Prussians, ordered the entire Quadriga packed into 14 boxes and sent to Paris. In 1814, after Napoleon's defeat, General von Blücher returned Quadriga to Berlin amid great celebration and mounted it atop the Brandenburg Gate on June 30. But the goddess, horses, and chariot remained covered. Berliners puzzled over the mysterious wrapping. When the coverings were removed in a festive August 7 celebration, the peace goddess Irene had been transformed to Victoria, the victory goddess. Schinkel had replaced Schadow's Roman eagle with a mean, martial Prussian eagle, and designed within the wreath at the tip of Victoria's staff the iron cross that was devised by Friedrich Wilhelm III during the previous year.

In 1868, the old Berlin wall was taken down and pedestrian paths built left and right of the Gate. During the Second World War, the Gate was severely damaged. Two and a half horses of Quadriga remained. East Berliners agreed to rebuild the Gate and the West Berliners undertook to repair Quadriga in 1958. The West Berlin foundry Noack cast a new Quadriga (which consists of a cast-iron skeleton supporting copper cladding) using the original plaster models of the damaged one. But Quadriga had changed. The East Germans declined to restore Schinkel's iron cross because of its associations with Prussian militarism.

Quadriga oversaw the divided city until its fragile copper cladding was destroyed by celebrants on New Year's Eve 1989, when happiness gushed over the Wall with no policing or control. Drunks mounted the horses bareback to express their glee during the party for the opening of the borders. They overdid it a bit.

For the third time, Quadriga was taken down. It was hoisted over the Wall and recast in the Transportation Museum (see Chapter 8). After 15 months work, the Berlin symbol was returned to site, but this time there was no Wall to impede its trip. On August 6, 1991, for Quadriga's 200th anniversary, fireworks, a laser show, and general merriment illuminated the Brandenburg Gate and Victoria's horses galloped above the unified city and after 33 years, the angry eagle and laureled iron cross had returned to the goddess's staff.

During its last restoration it was very interesting to view the Quadriga up close. The Quadriga comes apart. The upper surfaces are patina green; the undersides are black because they haven't been exposed to the weather. The realistic-looking four horses are separate items, each about 12 feet tall. Two have their left front hooves in the air; two have their right front hooves in the air. The chariot, which is no higher than the horses, has two wheels. On the yoke it has a Gothic lion's face. The one-ton winged goddess is assembled into the chariot with a stake, making the whole unit reach 85 feet (26 meters) above the street.

You can be married directly under the Brandenburg Gate. Since April 1997, the Berlin Transit Authority has been permitted to rent a special *Hochzeitsbus* ("Wedding Bus") for authorized marriage ceremonies here and at other sites of interest.

## PARISER PLATZ

Through the Brandenburg Gate, the first square you meet is **Pariser Platz**. Originally a parade ground for Friedrich Wilhelm's solders at the western end of the Linden street, the *Karee* ("Square") was renamed Pariser Platz in 1814 when General Blücher's armies returned the Quadriga from Paris, placed it atop the Brandenburg Gate and victory celebrations turned the city into a "sea of light."

You don't believe your eyes as you pass through the Brandenburg Gate from the *Platz vor dem Brandenburger Tor* (this square may be renamed *Platz des 18.März 1848* in honor of the workers' revolution of that date demanding more freedoms). East of the gate, Pariser Platz has cloned itself. Around the square the buildings look the same as those whose remains were piled into rubble mountains by the Trümmerfrauen. The 1997-98 buildings aren't exact replicas down to the last detail, but they present the same skyline that existed before the British bombs and Russian artillery shells of World War II. The aim of the architects was not to rebuild every detail historically, but to recall the history of the square. All buildings had to be of the same height and have the same structure: a ground floor, three main stories and a garret floor under a sloping roof. Only the Hotel Adlon and the buildings opposite were excused from this guideline because they were copied from the pre-war originals. The facades had to be mainly sandstone, blending in with the Brandenburg Gate. The windows were not permitted to constitute more than 30 percent of the facade and individual panes could not exceed a given size.

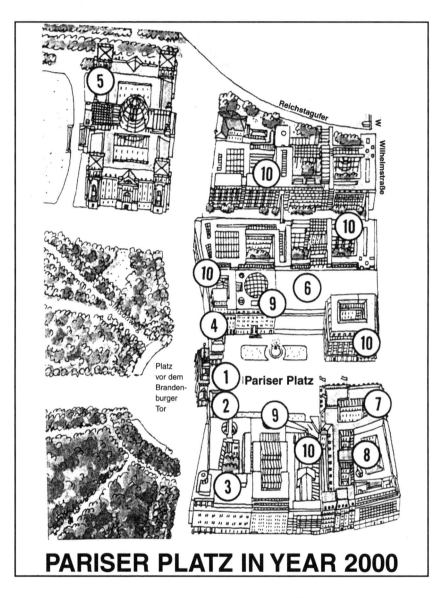

# PARISER PLATZ IN YEAR 2000

1. Brandenburg Gate
2. Haus Sommer
3. U. S. Embassy
4. Haus Liebermann
5. Reichstag
6. French Embassy
7. Hotel Adlon
8. British Embassy
9. Bank Building
10. Year 2000 offices

Pariser Platz was one of the most beautiful squares of old Berlin before the War, yet after the War the DDR made it worse than a desert. It became "no man's land" approaching the awful Wall, populated only by rigid armed guards and dangerous dogs on leash. Yet, you became so used to seeing the Brandenburg Gate in pictures and in person—it standing like a solitary jewel, before and after the Wende—that the new construction is a shock. Most Berliners are taking a wait and see attitude toward buildings they have never seen before, but are dubious. The present generation has come to love and honor the Brandenburg Gate as a symbol—and that symbol was not crowded by unfamiliar buildings.

Standing alone, the Brandenburg Gate made a statement—of history, of peoples' struggles for freedom, liberty, justice. Now amid the clutter of large, celebrated banks, expensive apartments, prestige hotels, museums, and embassies, it is lost. It is an interesting Greco-Roman gate, no more.

The square had been a desirable location from the time the gate was built. Historians can't tell you when construction of the square began. They say that possibly two palaces were built about 1729. For sure, they say, there were substantial buildings around the square by 1735, but that the square didn't begin to take its modern shape until 1842 when the royal court's master carpenter, Carl August Sommer, acquired addresses #6 and #7 and commissioned architect August Stüler to create the striking ensemble that the square came to know. Ebertstraße was formerly named Sommerstraße. House #6 was divided into 6 and 6a, which you identify from its square tower. In 6a, Giacomo Meyerbeer sought inspiration for his musical compositions below the tower's five windows while he lived there 1848-62. It later became the Dutch embassy. Other artists lived on Pariser Platz, but usually for short periods in order to take advantage of the prestigious address. House #7 was acquired in 1857 by calico manufacturer Louis Liebermann.

During reconstruction of these buildings, there was general agreement that the square in front of the Brandenburg Gate should maintain its representative function as a central point linking the two halves of the city and as an entrance to the historic district. The kaiser did not allow any trees on Pariser Platz so that people would concentrate on the architecture. The present Berlin Senate does not want any street cafés so that visitors are not distracted from the new run-of-the-mill buildings. In addition to the new Adlon Hotel and the Sommer and Liebermann buildings, the square houses the Academy of Arts, the American and French Embassies, and several bank buildings.

On the south, the Sommer House next to the gate is #1. Number 2 was given as a present by the kaiser to General von Blücher for his victory over

Napoleon. It was the western wing of this Blücher Palace that was purchased by the USA in 1930. Before the Americans could move in, the house was destroyed by fire. By the time workers had restored and rebuilt the building, the Second World War broke out. A new American Embassy is being reconstructed on the original site. The American architects, Moore, Ruble, and Yudell, have not agreed to maintain the classic style of architecture approved by the Berlin architectural bureau for the all the other buildings on Pariser Platz; instead, they have opted for a striking vertical cut in the facade. Many Berliners fear the American reconstruction may be an embarrassment.

The French Embassy on the north side of the square occupied house #5 since 1864 (off and on, depending on the state of hostility between the two countries). The neighboring palace at #5a was demolished in 1904 to make way for a French-styled edifice built privately. The Prussian Academy of Arts moved into Pariser Platz #4 on January 25, 1907. After the Second World War, the DDR thought it would be a good idea to return the several embassies to their former locations. No one else thought so. Which country would appreciate its embassy being located in a "no man's land" behind the Wall?

From the left (traveling in the same direction as the Quadriga horses), you see

• The tan sandstone reconstruction of the corner house **Liebermann Mansion** where Max Liebermann, the famous German painter, lived next to the Gate. When he saw the Nazi's four-hour torchlight parade at his door, he made the famous statement: "Pity, one can't eat as much as one wants to vomit."

• Jutting at right angles, with the Meyerbeer tower, to form the beginning of an "L" bordering Pariser Platz at number 6a is the larger yellow sandstone **Palais am Pariser Platz**. Because of its narrow frontage between the Liebermann house and the Dresdner Bank, it is hardly a palace, but the architect who thought up the name maintains that it has elements of a palace in its facade. The DM 46 million project is home to one of the owners, the Hypothekenbank. It would be exquisite to live in one of the apartments upstairs.

• The left flank facing the square has been extended by the new four-story tan with green upper story **Dresdner Bank** building at #6 Pariser Platz. The slightly curved roof is glass to allow lighting of the interior atrium.

• Beyond the Dresdner Bank, the new **French Embassy** is taking shape for completion in 2000. It was designed by Christian de Portzamparc, who also designed the Cité de la Musique in la Villette. It's an L-shaped building reaching around to Wilhelmstraße in back. Its Pariser Platz facade consists of a smooth, white stone bordered by seven tall windows. Inside there are two courtyards with the consulate, the residence of the ambassador, and a French cultural center, replacing the present **French Center** in Wedding at Müllerstraße 74.

• Finally, on the corner of Wilhelmstraße, the *Wohn- und Geschäftshaus am Pariser Platz*, a square business and apartment building.

On the south, to your right, you have

• The square **Haus Sommer**, Stüler's design symmetrical with his Haus Liebermann on the left. With Haus Sommer, Pariser Platz #1, the Commerzbank has acquired a prestigious address for its connection and diplomatic representation in Germany's capital city. Can you say, "lobbyist?"

• The American Embassy under construction.

• Opposite the Dresdner Bank, on your right, at Pariser Platz 3, the **DG Bank** anchors the multi-functional office and conference center with exclusive condominiums. The European Commission has taken the prestige garret floor. The three banks, the DG, the Dresdner, and the Commerzbank combine to make this *Bankenplatz Berlins.*

• Beside the DG Bank building will be the new home for the prestigious new **Akademie der Künste** ("Arts Academy"). This was the last argument on Pariser Platz to be settled. The cornerstone will be laid mid-1999. There will be less glass than originally planned and the reconstructed facade will match the architecture of the adjacent buildings, with a kind of balcony over the ground floor with letters that will announce what is on display inside.

• From the Haus Sommer, in front of the building runs a simple garden with fountain to the new **Hotel Adlon**. The hotel had such a magic name that for the week of the previews, Berliners stood in lines stretching around the corner more than 350 feet (100 meters) for a chance to view the interior of the hotel. Situated as it is, on the landmark site where an arsonist sent the 1907 Adlon, the last great, grand hotel, up in flames at the end of the Second World War, it has seen much history. The DM 430 million new Adlon is not a facsimile of the old house. The only things it has in common are its name, location, and prestige. The original Adlon was the last word in taste, luxury, and elegance. It should have been, for its patron was Kaiser Wilhelm II, who arranged for the acquisition of part of the land of the British Embassy, next door, to allow its construction. It was a battleground for the day beginning the Spartakus uprising of 1919, occupied in turn by Spartakists and Freikorps soldiers, both of whom paused to liberally sample the hotel's famous wine cellar. When Hitler was appointed chancellor, Hedda Adlon, wife of owner Lorenz, had the doors locked at 6 P.M. because every room had already been filled with guests wanting to watch the enormous parade down Unter den Linden.

On August 24, 1997, Federal President Roman Herzog cut the traditional ribbon to open the new Adlon. Percy Adlon, the great grandson of the hotel founder was there, remarking that the property had not reverted to the family after reunification. The name had been bought from Hedda Adlon by Kempinski Hotels.

• The dark-blue Rolls Royce turned left at the Hotel Adlon and stopped before a field barren except for a red carpet and a tent smelling of champagne. Out stepped Derek Fatchett to break ground for the new **British Embassy** on Monday, June 29, 1998. The British Embassy is being rebuilt around the Adlon corner at Wilhelmstraße 70 with a postmodern stone facade in the color of the Brandenburg Gate. Inside will be two courtyards with balconies, terraces, and a rounded tower. The British ambassador is expected to relocate from Bonn in fall, 1999. The British acquired this site in 1873 when the stock market crashed and the former owner went bankrupt. This may be the only embassy which will not be owned by the resident country. The British will take a 30-year lease on the building which will be built by a German consortium and owned by the Dresdner Bank.

## UNTER DEN LINDEN

Past Pariser Platz, you see that the Brandenburg Gate lies at the foot of the street famous from pre-War Berlin, **Unter den Linden** ("Under the Lime Trees"). Here were the great hotels; here were the great cafés. At the head stood the now-demolished **Berlin Stadt Schloß**, the "Berlin City Palace" of the Prussian-German emperors. All this was blown away by World War II, the Wall and the Communist vision of a workers' state.

Unter den Linden began as no more than a path under Linden trees between the palace and the Gate. For 400 years, no buildings stood here; it was simply a Linden path to the palace. Storybooks have it that in 1673, in front of the customs gate of the city, the elector's wife, Dorothea, planted with her own hands in the sand the first of 1,000 Linden trees and that was the beginning of Berlin's most famous street. In truth Elector Johann Georg laid out a path from where the Zeughaus now stands through the Tiergarten for a horse- and hunting path in 1573. After the Thirty Years War, the riding path was repaired, and in 1647 on the orders of Elector Friedrich Wilhelm a length of about 0.6 miles (942 meters) six rows of nut and Linden trees were planted according to the Dutch fashion. The elector's wife, Dorothea, was connected with the Linden in a totally different way. She had the architect J. E. Blesendorf divide the land into parcels and sold it for farmland thereby creating a new city section inside the gates. The name seems to have come from the orders given by the succeeding elector, who decreed in 1690 that "farmers must pen their pigs better 'Unter den Linden,' so they won't damage the trees." A hundred years later the street gained the character you recognize today.

Unter den Linden was lined with shops, cafés, and restaurants before the War. It is 0.86 miles (1,390 meters) long and 66 yards (60 meters) wide. Famous people like Marlene Dietrich and Max Liebermann, the painter, lived here. Now new apartments are being occupied for the first time. It will never be the same again. Berlin town planners have decreed the street will host banks, embassies, museums, and monolithic office buildings. It is hardly a place for conviviality. There are occasional sidewalk cafés, but little shopping.

Remembering the Kaiser-Wilhelm-Gedächtniskirche near the Zoo station, you now appreciate Wilhelm I, its namesake, who died in 1888. He was one of the few German kaisers who gained a certain popularity with the people although from the window of house #18, in 1878, Dr. Karl Nobiling shot and wounded him with a flintlock. Wilhelm I liked to stand at his corner window and greet the passers-by. He was a father figure. It's said that once a week he had a bathtub brought from the long-gone Hotel Rome at Unter den Linden 39 to his palace for splashing around.

At Unter den Linden Academy (#38) hung Berlin's first standard clock that was used to set all other clocks in the city. It's now in the Märkisches Museum.

The white, blue, and red tricolor of the Russian republic flies outside address 63-65 on the south side of Unter den Linden in the first block from the Brandenburg Gate. The biggest in the block and the first rebuilt after the War, 1949-51, the former Soviet Embassy that Stalin built is now the **Embassy of the Russian Federation**. The Soviet Union occupied the site after the Russian Revolution until December 25, 1991, when the building reverted to Russia. Other ex-Soviet Union republics also have offices here.

In 1837, Czar Nicholas I of Russia purchased the baroque marble palace on this site that had been the residence of the second sister of Friedrich the Great. At that time, one had to be a citizen of Berlin to own property so legally the Russian czar could not buy it. To resolve this dilemma, Nicholas was named an honorary citizen of Berlin. After World War II, Stalin's architects tried to turn it into a marble victory monument with stones taken from Göring's former Air Force Ministry (see Chapter 7). He had it built into a Communist palace unequaled outside the former Soviet Union. The steps built from three kinds of marble that lead up the column-supported colossus's exterior remind you more of Sanssouci (Chapter 13) than a Stalinist control center. The exterior was only overshadowed by the decoration of the interior. Until November 9, 1991, when it was dismantled by workers to mark the anniversary of the fall of the Berlin Wall, an enormous marble face of Lenin dominated the courtyard.

The corner of Friedrichstraße and the Linden, where the Grand Hotel now stands, was known as **Coffeehouse Corner**, where the Café Kranzler, Café Victoria, and Café Bauer faced each other. The Kranzler opened on this location in 1820 and quickly revolutionized society life in Berlin. It was so fashionable that confectioners flocked from Switzerland to share its popularity. Each café became a magnet to a particular clientele. The Kranzler was popular with lieutenants of the guard. D'Heureuse, on Breitenstraße, catered to liberal property owners. Courtin, near the stock market and post office, was frequented with bankers and businessmen. The Café Bauer was the site of the first electric light in Berlin.

The **Deutsche Guggenheim Berlin Museum** opened its doors in 1998 on the ground floor of the Deutsche Bank at Unter den Linden 13-15, Tel. 20-20-93-0, Fax 20-20-93-20, *http://www.deutsche-bank.de/deutscheguggenheim* (open daily 11 A.M. to 8 p.m; entrance DM 8, Mon. free; daily tours at 6 P.M., luncheon lectures Wed. at 1 P.M., and keynote tours Sun. at 11:30 A.M.). It features first-class exhibitions of contemporary art. Stroll in from Unter den Linden; the pure simplicity of the museum will enhance your enjoyment of the three or four yearly quality exhibitions. The museum occupies the ground floor of the traditional 1920 sandstone building of the Deutsche Bank. American architect Richard Gluckman (who also designed the Dia Center for the Arts in New York City and Andy Warhol Museum in Pittsburgh) created a vast, clear structural gallery. From the exhibition area you climb a stairway to the museum's shop and Café Kaffeebank, where you can see the interior of the bank. After the Peggy Guggenheim Collection in Venice, the Guggenheim Museum in Bilbao, Spain, and the two locations in New York City, the Deutsche Guggenheim Berlin is the fifth location of the Solomon R. Guggenheim Foundation, which is only appropriate because the Guggenheim family came originally from Germany and Hilla Rebay, the first director of the Guggenheim Museums, emigrated from former Prussia to New York.

In the middle of the street, the **Reiterstandbild Friedrich des Großen** ("Equestrian Statue of Friedrich the Great"), the monumental bronze created over ten years (to 1851) by Christian Daniel Rauch, was hidden until 1980 in the park of Sanssouci in Potsdam by East Germans determined to suppress Prussian history. The Communists wanted to break with Prussian tradition, but belatedly they realized that this was impossible, so Friedrich the Great shed his imperialistic militarist label, was transformed to a historic figure, and became quite a good Communist at the end.

The bronze statue looks bright and shiny because it was carted away on October 1, 1997, for renovation costing DM 2 million at a workshop in Tempelhof. Replaced on its stand in 1999, the green will come with age. The 44-foot (13.5 meters) statue depicts Friedrich on his favorite horse, Condé, wearing his coronation robes, tricorne and riding boots, and holding a crop. The four tablets at the base list 60 leaders of his reign. Above are life-size figures of generals; at the corners, cavalry commanders; and above them are bas-reliefs of scenes from his life.

The gray stone **Humboldt Universität** ("Humboldt University"), originally the neoclassical 1748 Prince's Palace built for the brother of Friedrich the Great, still stands proudly on the north side of Unter den Linden. It was opened by Baron Wilhelm von Humboldt in 1810 as minister of education under King Friedrich Wilhelm and named Friedrich Wilhelms University. When the Soviets reopened it after the War, on January 29, 1946, they renamed it Humboldt University. At the entrance you see busts of Wilhelm, the writer and politician, and his brother, Alexander, the famed naturalist and explorer of South America who is credited as the first European to realize the value of using bird droppings for fertilizer. The white marble statue of Alexander was fashioned by sculptor Reinhold Begas in 1883 to match Wilhelm von Humboldt's memorial. A Bremen wine wholesaler paid US$18,000 in 1998 to have it cleaned—which took four months. The parallel statue, Wilhelm, was restored the previous year. The university's present building is in the shape of an *H*. In the courtyard, there is a tree that was planted during the Humboldts' lifetime, a ginkgo tree. The men who taught here were among the greatest figures of their times—Fichte and Hegel; Albert Einstein, the brothers Jacob and Wilhelm Grimm; Helmholtz, the physicist; Ranke and Mommsen, the historian of the Roman Republic. Mark Twain, for one, was captivated by the sight of a whole roomful of Berlin students raising their sabers and rising to their feet in honor of the entry of Mommsen. Alumni include Karl Marx, Friedrich Engels, and Karl Liebknecht. The shrinking number of students, now 20,000, is a problem.

Humboldt is the oldest of the three universities of Berlin; the **Freie Universität** (Free University) in West Berlin's Dahlem district is the youngest. FU split from the Humboldt University in 1948-49 because of the political division. The Technical University in West Berlin evolved after the War from the old Technical High School. The Humboldt and the Free universities were not recombined after the Wende. Professors at the three universities continue education, but those who had preached Stalinistic ideology at Humboldt are long gone. Their dismissal was a difficult process.

The Behrenstraße and the Französische Straße were lined with bank buildings scarcely 90 years old, including the main office of the Dresdner Bank. These banks all fled to Frankfurt am Main during the Cold War.

One of the largest libraries in Germany, a typical grandiose building on the north side of Unter den Linden, is the **Deutsche Staatsbibliothek** ("German National Library"), housed in the former Prussian State Library Building (the old **Staabi**). It is a house with columns set back from the road. The huge complex with six interior courtyards (the prettiest faces Unter den Linden) was built 1903-14. It contains over seven million volumes. Next to Humboldt University, you can relax beside the students in the pretty courtyard by the fountain when you feel like a break.

Opposite the Opera House you find the **Neue Wache** ("New Guard House") Unter den Linden 4, built to accommodate the palace guard. It was architect Carl Friedrich von Schinkel's first major building assignment and resulted in one of the most successful works of German classicism. Schinkel built it in 1817-18 and based it on the plan of a Roman fort. He decorated the Doric portico with scenes of ancient battle.

It was here that the "Captain from Köpenick" (see Chapter 12), shoe-maker and embezzler Wilhelm Voigt, drove up three horse-drawn cabs and turned over the "arrested" mayor and city treasurer of Köpenick. City Kommandant Kuno von Moltke released the two men, but by then, the false captain had hailed a taxi and disappeared.

Until 1918, the Wache served as a royal police station for the palace. After 1918, when there was no longer a king, the government made it a memorial for those killed in the First World War.

After the Second World War, under the DDR, an eternal flame was installed inside and the Neue Wache became the "Memorial to the Victims of Fascism and Militarism." Now figure this: in order to show its anti-Fascistic and anti-militaristic character, they placed a pair of honor guards in uniforms and helmets in front of the building at stiff attention, each holding a perfectly vertical rifle before the left side of his chest. When an electric bell rang for five seconds, the guards, with stunning synchronization, switched their rifles to the right. They were relieved every half-hour with an elaborately stiff ceremony featuring Prussian-German-Fascistic goose-stepping. They made the ceremonial goose-stepping guard changing into an astonishing tourist attraction that would have rivaled the changing of the guards at Buckingham Palace except that in Berlin the crowds gasped at the show of militarism that recalled the victimizers instead of the victims.

As a second joke, they wanted to place inside the hall the body of an unknown German soldier who had fought against Hitler. We know of the revolt of officers against Hitler, but those were officers and not enlisted men, and so the DDR took the body of an unknown Russian soldier and placed him inside the Neue Wache. He was the world's first foreign unknown soldier. In order to solve this problem, the DDR placed next to him a German resistance fighter, a civilian. Therefore within the Neue Wache lay a German civilian and a Russian soldier.

After the Wende, in 1993, the Neue Wache was converted to a simple federal republic memorial to the victims of war. Gone are the goose-stepping soldiers, the unknown soldier/resistance fighter, and eternal flame, but the Neue Wache is not yet free from controversy. The marble statue that was chosen as the new centerpiece is greatly criticized.

**Maxim-Gorki-Theate**r is the neoclassical building behind the Wache on the street called Am Festungsgraben ("On the Fortress Moat") where the Great Elector's original fortifications had been filled in, partly with the remains of the Royal National Theater which had burned down in 1817. It was built 1825-27 by Karl Theodor Ottmar, one of Schinkel's students, according to Schinkel's original plans for the first dedicated concert hall. The former house of the Berliner Singakadamie was rebuilt and renamed in 1952 after the Russian writer. Sadly, the interior is totally without charm because it has never been satisfactorily restored following the War.

Next to the theater was the **Haus der Deutsch-Sowjetischen Freundschaft** ("German-Soviet Friendship House"), the exhibit hall for Soviet music, books, etc. This representative baroque building in back of the Neue Wache was once the Prussian Financial Ministry in the **Palais am Festungsgraben.** The ownership of the collection remaining inside, which includes valuable Prussian antiques, is, like so many things in the former DDR, the center of bureaucratic squabbling. The Prussian collection may eventually be transferred to Charlottenburg Palace.

The oldest building on Unter den Linden, the two-story **Zeughaus—das Waffenkammer der Preußisch-Deutsche Kaiser** ("Armory—the Weapons Depot of the Prussian-German Emperor") that was built between 1692 and 1706 as a arsenal and storage facility for war appropriations, is Berlin's largest and most beautiful baroque building. The monumental building with four wings has a beautiful facade. The damaged copper roof has been repaired and the figures on the roof restored showing ancient gods, a winged goddess of victory, and representations of flags, weapons, and armaments. The four allegorical figures on the entrance represent the sciences of Mechanics, Mathematics, Geometry, and Pyrotechnics. Inside it contains the beautiful court known as the **Schlüter Courtyard** because of his decorations and his 22 *Masks of Dying Warriors*. The DDR's reconstruction of the 300-year-old building after the War showed the full turning of the DDR's philosophies. Admittedly it is Berlin's finest baroque building, but it deals directly with weapons and wars and nothing else and one can't imagine a better symbol of Prussian militarism.

Between 1993 and 1996, Berlin spent an additional DM 40 million to repair the heating and electrical wiring, and to install handicapped access and air-conditioning. On December 30, 1998, it entered a new era. The building was closed to begin construction of a new annex designed by architect I. M. Pei to be completed by 2001. Judging from the architectural renderings, Pei's new annex promises to attract at least as much controversy as Pei's pyramid on the Louvre or his East Wing of the National Gallery in Washington, D.C. Look forward to the building's reopening in year 2002.

## BEBELPLATZ

An architectural highlight of Unter den Linden is formed at **Bebelplatz**, which has variously been called the Linden Forum and Forum Berolinum (the idea goes back to Rome), and Forum Fredericianum, to be the cultural heart of Prussia. Here the Old Palace, the German State Opera House, the University, St. Hedwig's Cathedral, and the former Royal Library gather together.

In the middle of the uneven, cobblestone square lies a flat, smooth pane of transparent safety glass (which has to be replaced three times a year because of scratches). When you look through, you see that it is a **Versunkene Bibliothek** ("Sunken Library"), a window on a library filled with empty white shelves. This dramatic view is the 1994/95 memorial to the event which took place on May 10, 1933.

On May 10, 1933, books were burned. Hitler assumed his dictatorship in March 1933, and two months later, here, and in other large cities in Germany, huge collections of books went up in flames. At about midnight a torchlight parade of thousands of students ended at Bebelplatz across from the University of Berlin. The reason was clear: Nazis wanted to demonstrate that Communistic, Jewish, homosexual, and everything non-Aryan would be destroyed in order to create a clean, Aryan, German culture. Books written by Thomas Mann, Heinrich Mann, Erich Kästner, Jack London, Upton Sinclair, and H. G. Wells went into the Berlin air together with the papers the Nazis confiscated from Albert Einstein's summer house after he fled Berlin. In the words of a student proclamation, any book was condemned to flames "which acts subversively on our future or strikes at the root of German thought, the German home and the driving forces of our people."

The illuminated room with empty books shelves has space for 20,000 books—the number of books that were burned on May 10, 1933. According

# BEBELPLATZ

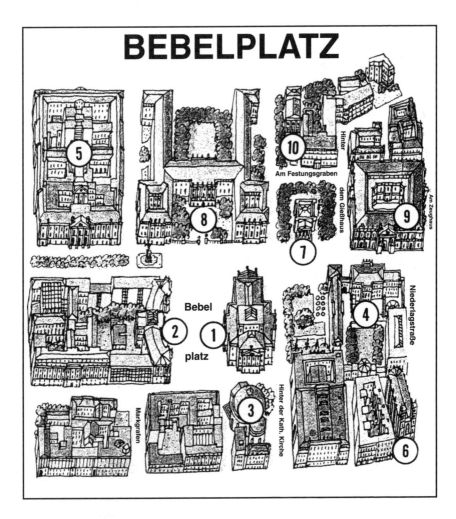

1. Deutsche Staatsoper
2. Royal Library
3. St.-Hedwigs-Kathedrale
4. Crown Prince's Palace
5. Alte Bibliothek
6. Schinkel Museum in Friedrichswerde Church
7. Neue Wache
8. Humboldt University
9. Zeughaus
10. Maxim-Gorki-Theater

to the metal plaque in the square: "That was a prelude. Wherever they burn books, sooner or later they will burn human beings also." Heinrich Heine, 1820. (There is talk that the **Heinrich-Heine-Denkmal**, the bronze statue of Heine created in 1958 will be relocated among the chestnut trees behind the Neue Wache.)

All the buildings surrounding this square were erected with the inspiration of Friedrich the Great, king of Prussia from 1740 to 1786, whose equestrian statue stands in the middle of the Unter den Linden. On the northwestern corner facing Unter den Linden stands the Alte Palais ("Old Palace"); on the western face was built the Königliche Bibliothek ("Royal Library"), known colloquially as the Kommode ("Chest of Drawers"); on the east facing Unter den Linden, the Deutsche Staatsoper ("German State Opera House"); and on the south face, the St.-Hedwigs-Kathedrale ("St. Hedwig's Cathedral"), the Catholic minority's cathedral.

The **Alte Palais** ("Old Palace") was so named because it was built between 1834 and 1837 by Carl Ferdinand Langhans in the neoclassical style. Kaiser Wilhelm I lived here until his death in 1888. Today it is used by Humboldt University.

The baroque building on the west side of Bebelplatz is the former **Königliche Bibliothek** ("Royal Library"), designed by Georg Christian Unger between 1775 and 1780 and copied from the Austrian Hapsburg 1730 Hofburg Palace in Vienna.

Due to its curved baroque facade which was restored in 1997-98, it is often known as the **Kommode** ("Chest of Drawers"). A plaque memorializes the student Vladimir I. Lenin, who read here in August 1895. Earlier, it was frequented by Friedrich the Great. Although Friedrich was king of Prussia, he didn't use the German language. The official court language was French. The Latin inscription reads: "Now you know what I'm studying." In the following centuries it was remodeled and during the War almost completely destroyed, but then restored and reopened in 1950. A plaque on the building recalls the book burnings in front of the structure. Today it is part of the Humboldt University.

**St.-Hedwigs-Kathedrale** ("St. Hedwig's Cathedral"), Tel. 200-47-61, at the back of Bebelplatz with a green roof, was the first Catholic church in Berlin. It is a copy of the 27 B.C. Pantheon in Rome. The Greek and the Roman empires were a model for cultural history in Germany and especially Berlin. Great powers such as Prussia wanted to follow in the cultural footsteps of Greece. The Brandenburg Gate was to be a copy of the imperial entrance to Berlin's Forum Romanum.

The peoples of North Germany and East Germany plus regions of Baden-Württemberg are principally Lutheran Protestants. St. Hedwig's

Cathedral was built by the Dutch architect Johann Boumann for Berlin's Catholic minority. Friedrich II made the first designs, which were completed by Georg von Knobelsdorff. It was completed in 1778, but destroyed during the War and rebuilt 1952-62 for the bishopric of Berlin.

The golden letters above the facade of the building facing Unter den Linden, the **Deutsche Staatsoper** ("German National Opera House"), Unter den Linden 7, Tel. 200-47-62, have seen rough going: FRIDERICVS REX APOLLINI ET MVSIS (King Friedrich, Apollo and Muse).

A few days after the burial of his hated father, Friedrich the Great asked his friend from Cossar an der Oder, Georg von Knobelsdorff, to build an opera house. Not any opera house. The Opera House. The most beautiful and mightiest in Europe. The first freestanding theater in Germany and France with a magnificent rococo Apollo ballroom. The king gave Knobels-dorff sketches down to the last detail. It was 1740.

While Knobelsdorff was finishing his plans, a new era in European history was evolving. The Hapsburg emperor of Austria, Charles VI, died; Prussia sent a well-supported 16,400-man army into Silesia; the First Silesian War broke out.

All was quiet in Berlin. The cornerstone of the opera house was laid on September 5, 1741, and the opera house opened on December 7, 1742, with *Caesar and Cleopatra* from Carl Heinrich Graun. The portico duplicates Palladio's design for the Villa Rotunda near Vincenza in Italy, but the grand staircase in front was only for the king's use. The public (1,800 standing and 1,500 in loges) used the side doors, but it wasn't until the king's death that tickets were sold to the general public. A loge ticket cost 32 Talers. The average worker earned 1 Taler for 10 days' labor.

Friedrich died. Napoleon marched in. And the opera house became a military storehouse. It burned down in 1843.

On the night of April 10, 1941, the opera house again burned without a word being printed in the Reich's newspapers. On February 3, 1945, it became a total ruin. The DDR wanted to impress the world during the Cold War. It was lucky to find architect Richard Paulick instead of one of the designers of sugary Stalinistic workers' buildings. Despite material shortages, Friedrich's jewel was authentically rebuilt except for the addition of new gold-foil hammers and sickles.

The rebuilt opera house was opened in 1955 and called the German National Opera House. By 1986, the DDR had rediscovered Friedrich. The letters FRIDERICVS REX APOLLINI ET MVSIS were restored over the entrance. The Prussian king had returned to the palace of the Communists.

The **Opern Café** evolved from the 1713 palace for General von Bescheffer and his stepson Grand Chancellor von Cucceji. In 1790 King Friedrich

Wilhelm acquired the property for his second son, Prince Ludwig. In 1798 King Friedrich Wilhelm III enlarged the house and attached the two-story baroque building to his Crown Prince's Palace next door by means of elevated walkways. After the death of Queen Luise in 1811, he had his three unmarried princesses, Charlotte, Alexandrine, and Luise take up residence here until their marriages. The palace then became known as the **Prinzessinenpalais** ("Princesses' Palace"). Since 1824 over a hundred associates of the royal house have lived here, ranging from government officials to Berlin citizens. It was the home of the Schinkel Museum from 1929 until the bombing.

The Princesses' Palace was also destroyed during the War, but was faithfully reproduced in 1962-63 to accommodate the Opera Café. Extending from the Opera Café to the Opera House, the garden is decorated with neoclassical sculptures from the school of Christian Daniel Rauch. The Scharnhorst memorial sculpture from across the Linden was moved here in 1964. It became a favorite location for both East and West. The back rooms were used by the ballet company of the German State Opera. A discotheque was opened.

In 1964 the adjacent garden was replanted. The Wende brought a general renovation in 1990. The latest addition was the installation of an unnecessary cast iron fountain next to the beer garden courtesy of a Bavarian bank.

Across King Friedrich Wilhelm III's elevated walkways, the **Kronprinzenpalais** ("Crown Prince's Palace"), Unter den Linden 3, Tel. 26-02-14-22, Fax 26-02-12-39, has had a tense history. Two years after the shocking "Katte affair" (see Chapter 12), Friedrich Wilhelm I commissioned architect Philipp Gerlach in 1732 to convert Johann Arnold Nering's 1663-64 townhouse into a two-story baroque palace with rich facade for him to give his son, Crown Prince Friedrich, later Friedrich the Great.

The building later was occupied by Prince Augustus Wilhelm, Friedrich the Great's brother, and from 1793 by Crown Prince Friedrich Wilhelm and his wife Louise. Friedrich Wilhelm III preferred to live here because the 30 rooms were homier than the Berlin City Palace.

After the further addition of a new floor, the Kronprinzenpalais became the residence of the future Kaiser Friedrich III and his wife Victoria (daughter of England's Queen Victoria) in 1856. His son, Wilhelm II, the last German kaiser, was born here on January 27, 1859.

After the First World War the Kronprinzenpalais was modernized and the modern painting collection of the National Gallery was hung in 1920. This gallery was closed immediately when Hitler took power and the paintings were either consigned to "Degenerate Art" or destroyed.

Having completely burned down during the last weeks of the Second

World War, the Kronprinzenpalais was the first of the historical structures in East Berlin to be rebuilt by the DDR (in 1968-69) for use as a guesthouse for prestigious state visitors, **Gästehaus des Magistrats**. You can detect the influence of the Communist party—after all, which Prussian prince had a hammer and sickle in his coat of arms? (This is now covered with a metal plate.) The treaty toward unifying East and West Germany was signed here on August 31, 1990. Use U-Bhf Französische Straße or bus 100.

In 1998, the **Museum für Deutsche Geschichte** ("German Historical Museum") began moving in. Originally a new building for the museum was supposed to be constructed near the Reichstag Building. The Italian architect Aldo Rossi had won the architectural competition in the year 1988. The sudden German reunification in 1990 changed everything. The federal government made the collections and properties of the East German **Museum für Deutsche Geschichte** available for use by the Western museum. The collections include extensive stores of posters and documents on the history of the workers' movement as well as a few remains from the former *Zeughaus* collection, which before World War II had been the largest collection of militaria from the history of Brandenburg and Prussia. The collections had to flee the *Zeughaus* to allow for construction of I. M. Pei's new annex across the street. Berliners called the move "from Pei to Palace." Unfortunately the Kronprinzenpalais provides only 13,000 square feet (1,200 square meters) of exhibition floor space and no room for administrators' offices. The curators have had to relocate into the *Prussian Raiffeisenbank* building (also known as the *Minol-Haus*).

Between the Crown Prince's Palace and the Spree, you see the scaly, green statue of Freiherr vom Stein, with "thanks from the fatherland," on the site of the former *Kommandantenhaus*, which was lost in action during the Second World War and buried by the DDR. In back of the token statue, which looks like it is set there just to fill in the space, stretching to the Spree is a poplar-planted square that was reborn or at least enlarged by the loss of buildings—Schinkelplatz. Marking its center, an attractive monument to the great man was restored and turned to this spot on August 21, 1996. Behind the statue, in back of the Crown Princesses' Palace, stands the **Friedrichswerdersche Kirche** ("Friedrichswerde Church"), one of the most important buildings by Schinkel. He proposed two possible designs for the building: an "antique" in the form of a Roman temple and (after his trip to England, where he fell in love with the neo-Gothic style) a neo-Gothic variation with a beautiful facade with Gothic windows forming the entrance and simple twin brick towers. This option was chosen by Crown Prince Friedrich Wilhelm and built from 1824 to 1830. It was Berlin's first neo-Gothic building. The church was so admired that it was used as a prototype for the many village churches that sprang up in the vicinity of Berlin as the population of Berlin grew. Later, these villages were incorporated into greater Berlin, so that now you see copies of this church throughout Berlin everywhere.

The church lay in ruins for many years after the War. Following its Communist reconstruction in 1987 for Berlin's 750th anniversary, it was no longer a church. It is now the **Schinkelmuseum,** Tel. 208-13-13 (open Tue.-Sun. 9 A.M. to 5 P.M.; admission DM 4, day ticket DM 8). Displayed inside are neoclassical sculptures of the time of Schinkel, some by Schadow, who designed the Quadriga on the Brandenburg Gate, as well as some by Rauch, a follower of Schadow, who also designed the equestrian statue of Friedrich II on Unter den Linden. It also houses a documentation of Schinkel's life and work as an architect and sculpture. Use U-Bhf Hausvogteiplatz.

On the Werderscher Markt, facing the present Schinkelplatz, is the Federal Republic's **Auswärtige Amt in Berlin** ("Foreign Office"). Construction of this Nazi building, built 1934-38 initially involved such noteworthy architects as Walter Gropius, Ludwig Miës van der Rohe, and Hans Poelzig, but the bid finally went to Heinrich Wolff. This was Hitler's **Reichsbank**. Upon the founding of the DDR, the Communist finance ministry moved in. The Central Committee of the Communist party of the DDR was of course the most powerful body in the DDR. Where did the Central Committee meet? Since 1959, in the Reichsbank, of course, a Fascist building, a melting together of Stalinism and fascism in Berlin. In 1990, when the Palace of the Republic (see below) was discovered to have asbestos, the DDR Volkskammer moved in, as well. The building has 1,000 offices and 2,000 windows, but that is never enough for bureaucrats, so they are covering the seven (!) courtyards with glass roofs and building a second five-story high-rise facing the Friedrichswerde Church. This one will only have three courtyards. Use U-Bhf Hausvogteiplatz.

## SCHLOßPLATZ

The **Berliner Stadtschloß** ("Berlin City Palace"), the palace of the Hohenzollern royal family, used to stand on what is now called Schloßplatz. The palace was Berlin's largest; a middle-age complex of different buildings that had grown over the centuries. Schlüter was commissioned to design a new, baroque facade to give it some unity and create a degree of grandeur. It had been quite the ugliest building in Berlin and even with Schlüter's facade, remained so. The palace was severely damaged at the end of the War, but it still would have been possible, easily, to rebuild it. But no, the DDR

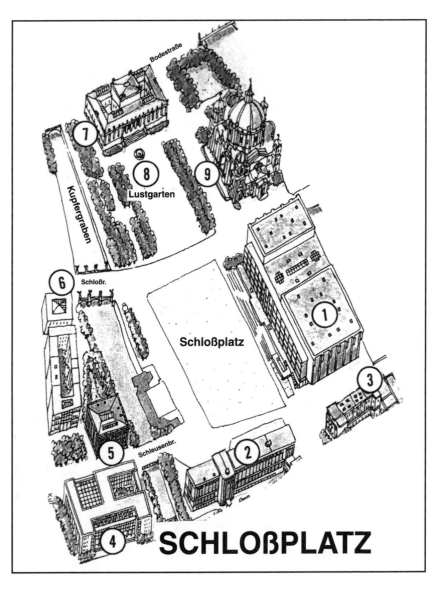

# SCHLOßPLATZ

1. Palast der Republik
2. Former State Council Building
3. Former Coach House
4. New Foreign Office Building
5. Year 2000 Building Academy
6. Schloßbrüke
7. Altes Museum
8. Lustgarten
9. Berlin Cathedral

government decided in 1950 to blow up the ruins by order of the first prime minister of East Germany, Mr. Walter Ulbricht, because of its militaristic significance. He saw it as a symbol of all that was evil in Germany and Prussia, a symbol for Prussian imperialism. Secondly, the government wanted to have, like their great big brother in Moscow, a great "Red Square." They tore up the old palace and used the square for a parade square and the mass rallies on the first of May every year. The political system preferred to build the Palast der Republik, which clashes with the Berlin Cathedral, opposite, and the old museums on Museum Island nearby.

Now Berliners debate whether or not they should rebuild the City Palace, as least the facade, not because they want another kaiser, but because it is part of their history. However, as they have no floor plans or details of the former Berlin City Palace, it would be difficult to recreate the old palace.

From 1973 to 1976, the DDR built a towering embarrassment to Berliners, the **Palast der Republik**, across half of the space of the former Berlin City Palace right in the historical center of what had been Cölln. The monstrosity of white marble and copper-tinted glass was the seat of the **Volkskammer,** the rubber-stamp People's parliament of the Stalinists which met only four times a year (for a week), a bowling alley, a 5,000 seat auditorium, several restaurants, a convention hall, and a discotheque. It was a prime example of how architects can blunder by building a modern structure on a historical site. Further, Communist engineers insulated it with asbestos. When asbestos was found to cause cancer, they had to close it in 1990. Taking the hammer and sickle out of the circular wreath over the side entrance didn't fool anyone. Berliner Schnauze refers to it as the "Ballast of the Republic."

It took seven years to decide to take the asbestos out of the palace. When this began in 1997, various historical interiors and relics were scavenged. The German Historical Museum wants to exhibit a part of the Volkskammer's meeting room. The Cuba gate taken from the original Hohenzollern palace is being preserved. Other interiors are being sent to the Historical Museum in Bonn. Details are being carefully documented so that they can be duplicated after the asbestos is removed. All this is leading to the eventual demolition of the palace. East Berliners want to reconstruct it. They say that the building is a symbol of Berlin's history. If it is gone, history is lost. West Berliners want to tear it down. It is a political issue. A decision about what to do with the skeleton has been postponed until after the 1998 elections.

In the back, the old building that you see next to the Palace of the Republic was the **Marstall** ("Coach house") created at the beginning of the last century for the City Palace. Horse-drawn coaches were stabled there for royal use. Spreeradio 105.5 now occupies the third floor.

The red and white, 1962-64, **Staatsratsgebäude** ("State Council Building") facing the Schloßplatz, near the Schleusen bridge over the Spree, was the former seat of the DDR State Council. Its main distinction is the asymmetrically-placed Portal IV from the former Hohenzollern Berlin City Palace that the DDR blew up in 1950-51. Eosander von Göthe's 1713 balcony was considered symbolic by the DDR because it was where Karl Liebknecht unsuccessfully called to arms workers and soldiers to establish a Free Socialist Republic after the resignation of the kaiser. They ignored the fact that it was also used by the kaiser to announce the start of the First World War. The balcony was extracted carefully from the palace before its destruction and kept in storage until it was incorporated in the new building in 1962. The portal is supposed to have used 30 percent of the original. For ideological reasons, the transferred balcony incorporates the Brandenburg eagle and the golden inscription "1713-1963." The State Council Building was the first new building after the War on the "island" in the Spree at the oldest part of Berlin, on site of the former Cölln (see Fischer Island, below). At 2,600 feet (800 meters) long and 1,200 feet (370 meters) wide, the State Council Building itself is larger than the beginnings of Berlin.

Erich Honecker maintained his office here, although he seldom used it, so it raised eyebrows when Chancellor Kohl announced he had decided to establish in 1997 the **Office of the Federal Chancellor in Berlin** temporarily in the same building. You can see the federal chancellor's office from the outside. It's on the first floor, left of the palace portal, directly adjacent to the diplomatic meeting room. The chancellor has a view of the Scholoßplatz and the Spree until his new offices in the bend of the Spree are completed at the end of 1999. Honecker, on the other hand, located his offices in the back, with a view of the garden, so he wouldn't be endangered by members of the working class while he was in office.

After the Wende, when in a democratically elected government Communists no longer governed East Germany, the building became headquarters for the PDS (Party of Democratic Socialism), the political party that evolved from the Communist party. You can still see the scars from the Communist-party emblem that once stood on the facade of the headquarters. It took three days to remove that 15-foot, multi-ton insignia showing two clasped hands that had once been a pet project of former Communist party chief Erich Honecker.

When the PDS moved out, it was replaced by the **Informations-Zentrum zur Hauptstadtplanung in Berlin** ("Information Center for Capital-City Planning"). On the ground floor you are treated to a free display of Berlin past and future. An enormous scale model of Berlin, with planned buildings indicated in white, shows Berlin in the future. The scale is so large you can almost pick out on the model the spot where you are standing. Everyone will enjoy browsing through the best collection of maps and sketches of Berlin growth through the past. On the second floor is an exhibition showing Berlin construction, living and traffic. Open daily 9 A.M. to 7:30 P.M. Admission free. Use U-Bhf Hausvogteiplatz, bus 147 or 257.

## BERLIN CATHEDRAL

The **Berliner Dom** ("Berlin Cathedral"), Tel. 2-46-91-11, adjacent to the Lustgarten has the distinction of being the only church in Berlin that charges admission, DM 5 (additional for admission to the dome), but on the first Sunday of the month you may pray for free (open daily 9 A.M. to 7:30 P.M.). You may find yourself hard-pressed to call it, "beautiful," but stature and presence it has, even though the exterior restoration, 1975-90, left it with an inconsistent cross assembly atop and cut its height to 320 feet (98 meters) from 374 feet (114 meters).

It seems to get prettier every time you see it, partially because its pretentious style begins to appeal to you more. The Berliner Dom, which cost about 11 million Gold Marks, was built as the state cathedral of the German kaisers by the brothers Julius Carl and Otto Raschdorff from 1894 to 1905 on the site of the smaller 1750 church commissioned by Friedrich the Great and designed by Dutch architect Johann Boumann (remodeled by Carl Friedrich von Schinkel in 1817-22). Known as the *Kaiser-Dom*, it was a pompous, corpulent, neo-Baroque building topped by a bigger and more ornate dome than on "old Fritz's teacup," which it replaced. They wanted at the turn of this century to show the strength of the Protestant faith by building a cathedral with a dome as compelling as St. Peter's in Rome. The neo-Baroque colossus was the largest and the main religious structure of Berlin's late Gründerzeit period. It contains the tombs of the Great Elector and his wife, Dorothea; Friedrich I and his wife, Sophie Charlotte; and Friedrich Wilhelm II.

After the War it was severely damage and its restoration questionable because of the DDR's scorn of religion, but by the 1970s, restoration took new life because the rulers of the DDR didn't want it to embarrass their boastful new buildings across the Linden. Finally in 1974, an agreement was reached with the Evangelical church in the DDR and the Dom's exterior was cleaned up. Even after restoration of the exterior was completed, the cathedral couldn't be consecrated for a second time until June 6, 1993, when West German engineers took over and repaired severe water damage inside that had caused staining and bleaching of the mosaics and allowed many stones to fall away. After the Wende, the extent of water damage had to be scientifically determined by West Germany's Materials and Testing Department. Jigsaw-puzzlelike restoration of the beautiful mosaic-tile artworks, including those measuring 128 square feet (39 square meters) and weighing 2.5 tons such as *Trumpeting Angels* and *Christ on the Throne*, was performed by 70-year-old Elisabeth Jeske in her single-family home in Schulzendorf, not far from Schönefeld Airport. With mosaics hanging on all walls and barrels and boxes filled with glittering gold, red, blue, and lavender stones, her living room looked like heaven-on-earth.

The fourth of formerly eight mosaic "pictures" was restored on August 15, 1998. Anton von Werner's "Blessed are the Peaceful" consists of 400,000 mosaic tiles in 2,000 different shades assembled like a jigsaw puzzle by a Tuscany, Italy, expert group. The central figure of the 430 square foot (40 square meters) mosaic mounted 164 feet (50 meters) above the floor, shows a king with crucifix held high in his left hand. The church is looking for corporate contributions to fund the restoration of the remaining mosaics.

The **Schloßbrücke** ("Palace Bridge") that Schinkel built in 1822-24) crosses over the river Spree now in front of the Berlin Cathedral formerly also in front of the Hohenzollern Palace. It is a work of art with cast-iron railings. When it was rebuilt in 1997, special care was given to preserving the eight white marble statues depicting the life of a Greek warrior that had been stored in the West during the War and traded back to the East in 1983. The original wooden bridge was called the Kavaliersbrücke (Knight's Bridge), because knights of the palace crossed the bridge to go into Berlin. Every time they crossed the toll bridge they had to pay a silver Groschen. Eventually a stone bridge was built, called the Kaiser-Wilhelm-Brücke. In DDR times it was called the Marx-Engels-Brücke because the Communists had blown up the palace.

Northeast of the Palace Bridge, the **Lustgarten** ("Lust" meaning "pleasure") is the name of the square in front of the Old Museum and Museum Island that was remodeled in 1998. Since 1653, when Elector Friedrich Wilhelm framed the Lustgarten into a Dutch garden with trees, marble sculptures, and—below ground—Berlin's first potatoes, the controversial square has experienced many changes. The "Soldier King," Friedrich Wilhelm I, made the Lustgarten into a drill field. At the construction of Schinkel's Old Museum (see below), he replaced the drill field with an elegant formal garden decorated with lawns, rows of poplar trees, and the memorial "Alten Dessauer." Hitler turned it back into a parade ground in 1935. The DDR preferred a casual, sandy expanse before it was returned to a formal setting by West Berlin landscape architects.

On November 9, 1918, the leader of the radical Spartacus League,

Karl Liebknecht, onetime member of the Reichstag turned Communist revolutionary, stood on a balcony of the now-defunct kaiser's palace facing this square from the south, and proclaimed a soviet of workers and soldiers, the Socialist German Republic. A red flag was hoisted overhead. At the same time Friedrich Ebert was announcing the Democratic Republic from the Reichstag. A clash on December 24 between the Democratic Republic's soldiers and a navy marine division returning from the front nearly sparked civil war.

The 47-year-old lawyer Karl Liebknecht, the agitator, and fellow Communist Rosa Luxemburg, the intellectual theorist, were dragged from a flat in Wilmersdorf on January 15, 1919, by officers of a marauding military, brutally murdered, and dumped into the Landwehr Canal at Lichtenstein Bridge near the zoo. Liebknecht and Luxemburg, who had given birth to the German Communist party, became heroes of the former DDR and during that administration many streets and monuments were named after them. West Berlin authorities placed plaques marking their ugly deaths near the Lichtenstein Bridge.

In 1942, the Baum Group from the Scheunenviertel attempted to burn the tents of an anti-Soviet Union exhibit on the Lustgarten between the Old Museum and the Palace of the Republic. Herbert Baum, the Jewish Communist leader of the group, was tortured and killed in custody one month later while his friends were sentenced to death and hanged. On this ground, the DDR erected on the Lustgarten a yellow sandstone memorial to Baum to show its solidarity with the Soviet Union. Baum's grave lies in the Weißensee cemetery (see Chapter 7).

## MUSEUM ISLAND

At the beginning of this century the German nation began building showcase national museums to gather together for display in Berlin the treasures German archaeologists had plundered from Greece, Asia Minor, and Africa. In this sense they are similar to the great museums in London and Paris. Sixteen of East Berlin's 26 museums were eventually located in buildings on a single island between the Spree and Straße Am Kupfergraben known logically as **Museum Insel** ("Museum Island").

The situation of Museum Island is almost like the site in Paris with Ile de la Cité and the Notre Dame—with two canal arms running left and right, forming a real island. Friedrich Wilhelm IV designated it as "a sanctuary of art and learning." Schinkel, the famous Berlin architect, planned to build only museums on this island. Friedrich Wilhelm's scheme was finally completed between 1912 and 1930 with the construction of the splendid

Pergamon Museum. Now the small area is home to five separate, splendid museum structures: Pergamon Museum, Bode Museum, Old Museum, National Gallery, and the New Museum. You don't have to walk far to get from one to another. They are located next to one another. Bus 100 is your best way here. Those museums and many of the most important others scattered throughout Berlin from Dahlem to Charlottenburg to Köpenick are managed by the *Staatlichen Museum zu Berlin* ("State Museums of Berlin"). Cost of admission to these state museums is among the lowest you will find in any city. Take advantage of their deal: admission to their most popular museums costs DM 8, while admission to those with less drawing power costs DM 4, but when you buy a ticket costing DM 8, it acts like a day pass and you can visit as many state museums as you can cram into one day—and not just those on Museum Island.

Because both East and West Berlin had separate, but not usually equal, parallel museum collections in parallel locations, one organization was awarded the heavy but rewarding responsibility of unifying them. This was the Staatlichen Museum and they are hard at work. Because of this some museums are being closed for renovation and to shift their prizes to other locations, and some are being opened with newly unified collections.

The **Pergamonmuseum** (open Tue.-Sun. 10 A.M. to 6 P.M.; Tel. 20-90-5555; one-day ticket DM 8 valid in other museums, as well) is Tourist Central. Most visitors make a beeline here, and rightly so. When you have time or the inclination to visit only one museum in Europe, this is the one. The short tour includes the first three rooms, and with the admission price, you receive earphones and a cassette in English guiding you through. You can spend many hours in the vast additional rooms filled with statues of various Roman and Grecian deities.

The Pergamon Museum, built between 1912 and 1930, contains the greatest treasures removed by German archaeologists. You can consider it an architecture museum because the things inside—the Pergamon Altar, an original Roman city gate, and the Ishtar Gate of Babylon—are huge architectural items. You pass through a sequence of, not rooms, it seems, but actual streets and public squares lifted out of ancient times and places and reassembled here. The Pergamon Museum's coup de theatre, by which you walk through the Roman market gate of Miletus and emerge on the other side among the blue and gold creatures of Babylon's Ishtar Gate, never fails to astonish. The processional avenue, built to provide a suitable passageway for Babylonian kings, is lined with high, turreted walls and adorned with glazed brick murals representing a procession of lions.

The Pergamon Altar is the most celebrated of the exhibits. It is a temple of such noble and harmonious proportions that everyone approaching it tends to fall silent, as if in deference to Zeus, to whom the people of Pergamon sacrificed on these very steps. The frieze of the altar is decorated, if such a prettifying word can be used to refer to something so powerful, with sculpted forms of men, gods, and demons writhing in battle.

Pergamon, in what is now Turkey, was the center of a once-great ancient kingdom, the site of the second-greatest library in the ancient world (after Alexandria), and one of the early centers of Christianity. The altar, nearly 2,200 years old, was erected as a victory monument under Eumenes II from about 180-159 B.C. It was taken apart piece by piece, shipped to Berlin, and reassembled by archaeologists around the turn of the century. It is a full city block in length, so huge it requires a cavernous room to itself.

More than 25 steps lead you from the museum floor up to the platform. The remarkable frieze around the building contains the largest figures that have ever been recovered. It depicts Hesiod's version of wars between Greek gods and giants. It required some 20 years of painstaking labor to piece it back together and reconstruct it inside the main hall of the museum. When the museum opened, it was impossible for a Berliner to climb into an airplane to visit Greece or Turkey. It was the first time in Middle Europe that one could see original, classical architecture on a 1:1 scale. It made this museum famous throughout the world.

In the museum's north wing, you find the original city gate (1:1) of Miletus, an ancient Roman seaport on the Aegean Sea. One of the nearby sculptures, a goddess dating from 575 B.C., had been encased in lead and buried more than 2,000 years. So well preserved is she that you can still see specks of the original pigment on her garment.

In the south wing, the prize monuments from ancient Assyria, Babylon, and Persia include the 2,600-year-old Processional Way of Babylon and, at two-thirds-size, the Ishtar Gate from Babylon (the Brandenburg Gate of Babylon), named after the most widely worshipped goddess of Assyria and Babylon. Also here is the glazed-brick throne room of Nebuchadnezzar.

Exhibits from the **Museum für Islamische Kunst** ("Museum of Islamic Art"), formerly in Dahlem, show tapestries, a Persian prayer niche with script friezes, fragments of a Koran from the ninth century, a 16th-century Turkish ornamental Koran, the dome from the Alhambra in Granada, Persian ceiling painting, and the diverse lines of development of Islamic art from the seventh to 19th century under the major Muslim dynasties from Spain to India.

The neoclassical **Antikensammlung** ("Antiquities Collection"), formerly in Charlottenburg before being returned, presents masterpieces of ancient Greek, Etruscan, and Roman art—in particular the Roman silver collection found at Hildesheim. The **Schatzkammer** ("Treasury") displays a silver collection and gold jewelry from about 2,000 B.C.

The sight of the big dome rising above the Spree immediately signals something special. Jutting into the Spree River on the north point of Museum Island, across from the rebuilt S-Bahn viaduct, is the 1898 **Bodemuseum** (open Tue.-Sun., 10 A.M. to 6 P.M., admission DM 4 or with a DM 8 day card). It is a museum of sculpture. The neo-Baroque museum, formerly the Kaiser-Friedrich, was renamed in 1956, in honor of Wilhelm von Bode, director-general of the royal museums from 1906 to 1920 who was largely responsible for its creation and who became world famous for organizing exhibitions and making it the model of what a good museum should be, with effective lighting and dramatic layout. In the domed staircase there is a bronze copy of Schlüter's equestrian Great Elector that stands in front of Charlottenburg Palace (see Chapter 5). Before the War it contained the greatest paintings of the ages. Most of those stored in the West during the War were first rehung in Dahlem (see Chapter 10) before moving to the new Paintings Gallery in the Cultural Forum in Tiergarten (Chapter 6).

Closed in 1999, it will reopen in year 2000, after extensive redesign, and you will be able to visit in the Bode Museum the **Museum für Spätantike und Byzantinische Kunst** ("Museum for Late Antiquity and Byzantine Art") and the **Skulpturensammlung** ("Sculpture Collection"), formerly in Dahlem (Chapter 10) which presents European sculptures from Early Christian and Byzantine periods extending through the end of the 18th century. Donatello's Italian Renaissance sculpture and Tilman Riemenschneider's *Four Evangelists* are highlights.

**Altes Museum** ("Old Museum"), Tel. 20-90-50 (open Tue.-Sun. 10 A.M. to 6 P.M.; admission adults DM 4, day ticket DM 8) is so named because it was the first one that was built in Berlin, in 1825 and 1830 by Schinkel, his greatest masterpiece, in the style of an antique, neoclassical temple with 16 lovely Ionic columns in the front of the rose facade flanked by splendid sculptures of youths and horses locked in gracefully violent struggle—copies of the Horse Tamers of the Piazza del Quirinale in Rome. The Hellenistic round dome is supposed to resemble the Pantheon in Rome. On top are gilded letters. If you translate the Latin inscription, you read "Friedrich Wilhelm III," who had the museum built to honor the liberal arts.

The Old Museum has always been used as a museum, now partially a museum for modern artists of all the world and Dadaists from Berlin, but also for traveling exhibits such as Rembrandt. Earlier, Honecker had insisted on DDR artists being shown here. Enter from the Lustgarten.

On the first floor you find the **Antikensammlung** ("Antique Collection") which moved here from Charlottenburg Palace on May 4, 1998, and until the end of 1999 you find on the second floor highlights of the paintings that formerly graced the wall of the Old National Gallery. During the War, 400 paintings were destroyed, sold by the Nazis, or lost, so that now the collection is much smaller than before the War. But it is very strongly represented by works from the time of classicism and romanticism, and includes Gothic paintings by Schinkel, German expressionists such as Kirchner, Cezanne, Rodin, de la Pena, many works from the beginning of this century, some modern art, items taken from the Berlin City Palace, and Schadow's famous bust of Goethe, which caused a scandalous argument between the erstwhile friends. Goethe insisted Schadow was too realistic and thought his bust should be more idealistic.

The **Alte Nationalgalerie** ("Old National Gallery") is built like a Greco-Roman temple. It will be closed until year 2001. Earlier, it was the museum for modern art in Germany. Following a design from Stüler, this 1866-76 building was a total ruin after the War, but now it has been restored and its magnificent exterior makes it one of Berlin's most impressive-looking museum/galleries. It is a monumental Grecian templelike building much in keeping with the nationalistic feelings of Germany. On top stand the letters *Der Deutschen Kunst MDCCCLXXI* and it has a patina-covered statue of Friedrich Wilhelm on horseback.

Originally curators had planned to exhibit French, Italian, and other foreign paintings in the Bode and other museums, and to reserve the National Gallery for German artists, but Liebermann, Monet, Malett, and many French impressionists were exhibited here in Berlin before becoming famous. It is a familiar phenomenon: famous abroad, but unknown in one's own country.

**Neues Museum** ("New Museum") was originally built as the Egyptian Museum by Stüler in the middle of the last century, but the whole museum island was bombed during the Second World War on February 3, 1945, and the East Germans didn't have the money to restore the museum. Now, an architectural firm is being selected to supervise the restoration. Its reopening has very tentatively been forecast as 2005, at which time you will be able to view Berlin's Egyptian collection together again.

It is the only remaining ruin on the museum island and the only remaining ruin in Berlin's inner city of great significance. Judging from its destruction, you can appreciate here how badly damaged was Unter den Linden—Berlin—after the War. It was very typical.

## GENDARMENMARKT

Unquestionably one of the most beautiful squares of Europe, the **Gendarmenmarkt** was originally planned as a place where Prussian soldiers

# GENDARMENMARKT

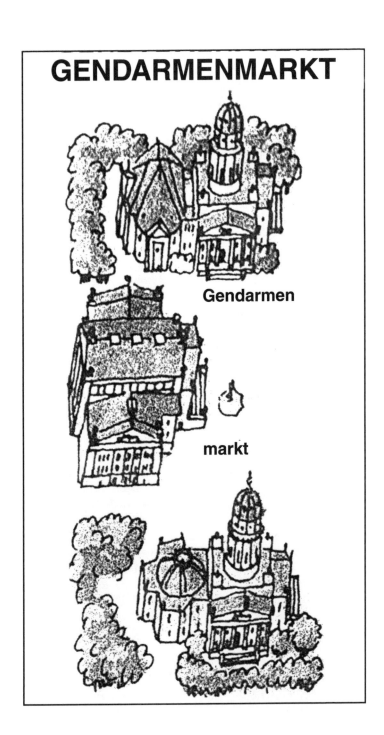

Gendarmen

markt

could rest between long marches. Stalls were installed at this square for the horses of the regiment *Gens d'armes,* hence the name of the square. To avoid military and Prussian associations, the DDR changed its name to **Platz der Akademie** at the time the Academy of Arts located on the left-hand side of the square celebrated its 250th anniversary in 1950.

The Gendarmenmarkt was nothing but ashes and rubble after 1945 when a heavily armed unit of the S.S. dug in here to resist the Russian army.

The square consists of a magnificent theater flanked left and right by lovely twin buildings, the French Church on the north side and the German Church on the south. Friedrich the Great wanted to create an imitation of the Piazza del Popolo in Rome, so he commissioned Karl Ludwig von Gontard to create 230-foot (70 meters) high domes atop each of the churches copying the domes of Santa Maria dei Miracoli and Santa Maria in Montesanto. The domes were completed in 1870-75.

The architectural and cultural centerpoint of the square is the grand **Konzerthaus Berlin** (formerly *Schauspielhaus,* "Playhouse"), Gendarmenmarkt 2, Tel. 203-09-0, Fax 2-04-43-70, separating two churches. From 1774 to 1776 on the north side of the Gendarmenmarkt, a comedy house was built for a French theater group. When the group moved on after two years, the building was used for storage. In 1786, it began a second life as the Royal National Theater until it was torn down in 1802. Parallel to this building, Carl Gotthard Langhans (who also designed the Brandenburg Gate) built a new National Theater that Berliners called the "Suitcase" because of its rounded roof. But when this burned in 1817, Friedrich Wilhelm III assigned Schinkel a follow-up to his successful, great Neue Wache. By 1821 Berlin had its present impressive neoclassical theater with enormous staircase, Ionic columns on the porch, reliefs, and rooftop sculptures.

Many experts consider this Schinkel's masterpiece. The sculptural decorations—Apollo with the chariot of the sun—were designed by Christian Daniel Rauch. It was reopened with Goethe's *Iphigenie.* During the first year the premiere of the opera *Der Freischütz* by Carl Maria von Weber was held here.

After its restoration from the bombing of the War, it was used since 1984 as DDR's concert hall, seating 1,900. After the fall of the Wall, Leonard Bernstein on December 26 performed Beethoven's Ninth Symphony here, but because of the overflow crowd, a huge screen was erected in front so that even those who couldn't get inside could see and listen to the performance.

"On the tenth of June, 1672, the Huguenots celebrated their first church service in their new home. A few years later, every fifth Berliner was a Huguenot," began Pastor Harmut Grüber in the French Church on the Gendarmenmarkt on the occasion of the 325th anniversary of their coming to Berlin. The **Französische Dom** ("French Church"), Gendarmenmarkt 5, Tel./Fax 204-15-06 (open Tue.-Sat. Noon to 5 P.M., Sun. from 11 A.M.; tours through the church, Tue.-Fri. at 3 P.M.; free hourly tours of the carillon, Sun. noon to 3 P.M.; viewing balcony, open daily 9 A.M. to 7 P.M., admission DM 3) was built between 1701 and 1705 by architect Louis Cayrat for the French Reformed Church as a symbol of the hospitality of Prussia for the French Protestant Huguenots. They had been persecuted in France under Louis XIV. Fifteen thousand Huguenots took refuge in Brandenburg, 5,327 in Berlin, when the Great Elector guaranteed freedom of religion in 1685 with his Potsdam Edict of Tolerance. The church is used still by the small French Huguenot community.

In its 230-foot (70 meters) tower, the French Church contains the largest of the three carillons in Berlin. Its 60 bronze bells span five octaves. The smallest bell weighs 44 pounds (20 kilograms) and the largest weighs 5.7 tons. It was built by the East Germans to honor Berlin's 750th anniversary. Carillonneurs play daily except Sat. at noon, 2, 4, and 6 P.M. (Tel. 498-93-690), climbing 160 feet (50 meters) above ground to give their concerts.

Inside the French Church you find a 66-foot (20 meters) high wine restaurant and the **Hugenotten-Museum** ("Huguenot Museum"), Tel. 229-17-60 (open Tue.-Sat. noon to 5 P.M., Sun. from 1 P.M.; entrance DM 3) with a permanent collection covering the Huguenots in France and in Berlin-Brandenburg. The circular staircase with 254 steps leads to the 130-foot high viewing balustrade where you have a good view over the historic city center.

On the south side of the square, the **Deutsche Dom** ("German Church"), Gendarmenmarkt 1, mirrors the French Church. Friedrich the Great commissioned Martin Grünberg to build the 1701-8 church for the Lutheran community. It was remodeled in 1881-82 in neo-Baroque architecture and contains the grave of Georg von Knobelsdorff, the architect of the Sanssouci Palace in Potsdam. After the War it sat for nearly 40 years accumulating rainwater, its destroyed interior serving as a set for the filming of war movies. The "lovely old lady" was finally restored and opened in 1995 as home for the politically correct exhibition, **Fragen an die Deutsche Geschichte** ("Questions Addressed to German History: Ideas, Strengths, and Developments from the 18th Century to the Present"), Tel. 22-73-21-41 (open Tue.-Sun. 10 A.M. to 5 P.M., admission free), although the Dom's exhibition space, 21,500 square feet (2,000 square meters) is only a quarter of the exhibition's former area in the Reichstag building. You can rent a cassette, which is especially useful if you can't read German. The government-sponsored exhibit covers the political breaking up of the old empire and the Vienna Congress, the revolution of 1848-49, the Industrial Revolution, and the formation of the empire, Imperial Germany from 1850 to 1918, the Weimar Republic from 1919 to 1933, the Third Reich from 1933 to 1945, and Germany from the end of the War until the present time. Use U-Bhf Französiche Straße.

Five years after the post-War reopening of the Konzerthaus, the white **Schiller-Denkmal** ("Schiller Memorial") by Reinhold Begas was set in front of the steps. Begas began his work in 1859 to mark the 100th anniversary of Schiller's death, but he toiled so patiently that he didn't complete his work until 1871.

The statue of Johann Christoph Friedrich von Schiller, one of the outstanding writers of German literature (he wrote the "Ode to Joy" featured in Beethoven's Ninth), had stood for 30 years in a park in Charlottenburg because during the Second World War all the art objects, historic books from the library, etc., had been sheltered in various safe places. Those that had been stored in West Berlin at the close of the War were embargoed by the West Berlin authorities. At the beginning of the 1980s, with the relaxation of tensions between East and West Germany, the Berlin Senate decided to return Schiller to the East because they heard that the DDR had an interest in rebuilding the Konzerthaus. Schiller belonged to the Konzerthaus because the statue had always stood in front of the building. So even before the Wende, Schiller was made a present to East Berlin. In return East Berlin gave West Berlin—for a trade—valuable collections from the Royal Porcelain Factory that had remained in East Berlin after the end of the War.

Around Schiller you can identify the four muses representing his main interests: **Euterpe** (poetry), **Melpomene** (drama), **Calliope** (philosophy), and **Clio** (history).

## ALEXANDERPLATZ

Alexanderplatz is the most controversial square in Berlin. During DDR tenure, it had almost no greenery. It was surfaced with nothing but concrete slabs, but because of its size it had a grandeur despite the deteriorating buildings surrounding it. One of its focal points was the wonderful fountain in the middle with plants, flowers, and birds.

During the Second World War Alexanderplatz was almost entirely destroyed. The DDR rebuilt it in 1966 to parallel big brother's Red Square in Moscow. It was designed bigger than life and seen as the center of modern Socialist Germany. Now, for all practical purposes, the Red Alex has vanished. West Berliners never liked the Red version. Western architects detested its

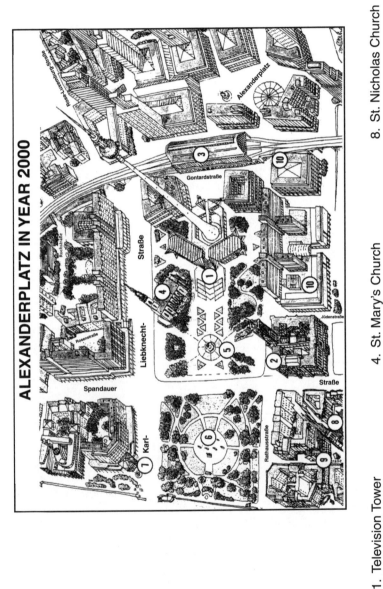

# ALEXANDERPLATZ IN YEAR 2000

1. Television Tower
2. City Hall ("Rotes Rathaus")
3. Alexanderplatz Regional Train Station
4. St. Mary's Church
5. Neptune Fountain
6. Marx-Engels-Forum
7. SAS Radisson Hotel Berlin
8. St. Nicholas Church
9. St. George & Dragon Sculpture
10. Year 2000 Construction

vast expanse of concrete with no greenery to speak of and felt it was militaristic. When they took control of the planning, they determined to break it up. They planted flower beds in giant burlap bags of imported earth laid over Alexanderplatz's tiles. They installed false lawns, potted trees, benches and basketball courts. They planted trees and overlaid portions of the striking square with unkempt tundra in some places, lawns in others, and out-of-place beds of flowers. The reconstruction of Alexanderplatz Regional Train Station and the rebuilding of the rooms at the foot of the television tower occupied vast footage. They lined benches around an ugly Neptune Fountain that the kaiser never liked and no wonder he never liked it. Streetcars began running along a new 1.8-mile (2.9 kilometers) line to Alex on December 18, 1998. You don't find it very interesting to see begonias growing in makeshift earthen mounds or a 1997 monument to bridge-building and tolerance or to sit around an ugly fountain. What was extraordinary, whether you liked it or not, is now ordinary and dull. It added another insult as well. The good impression of the important Red Rathaus (see below) is so lost now that the building seems like a footnote.

Alexanderplatz's focal point was the still-standing 24-hour World Clock. Dividing two distinct areas north and south of the Stadtbahn elevated railroad is the 1994-98 rebuilt Alexanderplatz Regional Train Station. Alexanderplatz was a pedestrian area. DDR ran its last streetcar there on January 2, 1967. The north side featured what was East Berlin's largest shopping center and a towering hotel, which was privatized and sold to Forum Hotel management who modernized it quite effectively. Scattered U-Bahn entrances lead through confusing underground passages like a giant spider. Riding the elevator to the top of the Television Tower is a prerequisite on a good day.

Hardly any other square in Berlin reflects the historic social changes in Berlin as does Alexanderplatz. During the Middle Ages Alexanderplatz was located northeast of Berlin on the trading roads to far destinations. Around 1272, St. George Hospital was formed and this gave the name to the city gate built there. Inside the city wall, the raising and marketing of cattle was forbidden, so a woolen and cattle market was built just outside the gate called *Ochsenplatz* ("Oxen Square"). During early Prussian times, the area was used for military exercise and parade grounds. The Russian Czar Alexander I visited Berlin in 1805 and after him Ochsenplatz was renamed **Alexanderplatz** ("Alexander Square").

The elevated **Stadtbahn** ("City Railroad") was built in 1882 and "Alex" (as Berliners call it) became a traffic hub with horse-drawn carriages and electric streetcars in 1896. The U-Bahn was built in 1913.

Karl-Marx-Allee was called Stalin Allee until 1961. It was here where the

East Berliners celebrated the birthday of the republic and held military parades past the tribunes of the East German government. On June 17, 1953, the building workers revolted here against the DDR government, which was defeated.

The elevated train station divides present-day Alexanderplatz in two. On the north you find in the center the **Brunnen der Völkerfreundshaft** ("Fountain of People's Friendship"), the 37-story **Forum Hotel** built by the DDR in 1970, with an entrance right on Alexanderplatz, and the **Weltzeituhr** ("World Time Clock"). When you make a date to meet on the "Alex," make it at the World Clock. The 32-foot (10-meter) high steel wheel covered with textured aluminum and enamel doesn't only tell the exact time in Berlin; the numbers you see show the local times in various famous world cities on all continents. After 30 years of non-stop ticking, the clock was repaired in 1997. At that time the names of Berlin's new sister cities were inserted on the ring and the names of cities whose names had changed were corrected. Look for artist Heinrich Zille, cast in bronze, sketch pad and pencil in hand.

Since 1998, the former 14-floor Intourist Hotel Berolina at Karl-Marx-Allee 31 is the **Rathaus von Mitte** ("District Hall for Mitte"). Where once tourists overnighted, 800 bureaucrats shuffle papers. On the east you can't miss the gaudy 12-story **Haus des Lehrers** ("Teacher's Building") on the site of the former Teachers Association's Building which stood from 1908 to 1945. The new building was the first erected on Alex, in 1964. The 22-foot (7 meters) high faded frieze, **Unser Leben** ("Our Life"), reflects the life that never materialized for happy Communist workers. It is made from glass, enamel, ceramic, and metallic elements.

The domed building is the **Kongreßhalle** ("Convention Hall"), with 1,000 seats and a design to complement the Teacher's Building. During its operation German and Eastern European conventions took place all year long. The puppet **Volkskammer** of the DDR met here until they moved to the disastrous Palace of the Republic.

While you are on Alex, cast your eye on the **Kaufhof am Alex**, the giant department store on the north with the white facade that Berlin Schnauze refers to as *Eierschalen* ("Egg Shells"). Opened on July 1, 1970, the store was part of the decoration and attraction of Alexanderplatz. Throughout the world, department store architecture adds or detracts from the ambience of the surrounding area. Remodeled in 1997-98 by the new owner, the Kaufhof company based in Cologne, the former *Kaufhalle* has 250,000 square feet (23,000 square meters) of floor space, including 21,500 square feet (2,000 square meters) for foodstuffs.

The south side of Alexanderplatz is bounded on the east by

Rathausstraße, which has been an important street since the Middle Ages. Originally named Oderbergerstraße, then Georgenstraße, and in 1701, Königstraße, it received its present name in 1951. Rathausstraße is a recreation and shopping venue for East Berliners with a cleverly designed terrace over the storefronts, but now it is so run-down that it is not very interesting to visitors.

**Bahnhof Alexanderplatz** was built in 1880-82 out of glazed yellow-brown brick as a station for the new Stadtbahn ("City Railroad"), but you are hard put to see the early structure because of its 1994-98 reconstruction. After nearly four years of reconstruction from the ground up, politicians finally got their opportunity to make their speeches at the reopening of Berlin's historic Alexanderplatz train station on March 12, 1998.

Berlin Mayor Eberhard Diepgen said, "Alexanderplatz is the pulsating heart of Berlin. The new station is a symbol of the growing together of the city." The reconstruction was such a success that the station is easy and comfortable to use. Automatic doors fly open so wide that they must know you are towing a fully-packed suitcase. The arch-covered through station is used by both S-Bahn and regional trains on elevated tracks. From this level you have interesting views through the windows on the south side on the close-by Television Tower and the activities on Alexanderplatz.

Underground, far removed from the elevated Alexanderplatz train station, U-Bhf Alexanderplatz is a junction of three U-Bahn lines. It is a complete, sprawling complex below Alex S-Bahn station.

A tower such as the West Berlin's prized Funkturm (see Chapter 5) was absent in East Berlin after its creation, so the DDR authorities built the **Fernsehturm** ("Television Tower") from 1965 to 1969 on Alexanderplatz as a symbol of the power of socialism. Looking like a faceted onion atop a skewer four football fields high, it is easily the tallest edifice in Germany. Its height measured 1,197 feet (365 meters, one for every day of the year) until the obsolete red-and-white antenna was replaced in 1997 with a 52.5-foot (16 meters) steel cylinder and 72.2-foot (22 meters) glass umbrella. This made the tower 1,207 feet (368 meters) high, 10 feet (3 meters) higher than before. Now it is 224 feet (68 meters) taller than the Eiffel Tower, but still the second tallest tower in Europe (after the one in Moscow). It was unthinkable that the DDR dared build one taller than Moscow's.

Built with Swedish assistance, the tower has a huge sphere covered in brown-tinted glass halfway up its long, tapering stem. After construction was complete, it was discovered that the sun setting in the west reflected from the complex globe to form a religious cross that was especially obvious from West Berlin. Berlin Schnauze called it "The Pope's Revenge" and "St. Walter's," after the DDR president, Walter Ulbricht, the man who had banned crosses from the roofs of East Berlin's churches. The globe consists of 140 segments and stretches seven floors between 656 and 760 feet (200 and 232 meters) above ground.

At 666 feet (203 meters), the **observation platform** (open 9 A.M. to 1 A.M., Mar.-Oct.; 10 A.M. to midnight, Nov.-Feb., admission DM 8, children to 16, DM 4), gives you a panoramic view of the city extending for 25 miles (40 kilometers) on clear days. One floor above the observation platform you find the **Tele-Café** seating 200 customers (open same hours as platform, Tel. 242-33-33). The café rotates once an hour around the axis of the tower.

In an emergency you might have to use the 986 steps spiraling down the tower shaft, but normally you will ride one of the two high-speed (20 feet—6 meters—a second) elevators to reach the top in 35 seconds. The "Telespargel" (*Spargel* meaning "asparagus," another Schnauze name for the tower) is the only one in the world located in the center of a major city. The two-story pavilion at the base was completed in 1972 with a café for dancing, restaurant, and self-service cafeteria.

Not exactly hidden in the shadows of the Television Tower, Berlin's small brick **St.-Marienkirche** ("St. Mary's Church"), Karl-Liebknecht-Straße 8, Tel. 2-42-44-67 (open Mon.-Thur. 10 A.M. to 5 P.M., Sat.-Sun. from noon), a part of historic Berlin, seems out of place among the post-War buildings on Alexanderplatz. It makes a splendid counterpoint to the tele-asparagus and a splendid picture when the two are photographed side by side from Karl-Liebknecht-Straße.

The cornerstone for St. Mary's, only the second church built in Berlin (after the Nikolai Church), was laid about 1270, and the church was consecrated in 1292. A tower was first added in 1418, but the church and the tower have been hit by fire after fire and each time they have been rebuilt and enlarged according to the style of the era. After a 1661 lightning strike, the parish register records that the fire was extinguished by worshippers carrying milk and water. In the tower hall a 1484 fresco, 72 feet long and 7 feet high (22 by 2 meters), portrays the "Danse Macabre," one of the oldest and most important murals in Germany. During the years it was painted over, but rediscovered in 1860.

Inside you see the baroque altar by Andreas Krüger and the four paintings by Bernhard Rode in 1762. The bronze baptismal font from 1437 is the oldest work of art in the church. When Johann Sebastian Bach visited Friedrich II in 1747, he loved to play the organ inside because of its excellent acoustics. St. Mary's tower was rebuilt for the last time in 1792 by Carl Gotthard Langhans, who also created the Brandenburg Gate. It is typically northern German, mixing neoclassical and Gothic influences, 300 feet (91 meters) high.

A few steps down the small Rosenstraße, which runs smack into St. Mary's Church, across the street from the preserved office buildings at Rosenstraße 16 and 17, you come to a notable red-sandstone **Sculpture Garden** marking the success of non-Jewish German women securing the release of their Jewish husbands. The final roundup of Jews remaining in Berlin began on February 27, 1943. Trains of cattle cars pulled out of Grunewald Station, heading east for the gas chambers and ovens of the extermination camps. Of the Jews that had remained in Berlin up until then, 4,700 Jewish men were partners in mixed marriages and had been segregated. On the Sunday morning of the roundup, their non-Jewish wives crowded around the building that held them, shouting and screaming for their men, hour after hour, refusing to leave, throughout the night and into the next day. By noon Monday, S.S. leaders decided not to machine-gun nearly 5,000 German women. All men married to non-Jewish wives were "privileged persons." These 4,700 together with some 1,400 underground Jews were the only ones to outlive the Nazi terror.

Below the Television Tower is the **Neptunbrunnen** ("Neptune Fountain"), one of the oldest fountains in Germany's capital. It was designed by Reinhold Begas in the fashion of a baroque fountain in Rome. On January 1, 1891, the fountain was placed in front of the Berlin City Palace, a gift from the city to Kaiser Wilhelm II, who never liked it, and no wonder: the figure on top is Neptune, Roman god of the sea, surrounded by sea creatures such as crabs and lobsters, while draped on the rim are four naked bronze ladies representing the four most important German rivers: Rhine (grapes and fishing net), Elbe (fruit and corn), Oder (goats and hides), and Weichsel (firewood).When DDR demolished the palace, the fountain was banished to Museum Island where it stood until 1969 when it was resurrected to complete Alexanderplatz. It is 33 feet (10 meters) high with a diameter of nearly 60 feet (18 meters). The remaining area in front of city hall is filled with rose beds, two kinds of benches (cement and wooden), and small forests of trees. Western landscape architects are doing their best to disguise the broad square that the Communists laid out and make it as routine as possible. They have made it into one of Berlin's least attractive.

The neo-renaissance-style **Rote Rathaus** ("Red City Hall"), Rathausstraße, Tel. 24-01-0 (open Mon.-Fri. 7 A.M. to 6 P.M.), on the southeast corner of Alexanderplatz is one of Berlin's most symbolic buildings. It has always been the seat of the governing Berlin mayor; the name has nothing to do with politics. The first meeting of the Berlin city council was convened here January 6, 1870. In 1933, Hitler dissolved the democratic proceedings.

When the Russian army arrived, they flew the Soviet flag from the tower on April 27, 1945, and installed their Communist government on May 19 in the partially destroyed building. After the Wende, on June 12, 1990, the West Berlin Senate and the East Berlin Council met together for the first time. The building was renovated, and in 1991, Eberhard Diepgen, the mayor of unified Berlin, and the deputy mayor, Christine Bergmann, together with the Berlin Senate's staff of 260 moved from Schöneberg Town Hall, took over 177 waiting office spaces, and hoisted the Berlin bear city flag that you see today. In 1999, the building will revert to the federal government when it arrives in Berlin in full strength because it was a DDR-government building during those bleak years.

It is supposed that, in 1290, Berlin's city hall was located on the present-day site of the Red Rathaus but there is little to support this. However historians insist there was in 1270 a city hall on Spandauer Straße. Although Schinkel, in 1814, called the city hall of the time "unsuitable," the city fathers declined to install his proposed facade. Then as Berlin grew with the incorporation of several suburbs and became the capital of the German Reich, City Architect Hermann Friedrich Waesemann (1813-79), who had made a name for himself with Stühler's New Museum, laid the cornerstone on June 11, 1861. He modeled his 245-foot (74 meters) tower after the Romanesque lantern-tower of the Cathedral of Notre-Dame in Laon, France. It soon became the logo for Berlin. A technological milestone was the electrification from within of the Red Rathaus's clock in 1866.

Waesemann constructed the mock Italian Renaissance building in terracotta and bright red brick using 920 different kinds of red stones which were copied during the post-War reconstruction. Red brick is the typical northern German building material for want of natural sandstone which limits its decorative ability. Take a special look at the 700-foot (216 meters) terracotta **Chronik Berlins** ("Berlin Chronicle") frieze from 1876-79 consisting of 36 tablets running around the building that shows events in the history of Berlin from the founding of the city to the formation of the German Reich. The DDR removed gilded bronze statues of King Friedrich I and Kaiser Wilhelm I, instead installing oversized sculptures over the entrance showing a famous **Trümmerfrau** ("Rubble Woman") and a "Reconstruction Worker" who worked endless hours without pay to remove 175 million cubic feet (5 million cubic meters) of war rubble. A statue of the revered Trümmerfrau stands by **Rixdorfer Höhe** ("Rixdorf Heights"), a 230-foot (70 meters) high mountain of rubble in Neukölln's Hagenheide Park.

Behind the Red Rathaus is the Molkenmarkt. As Berlin's original settlements began to grow, Berliners started a market for milk and dairy products. For a time, Berlin's police headquarters stood here. Now that is gone and the square is still known as the Molkenmarkt although after the War it became nothing more than a busy traffic intersection.

Across the Molkenmarkt you can't miss the imposing, but sad-looking **Altes Stadthaus** ("Old State House") designed by city architect Hoffmann in 1902-11 with a gray tower reminiscent of the towers of the twin churches on the Gendarmenmarkt. The building was restored in 1960-61 to become the seat of the Council of Ministers during DDR years, but again very gray, because it was linked to the Secret Police (Stasi).

Your access here is via **U-Bhf Klosterstraße** behind the city hall. The U-Bhf is decorated with a long series of delightful drawings of classic trains and trams on the walls. The capitals of the steel columns are Ionic to give a classical impression. At one end there is a model of a relatively new U-Bahn train coming out of a wall. This is meant to symbolize the impossibility of traveling by U-Bahn between the divided East and West sections of Berlin during the Cold War. All these stations on line U2 (i.e., Klosterstraße, Alexanderplatz, and Wittenburgplatz in the West) were designed by the same architect and opened at the same time, 1912-13.

The ruins of the former **Franziskaner Kloster** ("Monastery"), Kloster-/Grunerstraße, date from 1250 when Franciscan monks arrived to Christianize the heathens. The monastery was dissolved during the Reformation when Berlin became predominantly Lutheran. It was rebuilt and enlarged in 1813 by Schinkel in Gothic architecture, but was destroyed again during the Second World War. The ruins have been reinforced and made safe for use as a sculpture garden and memorial against violence and war. You can still admire the Gothic architecture. Use U-Bhf Klosterstraße.

Down the street you find the **Parochialkirche** ("Parish Church"), Klosterstraße 67, Tel. 2-47-59-50 (open April-Sept. 10 A.M. to 7 P.M., Oct.-Mar. to 4 P.M.). This baroque building, designed by Arnold Nering and built 1695-1703, the same time as the Zeughaus, was the first church built after the Reformation. It was severely damaged during the War. The tower survived the bombing, but its 1715 Dutch carillon rang for the last time in 1944.

Behind the church, on Waisenstraße behind a cyclone fence, you see a segment from Berlin's medieval **Stadtmauer** ("City Wall"). Experts judge that it was built between 1260 and 1280 and rebuilt in the 14th century as part of the wall surrounding the original settlements of Berlin and Cölln.

On the next corner, across from the Parish Church's cemetery, you arrive at the 1701-4, former **Palais Podewils**, Klosterstraße 68/70, Tel. 247-49-777 or 247-49-6, which is now used for open-air movies and musical performances. It was occupied by State Minister Heinrich von Podewil in 1732 and later became owned by the state. The Märkische Museum was founded here in

1875-80. The palace was reconstructed in 1952-54 and used for a Berlin youth club. Following a fire in 1967, it was again restored.

From here you might wonder about the building with A-frame windows and points like a maple leaf on the south side of Mühlendamm. It used to be called the "Maple Leaf Restaurant" and boasted Canadian flags, but became one of the largest discotheques of Europe in October 1991. Sadly, it had to be closed because authorities determined that plaster falling from the ceiling was caused by the vibrations set up by the disco music. It is empty, awaiting direction.

## MARX ENGELS FORUM

Across from the Nikolaiviertel and overlooked by the cathedral is the 690 feet by 690 feet (210 by 210 meters) **Marx-Engels-Forum**, a grassy square with quieting trees that hide it from the high-rise surroundings, muffle the sounds of the traffic on the highways, and provide a nesting place for songbirds, which makes it a relaxing counterpoint to the paved-over Alexanderplatz adjacent.

The bronzes for Marx and Engels standing in the center were designed by Ludwig Engelhardt in 1986. Although they were cast double life-size, someone has added realistic graffiti under the figures: *Wir sind schuldig,* which means, "We are to blame." As you would expect, these figures are controversial, but the government decided not to replace the DDR bronzes because they do not show the two subjects in a "victorious pose."

Walking along the Spree you come across a very beautiful dark red house. It looks like a house from a Thomas Mann story, but it is the famous Kurfürstenhaus, where the Great Kurfürst (Elector), the founder of the Prussian state, lived. It is preserved on the east side of the Spree, facing the river so that you must see it from the river.

The Kurfürstenbrücke was the most beautiful bridge of Berlin, leading from the Berlin Palace. It duplicated the one at the Charlottenburg Palace. It is gone, but perhaps it will be rebuilt; the cast is located in the Bode Museum.

The oldest crossing from Berlin to Cölln—the only one for 300 years—is the Mühlendamm Bridge. It was not only a bridge, but houses were connected to it for trading and sale of fish.

## NIKOLAI QUARTER

**Rathaus Café**, right across from the Red Rathaus, marks the beginning of the one-acre (4,000 square meters) **Nikolaiviertel** ("Nikolai Quarter"),

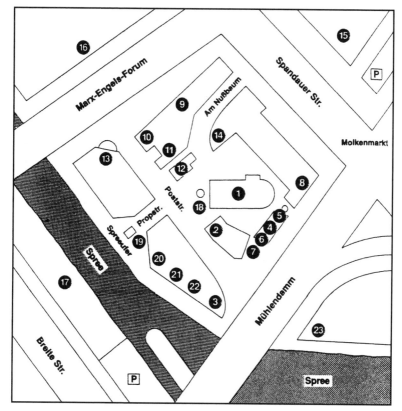

# NIKOLAI QUARTER

1. Nikolai Church
2. Knoblauchhaus
3. Epraim Palais
4. Berlin Handwerker Museum
5. Zum Paddenwirt
6. Zur Rippe
7. Kaffeestube
8. Musikhaus
9. Grand Hand
10. Weißbierstube
11. Judge's Passage
12. Zum Nußbaum
13. Am Marstall
14. Nikolai Café
15. City Hall
16. Marx-Engels-Forum
17. City Library
18. Tradesmen's Fountain
19. St. George Monument
20. Spree Buffet
21. Café Spreeblick
22. Fondue
23. Palais Schwerin

East Berlin's showcase quarter between Marx-Engels-Forum and Mühlen-damm. It has the ambience of a village, but is so out of character with the rest of Berlin that it seems artificial—it is, of course, because the houses are all new, or moved from somewhere else, because it was one of the areas restored by East German authorities as a tourist path for Berlin's 1987 anniversary. To save money, many of the houses had to be restored with prefabricated slabs that resemble the corrugated webbing inside a cardboard box torn apart. After 10 years, the DDR's concrete facades became stained and cracked and looked less attractive to visitors, so rejuvenation set in. The concrete blocks are being replaced with a friendlier look. The first project is the corner building at Post- and Rathaustraße.

The Nikolaiviertel supposedly looks like Berlin in the 17th century. You find outdoor cafés which are pleasant places to eat. Shields hang above the doors like those you see in the villages of southern Germany. The streets are cobblestone. The quarter has the oldest church. The **Bear Fountain** is the geographical center of Berlin. There is an ancient pump with water that can be drunk. Nearby is the Ephraim-Palais, the prettiest corner of Berlin, and the pink Knoblauch House which was regarded as the most beautiful residential house in Berlin.

The Nikolai Quarter's most famous café is the **Restaurant zum Nußbaum** ("Nut Tree Restaurant"). Reconstructed in 1986-87, the present café stands on the corner of Propstraße and Am Nußbaum. Below the shield outside—of a gilded beer mug—it has a few stand-up tables for beer drinkers. A placard on the wall beside the street remarks:

> Zum Nußbaum, destroyed in the Fascist World War, 1943, oldest restaurant of Berlin. Built in 1571 in Cölln, Fischerstraße 21. Visitors to the restaurant include Heinrich Zille, Otto Nagel, and others.

Walk toward the twin towers of the **Nikolaikirche** ("Nikolai Church"), Tel. 23-80-90-82 (open 10 a.m. to 5:30 p.m., admission DM 3), leading you to the heart of the Nikolai Quarter. The church is Berlin's oldest structure. It was begun in 1230 and completed in its present form in the 19th century with two towers, from the 13th and 14th centuries. They, too, were rebuilt in 1987 for Berlin's anniversary.

The church is now a museum because of the Communist animosity toward churches. It houses the permanent exhibit, "The Middle Ages Trading Town Berlin-Cölln: The Dual City from Its Beginnings until 1648." Berlin's third carillon (21 bells) is located here. Chimes play daily at noon, 3, and 6 P.M. and Saturdays at 11 A.M. It wasn't until 1997 that a new organ was installed to replace the one destroyed by the door to door fighting at the end of the Second World War. After more than 50 years, the church is blessed with the voice of the "Queen of Instruments." For the new instrument, more than DM one million went to the firm in Dresden that also built the organ in the Konzerthaus on the Gendarmenmarkt. The new organ is 30 feet (9 meters) tall and 23 feet (7 meters) wide. Its 3,227 pipes range in length from 16.4 feet (5 meters) to 3.8 inches (15 millimeters).

St. Nicholas was the traders' saint, saint of vendors, and saint of thieves, and on the nearby bridge across the Spree was the **Handelsmarkt** ("Trade Market").

When you follow Spreeufer to the beginning of Propstraße, you can't miss the green bronze St. George and the Dragon sculpture cast in 1853 by August Kiss, a student of Rauch (Schinkel Museum). It formerly stood in the courtyard of the Berlin City Palace before it was destroyed.

Baroque **Ephraim-Palais**, Poststraße 16, Tel. 24-00-20 (open Tue.-Sun. 10 A.M. to 6 P.M.) makes the corner of Mühlendamm and Poststraße the most beautiful in Berlin. Restored for Berlin's birthday in 1987, the balconies glitter in the midday sun. The museum features Berlin art since Friedrich the Great.

Designed by Friedrich Wilhelm Diterichs in 1761-66, the palace was a gift from Friedrich the Great to Nathan Veitel Heine Ephraim, the banker, manufacturer, and court jeweler who financed Friedrich's wars. With Tuscan columns at the main entrance and gilded balcony gratings, it is one of the most noteworthy architectural beauties of Berlin.

For Berlin's 750th anniversary, the building, which belongs to the Märkisches Museum, was taken stone by stone from its former location and rebuilt on its present site. Since 1987 it has been used for exhibitions. The standing exhibit is titled, "Berlin Portraits from Baroque to Biedermeier."

After the War, the finely detailed, gilded balcony gratings, the highlight of the building, were stored in the West (where authorities seriously considered reconstructing the whole building there) before finally being returned.

Across the street from the Ephraim-Palais you find the **Palais Schwerin** on the Molkenmarkt. This 1704 building was erected for Minister Otto von Schwerin. In 1937, in connection with the newer *Mint*, it was torn down and moved behind the old flood line, but the historic facade was replicated at its new site. It is interesting to look at the copy of the frieze that was created by Gottfried Schadow for the mint on the Werdeschen Markt in 1800. It tells the story of minting. During the DDR years the building was used for the Culture Ministry.

The **Knoblauchhaus**, Poststraße 23, Tel. 21-71-33-92, is one of the few houses in the quarter that survived the War. Johann Christian Knoblauch constructed it in 1759. In 1792, his son founded here the Karl Knoblauch Silk Factory and it became the commercial center of old Berlin. The remodeling of 1835 gave it its present early-neoclassical form. The second floor houses the exhibit titled "The Knoblauch Family—a Contribution to the History of Berlin in the 19th Century." On the ground floor is a historical wine Stube. It was restored for Berlin's 750th anniversary in 1987.

**Handwerkermuseum**, Mühlendamm 5, Tel. 21-71-33-25, south of St. Nikolas Church, displays the development of handwork from the 14th century until today. It is a branch of the Märkisches Museum.

## FISCHER ISLAND

The one-mile (1.5 kilometers) long "island" between the Spree and the Spree Canal is known as **Fischerinsel**. You've seen the northern part containing Museum Island, the Lustgarten and Schloßplatz, but at the southern end, across the Mühlendamm Bridge from the Nikolai Quarter, which was old Berlin, you reach the part of Fischer Island where Berlin's ancient twin city, Cölln, was settled in the 13th century. Cölln was so named because the first mayor came from Cologne (Köln) on the Rhine River. Berlin and Cölln did not like each other; they were rivals. In the early 14th century they were unified. Mayors of the time were called Schultheiss.

The **Mühlendamm-Schleuse** ("Mühlendamm Locks") in the Spree date from the Middle Ages when they were necessary to control the water level so that the Spree could be used for traffic. In the Middle Ages everything was made of wood, and the locks were hoisted by hand. Melting snow flooded the river, so that the Spree could not be navigated during the summer. Fishing and river traffic via the Great Elector's canal from the Oder and the Elbe from Poland to Hamburg flowed through these locks to the North Sea, so they were very important. Even now steamers along the Spree have to wait here to be raised or lowered 6.5 feet (two meters).

Here a Dutch settlement followed shipbuilding and shipping. The Jungfernbrücke, a drawbridge with chains, was built over the Spree Canal in 1798 of green iron. Formerly named Klockbrücke, it is the oldest remaining Berlin bridge, built in Dutch style, with a former Dutch name.

Bridges originally belonged to the king, but in 1850 the city began to buy and modernize them piece by piece. There were four toll bridges including Jannowitzbrücke, Herkulesbrücke, and Kavaliersbrücke, for which one had to pay a silver Groschen to cross.

In the 18th century, Breite Straße leading to Schloßplatz was the broadest street in Berlin. The maximum height of the rain gutters on the roofs was fixed so that they could not exceed that of the palace nearby. After 1870, when the German Reich was established, city planners allowed that they could be somewhat higher with the permission of the city architect.

As a tribute to Theodor Fontane, a visit to Berlin's only landmarked

Renaissance building is a must. The **Ribbeck House** on Breite Straße 31-34 has a restaurant and a Center for Berlin Studies for scholars. At Brüderstraße, a north-south street, you see a building that fits into the Berlin history. It is a narrow neoclassical house, **Nicolai-Haus,** which has nothing to do with the name of the quarter across the river. Friedrich Nicolai was a friend of Gotthold Ephraim Lessing, the first publisher of Berlin. He was a friend of Johann Wolfgang Goethe, who of course appreciated the printing of his books. Nicolai, the publisher, Lessing, and Moses Mendelssohn, the philosopher (see Scheunenviertel, below), formed a small group, the **Aufklarer,** after the French Revolution.

This is now the Neu Cölln quarter, only 10 minutes from the palace. It was a good neighborhood, on the edge of the city at the time. The city ended at Grünstraße, close by on the left bank of the Spree. Neu Cölln (the name Cölln has disappeared), Friedrichswerde, and Berlin now make up the historic district called Mitte. The architecture of the neighborhood here was a subdivision of German classicism, called Biedermeier (1850-70). Biedermeier was a definitive, friendly style. The interiors had beautiful furniture—mahogany was treasured. Daughters gave spinet or piano recitals; Heinrich Heine was sung; Goethe was read aloud.

## POSTAL MUSEUM (EAST)

The **Museum für Post und Kommunikation Berlin** ("Postal and Communications Museum"), formerly in the shadow of the Wall on the corner of Mauerstraße and Leipzigerstraße was originally the main post office for Berlin Mitte. It opened in 1872, making it the oldest postal museum in the world. The handsome corner building was damaged during the Second World War, but officially landmarked in 1977. The *Gigantengroup* ("Group of Giants") that you see on the museum, with three giants' arms wrapped around the earth ball to symbolize the global reach of the post office, was removed and then misplaced by the DDR because of the giants' association with Prussian militarism. In a change of party line, it was decided to replace the figures for the 750th anniversary of Berlin in 1987, but it never happened. A newly chiseled copy was placed on the building in 1997. The museum is scheduled for reopening in 1999. Until then, you can see exhibitions of its collections at the West Postal Museum on An der Urania (Chapter 3). Use U-Bhf Stadtmitte or U-Bhf Mohrenstraße.

## POTSDAMER PLATZ

The alien red box on stilts that you see on Potsdamer Platz may look like an earth-lander from outer space, but there are no extraterrestrials here,

# POTSDAMER PLATZ IN YEAR 2000

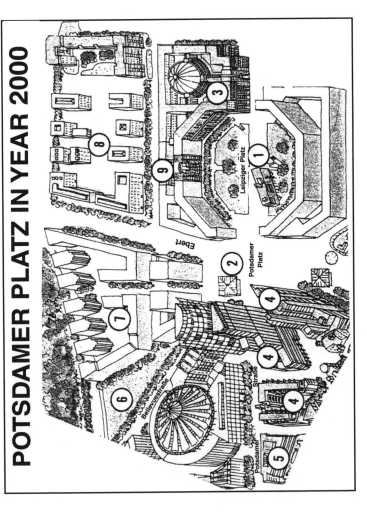

1. Info-Box
2. Gate House
3. New Shopping Arcade
4. New Office Building
5. New Hotel Building
6. New Parklands
7. Hertie Buildings
8. New State Buildings
9. New Mosse-Palais

just construction workers with yellow hard hats. Inside you can see the Berlin of tomorrow today. The **Info-Box**, Leipziger Platz 21, Tel. 22-66-24-0, Fax 22-66-24-20, *http://www.infobox.de*, the first building on post-War Leipziger Platz, was opened on October 16, 1995, to provide visitors with a tangible picture of Berlin in year 2000. The exhibition, which you can reach by Info-Box elevator, will remain standing until December 31, 2000 (open daily, 9 A.M. to 7 P.M., Thur. to 9 P.M., admission free). The real draw of the Info-Box; however, is the top-level observation platform which requires you to climb three flights of stairs and insert a DM 2 coin in the entrance turnstile. If the weather is hard or you are not up to scaling flights of stairs, you can view the construction site from Sorat hotel group's indoor second-floor cafeteria which requires no entrance fee. The panorama from the roof, however, is far superior.

"I recommend Potsdamer Platz because Potsdamer Platz has life. And life is the best thing that a large city offers," according to one of author Theodor Fontane's characters. (Fontane lived his last years on Potsdamer Straße.) Potsdamer Platz was laid out in the 18th century. In 1831, it received its name from Schinkel because it lay at the Potsdamer Gate. The traffic that once roared, raced, and rampaged through Potsdamer Platz is legendary. Potsdamer Platz was one jammed, gigantic traffic junction. In 1895, 244 horse-drawn wagons were counted trotting across the intersection. By 1904, 34 streetcar lines and six horse-bus lines served the square. Before the War 600 trams crossed every hour.

Near the red Info-Box you can see the old symbol of Potsdamer Platz—the traffic tower. Erected in 1924 in an attempt to control traffic on Potsdamer Platz, it was reconstructed in 1998 and reinstalled on the new Potsdamer Platz. The original hand-operated traffic tower was the first German traffic signal. It led to German prominence in the development of traffic signaling. The new tower is a copy of the 1924 original, which in turn was copied from New York. Like the original, the new one has a clock on each of four sides, a police call box, and a red-yellow-green signal. The gray-black tower consists of zinc-coated steel, weighs 5 1/2 tons, measures 8 1/4 feet (2 1/2 meters) across, and stands 28 feet (8 1/2 meters) high on five slender columns. This one isn't used to direct traffic.

Potsdamer Platz was once the center of Berlin's pre-War life. The biggest coffeehouses and largest department stores were here. Erich Mendelsohn's revolutionary 1931-32 *Columbushaus*, a totally functional design with glass walls around a steel frame, rose 10 stories. Its streamlined horizontal lines created a new standard for the whole world. Its first major tenant, suitably international, was the F. W. Woolworth company. Potsdamer Platz glowed with Europe's first electric streetlights. The War changed everything. Allied bombing aimed at Gestapo headquarters and Hitler's Chancellery, nearby, leveled Potsdamer Platz and created a wasteland. When the Wall sprang across the borders, Potsdamer Platz was left for dead. Berliners said that if you stood in the Potsdamer Platz you could hear the water lapping on the Volga.

Now after the Wende, Potsdamer Platz is again centrally located. It has grown into the major hub of new Berlin. Cartographers had to add 10 new street names to their maps of the city. There was a roar of protest when the properties on the square were sold. Berliners said they were "donated" to Daimler-Benz. For this reason, Berliner Schnauze calls it "PotsDaimler Platz." Daimler got the section of the square from Potsdamer Straße to Eichhornstraße. Sony Europa, Hertie (the department store chain), and Asea-Brown-Bovari (the heavy electrical equipment manufacturer) divided the remaining frontage.

The new Daimler-Benz project attracts every day 50,000 to 100,000 people with its 110 stores, more than 30 restaurants, bars and cafés, a musical theater, a casino, the multiplex **CinemaxX** with 3500 seats, an Imax theater, apartments, offices, and the Grand Hyatt hotel.

A team of international architects using Renzo Piano's master plan created the 17 new buildings and 10 streets, the 129,000 square feet (12,000 square meters) of water, and the central piazza named after Marlene Dietrich to the dismay of her fans in Schöneberg, her former home, where they wanted her name to be recognized. The site, covering 730,000 square feet (68,000 square meters), was the first building project to be completed at Potsdamer Platz. Costing DM 4 billion, it is also the largest.

It is hard to imagine that far below Daimler-Benz's high-rise structures, a new regional train station is taking shape. At the same time the new Lehrter Bahnhof (Chapter 6) opens for north-south train traffic in May 2003, the new two-level underground Potsdamer Platz regional train station will open.

The Sony Center is Potsdamer Platz's second-largest undertaking (178,000 square feet—16,500 square meters). It will be finished in year 2000. It consists of an architecturally cutting-edge ensemble of seven buildings. The slender 338-foot (103 meters), 26-floor glassed tower of the Chicago architect Helmut Jahn is the highest building of Potsdamer Platz, but the 43,000-square-foot (4,000-square-meter) covered Forum is the focal point of this office, entertainment and residential project. It is surrounded by restaurants, cafés, and shops, with space provided for cultural events. The center houses the European headquarters of Sony, the Berlin Filmhaus with the Marlene Dietrich collection, and the German Media Library.

Sony spent $35 million to restore the Grand Hotel Esplanade, incorporating landmarked parts of the hotel, including the facade and the gold- and red-trimmed two-story, neo-Baroque Kaiser's Hall where Kaiser Wilhelm II once held his renowned stags. Unfortunately Sony discovered that the Kaiser's Hall had become located right in the middle of a new street. This was the salon that Charlie Chaplin, Greta Garbo, and other names from the Golden '20s had enjoyed. During the War, Col. Claus Schenk Graf von Stauffenberg and his fellow conspirators waited there in vain for word that their assassination attempt on Hitler had succeeded. Workers had to hoist the 1,500-ton landmarked ballroom eight feet and roll it about 345 feet (105 meters) down the street to its new location. Not easily done. One-tenth of Sony's $35 million went toward towing the Kaiser's Hall.

You can see a few Wall segments, decorated with graffiti, below the Info-Box. Use U-Bhf Potsdamer Platz.

## JANNOWITZ BRIDGE AREA

The Jannowitzbrücke mainline and S-Bahn station was built adjacent to the **Jannowitzbrücke.** (The U-Bahn station is nearby.) A savvy cotton factory owner named Christian August Jannowitz built a private wooden bridge over the Spree in 1822 and collected tolls for its use. It has been rebuilt four times since. About 1880 a wrought-iron arched bridge was constructed. At the end of the 1920s, "Alte Jannowitz," as it had come to be called, was remodeled. It was destroyed in 1945 during the Red Army invasion of Berlin and rebuilt in 1952-54 as a steel-girder bridge. From the bridge you have an interesting view over the broad Spree as far as Fischer Island.

The huge building hulking west of Jannowitz Bridge is the Communist answer to West Berlin's ICC (Chapter 5), but is tiny by comparison. It is the BCC or **Berliner Congress Center**, Märkisches Ufer 54, Tel. 275-80, Fax 27-58-21-65. Conveniently located on the Spree embankment you can easily reach it from U- or S-Jannowitz Brücke.

**Märkisches Museum,** Am Köllnischen Park 5, Tel. 30-86-60 (open Tue.-Sun. 10 A.M. to 6 P.M.), documents the story of Berlin from the first traces of the first settlement 60,000 years ago until the present. Unfortunately, they do it in such a dark and dreary atmosphere that it becomes uninteresting.

The red brick building is imposing. It was finished in 1908 supposedly of characteristic Brandenburg architecture. The name comes from the state of Brandenburg surrounding Berlin which is known as Mark Brandenburg. The building recalls the Bischofsburg in the city of Wittstock and the

Catharine Chapel in the city of Brandenburg. The statue of Roland at the main entrance is a copy of the Brandenburg Roland from 1474.

You see displays of historic crafts and manufactured objects from the 17th to the 20th centuries including antique glass, porcelain, wrought iron, cast iron, and tin. You also see Berlin art from the baroque period to 1945, but the highlights include Berlin's theatrical history, the display on satirist Heinrich Zille (1858-1929), and especially the mechanical, sometimes coin-operated, music boxes and toys ("Automatophone"). There is also one of Schadow's copper horse heads from the original 1793 Quadriga atop the Brandenburg Gate. Use U-Bhf Märkisches Museum.

The nearby **Otto-Nagel-Haus,** Märkisches Ufer 16-18, Tel. 278-79-20 (open Sun.-Thur. 10 A.M. to 6 P.M., Wed. to 8 P.M.; admission DM 4, day card to SMB museums, DM 8), possesses the Bildarchiv Preussischer Kulturbesitz (Prussian photo archives). You have a glimpse of the life and work of proletarian revolutionary and anti-Fascist artists Otto Nagel (1894-1967), Käthe Kollwitz, Ernst Barlach, and others. Nagel was jailed by the Nazis in 1936. The museum was constructed in 1973 from two baroque residences, #16 (from 1790) and #18 (from 1730).

Take an admiring look at the houses at Märkisches Ufer 10 and 12, which are connected together in back. They blend harmoniously with the other handsome structures lining the riverbank although they were moved here from Breite Straße 11. The **Ermeler-Haus** (#10) is the last Berlin residence with an early neoclassical facade. Wilhelm Ermeler bought the house in 1824 from a tobacco manufacturer.

## FRIEDRICHSTRASSE STATION

Friedrichstraße station has been completely rebuilt from the ground up into a regional train station. Opened on December 13, 1998, it shines. Alive with trains rumbling, it is a hub of huge activity. Passengers scamper freely back and forth jumping aboard elevated regional trains and east-west S-Bahn lines, or up and down escalators to north-south S-Bahn and U-Bahn trains below ground. On the ground level auto and streetcar cross traffic along busy Friedrichstraße bisects the station.

The Berlin Transit Authority called it "rejuvenation." Commuters used harder words. GermanRail and the Berlin Transit Authority spent about one billion U.S. dollars to modernize the 5.5-mile, two-track S-Bahn and parallel mainline stretches. Key S-Bahn stations were open to traffic over the "rejuvenated" tracks, but closed to long-distance travel. They were noisy and dusty. Workers installed escalators. Stations Friedrichstraße and Alexanderplatz were realigned into regional train hubs. The original,

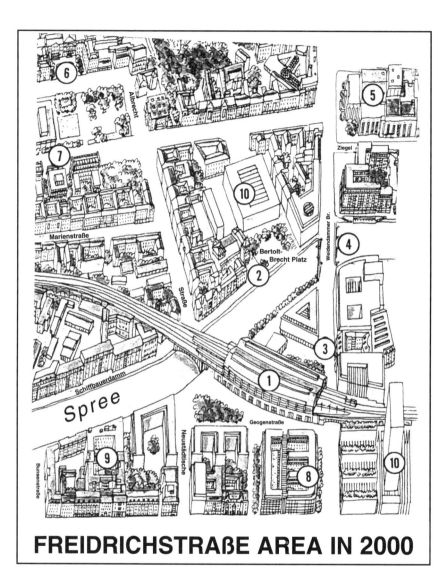

# FREIDRICHSTRAßE AREA IN 2000

1. Friedrichstraße Regional Train Station
2. Berlin Ensemble Theater
3. Metropol Theater
4. Weidendamm Bridge
5. Friedrichstadtpalast Theater
6. Deutsches Theater
7. Deutsches Theater Rehearsal
8. New Wintergarten Theater
9. Federal Press and Information Office
10. Year 2000 construction

estimated completion date was May 1997. That was before workers discovered the unexploded World War II bomb embedded in the brick Stadtbahn foundation and specialists from the bomb squad had to be called in to search the whole length for more. Then engineers discovered during renovation that the 1882 bridge across the Spree River next to Friedrichstraße station and the Bode Museum was not salvageable and they had to completely tear it down and build a new one for $20 million. Meanwhile, electricians completely electrified the stretch between Zoo and Hauptbahnhof and engineers widened the track area and platforms.

Now that it's a beautiful station with every modern convenience, you have to use your imagination to visualize what it was like before the unification and Friedrichstraße station was the only possible rail crossing point between East and West. Visitors from the West had to pass a solid iron wall right in the station and undergo heavy scrutiny and painstaking security inspections to visit East Berlin. You got out of the train, clutching your passport, climbed down into an underground cavern, and took a number to await clearance by the Grepo, who manned the barrier. If you didn't understand German when your number was called, you were out of luck. You sat on a bench for a half-hour or more. You had to pass gray-faced border guards sitting behind bullet-proof glass at several observation posts and surrender your passport to a succession of guards who studied it as if they were learning to read. They looked at it, looked at you, looked at the mirror in back of you, consulted a computer, took some mysterious notes, and eventually waved you on, always expressionless, without exchanging any talk. You had to have your film-loaded camera X-rayed. If you had a suitcase, guards passed it through a curtain to a back room for inspection. If you carried any Western books or newspapers, you had to leave them behind. You also had to exchange DM 25 at the official rate of one to one when you could get five times more on Alexanderplatz, but you could never find anything worthwhile to buy with them, so it didn't matter. And just when at last you thought you were finished with the inspecting and registering, you might be pulled out of line and taken to a small room for further interrogation.

Now you can't figure out where the labyrinth of guard posts and interrogation rooms might have existed. Everything is pastel.

Friedrichstraße, 200 feet (60 meters) wide and nearly one mile (1.5 kilometers) long, runs from Oranienburger Tor ("gate") to Mehringplatz. Between 1961 and 1989, it was closed because of the Berlin Wall at Checkpoint Charlie. Just north of Friedrichstraße Station is a lively **theater mini-district** including the Berliner Ensemble, Metropol Theater, Tränenpalast, Deutsches Theater, and Friedrichstadtpalast.

From Friedrichstraße Station, cross the magnificent imperial ironwork bridge, the **Weidendammbrücke** over the Spree. It is one of Berlin's most beautiful. In the 17th century a wooden bridge here was one of Berlin's first Spree crossings. It was replaced by a metal structure in 1824-26, which at that time was the only one of its kind in the world. Restored and regalvanized in 1992-24, the Weidendammer displays a cast-iron Prussian eagle on each of its railings. Make a sharp left on Schiffbauerdamm to **Bertholt-Brecht-Platz** with a fine bronze sculpture of the master playwright staring down at his famous words:

> Young Alexander conquered India.
> By himself?
> Caesar beat the Gauls.
> Didn't he at least have a cook with him?
> Philipp of Spain cried as his fleet sank.
> Didn't anyone else cry?
> Friedrich II won the 7-Years' War.
> Didn't anyone else win?
> Every side a victory.
> Who cooked for the victory celebration?
> Every ten years, a great man.
> Who pays his expenses?
> So many reports.
> So many questions.

The **Berliner Ensemble** is the famous **Bertholt-Brecht Theater.** Brecht first premiered his *Dreigroschenoper ("Threepenny Opera")* here in 1928. In 1949, this DDR playhouse was taken over by Bertholt Brecht and his wife Helen Weigel after he left asylum in the United States with an Austrian passport, a Swiss bank account, and a West German publishing contract. In the DDR the playhouse was turned into a play-museum for Brecht. His plays stagnated in this 1891-92 tower-topped house ornamented with alabaster tritons and dolphins and assorted nymphs and muses. The productions were merely pages from the past and for this the theater was severely criticized. Brecht is often performed in the West, but it is always modernized and made more meaningful. Now the Berliner Ensemble produces works, even premieres works, by other artists such as *Monsieur Verdoux* by Charles S. Chaplin.

It is planned to build along here a promenade along the Spree on both sides. Private properties will be recessed so that one can walk along the Spree from the Reichstag to Alexanderplatz and farther.

Just around the corner from the Berlin Ensemble in the theater on Schiffbauerdamm, the **Brecht-Haus**, Chausseestraße 125, Tel. 282-99-16 (open Tue.-Fri. 10 A.M. to noon, Thur. 5 to 7 P.M., Sat. 9:30 A.M. to noon, and 12:30 to 2 P.M., admission DM 4), was occupied by Brecht and Weigel starting in 1954. "Now that I'm closer to the theater, my people won't leave me alone." Next door is the Dorotheenstadt Cemetery where Brecht said he wished to be buried. After his death in 1956, Helene Weigel set up the Brecht Archives. The rooms Brecht and Weigel occupied have been maintained in the original condition and are open to the public, but Brecht's love affairs with his female associates did not make for harmony in his relationship with Weigel. When he was working at the Deutsches Theater, for example, he used to visit Ruth Berlau on Charitéstraße during his lunch breaks. A bookshop and literary forum are located at the front of the building, while in the basement you can visit the *Brecht-Keller*, a restaurant where meals are cooked according to Weigel's recipes. There are tours for up to eight individuals without reservations every half-hour. Use U-Bhf Zinnowitzer Straße.

Before crossing the Spree, right in back (to the north of) Friedrichstraße train station, just 15 feet from the exits of the mainline station and the U-Bahn station, you find the entrance to the now-closed **Metropol-Theater**, Friedrichstraße 101-2. The theater traces its roots to September 3, 1898, when it was named "Theater Unter den Linden" in the amusement center of the national capital. It became a light-opera house after the Wende where Germans enjoyed German-language translations of Broadway hits such as *Jesus Christ Superstar, My Fair Lady, Hello, Dolly!* and *West Side Story* before it ran into financial difficulties. When you have time, walk around to see the delightful rear of the theater decorated with maidens and scrolls. Use U-Bhf Friedrichstraße.

The Tränenpalast ("Palace of Tears") across from the Metropol Theater is tucked in close behind Friedrichstraße Station, station side of the Spree River. Farther north on Friedrichstraße you can't miss Europe's largest revue theater, Friedrichstadt Palast building, Art Nouveau with added pink decorations. Away to the left you find the Deutsche Theater. Particularly Schiffbauerdamm has been nicely spruced up with popular, trendy restaurants.

## HACKESCHER MARKT TRAIN STATION

S-Hackescher Markt is a small, covered, red- and blond-brick station constructed in 1882. Its heavily decorated, presumptuous exterior might remind you more of a palazzo than a train station. When the mainline route was reelectrified between Zoo and Hauptbahnhof in 1996-97, it was rebuilt and the interior was modernized and pleasingly restored. The exposed wood- and glass-arched ceiling is very attractive. In 1998, the ground-level areas below the station were rebuilt to provide space for new shops and cafés. Built as Bahnhof Börse ("Stock Exchange"), Bahnhof Hackescher Markt was the last link in the chain of train stations that set the

# HACKESCHER MARKT AREA

1. Hackescher Markt train station
2. Hackesche Höfe
3. Hackesche Höfe Office Project
4. Old Jewish Cemetery
5. Sophien Church
6. Monbijou Park

stage for a powerful expansion of industry in Berlin. It survived the War almost undamaged only to be called Marx-Engels-Platz train station during DDR times.

At Rosenthaler Straße 40-41, you find the **Hackesche Höfe** ("Hackish Courtyards"), the largest courtyard complex in Berlin. It is a labyrinth of eight courtyards in all, filled with businesses and living quarters. You feel like you are entering another world—a kind of fairyland which fills you with a sense of wonder. In the architecturally varied and somewhat garish inner courtyards you find assorted businesses of every kind (i.e., small boutiques, artistic shops, attractive pubs), all of which create a special ambience.

This ensemble of large industrial and living quarters built between 1905 and 1910 was named a historically landmarked area. Artisans produced handicrafts in the front two courtyards. After being heavily damaged in 1944, it was a poverty-stricken, almost falling-down wreck after the War. It was overlooked and neglected by the bureaucrats of the DDR who were more interested in sports stadiums. The state supported only the SophienClub at #6, a Jewish jazz club.

After the Wende, the Hackesche Höfe were restored with their striking Jugendstil facade and green, glazed-tile roof. Visitors came to admire the multiple courtyards decorated with magnificent glazed tiles of many colors and designs. The first courtyard is the showpiece. In 1906 the architect August Endell decorated the facade magnificently with glazed bricks, white and blue stones, green and brown ones arranged in curves, waves, in two-dimensional designs, and also in mosaic patterns composed of small pieces. Subcultural artists have installed galleries, performances, variety turns, dance halls and cafés, which has acted like a magnet for visiting artists and the curious. Since its restoration, it has become a shining, East Berlin tourist hub offering something for everyone—Ossi, Wessi and tourist. Visitors crowd the restaurants, cafés, bookshops, movie theaters, the SophienClub (jazz), the Chämeleon (varieté), and the HofTheater (Klezmer, which is Yiddish soul music from the east coast of the U.S. alien to Berlin Jews). By the time you wander into the back courtyards, you feel like an intruder. The city, even the front courtyards, seems to be a long way away. In these courtyards there are also some small businesses but without shop windows. The rest are apartments. At 10 P.M. doors to the residential courtyards are closed. Residents there need a little quiet and relief from the curious visitors. It is highly recommended. Use U-Bhf Weinmeisterstraße, S-Bhf Hachescher Markt, bus 348, or streetcar 1 or 13.

Directly opposite the Hackesche Höfe, developers are opening an eyesore ensemble of 12 large residential and commercial buildings with inner courtyards and side wings. The *Neue Hackesche Höfe* project comprises the typical Berlin residential/retail/trade mix which is to become a key feature of the post-Wende Scheuenviertel.

At Rosenthaler Straße 37, you find the **Hackescher Markt**. Its irregular shape gives some proof that it was hauled from the ramparts of the Spandauer Tor ("Spandau Gate") and installed here by City Commander Count von Hacke about 1750.

The path through the gate and courtyard of the three-story Jugendstil apartment house that was built in 1905 at Sophienstraße 6 opens up a striking array of courtyards used for living and business purposes such as was typical in the 19th and early 20th century.

The **Kulturamt-Mitte** ("Mitte Cultural Office") and the **Förderband/Kulturbüro** ("Cultural Promotion Office") are together in Kulturhaus Mitte nearby at Rosenthaler Straße 51 (open Mon.-Fri. 11 A.M. to 4 P.M.). Two cultural offices, one exhibit.

## SCHEUNENVIERTEL

The **Scheunenviertel** ("Scheunen" meaning "barns" and "Viertel" meaning "quarter"), or Spandauer Vorstadt, section in East Berlin is not an official city quarter, but the part of Mitte District between the former city wall now marked by the elevated Alexanderplatz train station and Prenzlauer Berg.

The name is more of a colloquialism. It comes from the fact that until the middle of the last century, this flat area was covered with fields of grain, windmills to grind the grain, and **Scheunen**—the barns, or sheds—that were used to store the straw. Scheunen were not allowed inside the city walls by the elector because of fire danger. Field workers living very close to the Scheunen worked hard and had little money, so it became the living section of the impoverished. It evolved into a slum at the beginning of this century. The streets were narrow; criminality and prostitution flourished. The sidewalks are still very narrow, a tip-off that the area was very poor.

Visitors find a slice of blue-collar Berlin, and memories recalling earlier times—of war and of suffering. It includes the great New Synagogue on Oranienburger Straße and the remnants of the old Jewish cemetery on the Großen Hamburger Straße. Visitors see an old street with a face-lift, an almost forgotten burial place honoring one of the heroes of the war of liberation, tenements from the industrialization of Berlin, and the streets of Alfred Döblin's novel *Berlin Alexanderplatz.*

The Scheunenviertel was known as a *Kiez*, a representative living quarter. The area was relatively untouched by the War because it was a residential quarter and had no strategic importance. After the War was over, it was ignored by the bureaucrats of the DDR who left it to take care of itself. The

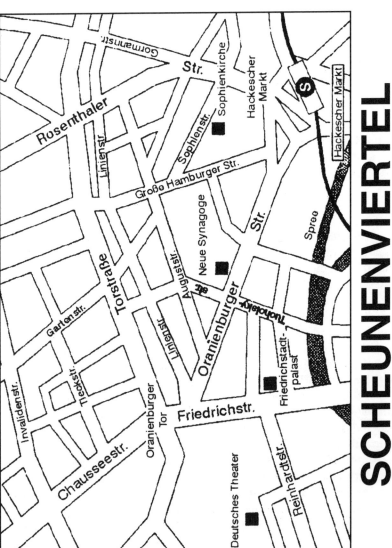

SCHEUNENVIERTEL

buildings were cheap, usually old, often with toilets outside. The entire quarter escaped Allied bombs and Russian tanks only to deteriorate slowly under an eastern regime more interested in building flimsy new towns than in repairing old ones.

When the Wende came, change was lightning fast and prices skyrocketed. Despite its disreputable housing, the Scheunenviertel's central location made it one of Berlin's most expensive districts and it became a construction site. Changing social patterns and the throngs of tourists changed the atmosphere. More than half of the present residents moved in after the Wende. They disdain the connotations of the name, "Scheunenviertel" and prefer "Spandauer Vorstadt." There had been strict assembly regulations under the DDR government. One could not go wherever one wanted or do what one wanted to do. Many in the DDR had to use their homes for concerts, theater performances, and exhibits. This led to a very strong subculture in East Berlin. For example, two young people living together in a one-room apartment with a kitchen might use their room for a gallery with paintings for sale that were changed periodically. In DDR times, it couldn't be advertised but everyone knew about it. Now, after the Wende, the same gallery has either been torn down or will have posters outside publicizing the artists on exhibit.

The old city walls are gone but now the S-Bahn viaduct separates the quarter from the city center. Instead of large residences and apartment houses north of S-Bhf Hackescher Markt, you see narrow alleyways and small old houses. Because of its isolation and because it has never been severely damaged, this quarter remained largely intact until the Wende. City dwellings 150 years old still stood, making it unique. While Berlin changed through the years, this quarter remained constant.

When industrialization began, the proletariat, or working class, moved in. When Berlin became the capital of Germany, floods of Eastern European Jews from Poland, from Russia, and from Vienna moved into the streets of Grendier- and Dragonerstraße (now Almenstadt- and Max-Beer-Straße) as well as Mulackstraße. Farms were torn down and buildings were constructed. The newcomers tried to make their area look like the small country villages from which they came. The well-off Jews already residing in Berlin had a beautiful synagogue and were not happy to see the poor Yiddish-speaking, spartan-living Eastern European Jews arrive. The new influx of Jews built their own cemetery and many buildings around it that were well cared for.

(It was a similar situation to the one in present-day Kreuzberg, where poor people arrived from Anatolia, the women wearing veils, and families carrying on traditional Turkish lifestyles.)

Only a few small synagogues or prayer rooms remain in the Scheunen-viertel; nearly all known Jews were murdered or deported by the Nazis. The Scheunenviertel earned a legendary reputation—an old quarter with many stories and traditions. Now the houses are old and gradually falling apart. Rebuilding of the houses is very difficult because it was a largely Jewish community and many of the rightful owners were murdered by the Nazis. In many cases, no one knows who owns them. Germans whose land was seized by the Communists can claim it (if it was not taken during the four years of the Russian occupation). Jews whose land was seized by the Nazis can claim it anytime if records exist. They often do not. For every house there are usually five applications of ownership. In this ghetto area, there are usually Jewish claims from 1938, and succeeding claims of ownership resulting from the War and DDR years. This all must be settled legally by the courts. It will take a long time. In the meantime the rent inflation scares the current occupants, who fear that this area will become limited to rich occupants.

Whenever you see a green space in East Berlin you can guess that it has its own story, because it signifies that something formerly there was destroyed by the War. In one case, a French Jewish artist looked through an old telephone book to find out the names of the people who lived at one time in a building that doesn't exist anymore. Then he looked at an old photo of the house to see how it once looked. He saw where the house stood, knew the names of the people who had lived there, and saw that the now empty space had a story, so the French artist painted the names of the former residents and their room numbers on the wall of the surviving house next door. It is now a document of history and a landmarked memorial, **The Destroyed House**, on Große Hamburger Straße 75.

At the turn of the century, the Scheunenviertel was the most densely populated section of Berlin. Crime was rampant. It became a hotbed of revolutionary fervor. Authorities refused to pave the roads with cobblestones for fear the inhabitants would rip them up and use them to build barricades.

In the heart of the Scheunenviertel, on the most famous street, at Mulackstraße 22, there is an interesting back courtyard where Heinrich Zille, the Berlin characterist, worked to capture the social character of the area. Nowadays they call it a Zille-milieu. You can see it.

On the other side of Mulackstraße was a famous restaurant that was torn down in the 1960s, **Restauration Zopfke.** In 1952, before the restaurant was torn down, a Berlin character, a well-known 70-year-old transvestite from the Scheunenviertel named Lothar Berfelde, saved the entire interior of the restaurant, the "Mulack Ritz," which had been frequented by Zille and others including Marlene Dietrich and Berthold Brecht, and installed it in Mahlsdorf in a late baroque house constructed around 1770 by David Gilly as a manor and moved from the former separate city of Köpenick. After much squabbling with the authorities and an incredible amount of idealism, Berfelde spent 13 years rebuilding the building and furnishing it piece by piece. Ultimately he received permission to open on August 1, 1960, the **Gründerzeitmuseum,** a private museum, Hultschiner Damm 333, Tel. 527-8329 (open Mon. and Fri. to 9 P.M., guided tours on Sun. at 11 A.M. and noon). *Gründerzeit* is the time of the formation of the German Reich, roughly the epoch from 1871 to 1894. This time period gave Berlin a special architecture, the transition to Jugendstil. For the Scheunenviertel, use U-Bhf Oranienburger Tor, S-Bhf Oranienburger Straße, and U-Bhf Weinmeisterstraße.

Many have seen the film or read the 1929 book *Berlin Alexanderplatz.* The author, Alfred Döblin, was a Jewish doctor who practiced on nearby Alexanderplatz. Döblin knew the Scheunenviertel through his patients. His protagonist, Franz Biberkopf, a petty criminal, came from here. All the streets in the novel still exist. Readers find it very interesting to reconstruct the book.

Gormannstraße played a major role in the book. The school on the corner of Rosenthaler Straße and Gormannstraße across from U-Bhf Weinmeisterstraße was built in the typical "Social Realistic" architectural style of the 1950s in the DDR. It shows the bountiful peaceful future of the happy workers of the Socialist state, with singing women, flag-waving workers, and farsighted leaders.

## NEW SYNAGOGUE

The glittering, golden dome you see from as far away as Friedrichstraße is the **Neue Synagoge,** Germany's largest synagogue at Oranienburger Straße 30, Tel. 28-40-12-50. The New Synagogue's grandiose design of elaborate domes and intricate decoration was based on Byzantine and Moorish influences, including the Moorish Alhambra in Granada. Construction began in 1859 using plans of Eduard Knoblauch of the Schinkel school and was completed by Friedrich August Stüler. Kaiser Wilhelm I was present when the New Synagogue was opened on September 5, 1866. It was built to demonstrate the distance that Jews had come during 200 years of discrimination. For the first time, the Jewish community felt that they were no longer Jews in Germany, but Jewish Germans.

The most beautiful Oriental-style building in Berlin, its beauty mostly saved it during the *Reichskristallnacht.* Reinhard Heydrich, the number-two man, after Himmler, in the S.S., had teletyped orders for "spontaneous

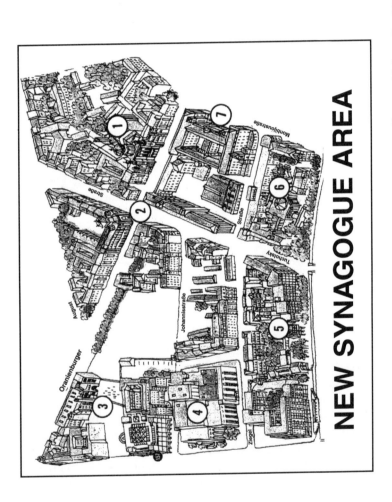

# NEW SYNAGOGUE AREA

1. New Synagogue
2. Former Postal Coach Building
3. Former Tacheles Ruins
4. Friedrichstadtpalast Theater
5. Former University Clinic
6. University Woman's Clinic
7. Former Telegraph Office

demonstrations" with the following guidelines: "Only such measures should be taken which do not involve danger to German life or property. For instance synagogues are to be burned down only when there is no danger of fire to the surroundings. . . . Business and private apartments of Jews may be destroyed but not looted. . . . As many Jews, especially rich ones, are to be arrested as can be accommodated in the existing prisons. Upon their arrest the appropriate concentration camps should be contacted immediately, in order to confine them in these camps as soon as possible."

On early morning of November 10, 1938, SA thugs broke into the New Synagogue, plundered the preciously decorated rooms and set them on fire, but because the building was landmarked as a national historic building, Berlin police office Wilhelm Krützfeld (1880-1953) called the fire departments to save the synagogue. It was a landmarked building. He didn't care whether or not it was Jewish. The firemen saved most of it. A plaque in front marks Krützfeld's conscience. The surviving rooms were then requisitioned by the German army in 1940 and used as a special arms depot. It was destroyed by aerial bombing in 1943, but by this time it was no longer a synagogue because Jewish worship had been forbidden by the Nazis. Only the dome and the reception area facing Oranienburger Straße were restored. The huge assembly hall, with seating for 3,500 worshipers that was destroyed by Allied bombs in 1943, was replaced by a simple, grassy area, with a large, glass superstructure protecting the ruins of the hall. Physicist Albert Einstein gave a violin concert in the synagogue on January 29, 1930. Presently there are about 10,000 Jews supporting four synagogues throughout Berlin. Most of them have emigrated from the former Soviet Union.

The simple, red-brick construction with a bust of Moses Mendelssohn next door is the **Centrum Judaicum**, Oranienburger Straße 29, Tel. 28-40-12-50 (open Sun.-Thur. 10 A.M. to 6 P.M., Fri. to 2 P.M.). Tours through the synagogue are arranged Sun. at 2 and 4 P.M. and on Wed. at 4 P.M. Adults pay DM 3; children DM 1.50. On the other side of the Neue Synagogue at Oranienburger Straße 31, is the **Jüdische Galerie** ("Jewish Gallery"), Tel. 282-86-23, Fax 282-85-29 (open Mon.-Fri. 10 a.m to noon and 4-8 P.M., Sat. 11 A.M.-3 P.M.). The red-brick building next to the Jewish Center is the Jewish-owned Oran Café. Built as a government administrative center, it was the home of the Jewish Museum before the opening of the Jewish Center. In the courtyard of Oranienburger Straße 32, you find the Café Orange. Use streetcar line 1 or 3 or bus 157.

You can see the Jewish collection formerly housed in the Martin Gropius Building in architect Daniel Libeskind's extension of the Berlin Museum on Lindenstraße (Chapter 8).

The original Jewish Museum was housed in the orange-brick Moorish *Postfuhramt* building down the street at the corner of Tucholskystraße. The striking building had been stables at the turn of the century for some 380 postal-coach horses. It was converted and opened in January 1933, six days before the take-over by the Nazis. Formerly there were no post-office mail delivery trucks. Mail was carried by horse-drawn postal coaches. In 1705-13, a **Postillionshaus** ("Stagecoach Driver's House") was built on the corner of Oranienburger Straße and Tucholskystraße where the horses were tended in the three-story, red-and-yellow glazed-brick **Postfuhramt** ("Postal Coach Office") built between 1875 and 1881 by Carl Schwatlo in a late neoclassical style recalling Lombardian early Renaissance—one of the most imposing public buildings in Berlin. The 25 reliefs on the facade show personalities from traffic and postal history. You still see parts of the old horse stalls and a horse's head over the gate. It quartered 240 horses in the courtyard, contained a coach house, and provisioned postal and parcel-post coaches. This War-damaged building is still used by the post office.

The Postal Coach Office is not the only post office installation on Oranienburger Straße. On the nearly opposite corner is the **Institut für Post- und Fernmeldewesen** ("Institute for Postal and Long-Distance Communication"). The two-story older part of the building was rebuilt by Friedrich Becherer as the **Große Landesloge der Freimauer** ("Great Freemason's Lodge"). In 1839 the building was remodeled and enlarged.

Next to it, on Tucholskystraße, the institute borders the red-and-black glazed-brick striped **Fernsprechamt** ("Long-Distance Telephone Office") from 1925. At the turn of the century, Berlin had the largest telephone network in the world. In 1865, a pneumatic-tube delivery service was also installed after having been tested between the main post office on Französische Straße and the Berlin stock market. Later the Pneumatic Post Central Office complex was built in 1910 at Oranienburger Straße 73-76.

When you want a tourist's-eye view of the Scheunenviertel or to take photographs, walk directly to **Sophienstraße.** It was restored by the DDR for the Berlin anniversary.

Sophienstraße is the oldest street in the area. Settlers, beginning about 1700, included craftsmen, day workers, shipbuilders and, later, workers at the textile factories. The street is now preserved because it was relatively lightly damaged during the War, but the passing years had done its work. The DDR prized manual workers and dotted the street with nicely rebuilt, small handicraft shops to convince German tourists and visitors from Eastern countries of the success of the Socialist system. The tourists were steered away from the back sides, which are not so picturesque.

Sophienstraße is nevertheless very pretty, and for East Berlin, a very pleasant place to live. Not only the facades were rebuilt and painted, but between 1981 and 1987, 473 apartments were modernized and 12 new ones built. Modern kitchens, central heating, and 442 baths were added. Residents who live in the apartments are very worried that their rents will increase beyond their ability to pay.

At Sophienstraße 10, there is the puppet theater, **Firlefanz**; house #11 at the intersection of Rosenthaler Straße is the oldest, dating from 1870; #17 is a firm that specializes in brass musical instruments; at Sophienstraße 18 you see the terra-cotta letters, **Berliner Handwerkerverein** ("Berlin Craftsmen's Guild") over the double gate. The guild was founded in 1844, but at this address on November 14, 1918, Karl Liebknecht chaired the first public meeting of the Spartacus group. It has a busy history of Communist gatherings. Sophienstraße 23 is the home of the **Heimatsmuseum Berlin-Mitte** ("Local History Museum"), Tel. 282-03-76 (open Mon.-Thur. 10 A.M. to noon and 1 P.M. to 5 P.M., Sun. 1 P.M. to 6 P.M.) with a collection of period maps, photographs, and documents.

**Oranienburger Straße** is one of the most interesting streets in East Berlin. It is lively—very recommended in the evenings. This street was known before the War, and is developing again, into a Toleranz Straße, where all faiths are accepted, in the middle of the Jewish community filled with occupied houses, experimental art, and contemporary lifestyles. The names of the cafés are hard to detect (many don't seem to have names in front), but you can see the activity. The first buildings were built about 1690, but no trace remains of them. Many of the buildings that give Oranienburger Straße its present appearance go back to about 1890 and you can trace them to that time. Look at the gray apartment at Oranienburger Straße 45. It has been landmarked because it is typical for the Scheunenviertel. It was built in 1890 with front, side, and cross buildings to form courtyards during the time of the rapid expansion of population into the Scheunenviertel in the 1880-90s. The mixed neo-renaissance and neo-Baroque facade was the idea of the builder. Address #37, as you see by the numbers above the entranceway, was built in 1885-86, but remodeled a few years ago. On the other side of the street, #67, now the **Henschel-Verlag** ("Henschel Publishing House"), was the residence of the scientist Alexander von Humboldt from 1843 until his death in 1859.

**Tacheles,** is the name of a young community group in the Scheunen-viertel at Oranienburger Straße 54-56a that occupied what was left of a historical ruin of a department store with theater. Late at night you could find the art community there. Finally, in 1997, 52 years of occupation after the War's end, and after years of bitter discussion, the residents were given one to two weeks to get out, the ruins were carted away, and investors looked forward to building on the site. Down the street is a rooming house that has been made over by young East Berlin artists into one of the neighborhood's favorite cafés and farther you see another very beautiful café in a former cellar apartment (a so-called souterrain apartment).

Just off Große Hamburger Straße the **Sophienkirche,** named for Queen Sophie Luise, is one of Berlin's finest baroque churches. It is one of the few architectural achievements remaining from the time of Friedrich Wilhelm I, the "Soldier King," who spent every cent on the military. It is surrounded by five-story neo-Baroque residences from 1904-5. The church was given by Prussian Queen Sophie Luise to the area in 1712 as a parish church. The richly decorated baroque tower from 1729-35 by Johann Friedrich Grael was used as a model by Schlüter for his Mint Tower. It's the only part to withstand the War relatively unscathed.

In the church cemetery you find a sandstone gravestone with rococo angels for marine architect Johann Koepjohann (d. 1792); an obelisk marking Carl-Friedrich Zelter (1758-1832), a friend of Goethe and director of the Berlin Singing Academy; and the grave of historian Leopold von Ranke. On the outer wall of the church there is an inscription by the novelist Anna Louise Karsch.

Churches in East Berlin played an important political role before the Wende. The DDR couldn't ban the services at the Sophie Church but they could make it very difficult to attend. The police and security forces closed off the street. Parishioners had to show passes to go in and out.

In a narrow area on this street you see evidence of three confessions: Jewish buildings, an Evangelical church, and the red building on the opposite site of the street which is the St. Hedwig's Hospital designed in 1851-54 by the architect of the Cologne Cathedral, Vincenz Statz, in neo-Gothic style.

Left from Sophien Church about 150 feet along the Große Hamburger Straße you reach a spot recalling the blackest days of German history and the Nazi extermination of the Jewish populace.

The **Alter jüdischer Friedhof** ("Old Jewish Cemetery"), the oldest in Berlin, was laid out in 1672 just one year after the arrival in Berlin of immigrants from Vienna. It was used until 1827, when the cemetery had filled and burials ceased. A bust of Mendelssohn stood in the cemetery until it was destroyed by the Nazis in 1938. In 1943, Nazis dug a slit trench through the cemetery, using gravestones to shore it up. From about 3,000 gravestones, there are only about 20 remaining with Hebrew inscriptions. It was the burial place of the homogeneous, poor Jewish community that clung together and maintained common religious beliefs. They all shared the same religious beliefs, lived close together, and all of them were discriminated against.

The philosophy espoused in France, that all men are created equal, spread to Germany. Lessing wrote a tract dealing with the problem of equality of man based on the philosophies of Moses Mendelssohn, a Jew born very poor in Dessau. In 1743, when he was 14, he came to Berlin, speaking only Yiddish, the Jewish dialect for the Jews who lived in Germany. He taught himself German, French, Latin, and English, and studied mathematics, literature, and philosophy. He became friendly with many learned men including Lessing, and Friedrich Nikolai, the Berlin publisher and novelist. He translated the Bible, one page in Hebrew, the facing page in German, but using the Hebrew alphabet because the Jews could not understand the Latin alphabet.

With his Emanzipationsedikt of 1812, Friedrich Wilhelm III granted the 70,000 Jews living in Prussia almost the same rights as Berlin citizens. There was economic flowering and the community grew. Some became rich and many more remained very poor. With economic change, religious traditions diverged so much that one could no longer speak of "the Jewish community." Many Jews integrated into the general life and lost their Jewish roots.

It was very difficult for the Nazis to define what is a Jew so they passed in 1935 a very complicated law to define a Jew.

For this reason there are rich and poor Jewish cemeteries in Berlin. The largest in Europe, with very beautiful burial markers of the rich, is in Weißensee (see Chapter 7).

After 1945 the Scheunenviertel's Jewish cemetery was rebuilt by the community. The memorial to Mendelssohn at the spot of his burial reads, "Moses Mendelssohn, born in Dessau on Sept. 6, 1729, died in Berlin on Jan. 4, 1786."

Next to the cemetery you find the first **old people's home** of the Jewish community of Berlin. In 1942 the Nazis converted it into a collection point for Jewish citizens. One-third of the city's community and 10 percent of Germany's Jewry, 55,000 Berlin Jews from babies in arms to the infirm, were transported to Auschwitz's and Theriesienstadt's work camps and gas chambers. Heavy fighting during the War destroyed it, but on this spot on the anniversary of *Kristallnacht* in 1987, a memorial was dedicated showing a group of gaunt figures with hollow faces.

Under the entrance at Große Hamburger Straße 27, you can still read the legend **Knabenschule der jüdischen Gemeinde** ("Boy's School of the Jewish Community"). Mendelssohn founded in 1778 the first free Jewish school in German so that children would have a better chance to learn the

German language, to give everyone equal rights, and to minimize the isolation of the ghetto. At first the community was not pleased with it, so it was financed by contributions, but it became so successful that the community took it over. In the beginning a parochial school of the Jewish faith and culture, it became a general high school not limited to Jewish students and without teaching the Jewish faith. In 1938 the Nazis forbade the intermingling of Christians and Jews and it became a pure Jewish school until 1942, when the deportations began and Jewish education was totally forbidden. It became a military installation. Now a trade school is located in the building.

The organization Freie Volksbühne ("Free People's Stage") was founded in the Scheunenviertel in 1890 by working-class citizens. From discounted theater tickets and donations, they accumulated enough money to build their own theater from plans by Oskar Kaufmann in 1912-13. With the words over the doorway, "The arts for the people," it opened on the edge of Berlin during the First World War with Max Reinhardt as the first manager. It was in the Scheunenviertel's Volkstheater that Artur Schnabel became the first pianist to play the cycle of all 32 Beethoven sonatas in 1927 on the occasion of the hundredth anniversary of the composer's death. The association was banned by the Nazis in 1933. Bombs destroyed the theater in 1943 and the remains burned in 1945. In April 1954, a new **Volksbühne,** at Rosa-Luxemburg-Platz (formerly Bülowplatz), was built with a dome and a huge line of Grecian columns which guard the front. It opened with a production of Schiller's *William Tell,* which celebrates fighting for liberty.

Across from the new Volksbühne is the **Karl-Liebknecht-Haus** at 28 Kleine Alexanderstraße where Ernst Thälmann, Communist candidate for president of the Weimar Republic who gathered more votes in Berlin than Hitler, and the Communist leadership of the 20s lived. As it was Communist-central until the Nazis came to power, there was many a confrontation and much blood letting during the Nazi demonstrations in the street. The plaque beside the door reads: "Ernst Thälmann, leader of the German working class and heroic fighter against fascism and war, worked in this house." The building is again headquarters for the PDS, the former Communist Party of Germany, making it a giant step downwards from the palaces the party commanded before the Wende.

Also on Rosa-Luxemburg-Platz you see the **memorial** honoring police officers Anlauf and Lenck, who were murdered during a Communist-inspired riot in the Scheunenviertel on August 9, 1931. The murderers fled immediately to Russia using already-prepared, forged passports, but one, Erich Mielke, who was 23 at the time of the murder, returned with the Red Army in 1945 and organized the political police of the Soviet sector. He advanced in 1950 to State Secretary, became Stasi-Minister of the DDR in 1957, and was awarded in 1975 the medal, "Hero of the DDR." Survivors called him "Master of Fear." At age 85, he appeared dazed and incoherent when, on October 27, 1993, a Berlin court found him guilty after a 20-month trial of murdering the two policemen 62 years ago. At the time he was the most senior official of the former East German Communist regime to be convicted by a court in unified Berlin. It was Berlin's turbulent history in microcosm: a former Communist leader was tried by a united German court for crimes committed during the Weimar Republic for which the Nazis had already sentenced him to death.

On **Auguststraße** there are various social buildings of the Jewish community, including an orphans' home and school. The pretty dark-red brick building was a 1929 Jewish middle school for girls. On the corner of Kleine Hamburger Straße, you see a red heart signifying a ballroom called Clärchens Ballhaus (see "Nightlife and Entertainment" below).

The plaque at the intersection of Auguststraße and Gipsstraße marks the house where the Baum Group resistance fighters lived (see "Lustgarten" under "Berlin Cathedral" above). Sala Kochmann was taken by the Fascists on August 18, 1942, and Martin Kochmann was taken in September 1943.

On the back side of the New Synagogue, the architecture of the **Judische Krankenhaus** ("Jewish Hospital"), Auguststraße 14-16, the heavy brick building with side wings, is different. It is late neoclassical, built by Eduard Knoblauch in 1860. It was used until 1914, when it became too small and a modern Jewish hospital was built in the Wedding district where the world's first kidney transplant was performed. This building is now used as a school.

At the corner of Joachimstraße and Auguststraße you come to Kleinen Rosenthaler Straße. The **Garnisonkirche** ("Garnison Church") was built in 1722. At the wooden door at Kleinen Rosenthaler Straße 7, see the **Garnisonfriedhof** ("Garnison Cemetery") for Prussian military. It was originally twice as large, but in 1899 the enlisted men's graves were taken away and only the officers' graves were allowed to remain. Under Prussian leadership, Germany was founded in 1870. Prussia's strength came primarily from a very strong military. In part these soldiers were forced into the army—they were not volunteers—and experienced terrible hardships.

## WALL MEMORIAL

On the border with the Western Berlin district of Wedding, at the corner of Gartenstraße and Bernauer Straße in Mitte, opposite the Nordbahnhof ("North Train Station") where only S-Bahn trains run, you see the

**Gedenkstätte Berliner Mauer** ("Berlin Wall Memorial") which was opened on August 13, 1998, the 37th anniversary of the day the Wall went up, under the sponsorship of the Berlin Senate which allocated US$1.2 million (DM 2.2 million).

Visitors to the memorial site are confronted by a 230-foot (70 meters) stretch of Wall flanked at right angels by two 23-foot (7 meters) high steel walls. There is no access to the former death strip. It can only be seen through observation slits in the back-up wall, which was built behind the Berlin wall proper. The slits also provide visual access to a closed-off area, which is designed to symbolize the oppressive atmosphere of the death strip. A documentation center is scheduled to open on November 9, 1999, in the parish rooms of the Evangelical Church of Reconciliation.

But it was difficult. The Berlin Senate wanted to create a memorial that would reflect the inherent brutality and contempt for man. Who wanted that on the street across from their house? Especially residents that had to accept for decades the real thing? The second problem was that politicians got involved, even down to the detail of the wording of the memorial plaque, which, in its final version, they changed to read: *In Erinnerung an die Teilung der Stadt vom 13. August 1961 bis zum 9. November 1989 und zum Gedenken an die Opfer kommunistischer Gewaltherrschaft* ("In memory of the division of the city from August 13, 1961, until November 9, 1989, and to the memory of the victims of Communist despotism"). The architects were furious, they wanted to know "which victims?" Stalinism in general? The Communist government in China? Cuba?

Nearby you see a fine section of the Wall sitting atop a trailer next to a mannequin of a soldier and a rusting Trabi automobile. This display is next to the **Berlin Flohmarkt** ("Flea Market"). Use S-Bhf Nordbahnhof, bus 245 or bus 328.

## 5. Sports

**Sport- und Erholungszentrum** ("Sports and Recreational Center"), Landsberger Allee 77 (Friedrichshain), Tel. 422-833-20/21 (open 9 A.M. to 10 P.M., except for bowling). The swimming area has swimming pools and diving platform, a wave pool, cascade and jet pools, an outdoor pool, a multipurpose pool for the handicapped, a sauna and a solarium, three fitness studios, a Polarium for ice-skating Oct.-Apr. or roller-skating and skate-boarding May-Sept., a bowling center with 16 lanes, a sports and leisure park with volleyball and badminton courts, ping-pong tables, and areas for boccia and miniature golf, as well as a children's sports garden. Seven restaurants. Use S-Bhf Landsberger Allee, bus 257, tram 5, 6, 7, 8, 15, 20, 27.

**Kinderbad Monbijou,** Oranienburger Straße, Tel. 282-8652 (open daily 9 A.M. to 7 P.M.). Swimming. Children's paradise in the Scheunenviertel with minilibrary, toys for loan, and baby changing room. Use S-Bhf Oranienburger Straße or U-Bhf Oranienburger Tor.

**Schwimmhalle Mitte**, Gartenstraße 5, Tel. 201-39-85 (open Mon. and Fri. 6:30 to 9 A.M. and 6 to 9:30 P.M., Tue. 3 to 6 P.M., Wed. 6:30 to 11 A.M. and 6 to 9:30 P.M., Thur. 6:30 to 9 A.M. and 3 to 6 P.M., Sat.-Sun. 2 to 9 P.M.)

**Schwimmhalle am Brandenburg Tor**, Behrenstraße 2, Tel. 229-15-51, special for children and elderly swimming and gymnastics.

**Schwimmhalle Fischerinsel**, Fischerinsel 11, Tel. 201-39-85 (Mon. and Thur. 6 to 9 A.M., Tue. 6 to 9 A.M. and 5 to 9 P.M., Wed. 7 to 10 P.M., Fri. 6 to 9 A.M. and 5 to 10 P.M., Sat. 9 A.M. to 3 P.M., Sun. 8 A.M. to 3 P.M.).

# 6. Shopping

You don't have to go to Paris to buy things Parisien. **Galeries Lafayette**, Französiche Straße 23, Tel. 209-48-0 (open Mon.-Fri. 9:30 A.M. to 8 P.M., Sat. 9 A.M. to 4 P.M.) was one of the first big names to rise in the East from a construction pit together with mixed-use buildings designed by I. M. Pei., but women of size should not look for French designer clothes. *Très petite!* It is appropriately at the door of U-Bhf Französiche Straße. The first week after its opening in spring 1996 was unbelievable. Friedrichstraße was filled with shoppers carrying G.L. bags. Many thanked Paris for sending to Berlin a second KaDeWe. Take a peek at the architecture inside.

Numerous boutiques have sprung up around the Lafayette department store and the Friedrichstadt-Passagen. They offer international fashion (**H&M**, **Benetton**), German elegance (**Escada**), American kitsch (**Planet Hollywood**) and Italian chic (**Gucci**).

**Meissner Porcelain,** Unter den Linden 39 (open Mon.-Fri. 9 A.M. to 6:30 P.M.). Famous for over 250 years, and a source of hard currency for East Germany since 1945, you can find the full range of Meissen products in the company's main shop in East Berlin.

The **British Bookshop**, Mauerstraße 83-84, Tel. 238-46-80/91, Fax 238-47-07. Near Checkpoint Charlie. (Open Mon.-Fri. 10 a.m to 6 P.M., Sat. to 4 P.M.) Use U-Bhf Stadtmitte or U-Bhf Hausvogteiplatz.

At **Hackeschen Höfe**, Rosenthaler Straße 40-41, shoppers can visit the off-boutique stores. The young ladies from **Kostümhaus, quasi moda**, and **Lisa D.** have spectacular designer clothes. **Hanley's Hair Company** and the shoe designer **Trippen** (open Mon.-Fri. noon to 6:30 P.M., Sat. 10 A.M. to 4 P.M.) in Hof 4, the *Brunnenhof* ("Fountain Courtyard") keep your head and foot with-it fashionable in these days of unconventional head and foot fashions. **Waahnsinn Berlin**, Neue Promenade 3, Tel. 282-00-29 (open

Mon.-Fri. 11 A.M. to 8 P.M.) has crazy fashion and oddities. Around the corner, **Orlando** gives you funky shoe fashions. Antiques are located in the fourth courtyard, known as the *Designareal.* Use U-Bhf Weinmeisterstraße, S-Bhf Hackescher Markt, bus 348, or streetcar 1 or 13.

**Berliner Antik- und Flohmarkt** ("Berlin Antique and Flea Market") Georgenstraße, located in Friedrichstaße train station's S-Bahnbögen ("S-Bahn overpass") (Wed.-Mon. 11 A.M. to 6 P.M.) where it is protected from the weather. Market dates from the 20s. It is the successor to the "Nolle," which was the a tourist attraction at Nollendorfplatz forced to close when the Wall came down. Stop by just to look and browse before visiting nearby museums. Sixty dealers specialize in quality second-hand furniture, antiques, curios, works of art, jewelry, and clothing from the 1920s. It is also home to restaurant **Zur Nolle, Café Odeon**, and the teddy bear stop **Bärenstark**. Use U- or S-Bhf Friedrichstraße.

**Antik- und Trödelmarkt** ("Antique and Second-hand Market"), Am Kupfergraben (open Sat.-Sun. 11 A.M. to 5 P.M.) is one of the most colorful and best known markets in Berlin. Located across from Museum Island you can find art, books, furniture, and DDR junk. Use U-Bhf Friedrichstraße.

**Berlin Flohmarkt** ("Flea Market"), corner Gartenstraße and Bernauer Straße (open Tue.-Sun. 10 A.M. to 6 P.M.). Use S-Bhf Nordbahnhof, bus 245 or 328.

**Flohmarkt auf dem Arkonaplatz** (every Sun.) Use U-Bhf Bernauer Straße.

**"Graf Hacke" Antik & Trödelmarkt**, Spandauer Brücke at the corner of Dircksenstraße, Tel. 445-61-32 (open 11 A.M. to 6:30 P.M.), offers nearly 10,000 square feet (900 square meters) in the train overpass. Look for furniture, household articles, and miscellaneous collectibles.

## 7. Nightlife and Entertainment

Nightlife doesn't share presence with the somber historical Prussian buildings, but booms in the busy Scheunenviertel centered on Oranienburger Straße. Here night people find many tiny galleries and cafés. Don't overlook the Hackesche Höfe.

Theater life in the East is excellent. It is in the German language, but musical events are enjoyable in any language.

## CLASSICAL AND LIGHT OPERA

**Konzerthaus am Gendarmenmarkt** (Gendarmenmarkt 2, Tel. 203-09-2101, Fax 2-04-43-70). Make Schinkel's concert hall your number-one ticket in Berlin. The resident Berlin Symphony Orchestra under head conductor Michael Schönwandt ranks as one of the most distinguished orchestras in Germany. Use U-Bhf Stadtmitte or U-Bhf Französische Straße. **Deutsche Staatsoper** (Unter den Linden 7, Tel. 203-545-55, Fax 203-544-83, *http://www.staatsoper-berlin.org*) is Knobelsdorff's 1741-43 neoclassical East German wedding-cake opera house. On the program you find opera, ballet, and concerts. Use U-Bhf Französische Straße or bus 100.

**Die Distel—das Berliner Kabarett-Theater** (Friedrichstraße 101), in the front building of the legendary Admiralpalast (see above), performs on the same stage as the Roland von Berlin cabaret troupe in 1926. At home here since 1953, the Distel cabaret has remained unmatched for political satire throughout Germany. Use U- or S-Bhf Friedrichstraße (U6 is closer).

Nestled behind trees farther north on Friedrichstraße, the **Berliner Ensemble am Schiffbauerdamm** (Am Bertholt-Brecht-Platz 1, Tel. 282-3160) was built by Heinrich Seeling as the *Neues Theater* in 1891-92. In a magnificent baroque interior, which just needs a little dusting, you can attend the most authentic productions of Brecht's, and others' plays in German. If you understand German, this is a must. Use S- or U-Bhf Friedrichstraße.

**Deutsches Theater/Kammerspiele** (Schmannstraße 13a, Tel. 28-44-12-22, Fax 28-24-117), a magical place built by Eduard Titz in 1849-50 and restored in 1983, was under the direction of Max Reinhardt from 1905 to 1933. It now presents a rotating German-language program including Brecht, Beckett, Shakespeare, Gorki, Molière, Ibsen, etc. In the Scheunenviertel at the end of Albrechtstraße. Use U-Bhf Oranienburger Tor, U-Bhf, or S-Bhf Friedrichstraße.

**Baracke** (Schummstraße 10, Tel. 284-41-222), near the Deutsches Theater and sharing the same box office, presents satirical and alternative plays. Use U-Bhf Oranienburger Tor, U-Bhf, or S-Bhf Friedrichstraße.

**Friedrichstadtpalast** and **Das Ei** (Friedrichstraße 107, for tickets Tel. 23-26-24-74, Fax 2-82-39-97, for information Tel. 23-26-22-03, for Fax-back 2-82-45-78). The "palace" five minutes down Friedrichstraße from the rebuilt Friedrichstraße Regional Train Station offers Europe's largest revue theater. You can enjoy 80-dancer extravagant revues, sometimes with international performers. Since February 1999, the audience has been enjoying *Elements*, the revue for the turning of the millennium. The "Egg" has small revues. Two minutes from U-Bhf Oranienburger Tor, or use bus 147, bus 157, or streetcar 1 or 50.

**Komische Oper** (Behrenstraße 55-57, Tel. 47-02-10-00, *http://komis-cheoper.line.de*) does not mean comic. It is Berlin's music theater, presenting classics. On Behrenstraße, which runs parallel to Unter den Linden, the

Komische Oper was originally the 1891-92 Metropol-Theater. Rebuilt in 1964-66, it still gives you a taste of the original ambience and is worth visiting for this reason alone. It presents a proven mixture of music and German-language theater. Use U-Bhf Französische Straße or S-Bhf Unter den Linden. **Maxim-Gorki-Theater** (Am Festungsgraben 2, Tel. 20-22-11-29), in the former building of the *Singakademie* designed by Karl Theodor Ottmer and built between 1825 and 1827, presents an excellent program of contemporary and classical drama including premieres in the German language. Use S- or U-Bhf Friedrichstraße. The entrance to the Gorki Studio is behind the Gießhaus. Use U- or S-Bhf Friedrichstraße.

**Volksbühne** (Am Rosa-Luxemburg-Platz, Tel. 24-77-694, Fax 30-87-46-42) is a must for theater fans. It presents a complete program of louder and shriller theater ranging from intense drama to classics to music. In addition to the main stage there are three small stages: *Roter Salon, Grüner Salon, and "3. Stock."* Use U-Bhf Rosa-Luxemburg-Platz.

**Podewil** (Klosterstraße 68/70, Tel. 247-49-777 or 247-49-6) presents theater, dance, concerts, literature; interdisciplinary projects with international and Berlin artists. Housed in the Podewilsches Palais, built in 1701-04, formerly the *Haus der jungen Talente.* During the summer it provides 500 seats for open-air movies next to the cloister ruins. Are you interested in a vampire film festival? Use U- or S-Bhf Alexanderplatz or U-Bhf Klosterstraße.

**Concerts in the Berliner Dom** (ticket office at doorway 9, Berliner Dom, Lustgarten side, Tel. 202-69-136). Evening organ and choral concerts. Use bus 100 or S-Bhf Hackescher Markt.

## CONTEMPORARY

Visit the Hackesche Höfe for the Sophienclub (jazz), the Chämeleon (varieté), and the Hoftheater's Klezmer.

**Sophienclub**, Sophienstraße 6, Tel. 282-45-52 (open 10 P.M. to 5 A.M.). Jazz, Brazil, House, Soul, Funk, Reggae, Techno. Billiards from 2 P.M. Use U-Weinmeisterstraße.

**Chämäleon** Varieté, Rosenthaler Straße 40, Tel 282-7118 (Tue.-Sun., 8:30 P.M.), provides diverse entertainment spoofing nostalgia: satirical, slapstick, juggling, acrobatic, and crazy, in a 1930s ballroom that was used by German television for a test studio. Midnight performances on Fri.-Sat.

In the Hackeschen Höfe you also can visit several theaters, including **Hackesches Hoftheater**, Tel. 283-25-87, which after sundown is a number-one location for pantomime theater and Yiddish music, and **PantoMime Theater** and hoist a brew at the **Irish Pub**. Use S-Bahn Hackescher Markt.

**Tränenpalast**, "Palace of Tears," Reichstagufer 17, Tel. 238-62-11, Top popular artists make their one night stands here in the steel/glass former DDR Checkpoint Hall where friends said good-bye to loved ones crossing the East/West border. Use U- or S-Bhf Friedrichstraße. Salsa fever rages Saturday nights in Club Chango. In addition to New York Salsa, dance to Cuban music, son and mambo.

**E-Werk**, for "electrical," Wilhelmstraße 43, Tel. 252-20-12. Bad news for those who haven't yet heard in Knoxville or Nagasaki or Perth: the world-famous E-Werk is dead. There was a three-day mega-party in July 1997 to mark its closing. It was Berlin's largest and most innovative Techno palace, the temple for Techno and Jungle in Mitte. Music hit first your stomach and then your ears. After renovation there are concerts and events and even a little dance floor for tourists. Use U-Bhf Französische Straße, opposite the Luftfahrsministerium building.

## BALLROOMS

There is an institution from pre-War times which continued to flourish during DDR times: *Ballhäuser,* or ballrooms which cater to those from 18 to 80. Ballrooms are not discotheques. They have full-fledged orchestras and traditional dancing. They are part of the Kiez atmosphere, for lonely hearts. Berliners say, "One goes in single, comes out double." Men must wear ties; they may be drunk, but as long as they are orderly and wear ties they can get in. Ladies are admitted free. On certain nights it is the custom for ladies to ask the men to dance.

**Clörchens Ballhaus** ("Little Clair's Ballroom"), Auguststraße 24-25, Tel. 282-92-95 (open from 7:30 P.M.). Everyone's here from elderly ladies of the night to the underworld. Use S-Bhf Hackescher Markt.

**Altdeutsches Ballhaus**, Ackerstraße 144, Tel. 282-6819, is open Sun., Mon., Tue., and Fri. from 7 P.M. to 1 A.M.; Sat. to 3 A.M. Use U-Bhf Rosenthaler Platz.

**Ballhaus Berlin,** Chausseestraße 102, Tel. 282-75-75 (open Tue.-Fri. from 9 P.M., Sat. from 8 P.M.), has telephones for table-to-table telephonic flirting and a grill for snacks. Thursdays are ladies' choice. Use U-Bhf Zinnowitzer Straße.

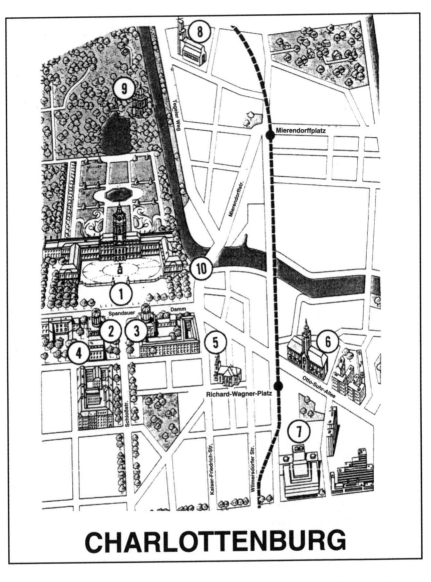

# CHARLOTTENBURG

1. Charlottenburg Palace
2. Berggrün Collection
3. Egyptian Museum
4. Bröhan Museum
5. Luisen Church
6. Charlottenburg Town Hall
7. Deutsche Oper
8. Gustav-Adolf-Church
9. Belvedere
10. Ship Landing

# 5

# Charlottenburg

## 1. Orientation

One of Berlin's finer districts, Charlottenburg was incorporated into Greater Berlin in 1920. At the time there were 340,000 inhabitants. Now there are about 180,000. The district is one of Berlin's largest, stretching west from the Tiergarten to Spandau, including Charlottenburg Palace, top museums, good theaters, and the German Opera. One of the streets, Kantstraße, is well known as a shopping paradise for Poles.

In 1705, Elector Friedrich III of Brandenburg, who became King Friedrich I in Prussia (the imperial law of the German Empire forbade the princes from assuming royal titles, but when the emperor bargained this right for the use of Friedrich's crack soldiers, Friedrich was crowned king in Prussia at Königsberg in 1701), changed the name of the village of Lietzow to Charlottenburg after his brilliant young wife, who had died that year at age 31 from a throat ailment. Further, he incorporated the small settlement he had set up for his senior court officials in the neighborhood of her former summer residence, and named himself mayor. In the following 215 years the summer residence of Sophie Charlotte grew to a splendid palace and Charlottenburg grew not only into a large city, but also into the richest city in Prussia.

Parts of Charlottenburg were formerly called the "wet" triangle, not because of the number of bars around, but because the foundations of the houses lie below the water level and so these flats used to be very wet. Berlin Schnauze says that one could catch a herring in a mousetrap.

## 2. The Hotel Scene

Many of Charlottenburg's hotels are situated in the heart of town in the Kurfürstendamm, Savignyplatz, and Zoo train station neighborhoods (Chapter 3), but you may want to stay in Charlottenburg in the neighborhoods of the Charlottenburg Palace and the ICC.

Across from the ICC and next to the Central Bus Station is the **Hotel Ibis Berlin Messe** (**Messe** meaning "convention," Messedamm 10, Tel. 30-39-30, Fax 30-19-536), a simple hotel which is only convenient for conventions held in the ICC. US$66-103, single; US$77-103, double; breakfast buffet US$8 extra. In the U.S., Tel. 1-800-668-6835.

**Kanthotel** (Kantstraße 111, Tel. 32-30-26, Fax 324-09-52, *http://www.utell.com*) is a 110-bed hotel in a pedestrian mall not far from the ICC. No restaurant. US$127-38, single; US$138-49, double; breakfast buffet included. Weekend special: US$89, single; US$111 double. In the U.S., Tel. 1-800-225-3456 or Utell at 1-800-207-6900.

Not far from the ICC is the **Hotel Seehof am Lietzensee** (Lietzenseeufer 11, Tel. 320-02-0, Fax 320-02-251, *http://www.utell.com*), on the Lietzensee. US$128-206, single; US$161-261, double; breakfast buffet included. Weekend special: US$94, single; US$122, double. In the U.S., Tel. Utell at 800-207-6900.

## 3. Restaurants and Cafés

Many of Charlottenburg's restaurants are situated in the heart of town in the Kurfürstendamm, Savignyplatz, and Zoo train station neighborhoods (Chapter 3), but restaurants in the neighborhoods of the Charlottenburg Palace and the ICC also lie in this district.

**Funkturm-Restaurant**, Messedamm 22, Tel. 3038-2996 (open 11 A.M. to 11 P.M.), the walnut-paneled a la carte restaurant-in-the-sky in the Broadcasting Tower at 180 feet (55 meters), was restored in 1986. It boasts "heavenly" food. Come Fridays for the Funkturm buffet. Reservations advisable. Admission costs DM 3.

**Heinrich**, Sophie-Charlotten-Straße 88, Tel. 321-65-17 (open Sun.-Fri. noon to 1 A.M., Sat. from 4 P.M.), on the fourth floor of the house where the master of the sketchbook, *Pinselheinrich* ("Paintbrush Heinrich") Zille lived (see text). Very good German cuisine on a worthy menu. On warm summer evenings, tourists, tipplers, and artists sit outside and watch the sun go down.

Across from the main entrance to Charlottenburg Palace are several pleasant cafés. Outdoor tables below tall plane trees blend harmoniously with the multitude of trees standing in front of Charlottenburg Palace. These are good for a beer or coffee and perhaps a pair of Wurst, but it is not worthwhile getting too deep into the dinner menu.

Across the Spandauer Damm is the **Eosander Restaurant,** Tel. 342-30-37 (open Mon.-Sat. 9 A.M. to 1 A.M., Sunday to 11 P.M.) with German cooking. For breakfast across from the palace, it shares the same quarters with **Café Lenné,** Spandauer Damm 3-5.

**Kleine Orangerie**, Spandauer Damm 20, Tel. 322-20-21 (open summer 10 A.M. to 11 P.M., winter to 8 P.M.). Fortify yourself for your explorations of the palace and gardens with coffee and cake. Also across from the palace on Luisenplatz:

**Luisenbräu**, Luisenplatz 1, Tel. 341-93-88 (open 11 A.M. to 2 A.M.) has many tables for many tourists. It serves fresh home-brewed beer and sausages with a view of Charlottenburg Palace's patina and the brewer's copper.

**Samovar**, Luisenplatz 3, Tel. 341-41-54 (open noon-midnight) is a Russian restaurant with live music. In summer, there is a terrace.

**Alt-Luxemburg**, Windscheidstraße 31, Tel. 323-8730 (open Mon.-Sat. dinner only). Here's your usual Michelin star restaurant away from Berlin's bustle. Reservations required. Closest to S-Bhf Charlottenburg, use taxi.

**Chez Martial**, Otto-Suhr-Allee 144, Tel. 341-1033 (open from 6 P.M.). French restaurant, French wine. Reservations strongly recommended. Use U-Bhf Richard-Wagner-Platz.

**Theodor**, Theodor-Heuß-Platz 10, Tel. 302-57-70 (open 9 A.M. to midnight) is not expensive, yet you savor very good German-French-Austrian cooking and professional service. Or enjoy the opulent Sunday brunch. Better make reservations, it's always full. Use U-Bhf Theodor-Heuß-Platz.

# 4. Sightseeing

## CHARLOTTENBURG PALACE

The most beautiful baroque building in Berlin is the **Schloß Charlottenburg** ("Charlottenburg Palace"). In what is now West Berlin, its major historical structure began in 1695 as a small, summer house for Sophie Charlotte, wife of King Friedrich I. You may visit a highly regarded gallery of Romantic paintings as well as the historical living quarters of the royal family. Plan a long walk in the beautiful French landscape garden and the English garden laid out by Peter Josef Lenné behind the palace.

Friedrich, at the coaxing of Sophie Charlotte, commissioned architect Johann Arnold Nering to build a small summer residence in Lietzow, five miles (eight kilometers) from Berlin's old walls. Nering died before the house was completed, and the work was turned over to Andreas Schlüter (ca. 1660-1714), who was later superseded by his Swedish competitor Eosander von Göthe, Sophie Charlotte's favorite. A modest 11-window central building was completed in 1699 with a small formal French garden behind. From here it grew to what it is today, a palace.

The largest wing, the oldest that belongs to the central building, was built according to Nering's plans, but now it is called the Nering-Eosander building, because Eosander von Göthe added the projecting veranda in the center of the facade to support his 165-foot (65 meters) copper-plated dome which forms the signature of the palace. Von Göthe had spent a good deal of time in France, had studied there, and thus brought a certain French influence to all his Prussian buildings. Schlüter added two less ornate wings on each side to form a courtyard and provide living quarters for the royal retinue and servants.

The palace passed from Friedrich to a succession of different royal owners. Other parts were added in the following decades. Friedrich the Great used the palace for family occasions and lived on the second floor until his palace Sanssouci was built in Potsdam in 1747. Then he never set foot in Charlottenburg again. The expanded cream-colored facade has a length of 1,655 feet (505 meters).

On top of the palace you can see a weathercock. That is the statue *Fortuna*, the Goddess of Fortune, symbolizing the fickleness of luck. It was designed so that Sophie could move it from inside the palace. It is said that she used the cock to show her lovers from which way the wind was blowing (i.e., whether her husband was at home or not). *Fortuna* had the bad luck to be destroyed by a nearly direct hit during the Second World War, but was replaced by American Richard Scheibe.

The palace was severely damaged on November 23, 1943, by bomb strikes. Prussia's largest porcelain collection was destroyed. The palace was in ruins. After the War the authorities were undecided about what to do with the palace—should they rebuild it or tear it down? In 1950, the DDR blew up the Hohenzollern Berlin City Palace in the East. That decided it. Charlottenburg Palace *must* be rebuilt. It was a successful decision. Much of what you see today has been restored, inside and out. The original character of the interior was recreated by scavenging precious objects from other palaces.

Do not use S-Bhf Charlottenburg. Use bus 109 from Zoo station, or either U-Bhf Richard-Wagner-Platz (signs will direct you to the palace and museums) or, best, U-Bhf Sophie-Charlotte for a delightful walk up Schloßstraße, whose first residents were the only service at the palace— particularly servants from foreign countries. It is a pleasant gambol up a green boulevard with interesting buildings on both sides and Berlin's sharpest boule players tossing their metal balls into the sand of the median strip. Almost everyone stops before landmarked #67, a lovely neoclassical Gründerzeit house built for the owner of a brick yard in 1873-74. A look to the east at Schloßstraße 55, at the **Kunstamt Charlottenburg** ("Charlotten- burg Department of Art") in Villa Oppenheim shows the wood-and-paint collage/mural which is part of the Schloßstraße/Schustehruspark Artistic Area, created by Gerhard Andreas in 1980-82, and installed in this location in 1989. The tiny green house at Schustehrusstraße 13 with the unimposing facade dates from 1712, the time of Friedrich I, making it the oldest house in Charlottenburg. The interior of this Eosander-Modell-Haus was gorgeously restored in 1997. Along storefronts on Schloßstraße you find a dynamic series of paintings—a **Bilderzylus** showing scenes from Berlin's recent history. They were originally painted by young artists between 1980 and 1983, and they were restored in 1994 by schoolchildren from Pomerania and Silesia.

The former **Wohnhaus Heinrich Zille** ("Heinrich Zille's Residence"), nearby at Sophie-Charlotte-Straße 88, is where the artist, the chronicler of working-class Berlin, lived from 1892 until his death in 1929. Visit the restaurant on the fourth floor. Zille didn't find his savage style and earthy social criticism until near the turn of the century when he was already over 40. One of everyone's favorites is the 1899 cartoon showing a drunken Prussian soldier, spiked helmet awry, holding up a wall under a street lamp. During the First World War, many of his anti-war cartoons were banned.

The **equestrian statue** of the Great Elector in front of Charlottenburg Palace is the most important statue of German baroque. Friedrich Wilhelm's son, Elector Friedrich III, commissioned the statue by Andreas Schlüter, who cast it in one piece in 1697, to honor the founder of the State of Brandenburg and Prussia. The Great Elector is shown partly in Roman and partly in contemporary dress with a bronze breastplate and a flowing wig. On the marble base you can see four slaves in chains symbolizing the enemies overcome by the Great Elector. In 1943, the statue was packed away from its original site on the Lange Brücke outside the former City Palace (see Chapter 4) for safety, but on its return in 1946 the barge carrying it was in a collision and sank in Tegel Harbor. The statue was recovered in 1949, but because its former location had been in the East, it was placed in the courtyard in the West in 1952. It's still in the wrong location.

The **Königliche Wohnraüme** ("Royal Residence") (open Tue.-Fri. 9 A.M. to 5 P.M., Sat.-Sun. 10 A.M. to 5 P.M.; entrance DM 5; a combined ticket for all buildings and historical rooms costs DM 15). The historical rooms throughout the palace's interior have been restored to their original glitz and dazzle. A shuffle through the royal living and entertainment rooms with slippers provided over your shoes to protect the floors brings you three centuries of Berlin history. In the west end of the central building you admire the living quarters occupied by Friedrich I and Sophie Charlotte, including the Oak Gallery and the Chinese porcelain cabinet. In 1740-46, the **Neuer Flügel** ("New Wing"), with a concert hall, was built onto the east end of the palace by Georg von Knobelsdorff, forming a counterpart to the Orangerie. Here you visit the quarters where Friedrich Wilhelm II ("the Fat") passed the summers from 1788 and the living quarters of Friedrich the Great. The rococo, 140 foot (42 meters) long **Goldene Galerie** ("Golden Gallery") with green-gold decoration on the east is the architect's masterpiece. Throughout you see royal tapestries and fabrics, Chinese lacquer furniture, paintings, and porcelain.

The **Galerie der Romantik** ("Romantic Gallery") on the ground floor (open Tue.-Fri. 10 A.M. to 6 P.M., Sat.-Sun. from 11 A.M.; entrance DM 4, day ticket to all SMB museums including those across the street, DM 8) in the Knobelsdorff east wing contains a highly regarded collection of German and European Romanticism. The furniture, including rococo and Biedermeier, is not the original furniture, which was destroyed in the Second World War.

In the West Wing of the Langhans Building you find the **Museum für Vor- und Frühgeschichte** ("Museum of Pre- and Early History") (open Mon.-Thur. 10 A.M. to 6 P.M., Sat.-Sun. from 11 A.M., admission DM 4, day card for all SMB museums DM 8), in what was originally the **Schloßtheater** ("Palace Theater"). Heinrich Schliemann's collection of Trojan antiquities was decimated during the War, but the museum presents archaeological finds from the Berlin area from the Old Stone Age through the early Middle Ages. Arranged in chronological order, the displays begin with Paleolithic cave paintings and progress to the creation of the written language, the Iron Age, and early Germanic tribes to give it a range and diversity unequaled by any other museum of its kind.

Sophie Charlotte loved nature, so she immediately ordered the construction of a large baroque French-style **garden** laid out in 1697 by French landscape architect Siméon Godeau with clear, orderly, geometric forms surrounding an enchanting lake favored by swans. In the early 19th century it was mostly remodeled by Peter Josef Lenné into a very wild English-style garden. In the course of reconstruction following the Second World War, both styles have been restored.

Located in the park are the Schinkel pavilion, a belvedere teahouse, and Schinkel's mausoleum for Queen Luise. The present view from the bridge overlooking the lake back onto Charlottenburg Palace is breathtaking.

The **Neue-Pavillon** (open Tue.-Sun. 10 A.M. to 5 P.M.) at the end of the Knobelsdorff wing of the palace, east entrance to the gardens, was built in 1824-25 by master architect Schinkel for Friedrich Wilhelm III and his second wife, Princess Liegnitz, in the style of a Villa Reale Chiatamone near Naples, where the king had enjoyed a pleasant stay in 1822. It is a delightful little, charming summer house, a simple cube on two floors, with a fireplace in the corner of every room and lovely views over the river and palace gardens. It holds a collection of paintings, sculptures, furniture, and crafts of the early 19th-century Schinkel period along with paintings by Schinkel, Blechen, and Eduard Gärtner, the local artist who painted lifelike street scenes and striking panoramas of Berlin.

At the northern point of the park near the Spree, the **Belvedere** (open Tue.-Sun. 10 A.M. to 5 P.M.) contains a porcelain collection. It was built by Carl Gotthard Langhans in 1788 as a teahouse for Friedrich Wilhelm II.

On the west side of the park at the end of a line of firs you find Schinkel's second contribution to Charlottenburg Palace in the form of a small Doric temple with columns of Brandenburg granite. This **Mausoleum** (open Tue.-Sun. 10 A.M. to 5 P.M.) was built in 1810 by Friedrich Wilhelm III for the resting place of Queen Luise. Thirty years later her husband, Friedrich Wilhelm III, was laid here. Later burials include Prince Albrecht (1837-1906), Kaiser Wilhelm I (1797-1888) and his wife Augusta (1811-90). The building contains Christian Daniel Rauch's sculpture of reclining Queen Luise.

The **Orangerie** ("Hothouse") was built at the west end of the palace by Eosander von Göthe in 1709-12 to store the potted orange trees for the winter. During the reign of Friedrich Wilhelm II a small theater was built by Carl Gotthard Langhans in the west end of the Orangerie (1788-90). The Orangerie is now a coffee restaurant and a place for special exhibitions.

## CHARLOTTENBURG'S MUSEUM MILE

Across the Spandauer Damm from Charlottenburg, left and right on Schloßstraße, you find a dotting of museums. The Egyptian Museum has collections from the Prussian Cultural Heritage Foundation. Directly south of the Egyptian Museum at Schloßstraße 69 is the **Heimatmuseum Charlottenburg** ("Heimat" meaning where one lives; open Tue.-Fri. 10 A.M. to 5 P.M., Sun. from 11 A.M.; entrance free), with maps, photos, and models charting the development of Charlottenburg to the Weimar and Wartime periods. The Bröhan Museum and the Berggrün collection on display across the road are private. Across Sophie-Charlotte-Straße to the west of the palace is the Plaster Cast House. Reach them all by U-Bhf Richard-Wagner-Platz or U-Bhf Sophie-Charlotte-Platz or by bus 109, 121, 145, or 204.

The most important is the neoclassical **Ägyptisches Museum** ("Egyptian Museum"), Schloßstraße 70, Tel. 32-09-12-61 (open Mon.-Fri. 10 A.M. to 6 P.M., Sat.-Sun. from 11 A.M.; admission DM 8—day ticket valid in other museums), originally constructed in the 1850s by Schinkel's pupil August Stüler as barracks for the officers of the royal bodyguards. You can tell it by the array of sphinxes aligned in front. Among the turquoise hedgehogs, nibbling baboons, striped mice, and a monkey playing a harp, you see art classes sketching the illuminated, lovely bust of Nefertiti from tell el-Amarna on the Upper Nile. Berliners will tell you that she is the most beautiful woman in the city despite being 3,400 years old and having only one eye. She was unearthed in 1912 by a team of German archaeologists headed by Ludwig Borchardt. In adjacent rooms you see smaller likenesses of Nefertiti's husband, King Akhenaton, and their daughter, Princess Meritaton. The reconstructed Kalabasha Monumental Gate built for the Roman Emperor Augustus around 20 B.C. shows him as a pharaoh. It was given to the museum by the Egyptian government in 1973 after the flooding of the site by the Aswan High Dam.

Across the street, at Schloßstraße 1, Tel. 20-90-55-55, the **Berggrün Collection**, "Picasso and His Era" (open Tue.-Fri. 10 A.M. to 6 P.M., Sat.-Sun. from 11 A.M.; admission DM 8, including day ticket to SMB museums) opened in 1996 in the western *Stülerbau*, Stüler's second officers' barracks building. You can see more than 120 works from the collection of Werner Berggrün, including 72 by Picasso—paintings, sculptures, and drawings from his time of study in Madrid until late in his creative career. Cézanne is represented by two Provence landscapes and van Gogh by his *Autumn Garden*, which he painted while waiting for Gauguin's arrival. You can see Picasso's *Sitting Harlequin* for the first time in more than 70 years. A tape-recorded description is available to guide you through the exhibition in English, German, or French for DM 6. Bring your passport for deposit.

The **Bröhan-Museum**, Schloßstraße 1a, Tel. 321-4029 (open Tue.-Sun. 10 A.M. to 6 P.M., Thur. to 8 P.M.), opposite Charlottenburg Palace features about 1,600 Jugendstil ("Art Nouveau") and Art Deco paintings, sculptures, furniture, graphic designs, arts and crafts, and industrial designs from 1889 to 1939. They were given to Berlin in 1983 by Professor Karl-Heinz Bröhan, who started the collection, one of the finest of its kind in the world. Anyone interested in Jugendstil and Art Deco should not miss it.

The **Gipsformerei** ("Plaster Cast House"), Sophie-Charlotte-Straße

17-18, Tel. 3-21-70-11 (open Mon.-Fri. 10 A.M. to 6 P.M., Sat.-Sun. from 11 A.M.; admission DM 4, day card DM 8), is a branch of the Staatliche Museen Berlin. For museum visitors and scientists it is a treasure—and a valuable resource. Friedrich Wilhelm III and his Secretary of State von Humboldt created something unusual in 1830. You can buy plaster casts of some 7,000 ancient masterworks in the custody of the *Staatliche Museen zu Berlin*: small Egyptian sculptures, Roman reliefs, multifigure, 13-foot (4 meters) tall sculptures from Naples, death masks, busts (including Nefertiti), and statues—all true to the originals within a fraction of an inch.

## CHARLOTTENBURG GATE

The neo-Baroque **Charlottenburger Tor** ("Charlottenburg Gate") over the Landwehr Canal was the grand entrance to the city of Charlottenburg on what is now called the Straße des 17. Juni, for the date of the uprising in East Berlin (see Chapter 7) from the Tiergarten district of Berlin. In 1905, on the 200th anniversary of the death of Sophie Charlotte, the wealthy citizens of Charlottenburg hoped to flaunt their wealth and independence by creating a sandstone counterpoint to Berlin's Brandenburg Gate. The creation of Greater Berlin 15 years later robbed the gate of its original purpose.

On the left you see Friedrich I, the first king in (not "of," because he was not internationally recognized) Prussia who was crowned in 1701 in Königsburg (before his crowning he was Elector Friedrich III). On the right is his wife, Sophie Charlotte, showing the way directly to Charlottenburg Palace. The present gate is a smaller version of the original because Hitler's architect, Albert Speer, in 1937, had to reduce the thickness of the columns and the grandeur of the original to make room for his grand avenue, Charlottenburger Chaussee, that he was creating for the great east-west axis of Berlin and the route for Nazi victory parades. The street is now called Straße des 17. Juni for the 1953 workers' uprising in East Berlin.

The large, circular **Ernst-Reuter-Platz** was renamed for the first mayor of Berlin after the War, 1949-53. Mayor Reuter was the flame of hope for many Berliners during the hard times after the War and he is still remembered for his many famous speeches encouraging the Berliners during the dark days of the Berlin Airlift. Ernst-Reuter-Platz is surrounded by the flags of countries of the European community. These flags were installed here in 1988 when Berlin became the Cultural Capital of Europe for that year. Because Reuter did a lot for the development of West Berlin, a metal sculpture monument was dedicated to him with a flame 16 feet (five meters) high that burned until Berlin was reunited. The sculpture, pools, and fountains in the middle of the square are accessible through pedestrian tunnels connected under U-Bhf Ernst-Reuter-Platz. This intersection used to be called the **Knie** ("knee") for the way it breaks the junction between Bismarckstraße and Hardenburgstraße.

From Ernst Reuter Square you can appreciate the Nazi parade route from the Funkturm to the Red Rathaus. To celebrate Hitler's birthday in 1939, a set of new streetlights designed by Albert Speer were installed. They became a symbol for the entire Nazi episode. Speer took a traditional, classic form (two arms) and modified it with the latest technical development (neon bulbs), to create the world's first neon streetlights. The lights formed a strip of bright. After the parade, Hitler told his commanders-in-chief that he intended to go to war that year. The lights still stand, resistant even to Love Parades.

Around Ernst-Reuter-Platz you see buildings of the **Technische Universität** ("Technical University"). The Technical University was founded as the Technical High School of Charlottenburg. There are about 35,000 students. At Berlin's largest university, the Freie University in southwest Berlin (Chapter 10), there are about 60,000 students. Taken together in Berlin there are about 134,000 students, making it the largest university city in Germany.

Past Ernst Reuter Square, the branch to the right, Otto-Suhr-Allee, leads past the beautiful 1905 **Rathaus Charlottenburg** ("Charlottenburg Town Hall"), Otto-Suhr-Allee 96-102. Kaiser Wilhelm II on his way to Charlottenburg Palace always made a wide detour around the Jugendstil- ("Art Nouveau") and new Gothic town hall because its striking, imported Polish sandstone, 290-foot (88 meters) high tower angered him because it rose higher than his palace. It is the highest town hall bell tower in Berlin. In summer, falcons nest there and give birth to their young, but just like tourists, they fly away to Spain in the winter. Every district has its own town hall and the Charlottenburg residents wanted theirs to be the most impressive because they wanted to be independent so the city fathers of the richest city in Prussia hired architects Heinrich Reinhardt and Georg Süßenguth in 1898 to build a new city hall for the rapidly growing city. Charlottenburgers didn't like the Berlin mentality; they didn't like the Berlin dialect; and they didn't like to pay Berlin taxes. In 1920, they became Berliners. In 1998-99 their taxes and then some went to cleaning and restoring the city hall for US$1.4 million (DM 2.5 million).

Between Charlottenburg Town Hall and Palace you can make a detour to the south to see **Luisen-Kirche** ("Luisen Church"), Am Gierkeplatz. It comes from 1712-16, but the wooden-roofed building was remodeled from 1823 to 1826 according to the plans of Schinkel with a yellow tower in the

Biedermeier style. Life around Gierkeplatz is colorful and lively. The buildings have been sensibly modernized without destroying the feeling of the neighborhood.

**Charlottenburg train station** was not extensively rebuilt after the Second World War. The simple, red brick, station with bicycle parking places in front has only very primitive platforms. Inside you find only ticketing counters and a few lockers. On the corner is an Imbiß serving Schultheiss beer as well as take-away snacks.

Charlottenburg train station was a major train station at one time. Its construction confirmed the national recognition of Charlottenburg as an autonomous city and brought a building boom and population explosion. Now it is just a collection of partially covered platforms. Two are reserved for S-Bahn trains. Mainline trains don't stop here any longer, but two Regional Bahn (RB) lines (see Chapter 1) originate here. Charlottenburg station was used for British military trains during the Allied occupation.

## LIETZENSEE

At the upper end of Kantstraße you find **Lietzensee,** with its idyllic park divided into two by the street. Such a green oasis in the middle of the city exactly fits the Berliners' taste, and they take to rowboats for rent and the beautiful walking paths. It is one of the popular recreation areas in West Berlin.

## OLYMPIC STADIUM

The undistinguished **Olympia-Stadion** ("Olympic Stadium"), with the intertwined four rings, was erected in 1936 for the 11th Olympic Games. It seats 76,000 spectators for all sorts of events: soccer, National Football League exhibition games, Rolling Stones concerts, etc. It is enormous, covering 66 acres, and these large-scale events don't even intrude into the Olympic swimming pool and athletic areas. Use U-Bhf Olympiastadion.

The **Glockenturm** ("Bell Tower," open daily Apr.-Oct. 10 A.M. to 5:30 P.M.), which was reconstructed in 1962, contains a bell weighing seven tons, with the inscription "I call the youth of the world." The express elevator takes you to the 256-foot (78 meters) observation platform in 25 seconds. The view over the stadium, the nearby Waldbühne, and the Havel lake region is super. Nearby is Jesse-Owens-Straße, which was named for the athlete who won four gold medals in 1936 and so enraged Hitler that he stormed out of the stadium. A new roof over the southern gate was added in 1974. Use U-Bhf Olympia-Stadion.

A large apartment house, rather square, with colored balconies is the **Corbusier Haus,** constructed for the Third International Building Exhibition in 1957 according to plans by the famous French/Swiss architect. The building is 450 feet (135 meters) long, 17 stories high, and has 350 apartments. It is located at the turnoff from the main highway (Heerstraße) to the south of the stadium.

The **Georg-Kolbe-Museum,** Sensburger Allee, Tel. 304-21-44 (open Tue.-Sun. 10 A.M. to 5 P.M.; entrance DM 2.50), is the studio of sculptor Kolbe, who died in 1947. It is used as a museum for some 180 bronze figures and numerous drawings. Special exhibitions are held here. Use U-Bhf Theodor-Heuss-Platz or bus 149.

# INTERNATIONAL CONVENTION CENTER

In outer Charlottenburg between U-Bhf Kaiserdamm and U-Bhf Theodore-Heuss-Platz you find a visitors' complex of overwhelming proportions. Centered on the West Berlin broadcasting tower, you find the Deutschlandhalle, the Eisstadion, SFB, radio headquarters, Palais am Funkturm, the international bus station, and bigger than Godzilla, the enormous International Convention Center, which dominates everything else.

The **International Convention Centrum** (ICC), Messedamm 2, Tel. 3038-3049, Fax 3038-3032, opened in 1979, still remains Europe's largest convention center and one of the most modern in the world. For its construction, DM 250 million were budgeted, but in the end it was Berlin's most expensive post-War building to that time, costing DM 1 billion, and no wonder: the Convention Center and garage are 1,130 feet (315 meters) long, 280 feet (85 meters) wide, and 131 feet (40 meters) high. Its 80 convention areas in 26 halls accommodate 10,000 visitors at the same time. It will get bigger in 1999. No wonder that Berlin Schnauze calls it "Battlestar Galactica." About 800 conventions are held here every year. Use S-Bhf Westkreuz.

The French sculptor Jean Ipousteguy built in the forecourt his monumental work, *Ecbatane,* but you can see why Berlin Schnauze refers to it as "King Kong Using the Toilet."

Opposite the main entrance to the ICC grounds on Hammarskjöldplatz is the large building complex of SFB, **Senders Freies Berlin** ("Radio Free Berlin"), and a new transmission tower. In front of SFB's skyscraper is a nice piece of the Wall. On the backside of the Wall, facing SFB, an artist has drawn a cartoon showing the DDR's last head, Erich Honegger, pinning a note to a painted hole in the Wall: "Erich, last one out turns off the light." The maroon-colored, glazed brick building in the same block—it resembles a modern factory—is the **Haus der Rundfunk** ("Radio House"), the oldest broadcasting building in the world (1931).

Scratching for existence somewhere in the middle of the sprawling and ever-growing ICC buildings is the steel-girder **Funkturm** ("Broadcasting Tower"), one of Berliners' favorite structures, a copy of the Eiffel Tower in Paris. Known affectionately as **Langer Lulatsch** ("Bean Pole"), it has always been a little mascot of Berliners akin to the Empire State Building in New York. It was placed on the list of landmarked historic structures in 1958.

The Funkturm was erected in 1924 to the plans of Heinrich Straumer and was put into operation as a broadcasting tower for the Third German Broadcasting Exhibition in 1926. It rises 450 feet (138 meters) high in the midst of grounds where many important German fairs are held. In 1937, almost four million visited the exhibit—almost as many as lived in Berlin at that time. The panoramic platform, visited yearly by about a quarter-million people, is 413 feet (126 meters) high, which you reach by high-speed elevator (daily 10 A.M. to 11 P.M.; adult admission DM 6, child DM 3; Tel. 3038-1905). It gives you not-so-very-interesting views over the fairgrounds, Olympic Stadium, Avus, and Grunewald (see Chapter 11).

At night the Broadcasting Tower is illuminated by 52 floodlights. It acted as a lighthouse for the approach of Allied *Rosinen-Bomber* ("Raisin Bombers") during the Soviet blockade of the divided city.

At the foot, the **Deutsches Rundfunkmuseum** ("German Radio Transmission Museum") Hammarskjöldplatz 21 am Funkturm, Tel. 3-02-81-86 (open Wed.-Mon. 10 A.M. to 5 P.M.; adult admission DM 3, children DM 1.5), documents the tower's role in the history of radio technology, the first television picture broadcast in 1929, and the first television test in 1932. Access to the tower, the museum and the Funkturm Café is complicated because you must pass through the outer ICC arm circling them like an octopus. Use U-Bhf Kaiserdamm or (better) bus 109, 104, or 149.

**Theodor-Heuss-Platz** along the long east-west axis (here named Heerstraße) is called by Berliners the square of the thousand names because first it was named *Reichskanzlerplatz* ("Imperial Chancellor Square"), then *Adolf-Hitler-Platz*, then—for a few days—*Stalinplatz*, then again *Reichskanzlerplatz* and finally today, *Theodor-Heuss-Platz*. At the apex, an eternal flame burns for freedom, justice, and peace. The center area is graced with a curious, transparent 1995 fountain. The 50-foot (15 meters) obelisk by Hella Santarossa is a play of light, symbols and myths. With its many tales and blue reflections, it invites you to take a break during your walking tour.

Looking down the Kaiserdamm along the east-west axis to see the Red Rathaus, the Brandenburg Gate, and the Victory Column presents one of the most staggering perspectives in Berlin. The area between Theodor-Heuss-Platz, Spandauer Damm, Steuben- and Branitzer Platz is a conservative neighborhood known as **Westend**. Even at its formation in 1866, the area—a villa colony of prestige addresses—inherited a "Very British Touch of Class" because it was named after the classy London neighborhood. It was not merged into Charlottenburg until 1878.

Two actual **Cadillac automobiles** buried in concrete mark Rathenau-platz, the beginning/end point of Kurfürstendamm. Berlin artist Wolf Vostell's commentary for the 1987 Berlin anniversary expresses his dislike for concrete and automobiles. It is known as *The 24-hour Laughing Dance around the Golden Calf.* Graffiti scrawled on the side reads, "Money isn't everything," but costing DM 150,000, this commentary would look good in a rock café.

## 5. Sports

**Olympia-Schwimmstadion,** Olympischer Platz (east gate), Tel. 304-0676/78 (open. 7 A.M. to 7-8 P.M.). Swimming. Use U-Bhf Olympia-Stadion.

**Freibad Jungfernheide,** Jungfernheideweg 60, Tel. 380-5351 (open 8 A.M. to 7 P.M.). At Volkspark Jungfernheide (west side). Use U-Bhf Siemensdamm, bus 123.

**Deutschlandhalle**, Messedamm 26, the traditional venue for sporting events such as the International Horse Show in November and the six-day bicycle race in October is closed. It is estimated it would cost US$ 4.2 million (DM 7.5 million) a year and three months to reopen it. Use U-Bhf Westkreuz.

**Eissporthalle** ("Ice Stadium"), next to the ICC on Jaffee Straße, Tel. 30-38-4223 (open Mon. 7:30 to 9:45 P.M. for ice disco, Tue. noon to 1:30 P.M. for senior skating). Use U-Bhf Westkreuz.

**Kunsteisbahn des Berliner Schlittschuh-Clubs** ("Artificial Ice of the Berlin Skating Club"), Glockenturmstraße 21, Tel. 305-50-20. Use bus 218.

**Sporthalle Charlottenburg,** Sömmeringstraße 9, Tel. 783-2732. Use S-Bhf Charlottenburg.

**Stadtbad Charlottenburg** includes two arenas for swimming: the **Neue Halle,** Krumme Straße 9, Tel. 34-30-324 (open Mon.-Tue. 2 to 9 P.M., Wed. to 6 P.M., Thur. to 5 P.M., Fri.-Sat. 7 A.M. to 4 P.M.; Sun. 8:30 A.M. to 1 P.M.), and the **Alte Halle,** Krumme Straße 10, Tel. 34-30-3214 (open Mon. 7 A.M. to 3 P.M., Tue. 7 to 10 A.M. and 3 to 6 P.M., Wed. 11 A.M. to 7:30 P.M.; Thur. 7 A.M. to 2 P.M. and 6 to 9 P.M.; Fri. 7 A.M. to 2 P.M. and 4 to 6 P.M.; Sat. 7 A.M. to 4 P.M.). Use U-Bhf Deutsche Oper or U-Bhf Richard-Wagner-Platz.

# 6. Shopping

Always wanted a true copy of a small Egyptian sculpture, Roman relief, multifigure, 13-foot (4 meters) tall sculpture from Naples, death mask, bust (including Nefertiti), or statue? You can buy plaster casts of some 7,000 ancient masterworks at Charlottenburg's **Gipsformerei** ("Plaster Cast House"), Sophie-Charlotte-Straße 17-18.

**Zille Hof,** Kastanienalle 43 (open Mon.-Fri. 8:30 A.M. to 5:30 P.M., Sat. to 1 P.M.) is a charming secondhand shop named after Heinrich Zille, who was famous for characterizing social life during the first third of this century. You can find everything from kitsch to antique.

**Kiepert** book store on Ernst-Reuter-Platz caters to the Technical University students. You will probably find what you need.

**Russiche Samoware**, Marburger Straße 6, Tel. 211-36-66 (open Mon.-Fri. 10 A.M. to 6:30 P.M., Sat. to 2 P.M.). It sparkles and shines as far as the eye can see: brightly polished silver, brass copper.... Heinz Amann's store is stuffed with samovars dating back to the czars. Don't miss the other precious antiques.

**Nobelmarkt**, Preußenallee (open Tue. and Fri. 8 A.M. to 1 P.M.), is Charlottenburg's weekly market where you will pay a few Marks more. You get what you pay for. Use U-Bhf Neu-Westend.

# 7. Nightlife and Entertainment

**Deutsche Oper Berlin**, Bismarckstraße 35, Tel. 341-02-49. Opened in 1912 as the *Deutsches Opernhaus,* for the opera-hungry crowds who couldn't get into the State Opera on Unter den Linden, Bruno Walter was director. It was destroyed by bombs in 1943, rebuilt and reopened in 1961 as one of Berlin's three opera houses. The site presents classical and modern opera, ballet, and international concerts. Use U-Bhf Deutsche Oper.

**Schiller-Theater**, Bismarckstraße 110, Tel. 31-11-31-11. Wolfgang Bocksch, who has been the owner since 1997, imports Broadway's most popular shows. More than a million Berlin fans have come to the Schiller Theater to be entertained by the American musical. The 1100-seat, 1951 house belongs to the city of Berlin. Use U-Bhf Ernst-Reuter-Platz.

**Tribüne**, Otto-Suhr-Allee 18, Tel. 3-41-26-00, Fax 3-41-16-86, built in 1914-5 from plans by Emilie Winkelmann for a boarding school, it was the first theater to open after the Second World War. During renovations in 1982, the front section of the building was added. Presenting contemporary pieces, social comedy and musicals, some are in Berlin dialect. Use U-Bhf Ernst-Reuter-Platz.

228 MAVERICK GUIDE TO BERLIN

The **Waldbühne** ("Woodland Stage"), Am Glockenturm, Tel. 23-08-82-30, may be the finest open-air theater in Europe. It is the biggest show in town. During the summer months you can be among the 22,000 fans each evening to the semicircular Greek outdoor amphitheater to enjoy classical and rock music events and open-air movies. Close to Olympic Stadium, it was built at the same time as the stadium in 1936 by Werner March. At a Rolling Stones concert in the 1960s the amphitheater was badly ravaged. Use U-Bhf Olympia-Stadion (Ost), S-Bhf Olypiastadion, or bus 218.

# 6

# Tiergarten

## 1. Orientation

The Tiergarten wasn't created from an existing village like so many other Berlin districts. It was incorporated into Berlin in 1861. It is Berlin's sixth smallest district, 5.4 square miles (1,341 hectares), and one of the least populated, 93,000, because it comprises primarily the Tiergarten Park on the Spree River, making it one of Berlin's greenest, most beautiful, and most centrally located recreational districts. Nevertheless it contains one of Berlin's prime attractions, the Reichstag building, and West Berlin's artistic center, the Cultural Forum. On the east, visitors seek memories of the Wall.

Tiergarten Park itself contains many important attractions such as the new Chancellor's Office, the Federal Court, and the Reichstag, which are respectively, the executive, the judicial, and the legislative buildings of the new Berlin metropolis. The Victory Column marks the **Großer Stern**, the center of Tiergarten Park, with avenues leading in every direction, one along a route earmarked for the victory parades of the Third Reich by Hitler's architect, Albert Speer. Tiergarten offers a pier for boat departures on the Spree River. On the southern edge, you come across the Cultural Forum, with modern, controversial architecture.

## 2. The Hotel Scene

Hotels in the Tiergarten that are part of the Heart of the City (Chapter 3) are listed there. Many hotels in Mitte (Chapter 4) are not far from the Reichstag, the must-see prize in Tiergarten.

**Grand Hotel Esplanade** (Lützowufer 15, Tel. 254-78-0, Fax 265-11-71), opened in 1988, is one of Berlin's deluxe hotels: very elegant, very modern, very expensive. It is a handsome, chic hotel with a steel and glass courtyard right across the Landwehr Canal from the Bauhaus Archives, but too far from the Europa Center to be considered central. It has a Harry's Bar and the feeling of a resort hotel; facilities are excellent and service is faultless, but at the same time it seems remote from the excitement of Berlin. US$211-67, single; US$239-94, double; US$16, breakfast buffet. In the U.S., call Utell International, Tel. 800-448-8355, or Leading Hotels, Tel. 800-223-6800. Use Bus 100. The original Hotel Esplanade is being restored as part of the Sony Center, Potsdamer Platz (Chapter 4).

**Sorat Hotel Spree-Bogen Berlin** (Alt-Moabit 99, Tel. 030-399-20-0, Fax 030-399-20-999) lies north of the Spree River with the Tiergarten Park on the south. This hotel, located on the site of a traditional dairy factory next to the new location of the federal interior ministry, has a jetty on the River Spree. US$117-67, single; US$156-206, double; breakfast buffet included.

## 3. Restaurants and Cafés

**Caféteria am Bauhaus Archiv**, Klingelhöferstraße 14, Tel. 262-57-00 (open Wed.-Mon. 10 A.M. to 6 P.M.), has some of the best cakes in Berlin with simple dishes for lunch. Use bus 100.

**Caféteria der Staatsbibliothek**, Potsdamer Straße 33 (open 10 A.M. to 7 P.M.). A cup of coffee speeds the research.

**Schwangere Auster** ("Pregnant Oyster"), John-Foster-Dulles-Allee, Tel. 394-23-77, Fax 39-78-32-23 (open in summer 10 A.M. to 10 P.M., in winter to 8 P.M.), in the Haus der Kulturen der Welt sits above the Spree boat landings, which may well bring you here. When you come, allow extra time to enjoy the café's wonderful terrace directly overlooking the Spree River and the good, but overpriced, Wiener Schnitzel and Italian specialties. Use bus 100.

**Café am Neuen See**, Lichtensteinallee 1, Tel. 254-49-30 (open Feb.-Oct. 9 A.M. to midnight daily; Nov.-Jan. 10 A.M. to 10 P.M. on Sat.-Sun. only). Relax in summer under the tall trees of the Tiergarten; in winter, ice skate. Serve yourself in the beer garden, but cheerful table waiters and waitresses serve you your choices from a limited menu. It is one of Berliners' favorite locations only a few minutes by foot from Zoo train station.

# 4. Sightseeing

## REICHSTAG

The building called the **Reichstag** ("Reich's Parliament") has a history reflecting all of the violence and agony of modern Berlin. Now that Berlin is the seat of the German government and the post-War German parliament (*Bundestag*) is taking occupancy, should the building be renamed Bundestag or should Berlin have the Bundestag in the Reichstag building?

The history of the unified German nation-state begins on January 18, 1871, when in a ceremony in the Hall of Mirrors at Versailles, King Wilhelm I of Prussia was proclaimed Kaiser of the German Reich. Only a few weeks later, on March 21, the newly elected Reichstag met in Berlin and decided to build for themselves a magnificent parliament house in Berlin. The Reichstag building was built between 1884 and 1894 in Italian Renaissance as the seat of the German parliament. On November 9, 1918, following the resignation of the chancellor, Prince Max of Baden, the Social Democrat Phillipp Scheidemann dashed to the window of the Reichstag overlooking Königsplatz and without consulting his comrades proclaimed Germany's first republic, the Weimar Republic, to the gathered throng below.

On January 30, 1933, Hitler took power as the legally elected German chancellor, and then, 27 days later, on the night of February 27, the Reichstag burned. A half-witted Dutch Communist named Marinus van der Lubbe was arrested, found guilty, and decapitated. Whether or not van der Lubbe was solely responsible or whether the arson was committed by a small band of Nazi storm troopers, on the next day, Hitler produced a presidential decree imposing "restrictions on personal liberty, on the right of free expression and opinion, including freedom of the press; on the rights of assembly and association." He broke up all political parties (excepting his own) and arrested their leaders. On March 23, at the Kroll Opera House, the so-called Enabling Act was passed and Germany became a dictatorship. The Reichstag was not restored. Hitler ran the country. The building remained a burned-out ruin. It was heavily damaged during the Second World War. Beginning in fall 1944, Americans and British bombed Berlin day and night to force a surrender.

From April 21 to May 3, 1945, Berlin was a battlefield. Everything above ground was leveled. The subway tunnels were flooded. Some 120 of Berlin's 258 bridges were destroyed. The Russian Red Army arrived under the command of Generals Zhukov and Koniev and on the square before the Reichstag set up their artillery and began, with tanks, the last battle for Berlin on April 29. At 10:50 P.M., on April 30, with the Reichstag taken by soldiers of the Red Army, the hoisting of the Soviet flag on one of the

Reichstag's corner towers marked the end of the battle for Berlin. The War was over.

The building was almost not even there after the fire of 1933, the bombings, and finally the battle with the Russians. It remained a ruin until the beginning of the 1960s. Then the West German parliament decided to rebuild the Reichstag at a cost of DM 110 million as a symbol of the wish to reunite Germany, and to have a parliament here for all of Germany, but to save money they didn't rebuild it for permanent use as a parliamentary building and didn't replace its huge dome.

The Reichstag is a monumental stone edifice, its roof-line abundant with statuary, a heavy square turret at each corner, originally with a neo-Baroque squared dome, and an imposing pediment supported by six Corinthian columns. Before 1918, the words *dem Deutschen Volke* ("To the German People") were not inscribed over the north entrance. The Reichstag was a democratic facade for a militarist autocracy ruled by the king of Prussia, who was also emperor. It was a debating society. The throne had the power—by divine right. In 1914, German parliamentarians voted for the kaiser's war loans and for World War I. In 1918 there was a power struggle between the ineffective, puppet parliament and the powerful German kaiser, Wilhelm II. He abdicated and the first republic took power in 1918. When the Reichstag really became a parliament for Germany, the words were inscribed.

Left of the entrance in the mural is a man with a beard. After him comes water. On the right is a naked woman, also with water. A hundred years ago, one prophesied today's German boundaries. The man is the Rhine River; the woman is the Oder River—the two important north-south rivers of Germany. Father Rhine is the boundary with France; Mother Oder is the boundary with Poland.

The original 1894 dome that Berlin Schnauze called "Pickelhaube" (Prussian spiked helmet) withstood both the Hitler-inspired burning in 1933 and the final battle for Berlin, but the rusting steel of the dome was blown up in 1954 (after two attempts), hauled to the scrap yard, and replaced with a rather undistinguished dome.

After an international competition to rebuild the Reichstag with modern comforts for a modern legislature, the German parliament selected the DM 1 billion design featuring a prominent, illuminated egg-shaped dome submitted by British architect, Sir Norman Foster. The new oval glass cupola is accessible by two 750-foot (230 meters) spiral ramps so visitors can view the chambers of the parliament below from a platform 130 feet (40 meters) high. The new circular, steel-and-glass dome, weighing 800 tons, with a 130 foot (40 meters) diameter, rises 75 feet (23 meters) above the building. The original steel, bronze, and glass dome weighed 370 tons and measured 100 feet (30 meters) by 118 feet (36 meters) at its base because it was not quite round. With lantern on top, it reached 243 feet (74 meters) high. During the reconstruction, workers discovered graffiti left on the walls of the Reichstag by Red Army soldiers in 1945.

The interior is dominated by a giant aluminum eagle 22.3 feet (6.80 meters) high and 27.8 feet (8.50 meters) wide copied from the 1953 one in the Bonn Bundestag but one-third larger. Berlin Schnauze refers to it as the "fette Henne" (fat hen).

Some 150 freshmen members from the 1998 German Bundestag election arrived in Berlin in November 1998. (The Bundestag is online at *http://www.bundestag.de.*) They met for the first time in the new building on April 19, 1999, and elected the new federal president in the Reichstag building on May 23, 1999. In autumn 1999, the Bundestag returns from its summer break and takes up residence and legislation in earnest in its new high-tech quarters. Take bus 100 to the Reichstag.

The **wrapping of the Reichstag** was one of the pleasantries of the decade. The Bulgarian-born New Yorker, Christo Javacheff, known as Christo, and his wife, Jeanne-Claude, received, after emotional debate with Chancellor Kohl in opposition, permission from the German parliament to surround the Reichstag building with plastic wrap, and did so. From June 17, through June 23, 1995, some 200 workmen, backed by 600 crowd controllers, coordinators, and caterers, enveloped the Reichstag building with $700 million worth, 807,000 square feet, of rough polypropylene cloth faintly coated with aluminum. The silvery-appearing and surprisingly revealing shroud was left in place for two weeks. During this time Berlin Hotels experienced a boom. The area around the stupendous tent was open 24 hours with no admission charge. Visitors approached the wrapping and touched the fabric and the blue polypropylene ropes which secured it. Monitors circulated through the crowd with patches on their sleeves to indicate which languages they spoke.

## NEW GOVERNMENT QUARTER

Additional conference rooms and offices for parliamentary groups, committees, and members of the new parliament, as well as for the administrative apparatus of the German Bundestag are to be located near the Reichstag in the Alsen, Luisen, and Dorotheen blocks and in several renovated old buildings. Having learned their lessons from the past, designers of the Reichstag provided secure underground tunnels to and from the new presidential palace, chancellery, and Federal Council building.

234	MAVERICK GUIDE TO BERLIN

The future government and parliamentary quarter on the **Spreebogen** ("Bend of the Spree River"), with the Reichstag Building as its centerpiece, is called **Band des Bundes** linking East and West Berlin. Some 325 feet (100 meters) wide and one mile (1.5 kilometers) long, it stretches from Friedrichstraße train station in the East to Moabit in the West. The legislative quarter will be on the Eastern side of the Spreebogen and the executive quarter will be on the Western side. To the north of the Reichstag in the Spreebogen, the Paul Löbe Building (Alsenblock) will house offices for members of the Bundestag and for administrative staff. This ensemble of six-story buildings will not exceed Berlin's traditional maximum height of 72 feet (22 meters). In total, the complex will provide about 1,700 offices for members, committees, archives, visitors' services, and a restaurant. The complex will be extended from the Paul Löbe Building across the Spree. The last building to be built, on the opposite bank, the Marie Elisabeth Lüders Building (Luisenblock) will house the central parliamentary library, archives, and the research and reference services. With 1.2 million volumes and 11,000 periodicals, the public will not be welcome.

## BERLIN WALL

The instant the **Berlin Wall** began to rise across from the Reichstag, there was a last-minute flight of citizens determined to jump over the barbed-wire barricades, clamber over the walls a-forming, leap from still-open windows, and sprint through sewers and underground train tunnels. There was a frenzy of tunneling below street level. In all 80 people are known to have been killed. The last fatality occurred in February 1989, only a few months before the opening of the Wall.

August 13, 1961, was a Sunday. This was one reason why politicians in West Berlin, Bonn, and Washington were caught completely unawares when the East German government sealed off the Soviet sector of the city and erected street barricades and fortifications against West Berlin.

At 1 A.M., when most Berliners were sleeping, the DDR began building the Wall. At 1:30 A.M. S-Bahn and U-Bahn train connections were interrupted and 68 of the 80 road crossings were closed. Several hours passed before Berliners and the rest of the world learned of this nasty surprise on the radio and television and in newspaper extras.

The initial breeze blocks were replaced by heavy reinforced concrete sections, each of which was 11.7 feet (3.6 meters) high, 4 feet (1.2 meters) wide, 6 inches (15 centimeters) thick, and weighed 2.5 tons. The Wall was topped by a thick rounded cap that was later crowned with barbed wire.

On the opposite shore of the Spree from the Reichstag you can see a few remnants painted black and white. These are grim, but not very authentic and belong to the "kitsch" category because they were painted in 1990, after the Wende and demolition of most of the Wall. The Reichstag shore of the Spree belonged to West Berlin, the opposite shore to East Berlin (see Chapter 7 for more on the Wall).

In back of the trees, on the Straße des 17. Juni, a stone's throw westward from the Brandenburg Gate, you find the **Sowjetisches Ehrenmal** ("Soviet War Memorial"). It is clear why it was built here. Here was where the Second World War ended. Victory was achieved here and they immediately built a memorial to the 20 million Soviet victims of the Second World War. Until the end of 1990, an honor guard of the Red Army stood here day and night (guarded by British soldiers). It stood within West Berlin, but the property was like an embassy: extraterritorial. The Soviet guards have been withdrawn, but the burden of maintaining this Soviet memorial falls on Germany.

The two tanks on the marble pedestals are the first to have entered Berlin. The two cannons could tell an ironic story of the fate of war. They were produced by the German Krupp company and sold to the Soviets, who used them against Germany during World War II.

One report says that the Soviet government used the stone of the Reichstag to build the memorial, but this is not certain. Reichstag stone was, however, used to build the Soviet Memorial in East Berlin (Treptow).

In 1938, Hitler's armies marched into Austria. Was Austria a victim of Hitler or was Austria an ally? Many Austrians welcomed the annexation by Germany. Austrian soldiers fought side by side with Germans. A similar monument is built in Vienna.

## TIERGARTEN PARK

The **Tiergarten** ("Animal Garden"), the Central Park of Berlin, was until the 17th century, some 400 years ago, a bountiful hunting area in the west of Berlin for Berlin's electors and Prussia's kings. Thus its name—although in modern German "Tiergarten" is simply a synonym for "Zoo."

In 1833, Peter Josef Lenné (the same man who created Potsdam's gardens) transformed it into a 1.2-square-mile (3 square kilometers) green area, one of the most beautiful landscape gardens in Europe with numerous sculptures, the rose garden, and an English garden.

You don't see the War damage any longer, but almost all of the trees were chopped down after the War for firewood. In 1949, on only an eighth of the area, one million saplings were planted, most of which were presents from other German cities.

Because of this, Berliners have a regard out of all proportion for the

Tiergarten. Its significance transcends that of just a nice place with pretty trees to picnic. It signifies the city's rebirth.

Thus there is great criticism for the route chosen for Berlin's annual **Love Parade** which passes through the park. Some one million ravers, as these dancers are called, begin arriving on a Friday in the middle of July and at 2 P.M. on Saturday, one million people dance through the park. Berlin turns into a 341-square-mile pulsating disco. Some 50 flat-bed trucks covered to overflowing with gyrating ravers and equipped with speakers pounding out untold watts of energy, almost enough to blast the leaves off the trees, vibrate along the parkway.

The event says much about the tolerance of the Berliners. Try to think of another world city which would tolerate, no, *welcome* and encourage one million energized and unpredictable visitors. Calling on the English language, the transit authorities even issue special "No Limit Tickets" for DM 10 allowing ravers to ride anywhere for the 54-hour party. But the tickets aren't the usual paper stubs, they are fluorescent armbands that ravers take home as souvenirs of the event. See *http://www.bvg.de/love.htm.*

Many Berliners fear that the waste from one million ravers dancing through the park will destroy its ecosystem. They want to reroute the parade. Despite criticism that the parade is an ecological disaster, a political prank, an advertising stunt, or simply a reflection of the end of the techno movement, one forgets that one million people come to Berlin and have a great deal of fun. Berlin becomes "Rave City." The day after, the Tiergarten looks disgusting. You can walk the length of the parade route upon discarded aluminum beer and soft drink cans and empty brown bottles, but on Monday morning the Tiergarten and parade route have miraculously been returned to virgin condition by private contractors working in shifts.

The parade traces its roots to Detroit, Michigan, where techno music started in the '80s. The raves came to Berlin in 1990. It was a natural combination. For a right rave you need big, empty spaces. Techno music became hip by 1990. Drugs, especially Ecstasy, were readily available. The idea was to have a few hundred people gathered around trucks carrying nothing but sound machines. The police busted them. They caused traffic problems.

The rave promoters called it a political demonstration because political demonstrations are a tradition in Berlin. Authorities said they needed a political platform. "We have it! Love, peace, unity!" The tourist office seized its appeal to young visitors and helped promote it. Now it has grown to such a large institution that its popularity threatens to destroy it.

Berlin becomes one huge open-air disco. The parade begins at Ernst-Reuter-Platz (Charlottenburg) and proceeds along the Straße des 17. June past S-Bhf Tiergarten (where someone changes the signs to read S-Bhf

Ravegarten) around the Victory Monument on Großer Stern to the Brandenburg Gate where it turns around and goes back to the Victory Monument. Students fence in a raver-free zone in front of the Technical University. Authorities launch rescue boats on the Spree and Landwehr Canal to fish out wayward ravers. There is minimal drunkenness and little smoking, but the chemical laboratories must be working overtime. After the parade visitors flock to countless parties (you can stop counting at 130) such as *LoveInsel Galaktika* ("Love Island Galactica"), *No Ufos—the Metropolis of Tomorrow,* and *Metallheadz.*

Berliners expect a counter demonstration for every demonstration, so it is with a laugh that Berliners greet the **Hate Parade** which began in 1997. It starts at 3 P.M. at the bunker on Reinhardtstraße and winds its way through East Berlin to the Red City Hall. Only the music is harder (200 beats per minute vs. 130). Fascists and skinheads are not to be seen.

The Tiergarten has become one of Berlin's most popular recreation areas, especially on the weekends when the Turkish *Gastarbeiter* ("Guest workers") families like to meet here for barbecues ("under every tree, a fire") and sports and to use the children's playgrounds and enjoy the wonderful, green atmosphere. The park is literally filled with smoke.

**Großer Stern** ("Big Star") is the center of the Tiergarten, a traffic circle with streets radiating in six directions. In the center of the circle towers the striking **Siegessäule** ("Victory Column"), Tel. 391-29-61 (open Tue.-Sun. 9 A.M. to 5:30 P.M., Mon. from 1 P.M.) with Victoria, the Goddess of Victory, atop. Victoria is known to Berliners as "Golden Elsa," the heaviest lady in Berlin, 1,500 pounds. When it was erected, initially on the Königplatz, Berliners called it the *Siegesschornstein* ("Victory Chimney") and Victoria became known as the *Siegestante* ("Victory Auntie"), the most respectable woman in Berlin because she has no lovers.

The 222-foot (67 meters) column was built in 1873 to mark the Prussian victories over Denmark (in 1864), Austria (1866), and France (1870-71). There is a 157-foot-high (48 meters) observation platform, but you must climb a spiral staircase 285 steps for the view. Victoria on top is 26 feet (8 meters) tall. In 1938, Hitler's architect Albert Speer had it moved to its present location from the Königsplatz, today's Platz der Republik, directly in front of the Reichstag. Speer wanted to create a great east-west axis through the Tiergarten on which to hold victory parades crossing the whole city of Berlin and the Victory Monument was to be its centerpiece. (He didn't realize he was creating the route of the present-day *Love Parade.*) In 1945, when the Allies took Berlin, France wanted the Victory Column blown up because the column was cast from eight French cannons.

Ringing the Großer Stern are monuments of Prussian General Helmuth

# GROßER STERN

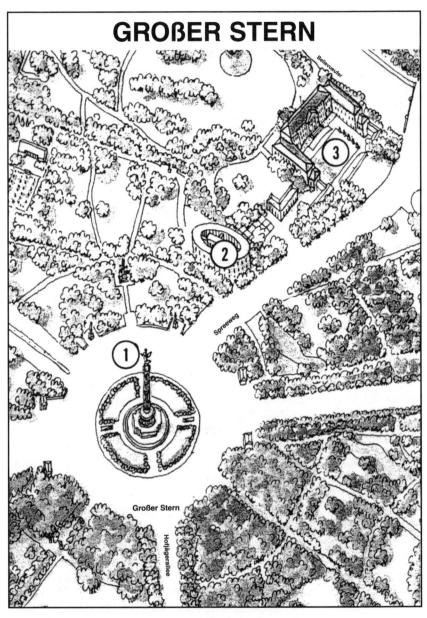

1. Victory Column
2. Bundespräsidialamt (Federal President's Staff Building)
3. Bellevue Palace (Federal President's Residence)

Moltke, Bismarck's war minister, Albrecht Roon, and—the largest—one of Germany's 500 monuments to the "Forger of the German Reich," Chancellor Otto von Bismarck, who took various kingdoms, duchies, principalities, and Hanseatic states and forged them together under Prussian rule in 1871. Over one million Marks were collected for the Bismarck memorial, which was also removed from around the Reichstag, in ruins at the time. Use bus 100 or bus 341.

The **Straße des 17. Juni** ("Street of the 17th of June") is the main highway through the Tiergarten connecting Unter den Linden at the Brandenburg Gate, running past the Victory Column, and entering Charlottenburg at the Charlottenburg Gate. It was named for the date of the workers uprising in East Berlin. It belongs to the east-west axis of Berlin laid out by Hitler's official city architect, Albert Speer, for military parades. The axis crosses all of Berlin under various names and is extremely straight without any curves, eight miles (12 kilometers) long from the shores of the Havel River to Alexanderplatz. It effectively aligns the Red Rathaus, the Brandenburg Gate, the Victory Column, Ernst-Reuter-Platz, and Theodor-Heuss-Platz.

Originally called Charlottenburger Chaussee, it is now unofficially called the Street of the 9th of November for the date of the opening of the Wall.

**Schloß Bellevue** ("Bellevue Palace"), Spreeweg, Tel. 390-84-0, was erected in neoclassical style by Philipp Baumann in 1785 as a "modest" birthday present from Friedrich the Great to his youngest brother, Prince Augustus-Ferdinand. Used by the Nazis as a guest house (Soviet Prime Minister Molotov was one of the first guests, in 1940), in 1954 the federal republic startled the Soviets by making it the official residence in Berlin of the federal president. In February 1994, the office of the federal president had the honor of being the first constitutional body to move to Berlin when the president's *principal* office was relocated here. To the south of the palace you can see the new building for the staff of the office of the federal president.

You can tell whether he is at home or not. If the flag flies, he is in Berlin. Tours of Langhans' 1791 oval hall inside the palace are by appointment only, but the park is accessible. Use bus 100, not S-Bhf Bellevue, which is not convenient to the palace.

On November 23, 1998, Federal President Roman Herzog and his staff began moving into the building between Bellevue Palace and the Großer Stern that is something of a joke in Berlin. It is known as the "President's Egg." In fact, the four-story building is oval, but Berlin Schnauze labels it an "egg" because of the German-language word play on its official name:

**Bundespräsidialamt** ("Office of the Federal President"). The DM 94 million "Oval Office," as it is also called, provides 138 offices in 193,750 square feet (18,000 square meters) of working space for the 150-member staff of the federal president and access via a vine-covered latticework tunnel to the Bellevue Palace.

The former *Kongreßhalle* ("Congress Hall"), John-Foster-Dulles-Allee 4, Tel. 39-78-70 (open Tue.-Sun. 8 A.M. to 6 P.M.), now known as **Haus der Kulturen der Welt** ("House of World Cultures"), was opened in September 1957 after only 14 months' construction as an American contribution to the Third International Building Exhibition in Berlin. Because of its avant-garde 1950s architecture, Berlin Schnauze immediately dubbed it, "the Pregnant Oyster," but it looks for all the world like the smile of President Jimmy Carter. In 1980 part of the roof caved in, killing one man. After its restoration it is being well used as a forum for non-European cultures: African, Asiatic, and South American.

The decorative pool in front of the building features a Henry Moore bronze called "Madame Butterfly" by Berliners. The water is pumped directly from the nearby Spree River to save money—and because the Spree is packed with algae, it causes major clean-up problems. Yearly, over 2.6 million gallons (10,000 cubic meters) run through pipes into the pool. After 1979, the larger and better equipped ICC (see Chapter 5) became the site of most conventions. Use bus 100.

Wandering through Tiergarten Park, you might hear the chiming of bells floating from the shiny, black Norwegian Labrador granite, 138-foot (42 meters) **carillon** tower overlooking the former Congress Hall. It chimed for the first time in October 1987, on the occasion of Berlin's 750th anniversary, a gift from a major automobile company to Berlin. You can guess which company it is when you hear the Berlin Schnauze nicknames: "Big Benz" and "Notre Daimler." Having cost DM 4 million, of which Daimler-Benz paid DM 1.5 million, it's a marvel it does not have a Mercedes star atop.

Carillons originated in Flanders. The Great Elector, Friedrich Wilhelm I, heard such music for the first time in the Netherlands in the 17th century. With his wife, Luise Henriette, a Dutch princess from the House of Orange, he introduced this music to Brandenburg. His son, the later Prussian King Friedrich I, commissioned the architect of baroque, Andreas Schlüter, to develop a carillon tower in Berlin at the beginning of the 18th century. Difficulties however forced installation of the first carillon in the tower of the Parochial Church, which was damaged during the Second World War.

Now there are three carillons in Berlin. The other two are in East Berlin (see Chapter 4). The one in the Nikolai Church has 21 bells and the one in the French Church has 60 bells. With 68 bells (which were cast in the Netherlands), the Tiergarten carillon has an unusually wide range of five and a half octaves. It is the largest and heaviest (48 tons) in Europe; the fourth largest in the world.

During the summer months the American carillonneur, Jeffery A. Bossin, gives regular concerts, playing by hand and foot from a keyboard and special pedals. The carillon sounds regularly at noon and 6 P.M., controlled by computer.

In back of the trees, the area between the carillon and the Spree, fronting on Große Querallee and facing the Reichstag building across the green lawns of the Platz der Republic in a fashion similar to the mall in Washington, D.C., is the new home of the German **Bundesrat** ("Federal Court"). It has replaced the **Tempodrom,** which was a mammoth tent used for rock concerts. Rock concerts had been totally appropriate because the name of the side street, "In den Zelten" (*Zelt* meaning "tent"), came from the days when tented booths and beer gardens catered to park visitors.

Along the northwestern edge of the Tiergarten Park, the **Hansaviertel** ("Hansa Quarter") is a planned community of single family dwellings and apartment houses interesting for its modern architecture. A residential area from before the turn of the century, it was almost completely destroyed during the War. It was the first area rebuilt after the War within the context of the 1957 International Building Exposition (IBA) held in Berlin. The Berlin Senate invited and approved proposals from 50 architects, including Finland's Alvar Aalto, Germany's Walter Gropius, and France's Le Corbusier. Each architect designed a different building. Now about half of West Berlin's buildings have been built since the War.

The Hansa Quarter contains, among other buildings, the Akademy of Arts, the children's and young people's **Grips Theater,** the Lutheran Kaiser-Friedrich-Gedächtniskirche, and the Catholic St. Ansgar-Kirche.

One building you probably wouldn't pay attention to—except that it catches your eye on the north side of the S-Bahn line—is the blue building with a pink tube. You would hardly guess that it is one of the most important research centers in Berlin, the **Institut für Wasser und Shiffbau** ("Institute of Water and Shipbuilding" or "Institute for Hydraulic Engineering"). It is open to visitors on Saturdays and Sundays.

## BAUHAUS ARCHIVES

Once you have walked down the corkscrew ramp and passed through the door inside, you feel like the whole thing is about to cast off, ferrying you along with the Feiningers and Kandinskys down the Landwehr Canal for a class in architectural design. The **Bauhaus Archiv,** Klingelhöferstraße 13-14, Tel. 254-00-20 (open Wed.-Mon. 11 A.M. to 5 P.M., Fridays until 8 P.M.; entrance DM 3.50) is a treat for anyone interested in design. It contains collections from the history of the Bauhaus in Weimar and Dessau.

The Bauhaus School of Design was founded in Weimar in 1919 when republican authorities summoned Walter Gropius from Berlin to take charge of an art academy and an arts and crafts school. He started by giving the institution a new name: the Bauhaus. Although the Bauhaus itself was located in Weimar, Gropius and his associates, Miës van der Rohe and Eric Mendelsohn, carried out most of their work in their Berlin studios. Because of local hostility Bauhaus moved to Dessau in 1925, where it was closed by the Nazis in 1932. It tried to reopen in Berlin but closed permanently in 1933. Wassily Kandinsky and Paul Klee (see *www.artchive.com*) taught in Dessau during Berlin's Golden Years in the 1920s.

The Bauhaus Archiv was built in 1976-78 after Gropius' death in 1969 based on his design. It is surprising to see that furniture, tube chairs, tapestry, and designs still modern were being sketched and built some 70 years ago. There are paintings by Kandinsky and Klee and interesting advertisements of the day. Disgracefully, vandals have defaced the Mediterranean white walls of the Bauhaus edifice with graffiti. The library and collection of documents is open Mon.-Fri. 9 A.M. to 1 P.M. Use bus 100.

## CULTURAL FORUM

A cluster of controversial modern buildings and a forlorn church stand, out of place, on the south edge of the Tiergarten Park on a site which had been earmarked by Hitler for a triumphal north-south axis from the Brandenburg Gate to a new complex of Fascist buildings. Flattened during the Second World War, it was selected as the perfect place for Germany's post-war architects to flex their creative muscles.

Poked into a corner of the Tiergarten where it would seem no one would notice, and snug against the hated DDR Wall, Berlin architects felt free to break away from Prussian (Schinkel) influence. Unfortunately they created an eyesore in this out-of-the-way pocket. Wessis hated it. *Voilà!* The Wall was torn down. The area became exposed. What was once a neglected corner became an open secret. The new buildings found themselves on a thoroughfare to the Potsdamer Platz construction site. Suddenly they didn't seem so horrible after all. Modern architecture that seemed to belong on Mars fit in nicely with the new buildings rising on Potsdamer Platz.

The Tiergarten seems an odd place for the two golden buildings of the Philharmonic Hall and the Chamber Music Hall. They stand near the

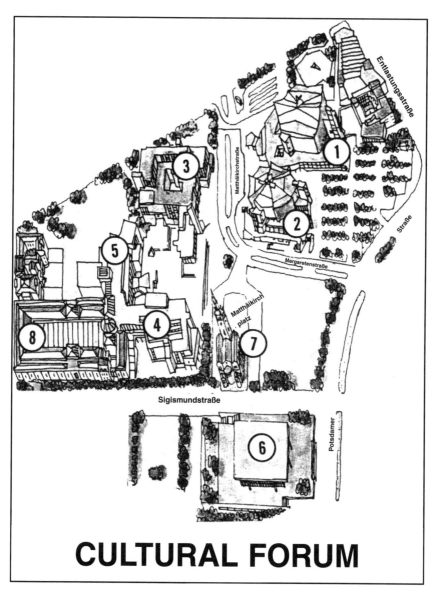

# CULTURAL FORUM

1. Philharmonie
2. Chamber Music Hall
3. Arts and Crafts Museum
4. Engravings Museum and
   Art Library
5. Paintings Gallery
6. New National Gallery
7. St. Mathias Church
8. Art Gallery

Engraving Museum/Art Library to the left, the Arts and Crafts Museum to the right, and the new Painting Gallery in the center. The New National Gallery is located just behind, to the south.

When architect Hans Scharoun died in 1972, he left behind him the conceptual plans he completed in 1959 for an imaginative cultural center in a quiet corner of the American sector of Berlin. Construction began ambitiously with the Philharmonic Hall, the National Gallery, and the National Library.

After Scharoun's death, a competition was held among his followers for a visionary area design. Winner Viennese Professor Hollein conceived a long, narrow canal along the National Gallery, the St. Mathias Church, and the already built Arts and Crafts Museum together with a so-called City Cloister, a four-story hotel, and a Bible museum. According to Hollein's plan, the St. Mathias Church, Cloister, Bible building, and Chamber Music Hall would surround the Philharmonic Hall to form a completed Cultural Forum. What this would have looked like, we will thankfully never know.

The large building that first insults your eye is the gold-colored **Philharmonie** ("Philharmonic Hall"), Matthäikirchstraße 1, Tel. 261-43-83, built between 1960 and 1963, home of the Berlin Philharmonic Orchestra. It has an asymmetric exterior with a tentlike concrete roof resembling a great wave from the sea that covers an unconventional interior in the shape of a Greek amphitheater seating 2,200. The podium is almost in the center of the hall so that the public sits in ascending, asymmetrical pentagonal terraces on nine levels surrounding the stage. The acoustics are near-perfect, not only for classical music, but also for popular music.

From 1954 to 1989, when he retired a few months before his death at age 82, Herbert von Karajan was artistic director of the Berlin Philharmonic, a highly successful recorder of classical music for the Deutsche Gramophone label, and the center of so much controversy that the press called this site "Karajan's Circus," ostensibly because of its asymmetrical tent-like roof. Karajan had been a favorite of Hitler. On one occasion he seated the audience in the shape of a swastika. Following renovation of the Philharmonic Hall, his successor in 1990, the Italian Claudio Abbado (the first non-German to assume the directorship), led the gala reopening ceremony of Arnold Schönberg compositions in April 1992.

The smaller golden building, the **Kammermusiksaal** ("Chamber Music Hall"), Matthäikirchstraße 1, Tel. 261-43-83, was a present from the former German capital, Bonn, to Berlin. Based on Scharoun's plans, it was built from 1984 to 1987 by Scharoun's partner, Edgar Wisniewski.

There is a third golden building. When you compare the two Philharmonic buildings with the one on Potsdamer Straße you have no doubt that it is the mark of Mr. Scharoun. The 1967-68 **Staatsbibliothek** ("National Library"), Potsdamer Straße 33, Tel. 266-1 (open Tue.-Fri. 9 A.M. to 9 P.M., Mon. from 2 P.M.; Sat. to 5 P.M.; entrance free), is known as the "Staabi." It is the fourth largest in the world after Moscow, St. Petersburg, and Washington, D.C.

The library is a pleasure to visit whether or not you want to do serious work. You can visit presentations, concerts, and exhibitions. It contains 3.6 million volumes, 63,000 letters, and more than 30,000 current periodicals including a wide selection of English-language newspapers.

The core of the library's collection comes from the *Preußische Staatsbibliothek*, the former Prussian State Library that was founded in 1661 as the Elector's Library and then became the Royal Library in 1701. After the War volumes were stored in Marburg and at the Tübingen University Library but now all have been returned to Berlin.

Also according to Scharoun's plans the neighboring building housing the **Staatlichen Institut für Musikforschung** ("National Institute for Music Research") contains the angular, white **Musikinstrumenten-Museum** ("Musical Instruments Museum"), Tiergartenstraße 1, Tel. 254-81-0 (open Tue.-Fri. 9 A.M. to 5 P.M., Sat.-Sun. 10 A.M. to 5 P.M.), with examples from Renaissance and baroque periods including ornately decorated harpsichords and 17th-century trumpets and trombones.

Even before the June 14, 1998, opening of the **Gemäldegalerie am Kulturforum** ("Paintings Gallery in the Cultural Forum") Matthäikirchstraße 8, Tel. 20-90-55-55 (open Tue., Wed., Fri. 10 A.M. to 6 P.M., Thur. to 8 P.M., Sat.-Sun. from 11 A.M.; admission DM 4, day-ticket DM 8), a line of 800 patrons waited outside for admission. The newest prize of the Cultural Forum is the modern centerpiece between—and connecting—the wings harboring the Arts and Crafts Museum and the Engraving Museum. This space was planned by architects Heinz Hilmen and Christoph Sattler long before the Wende could even be imagined. The museum unites under one roof the world-famous royal German painting collections from East Berlin (Bode Museum) and West (Dahlem).

Berlin, March 1945. The Red Army has just crossed the Oder River and is bearing down on Berlin. The evacuation of the valuable collection begins much too late. Smaller works are transported at great risk overland to a salt mine in Thuringa. Larger paintings have to be left behind in a flak bunker in Friedrichshain because they can't fit into the mine cage. Later, fires break out (their origin unknown to this day), destroying monumental works by Rubens, Van Dyck, and Caravaggio, as well as Signorelli's famous *Pan*. The calamitous history of Germany wreaks disaster upon Berlin's priceless collection.

After the War, American troops take part of the Berlin collection back to the United States. Russians take what they find in the cellar of the Kaiser Friedrich Museum to the Soviet Union. The Western portion finds a new home in the Dahlem Museum in Zehlendorf. The Russians install their booty in the Bode Museum.

Despite great losses in the War and the division of the collection, the Gemäldegalerie's still vast combined collection contains over 2,000 canvases including 25 by Rembrandt, making it Europe's second largest, after the Rijksmuseum in Amsterdam. It offers an overwhelming view of European painting from the 13th to the 18th century. You enter the Gemäldegalerie—which makes exclusive use of natural light—through a high rotunda leading to the exhibition rooms and an atrium with a modern water sculpture by Walter de Maria. This central hall incorporates stylistic elements of the Middle Ages and Renaissance and prepares you for a mental flight back through time.

The heart of the museum is the octagonal Rembrandt hall. At long last, the historical paintings of the Dutch master, with their striking chiaroscuro effects of light glowing out of darkness, can be seen together with the works of his students. You see Berlin's second most famous work of art (after the bust of Nefertiti), *The Man in the Golden Helmet,* which is not by Rembrandt after all, but from his studio.

Treasures include the Dutch and Flemish paintings that the Great Elector received when he married Princess Dorothea of Orange (including the works of Bruegel, van Eyck, and Rembrandt) and a group of some 3,000 Italian masters received in the 1820s. Its most famous painting is Bruegel's delightful *Dutch Proverbs.* Room after room offers you Dürer, Botticelli's *San Sebastian,* Vermeer's *Glass of Wine,* van Eyck's *Madonna in the Church,* Lippi's *Adoration in the Forest,* Rubens, Titian's *Reclining Venus.* The numbers are monumental: 900 paintings in the Main Gallery, 400 in the Gallery of Studies, and 1.7 miles (2.8 kilometers) of wall space. Preparing for the opening of the Cultural Forum's Gemäldegalerie, experts restored one of the best known late Middle-Age paintings in Germany, the eight panes of Hans Multscher's (1400-1476) *Wurzacher Altar,* from 1427. Half of the restoration's cost was covered by a grant from the J. P. Getty Foundation in Los Angeles.

Across the street from the Chamber Music Hall you find the lumbering, red-brick-and-concrete, vine-covered, modern **Kunstgewerbemuseum** ("Arts and Crafts Museum"), Matthäikirchplatz 10, Tel. 20-90-55-55 (open Tue.-Fri. 10 A.M. to 6 P.M., Sat.-Sun. from 11 A.M.; entrance DM 4, day ticket DM 8), which was opened in 1985 with treasures transferred from their temporary home in Charlottenburg Palace. It is more interesting to visit the interior than to look at it from outside because the museum contains the fabulous Guelph Treasure of the Middle Ages, a translucent opal and enamel box by Eugene Feuillatre, and other eclectic examples of the Staatlichen Museen zu Berlin. While the Kunstgewerbemuseum in Köpenick (Chapter 12) is closed, displayed in the Tiergarten museum is the highlight of the Köpenick museum's collection, the silver sideboard moved from the former Berlin Palace. The silver treasure was hammered in 1695-98 in Augsburg, probably from a sketch of Andreas Schlüter for Elector Friedrich III.

Across the severe, inclined plaza you find the Arts and Crafts Museum's counterpoint, the similar red-brick building which houses the **Kupferstich-kabinett** ("Engravings Museum") and **Kunstbibliothek** ("Art Library"). These sites of culture also sponsor exhibits in the Hamburger Bahnhof (see below).

The Kupferstichkabinett, Matthaikirchplatz 6, Tel. 20-90-55-55 (open Tue.-Fri. 10 A.M. to 6 P.M., Sat.-Sun. from 11 A.M.; entrance DM 4, day ticket DM 8) goes all the way back to 1831 when King Friedrich III decided that engraving was so important it deserved to be collected and 2,500 drawings from as far back as 1652, the Great Elector's time, were assembled in the present-day Old Museum. The collection shows a beautiful collection of drawings, prints, graphics, and illustrated books from the 15th through the 20th centuries. Prominent are Dürer's and Rembrandt's drawings as well as graphics by Bruegel, Botticelli, Holbein, Cranach, Goya, and Michelangelo.

Sharing the same building is the Art Library, Tel. 266-2028, Fax 266-2958 (open Tue.-Fri. 9 A.M. to 8 P.M., Mon. from 2 P.M.), which was created in 1867 as part of the German Arts and Crafts Museum. It was housed in Dahlem until its relocation here in 1994.

Behind the Mathias Church (see below) stands incontrovertible proof that modern architecture can be graceful as a swan. The architectural highlight of the Cultural Forum is van der Rohe's rectilinear, black **Neue Nationalgalerie** ("New National Gallery"), across Sigimundstraße from the Staatsbibliothek at Potsdamer Straße 50, Tel. 20-90-55-55 (open Tue.-Fri. 10 A.M. to 6 P.M., Sat.-Sun. from 11 A.M.; admission DM 8, which includes admission to all other SMB museums), over a concealed lower floor more than twice its size. It was built to unite the collection of French impressionist and German expressionist paintings expelled from the Crown Prince's Palace (see Chapter 4) by the Nazis with the municipal Gallery of the 20th Century. You can make an interesting comparison of the French impressionists, including three canvases by Manet (including *The Conservatory*) and landscapes and portraits by Renoir, Pissarro, and Monet, with their German contemporaries, Liebermann and Slevogt. Also look for canvases by Menzel, Kokoschka, Klee, Ernst, and works from Picasso's various periods.

The building was designed in 1965 by Ludwig Miës van der Rohe, the last Bauhaus director in Berlin before its closing by the Nazis in 1933 (see "Bauhaus Archives") who returned to Germany after a long residence in the United States. It was completed in 1969, the year of van der Rohe's death.

The old section above ground, a 213-foot-square (65 meters) glass box on a broad terrace, is the tip of the iceberg. It contains only occasional exhibits. The gallery itself is hidden below street level. The trademark of the gallery is the mobile *Four Squares in Geviert* by American George Rickey.

Take your cameras. The view from the terrace of the gallery juxtaposes the bizarre *Heads and Tails* of American Alexander Calder in the foreground, the modern New National Gallery building in the center, and the austere silhouette of the 1846 St. Mathias Church in the background. Don't be intimidated by busy skateboarders.

**Matthäikirche** ("St. Mathias Church") stands as a beacon of architectural reason, an echo and fragrance of Sienna. It is the only building on the site from the 19th century. The red- and white-brick church was known as "the Diplomat's Church" because diplomats stationed before the Second World War in their nearby Tiergarten embassies attended the church to worship and no doubt to exchange rumors and diplomatic confidences on the sly. The church was built in 1846 by Stüler, and remains a lovely example of Prussian neoclassicism.

## DIPLOMATIC QUARTERS

South of Tiergarten Park on Tiergartenstraße on an expanse of land next to the Cultural Forum, the **Diplomatenviertel** (the former "Diplomatic Quarter") now consists of only six of about two dozen pre-War diplomatic missions from countries around the world. The six are Argentina, Greece, Italy, Japan, South Africa, and Turkey. Owing to their extraterritoriality (even as ruins), they did not fall to the leveling of the area, but about half subsequently passed to Berlin and the other half remain extraterritorial property. One exception is the former Japanese embassy, which had to be completely rebuilt in 1988 at a cost of DM 60 million in the 1938-42 style of Ludwig Moshamer to become the German-Japanese Center, Tiergartenstraße 22-27, a foundation for the promotion of German-Japanese cooperation. With the relocation of Germany's government, it is being rebuilt once more to welcome back an ambassador. One wing of Mussolini's gigantic state palace—the former Italian embassy by Friedrich Hetzelt in 1938-42—is now the Italian general consulate, just across the street from the Japanese building. The Greek government is reconsidering rebuilding their embassy on Graf-Spree-Straße despite high costs. The Portuguese have begun design studies. The former Danish legation became in 1988 an institute of advanced training of the West German post office.

The desolate area has new life as a center for representation of the German states such as Bremen and Baden-Württemburg that are building here. The new building for the Konrad Adenauer Foundation is completed. The Friedrich Ebert Foundation's building is well underway. The **Villa von der Heydt,** down the street from the Bauhaus Archives, is an elegant neoclassical mansion designed in 1861 by Hermann Ende that was once the Chinese embassy.

West of the former Diplomatic Quarter on Tiergartenstraße at Klingelhöferstraße, the successor to the destroyed diplomatic quarter, a new city quarter called the **Tiergarten-Dreieck** ("Tiergarten Triangle") will be the home of the brand new Mexican embassy and, next to it, the five Nordic embassies (Denmark, Sweden, Norway, Finland, and Iceland) in a complex with a facade of glass, blonde wood, and limestone designed to demonstrate Scandinavian sincerity. Completing construction of the triangle—with plans from 17 architects—will be the new headquarters for the CDU political party, deluxe apartments, a promenade, and sculpture garden. Use bus 100.

## MUSEUM FOR CONTEMPORARY ART

Another Tiergarten museum which is oddly placed, is the **Museum für Gegenwart Berlin** ("Museum for Contemporary Art"), Invalidenstraße 50-51, Tel. 20-90-55-55 (open Tue., Wed., Fri. 10 A.M. to 6 P.M., Thur. to 8 P.M., Sat.-Sun. from 11 A.M.; admission DM 8, which is a one-day ticket valid in all SMB museums, students DM 4). The museum was opened on November 3, 1996, north of the Spree River and beside the Schiffahrtskanal ("Shipping Canal") in the **Hamburger Bahnhof** ("Hamburg Train Station"). The building, the oldest train station in Berlin, had been the terminus of the 180 mile (300 kilometers) stretch connecting industrial Berlin with port-city Hamburg. When traffic dwindled at the end of the 19th century, a new Traffic and Building Museum moved in. Hamburger Bahnhof was restored for Berlin's 750th anniversary in 1987 after it came to the West as part of the DM 3 million package that the West Berlin transport authority paid to take over the run-down S-Bahn system in 1984. The Hamburger Bahnhof, like the S-Bahn, had been owned by the East German railroads despite being situated in the West's Tiergarten. The original purpose of the building is quickly revealed when you enter and see the high glassed roof designed for steam engines and the slightly elevated areas that were boarding platforms.

The international collection of Erich Marx is a multi-media artistic knock-out. You are treated to dynamic art; specifically art completed after the Second World War. There are wonderful exhibits, paintings, and multi-media, but nothing traditional. You see Andy Warhol's classic *Mao* and hear/watch "The audiovisual Joseph Beuys archive" contributed by the National Gallery. In addition to Warhol, representative work from Anselm Kiefer, Lichtenberg, Joseph Beuys, Robert Rauschenberg, and Cy Twombly enliven the walls and floor space. You find collections of Italian Transavanguardia and Minimal Art. Pride of show is Beuy's "The secret block for a secret person in Ireland" which comprises 450 drawings.

It's a wonderful trip. Use U-Bhf Zinnowitzer Straße and walk west on Invalidenstraße, passing along the way, at Invalidenstraße 44, the Prussian building occupied by the DDR's Geologic Ministry during the Cold War. The **Bundeministerium für Verkehr** ("Federal Traffic Ministry") is moving in after modernization 1997-99 by Swiss architect Max Dudler. Adjacent is the 1997 **Invalidenpark**. The building across the Schiffahrtskanal from the Hamburger Bahnhof, at Invalidenstraße 48/49, is the **Bundesministerium für Wirtschaft** ("Federal Ministry of Economics"), which occupies the site of the Military Medicine Academy which had to be dissolved as a condition of the Versailles Treaty ending the First World War. When Hitler assumed power, he returned it to its original purpose. During the Cold War, it faced the Wall's no-man's-land at the Schiffahrtskanal. When you cross the *Sandkrugbrücke* over the Schiffahrtskanal, you cross the fortified dividing line between East and West Berlin.

## LEHRTER BAHNHOF

On March 29, 1890, resigned Chancellor Otto von Bismarck left Berlin while a squadron of hussars lined the platform, a military band played, and ministers, ambassadors, generals, and thousands of admirers cheered and sang as his train steamed out of the Lehrter Bahnhof. Elevated S-Bhf Lehrter Stadtbahnhof, a classy stop that already has been rebuilt for over DM 20 million since 1987, is doomed. By May 2003, Lehrter Bahnhof will be rebuilt into the largest train station in Europe. Platforms 50 feet below ground will be crowded with passengers on the new north-south traffic route that will run in tunnels below the new federal chancellor's office, the Tiergarten Park, and the new city quarter at Potsdamer Platz. New platforms rising 30 feet over the street will continue to carry mainline, regional, and S-Bahn trains in the usual east-west direction. An estimated 240,000 travelers daily will pass through the new crossing, allowing those from the north and south to reach Berlin's center without skirting it.

With trains newly routed via a north-south tunnel through Berlin's center and a junction at a mammoth new Berlin station at the site of the present Lehrter Bahnhof, it was widely believed that Lehrter (the name of a city nearby) Bahnhof would be renamed "Central Bahnhof." Not so, its name will be (drum roll, please) Lehrter Bahnhof. On September 9, 1998, the first sod was cut on the site of the new station. Passengers boarding at the new train station will cross through the new two-mile-long (3.5 kilometer) north-south tunnel below the Spree River and the Tiergarten Park that ends south of the Landwehr Canal. While the tunnel is being built, a 660-foot (200 meters) stretch of the Spree River has been moved 230 feet (70 meters) north because the river bed is only three feet (one meter) above the new tunnel, making it too difficult to dig from below. The new tunnel will allow passengers to get on and off at stations along a nearly 5.5 mile (9 kilometer) travel corridor through Berlin's new Potsdamer Platz central area.

## 5. Sports

**Tiergarten Park** is the largest and most beautiful park of Berlin for jogging, playing ball, bicycle riding, frisbee throwing, etc. Use bus 100 or 148.

**Sommerbad Poststadion,** Seydlitzstraße 6, Tel. 39-05-4013/1 (open Mon. 9 A.M. to noon and 2 to 7 P.M., Tue., Thur., and Fri. 2 to 7 P.M., Wed. 9 A.M. to 2 P.M. and 2 to 4 P.M., Sat. 9 A.M. to 5 P.M., Sun. 9 A.M. to 1 P.M.). Use S-Bhf Lehrter Stadtbahnhof, bus 187, 227, or 245.

## 6. Shopping

**Großer Berliner Trädel- und Kunstmarkt** ("Larger Berlin Second-hand and Art Market") takes place every Saturday and Sunday from 8 A.M. to 4 P.M. on Straße des 17. Juni. The array of secondhand and antique wares, china, silverware, small art and jewelry, offered at about 200 permanent and 300 open stands is impressive, but has also become a bit commercial. It is Berlin's most popular. There are bargains here, but you have to scout them out. Collectors and art buffs will find something suitable here. Use S-Bhf Ernst-Reuter-Platz.

## 7. Nightlife and Entertainment

**Philharmonie**, Herbert-von-Karajan-Straße 1, Tel. 254-88-132, Fax 261-48-87, is your first address for classical music. The orchestra and acoustics are unexcelled. It is hailed as an acoustic masterpiece. The adjacent

**Kammermusiksaal**, "Chamber Music Hall" offers no less incredibly excellent acoustics. Use U-Bhf or S-Bhf Potsdamer Platz, bus 348 or 148.

**Grips Theater**, Altonaer Straße 22, Tel. 391-40-04, in the Hansa Quarter, presents contemporary, socially-critical German-language theater for children and young adults. Use U-Bhf Hansaplatz.

**Berliner Kammerspiele**, Alt-Moabit 98, Tel. 391-55-43. Youth theater with productions of important plays by modern authors such as Dürrenmatt, Miller, Sartre, etc. Use U-Bhf Turmstraße or S-Bhf Bellevue.

**Hansa Theater**, Alt-Moabit 48 (Alt-Moabit), Tel. 391-44-60. Use U-Bhf Turmstraße.

**Harry's New York Bar** im Hotel Esplanade, Lützowufer 15, Tel. 254-78-21 (open from noon), is one of the handsomest bars in Berlin. A good place to meet for a cocktail, it shares the Grand Hotel's floorspace with the **Eckkenipe** pub and the **Harlekin** Michelin-star restaurant. Use bus 100.

**Kumpelnest 3000**, Lützowstraße 23, Tel. 261-69-18 (open daily 5 P.M. to 5 A.M.), is a classy Szene hangout in a former bordello. Use U-Bhf Kurfürstenstraße.

**Wintergarden**, Potsdamer Straße 96, Tel. 230-88-230, Fax 25-00-88-55, *http://www.berlin-entertainment.de*. In the Wintergarden's nighttime sky, 4,564 stars twinkle. Precious woods, brass, dark-red velvet, and mirrors give the theater its unique look. In beautifully restored quarters, you see varieté at its best—turbulent, colorful, and daring. Magicians, clowns, jugglers, and acrobats present a program of stunning and spectacular acts. Some look impossible. Use U-Bhf Kurfürstenstraße.

# 7

# The Berlin of Fascism
# and Cold War

## 1. Orientation

In the Heart of Berlin you found the Berlin of the '90s; in the Tiergarten, you found buildings that will house the government of the 21st century; Historic Berlin is covered with the best of historic Prussian architecture; but there is no ignoring that Berlin is also notorious for the atrocities of the Nazis and the murder of the Cold War.

Berlin's nightmare days began with Hitler's taking office in 1933 and continued until the falling of the Wall. Berlin lived under the terror of the Nazis, saw its destruction by the Allies' bombings and the Red Army's artillery, and felt Stalin's imprint and the division of the city into hostile camps. In the area along the course of the former Wall separating Berlin Kreuzberg and Berlin Mitte, you find the rubble and ruin of Nazi terror and Cold-War confrontation. This scarred earth includes the bunker of Hitler's command center, his chancellery, the headquarters of the Gestapo, and more. In the outskirts is the abominable Sachsenhausen concentration camp where Jews were slaughtered. On Normannenstraße, the headquarters of the DDR secret police, spies turned man against man with hateful snooping.

# TOPOGRAPHIE des TERRORS/CHECKPOINT CHARLIE

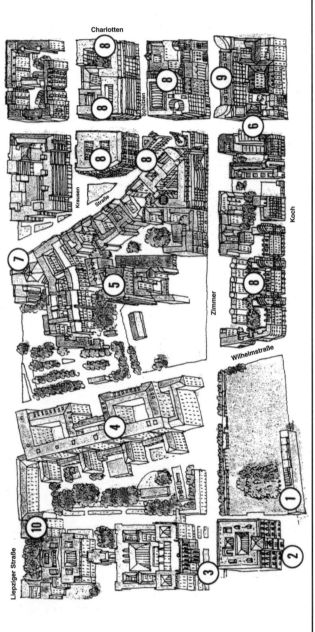

1. Topographie des Terrors Exhibition
2. Martin Gropius Building
3. Berlin City Council
4. German Finance Ministry
5. Former E-Werk Techno-Disco
6. Haus am Checkpoint Charlie Museum
7. Postal Museum (East)
8. New business building
9. New shopping arcade
10. Federal ministries

Use S-Bhf Anhalter Bahnhof or S-Bhf Potsdamer Platz to reach the former Nazi headquarters buildings. In the outskirts you can use public transportation to find Plötzensee Prison, Sachsenhausen Concentration Camp, Weißensee Jewish Cemetery, former Stasi headquarters, and the Soviet Memorial.

## 2. The Hotel Scene

**Hotel am Anhalter Bahnhof** (Stresemannstraße 36, Tel. 2-51-03-42, Fax 2-51-48-97) has 33 rooms with or without shower/lavatory. US$44-78, single; US$61-100, double; breakfast buffet included. Weekend special: US$39-56, single; US$56-78, double.

**Hotel Stuttgarter Hof** (Anhalter Straße 9, Tel. 2-64-83-0, Fax 26-48-3-900). Brick property around the corner from the Anhalter Bahnhof and near the Martin Gropius Building. US$92-164, single; US$114-206 double; breakfast buffet included. In the U.S., call Best Western, Tel. 1-800-528-1234.

## 3. Restaurants and Cafés

While you are sightseeing in the area of Checkpoint Charlie, the Martin Gropius Buildings and Topographie des Terrors, there are places for good and inexpensive light meals.

The **Café Adler**, Friedrichstraße 206, Tel. 251-89-65 (open 9 A.M. to midnight) in the building famous for housing the American military overseeing Checkpoint Charlie, you can stop in here for milk coffee while the tour buses roll past outside. Use U-Bhf Stadtmitte or U-Bhf Kochstraße.

**Lekkerbek Café**, Friedrichstraße 211, Tel. 251-72-08. A quick and inexpensive restaurant near Checkpoint Charlie. Point at your selection of Italian pasta or sandwich and take it to your table. The coffee is very good. Open for breakfast and lunch. Use U-Bhf Kochstraße.

**Sale E Tabacci**, Kochstraße 18, Tel. 252-11-55 (open Mon.-Fri. 8 A.M. to 2 A.M., Sat.-Sun. from 10 A.M.). Trattoria am Checkpoint Charlie, the large fashionable space makes you imagine you took a wrong turn at the Brenner Pass. Berlin newspapers hang on poles for your reading at your table. Use U-Bhf Kochstraße.

**Gropius** in the Martin Gropius Building, Stresemannstraße 110, Tel. 262-76-20 (open Tue.-Sun. 11 A.M. to 8 P.M.) provides a rustic café with typical museum cakes and coffee, and also vegetarian cooking, not only for museum visitors. You can visit the café without paying exhibition admission.

# 4. Sightseeing

## THE WALL

The Wall has become a curiosity. Once the East was opened, hammers, crowbars, and pickaxes appeared from storage. Wessis chipped away at the concrete of the suddenly valuable, souvenir Wall. Ossis protested that Wessis couldn't sell it, "It's *our* Wall." Vendors still sell chunks of rock on their collapsible card tables lining the tourist hubs near former Checkpoint Charlie and the Brandenburg Gate. The more traces of purported graffiti per rock, the greater its sales price. Who knows whether the coloring was daubed last night in some artist's atelier? About one in ten Germans has a chunk at home.

Follow the tourist office's red line between the Reichstag (Chapter 6) and the Brandenburg Gate (Chapter 4). You have to search to see indications of the former Wall which divided these focal points. The Reichstag used to be in West Berlin; the Brandenburg Gate in East. Try to imagine the watchtowers, barbed wire, scowling machine gunners, and the nearly impenetrable wall confining East Germans.

When Berlin was divided after the end of the Second World War, the Four Powers took a city map and separated the city according to pre-War districts along red lines on the map. When the Wall was eventually built it therefore separated, for example, the districts of Mitte from Tiergarten. However the Wall wasn't constructed exactly on the map's red line. Builders slightly offset the Wall, so that DDR border guards could work on both sides. The sidewalk near the Reichstag lies in the Tiergarten district; the street itself in Mitte. That meant that Mitte authorities had to keep the street repaired and Tiergarten employees had to keep the sidewalk swept.

During the early hours of August 13, 1961, guards unrolled bales of barbed wire, masons cemented closed the windows of houses fronting on the West, and bulldozers forced into place the foundations of what came to be an effective barrier between East and West. When Berliners awoke that morning, they were shocked—East and West—to hear on the radio newscast that their city had been sliced.

This followed nine years during which 1.5 million DDR citizens, mostly young and skilled, had left their country for the high wages and creature comforts of West Germany's Economic Miracle. The exodus, which had reached 30,000 a month, was robbing the DDR of a substantial part of its working population, causing an increasingly widespread shortage of labor, and turning the DDR into a nation of old-age pensioners.

The June 1961 summit meeting between Khrushchev and Kennedy in

Vienna had been a disaster, so the DDR government concluded that its best course was to close the border with West Berlin and build the physical barrier supported by 252 watchtowers and 136 bunkers separating Berlin for a length of 27 miles (43 kilometers) and surrounding the city of West Berlin for a total length of 97 miles (155 kilometers). The barrier blocked 62 city streets and 131 roads. Before the Wall, there were 81 crossing points between the Berlin sectors; afterwards there were 8, including one for mail vans and one for coffins that were allowed through on Wednesdays. All U- and S-Bahn crossings were closed except for Friedrichstraße station.

When at last the expiring DDR permitted East Berliners through the Wall, enthusiastic merrymakers began to tear it down starting at the Reichstag, where it had stood 13 feet (4 meters) high. After the fall of the Wall, Berliners left only fragments intact. *Mauerspechte* ("Wall Woodpeckers") hammered to oblivion concrete walls, caged dog courses, and observation towers. They only missed a few. Original parts of the Berlin Wall have been preserved in back of the Martin Gropius Building (see below) and below Potsdamer Platz's Info-Box. The red line tracing the Wall's former path through the city is taking longer to complete than the Wall's original construction.

## CHECKPOINT CHARLIE

It's quiet now at the corner of Friedrich- and Zimmerstraße. Through the rolled-down windows of passing automobiles and buses, cameras no longer click and video cameras no longer hum. This was **Checkpoint Charlie**, where observers of world history held their breath. Former Checkpoint Charlie was the media star of the Cold War. The 10-lane checkpoint of the American forces for diplomats and foreigners became the center of world attention on the dramatic days between October 25 and 28, 1961, when American and Soviet tanks faced each other with running motors, and the building of the Wall went on. Now there is no more Checkpoint Charlie, no more wall segments, no watchtower, no barbed wire, no tank traps, no bunker, and no guard shack. The corner has all the charm of a parking garage.

One could only enter East Berlin after the passports for pedestrians and buses were checked. Only foreigners were allowed to enter here, not Germans. It normally took at least a half-hour before one received an East German visa, then one was subjected to customs inspections and mandatory money change to East German Marks (OstMarks)—and that took another half-hour, so one could count on at least an hour of paperwork to cross the border. It took slightly less time to leave, about a half-hour, but everyone had to get out of the bus, the hood lifted, the trunk opened, and the seats tilted forward. Clever people had figured out how to install a tiny motor in a large automobile to make place for smuggling Easterners to the West. Others had taken out their gas tanks, put a half-gallon container of gasoline under the hood, and stashed fugitives where the gas tank ought to be. All possibilities were checked.

English, French, and American diplomats and soldiers crossed without the control of the DDR authorities from West Berlin to East Berlin and back. Similarly Red Army officers drove from East Berlin to West Berlin and returned. Although the city was divided, Berlin was the property of all four governments. The four military victors, despite walls, could travel in every corner of East and West Berlin without control. When passing through the Wall, American soldiers, even in civilian dress, simply showed their military papers. The DDR had no authority over the four occupying forces, only over citizens of West Germany. During the entire Cold War, American, British, and French soldiers went into East Berlin for shopping, sightseeing, and spying. According to agreements, East Berlin was not part of East Germany. It was the Soviet sector of Berlin.

In the middle of the street, Checkpoint Charlie was merely a shack where allied military personnel had to check out with their own army for security reasons so there would be some record of their traveling to East Berlin in case they were arrested or detained there.

The origin of the name, Checkpoint Charlie, is simple. It came from the NATO alphabet. Checkpoint Alpha lay at the entrance to the Autobahn Hannover/Helmstedt-Berlin. It was the only Autobahn that American troops were allowed to use. At Checkpoint Alpha, they checked out. At Checkpoint Bravo, at the entrance to West Berlin, they checked in. Alpha, Bravo, Charlie . . .

Checkpoint Charlie was one of the most eagerly visited tourist attractions for nationals of all nations. It is a pity there is little left to see. On June 22, 1990, U.S. Secretary of State James Baker, during a meeting of foreign ministers, watched while the Checkpoint shed was hoisted away by a giant crane. The intersection has been realigned to accommodate through automobile traffic. It is now hardly even a curious tourist's attraction. Entrepreneurs have folded up their tables where they sold Russian and DDR officers' hats, bits of military uniforms, boots, dolls, postcards, souvenirs of the divided city, and "authentic" fragments of the former wall that were mounted on stone with inscriptions: "Berliner Mauer/1961-1989."

Friedrichstraße used to be a commercial trade road. At the beginning of this century it was Berlin's most important shopping street with department stores situated here, but the street was completely destroyed in the Second World War. Restoration has assumed an American flavor. Will

Friedrichstraße become Manhattan-on-the-Spree? Use U-Bhf Stadtmitte or U-Bhf Kochstraße.

**Museumhaus am Checkpoint Charlie** ("Checkpoint Charlie Museum"), was forced to move from its original, cheap storefront entrance facing the checkpoint where it opened on October 19, 1962, documenting the tragedy of the Wall and humanity's struggles for freedom. Now in a corner location (with café) at Friedrichstraße 44, Tel. 25-37-25-0, Fax 251-20-75 (open daily 9 A.M. to 10 P.M.; entrance DM 8, students DM 5), you see the haphazard archive in larger but less immediate quarters and its impact is lessened. It has a decorated Wall segment beside the entrance outside so you can see it even when the museum is closed. The inside of the museum is a curatorial disaster. There are four permanent exhibitions: 1) The Wall from August 13, 1961; 2) Painters Interpret the Wall; 3) Berlin: Front Line Town to the Bridge of Europe; and 4) Freedom Fighters from Gandhi to Walesa: Non-violent Struggle for Human Rights. The museum includes the large, stark, black-and-white sign, "You are leaving the American Sector," repeated in Russian, French, and German, bequeathed by American army commanders before pulling out of Berlin, and the red-and-white striped crossing gates given by Lothar de Maiziere, East Germany's last prime minister.

Among the other interesting exhibits are the balloon which one family flew to the West and the dummy motorcycle fuel tank where a Wessi hid his Ossi girlfriend. There are films documenting the killing of some of the 75 attempted escapes, photos of escape tunnels, and one section devoted to Gandhi, the U.S. civil rights movement, and Solidarity in Poland. Use U-Bhf Kochstraße. Use bus 129, U-Bhf Kochstraße or U-Bhf Stadtmitte.

Only 260 feet (80 meters) north of the **Museumhaus**, you see, facing Friedrichstraße, the preserved DDR **Kontrollhaus** ("Control House") in which border guards of the DDR checked those traveling outwards.

The **American Business Center** displaced the original museum location with a $400-million construction project involving five different buildings (Friedrichstraße 48, 50, 20; the Philip Johnson Haus/Checkpoint Charlie Marketing Center, 205, and Checkpoint Plaza). The project had clout. Until 1997, it was headed by Ronald Lauder, the American cosmetics heir who ran unsuccessfully in 1989 for mayor of New York after serving as U.S. ambassador to Austria. After Lauder's departure, the incomplete parts of the project were put on ice. The whole complex was designed to provide 1,760,000 square feet (100,000 square meters) of office, atrium, shops, and restaurants. The complex was designed by Philip Johnson, the New York architect responsible for Lincoln Center and the AT&T Building in New York and London's tallest building, the Canary Wharf skyscraper.

It was such a historic site that the Checkpoint structures should have been kept there. The sad irony is that it was American investors who really helped get rid of it because they wanted to put up the monstrosity business center. Berliners regard it as Philip Johnson's monument to his own ego.

One and a half blocks down Zimmerstraße east from Friedrichstraße (notice the red line marking the perimeter of the former Wall) you come to the **Peter Fechter Memorial** as closely as possible (because of the new street) to the spot where he was shot dead by East German border guards. "Help me," the 18-year-old cried after being shot climbing the Wall and falling on the West side but still within DDR territory. For 50 minutes he lay there bleeding, without medical assistance, without American soldiers interfering. He could easily have been rescued. A crowd gathered and watched with horror as he died. When he was dead, DDR soldiers carried him back through an opening in the Wall. After the Wende, authorities erected a 10-foot (3 meters) tall wooden cross and placed a wreath in memory of Peter Fechter on the spot. Whether the cross will remain standing or be replaced by a memorial tablet depends on public opinion and the architects erecting massive new shops and apartments on the site.

What do you think of the rainbow-colored office buildings, now opposite, standing where killer dogs once patrolled no-man's land? The **Aldo-Rossi-Haus** on Markgrafenstraße is a raging success both in public opinion and in renting space to supermarkets, bakers, flower shops, tea parlors, cobblers, key makers, and an Italian restaurant. Since the fall of the Wall, monstrous, monotonous buildings have risen all over Berlin, often taking over whole city blocks. Given this pattern, the DM 430 million project by Munich developers located between Zimmer-, Schützen-, Markgrafen- and Charlottenstraße will catch your eye. The block is not covered by a single building, but by 12 different green, yellow, red, and gray houses. They are linked by partly public, partly private courtyards and gardens. From the outside you have the impression that the garish houses were built at different times instead of all at once. The only original is the house at Schützenstraße 11 from the *Gründerzeit*. It was modeled after the Palazzo Faranese designed by Michelangelo in the 16th century. The bizarre thing is that tourists march through the courtyard to the structure three houses to the left which is another copy, formed a hundred years later, of the Roman Palazzo.

The flip side of the memorials to those killed trying to flee from the East, and nearly as great an indictment of the Wall, exists at the nearly abandoned corner of Jerusalemer Straße and Reinhold-Huhn-Straße, where East Germans once inspected passports. Here four cement blocks form the **Denkmal für ermordete Grenzsoldaten** ("Memorial to Murdered Border Soldiers"), to remember the 25 border guards who were killed in the line of duty supporting the Wall. The inscription reads: "Here death is our duty." But now you see no trace of the DDR passport control point, only the neglected memorial and a parking lot.

## WILHELMSTRASSE

The stretch between Unter den Linden and Leipziger Straße is known as the **Geschichtsmeile Wilhelmstraße** ("Historical Mile Wilhelmstraße"). Before the end of the Second World War, it had the importance of London's Downing Street or Paris' Quai d'Orsay. (See *http://www.dhm.de/museen/ wilhelmstr.*) Imperial Berlin, Weimar Republic, Third Reich, DDR, and reunited Berlin are all represented. A walk down Wilhelmstraße through the districts of Mitte and Kreuzberg recalls ugly history. Wilhelmstraße was the famous Nazi government street of Berlin.

The **Altes Regierungsviertel** ("Old Government Quarter") was the power base of the Nazis and their bureaucrats, mostly along Wilhelmstraße, which served as a parade route in front of Nazi government buildings. Until 1945, the most important chancelleries, palaces, and ministries lined Wilhelmstraße. Here you found the **Neue Reichskanzlei** ("New Reich Chancellery"), the **Ministergärten,** the **Palais mit den Ministerien,** and the notorious **Hotel Kaiserhof**. After the War and before the opening of the Wall, Wilhelmstraße was a dead-end street. During DDR times the street was dead. The U-Bahn terminated here. Present-day Wilhelmstraße has an entirely new face. Boutiques, bakeries, and Berlin bars moved in. There are 1,060 apartments. A kindergarten and a grammar school are integrated into the complex.

**Hitler's Bunker** which was 50 feet deep behind the former New Reich Chancellery on Wilhelmstraße is now filled with water below a weed-grown field. You see only a heap.

Shortly after the Red Army, at noon on April 30, 1945, took the Reichstag, Hitler fled at 3:30 P.M. and committed suicide together with Eva Braun (Hitler's wife of one day). He had given orders that after his suicide, his body should be taken out of the bunker, burned in the garden before the Reich Chancellery, wrapped in a sheet, and then crushed into a shell crater. At 8:30 P.M. on May 1, Joseph Goebbels and his wife were shot, at his orders, by an S.S. orderly, and then their bodies were set on fire. Experts definitely identified Goebbels' burned body from X rays of his teeth, but Hitler had never allowed X rays of his teeth so scientists could not identify his corpse with certainty.

The concrete shielding of the Hitler Bunker reached high on Behrenstraße. The bunker with four-meter-thick steel-and-concrete walls was built in 1944 within a year by forced labor. The walls were blown up together with the foundations.

In the first months after the Second World War the ruins of Hitler's New Reich Chancellery on Wilhelmstraße were demolished to leave no memorial for potential neo-Nazis. The communists schlepped marble slabs from the chancellery to U-Bhf Mohrenstraße where they were put to use covering the walls and columns. Hitler's bunker was blown up, filled with rubble, and promptly flooded by subsurface ground water. In 1985, when DDR architects returned to build apartment houses here, the foundation of the bunker had to be cleaned out. At that time they found personnel office rooms, but no place where Hitler or his staff had worked.

At Wilhelmstraße 97/Leipzigerstraße 5-7, the historic **former Reichsluftfahrtministerium** ("Air Force Ministry"), built in 1935-36 on the site of the 1819 Prussian War Ministry, the largest office building in Berlin, was Göring's headquarters in his capacity as minister of aviation. It was the first large building of the Nazi period, light brown with some 2,400 office spaces, 4,000 square windows, columns similar to the Olympic Stadium in Athens, and socles on the two-foot (60 centimeters) thick concrete roof for bombproofing. The architecture, very typical for the Third Reich, was almost identical to the former Reich Chancellery. The same architect designed Tempelhof Airport. Göring's building is the only one in the area that was not severely damaged by bombing during the War. After the War, it was occupied by the headquarters for the Soviet military administration. In 1949, it was transferred from Soviet occupation to DDR administration and became, in 1950, the **Haus der Ministerien** ("Ministry") for the government of the DDR. It is ironic that the Stalinistic DDR government was located in a building built by Fascists.

The first uprising against Stalinism, the first in Europe, occurred here in Berlin in 1953, when this building was a ministry for the Stalinist government. On June 16, 10,000 Berlin workers marched to the building demanding free elections, the reunification of Germany, the return of German prisoners of war still held in Soviet camps, and the removal of Walter Ulbrecht and his clique. They called a general strike for June 17. The Soviet military commandant declared martial law and sent in Soviet tanks, T-34s, with orders to avoid casualties. Some 100 to 200 were killed, 4,000 were arrested, and 1,400 were sentenced to life imprisonment. The Western powers made no more than token noises of disapproval. Eventually, the Straße des 17. Juni in Charlottenburg/Tiergarten was named for this historic event.

After the Wende, from 1991 to 1996, the building became headquarters for **Treuhandanstalt,** the German federal agency charged with privatizing DDR property. Now, the enormous reception hall with the massive columns and the stone walls which Göring built for intimidation is being used for the **Bundesministerium der Finanzen in Berlin**, the federal taxation ministry that has moved to Berlin. Berlin Schnauze says that the building attracts criminal elements.

The building is now named **Detlev-Rohwedder-Haus**, after the murdered Treuhand president. During Treuhand's tenure, more than 3,800 staff members were occupied privatizing the leftovers of the 10,000 (900 in Berlin alone) industries along with 20,000 farms, forests, shops, services, and parcels of real estate that they received from the former Communist monolith. All told, 40 percent of East Germany's surface and 50 percent of its work force were put in Treuhand's care. At the halfway point in 1992, after about 21 months, Treuhandanstalt had privatized some 5,500 manufacturing and service companies and nearly 15,000 retail outlets. At the outset, no one knew even where to begin transforming the DDR's 270 *Kombinate* (vertically integrated public-sector holding companies) and 8,000 VEBs (individual economic units), but the Kombinates were transformed into joint-stock companies by affixing the suffix "AG" (*Aktiengesellschaft*) to their corporate names with East Germany's citizens as their shareholders. After Treuhand had completed most of its assignment, it was disbanded and the Bundesanstalt für vereinigungsbedingte Sonderaufgaben (BvS) took on the odds and ends.

On the outside face you see a 1952 Communist mural that is as impressive in its way as the interior. It shows the party of the working class—the party of Lenin, not of Karl Marx. One had to be invited to join the party, therefore it was an elite class. The mural is interesting because it shows so many different scenes and its scope is Utopian. It is done in chalky colors, showing happy farmers, clever scientists, and diligent workers.

Across Niederkirchnerstraße from the Detlev-Rohwedder-Haus, you see a 800-foot (250 meters) section of graffiti-covered **Wall**, thanks to an initiative of an East Berlin citizen's action committee, but this is not the "real" Wall, because the barrier between East and West normally consisted of a high wall, a danger area, and a smaller inner wall (see the model in the Berlin Museum). The section here is part of the inner Wall.

This part of the Wall was rescued none too soon from the Wall-tearing frenzy that followed the opening of the border. It is landmarked as a national monument. It will remain there, and of course it doesn't have the moving graffiti that covered the surfaces facing the West. These are preserved on the postcards on sale all over the city. Beyond this section of the "inner" Wall came the death strip and then the bigger, long-gone west Wall. Embedded in Niederkirchnerstraße you see the two-inch (five centimeters) wide, copper strip engraved *Berliner Mauer 1961-1989*. This was the first length to be marked with the red stripe showing the path of the Wall through Berlin, but here it is the much more appropriate copper strip.

## MARTIN GROPIUS BUILDING

Grouped together geographically among the remains of fascism and failed communism stands the innocent, extravagant, 1881 red-sandstone, Grecian-appearing building with red shutters, the **Martin-Gropius-Bau** ("Martin Gropius Building"), Stresemannstraße 110, Tel. 25-48-67-14, Fax 265-1371, *http://www.zeitgeist-berlin.de*, but closed until the middle of 1999 for reconstruction of the rear and remodeling the interior. It stood only 15 feet from the Wall. Predating the bad days of Berlin, it is one of the city's most beautiful exhibit halls. Although the Martin Gropius Building was considerably more damaged than the Nazi buildings nearby, the others were torn down after the War because of their ugly history while the Gropius Building was restored because it had always been a museum. It was designed by Martin, the uncle of Bauhaus founder Walter Gropius (see Chapter 6), in 1881, the most significant work of the younger Schinkel school. It is tattered outside, still pockmarked with bullet holes on its east face, so its interior comes as an exhilarating surprise, shining with black marble and gilt. The exhibitions take a life of their own in the splendid, airy interior.

You see on the exterior that was intended for the original Berlin Handicrafts Museum collection. The mosaics on the north, west, and east facades consist of epochs in the history of art. The frescoes over the windows display various crafts. The collection which remained here until 1921 is now in the new museum in the Cultural Forum (see Chapter 6). The building is now used primarily for block-buster exhibitions, but art lovers must not bypass the permanent collection of the **Berlinische Galerie** of modern art, photography, and architecture located here (open Tue.-Sun. 10 A.M. to 8 P.M.). It boasts excellent works of Max Liebermann and members of the **Berliner Sezessionist** school of painting.

In the Martin Gropius Building you also find the **Werkbund-Archiv** ("Museum of Everyday Life in the 20th Century") from the Berlin Gallery. Use S-Bhf Anhalter Bahnhof—follow the signs in the station—or U-Bhf Möckernbrücke.

The building with three flags flying (German, Berlin, and European) directly across the street from the Martin Gropius Building at Niederkirchnerstraße 3 (open 9 A.M. to 3 P.M.), is the sandstone Gothic, Greek-accented building that was formerly the **Preußische Landtag** ("Prussian Legislative Assembly Building"), taken over by Heinrich Himmler, who occupied house after house in the neighborhood for his S.S. institutions so that the whole area became the major S.S. complex. During the '50s and '60s it was the home of the (East) German Academy of Sciences with meeting rooms for Humboldt University. After the Wende it was renovated at a cost of DM 120 million for the **Abgeordnetenhaus von Berlin** ("Berlin City Council"). The members have made their home here since August 1993, when they moved from their "temporary" chambers in the Schöneberg Town Hall which they had used for 40 years.

As soon as they moved in, the Berlin legislators had to cope with a typical post-Wende Berlin situation. Their address was on Niederkirchener Street, but Käthe Niederkirchener was a German Communist woman who had served famously in the Soviet Red Army. How could the Berlin representatives from the West have an address on a street named for a Communist? In democratic fashion, they asked Berliners to vote to rename the street. Legislators lost. Käthe won.

Only a few steps from the patched-up Martin Gropius Building you meet a weed-overgrown field, without buildings. This is the **Prinz-Albrecht-Gelände** ("Prince Albrecht Grounds") that stretches between Niederkirchnerstraße (formerly Prinz-Albrecht-Straße), Wilhelmstaße, Stresemannstraße, and Anhalter Straße. On this site, between 1933 and 1945, the most important terror organizations of the Third Reich had their headquarters. The Gestapo had its headquarters in the **Prinz-Albrecht-Palais,** only a block from Hitler's Reichs Chancellery. It was the power center of Nazi terror. The desks of Himmler, Heydrich, and their S.S. toadies overflowed with records of atrocities. It was here that the plans for the Jewish Final Solution and the Germanization of the East were developed. Suspected conspirators in the Stauffenberg assassination attempt (see below) were tortured in the dungeons. Here the Gestapo imprisoned Jews, Communists, homosexuals, Gypsies, and Freemasons for interrogation, torture, murder, or deportation to concentration camps.

In 1926 on the western third of Prinz Albrecht Park, construction began of what came to be called the Europa-Haus. The rest of the site was bordered by a wall of which a part still exists, as does the gate from which a path led to the park in the direction of the Wilhelmstraße towards Prinz Albrecht Palace. It was along this garden path right next to the walled-in courtyard of the Gestapo prison that the Gestapo forced prisoners from Sachsenhausen Concentration Camp (probably in 1943-44) to build an annex containing a kitchen and mess hall. During excavation work for the foundations for the temporary exhibition pavilion in 1987, the basement of this building was uncovered. The pavilion was then built directly on top of the basement vaults but based on a modified floor plan.

On former Prinz-Albrecht-Straße 8, Southern Wing, the Gestapo set up its private prison with 20 one-man cells in late summer 1933. Three years later, 18 additional one-man cells and a communal cell were added. Interrogations were held on the floors above, where inmates were often brutally tortured by Gestapo officials and S.S. guards. The clearing after the War has left little of the Nazi terror center. Things have been blown up, plowed under, and not forgotten. In 1984, it was decided to cover the whole area with cast iron and spot in a few chestnut trees as a memorial, but the Berlin Senate got cold feet and nipped the idea a half year later. The mayor of Berlin, Eberhard Diepgen, wanted to rebuild Prinz Albrecht Palace, but students conducted a "dig-in" to protest the development and thus discovered underground cellars. The site was kept in rubble for the exhibit titled **Topographie des Terrors** of the Gestapo (S.S.) and *Reichsicherheitshauptamt auf dem Prinz-Albrecht-Gelände*. A temporary, prefabricated **Documentation Center** was opened on July 4, 1987, in the underground remains of Nazi interrogation rooms, but it had to be dismantled for constuction that began in July 1997, on a new permanent building for exhibition and visitors' center. The new building is expected to open in November 1999. During the period of construction you can see the exhibition of photographs and documents along excavations behind the Wall segment on Niederkirchener Straße with entrance next to the Martin Gropius Building. Admission is free. Open 10 A.M. to 6 P.M. in summer; during daylight hours in winter. Tel. 254-50-90, Fax 262-71-56. Use bus 341 or 129.

The new **Dokumentations- und Besucherzentrum** ("Documentation- and Visitors Center") was designed by Swiss architect Peter Zumthor for the Topographie des Terrors Foundation. You can see exhibits, a library, a photo archive, a media room, and an auditorium with the understanding that it will be a last presence on the site. It is hard to imagine that only a few years ago this site was used for the "Autodrom," for driving practice, owned by a well-known Berlin character named "Straps-Harry," who also operated a transvestite theater named the "Dream Boys Lachbühne" ("Laugh Stage").

The exhibit floods so many horrific photographs upon the visitor that the magnitude of the enormous outrage numbs the average visitor. Nevertheless, about 1.5 million passed through the turnstiles in the 10 years following its opening.

Drawings help you identify the former locations of Nazi buildings. You can see the former headquarters of the Gestapo. There is a drawing of the Askanische Platz, where the Anhalter Bahnhof stood; Saarlandstraße (since 1945 called Stresemannstraße) was a tourist center where the Hotel

Excelsior was located. On Hademannstraße was the headquarters of the Nazi party in Berlin from May 1930 to October 1932 and the seat of the editorial offices of Dr. Goebbels' propaganda newspaper. After the Reichstag fire in February 1933, Hademannstraße 31 served as one of the most infamous unofficial concentration camps. The building at Wilhelmstraße 20 was the seat of sections of the Reich's security main offices that were responsible for the personnel files of the members of the Gestapo and the criminal investigation division.

At Puttkamerstraße during the night of April 23-24, 1945, the S.S. used a bombed-out property on this street for the mass execution of inmates of the Gestapo prison. Looking west on Mauerstraße 82 (which is no longer there) you can see the Berlin Konzerthaus Klau, where Hitler delivered his first speech in Berlin on May 1, 1927. On February 27, 1943, it was one of the collection points during the so-called Factory Operation, the deportation of several thousand Berlin Jews who were arrested at their places of work by the Gestapo.

In back of the Martin Gropius Building was Zimmerstraße 88-91, the Berlin branch of the *Zentral Verlag* ("Central Publishing House") of the Nazis where Goebbels' Berlin newspaper, *Der Angriff,* the *Offizialer Beobachter, das Schwarze Korps,* and other Nazi publications appeared.

Germany has been virtually alone among Western nations with no central **Holocaust Museum** or memorial. In Berlin, it became a political football. Where, when, how, and whether had to be debated at great length in Bonn in Germany's parliament and considered in every detail by Berlin's politicians. Design became polarized along political lines. Some designs were compared to Albert Speer's Nazi concepts. Location grew to become a major controversy. Near the Brandenburg Gate? No. On the wasteland of the former Ministergärten, in the midst of the relics of the Nazi time, including the **Goebbels Bunker** which was not discovered until 1998, and gave an excuse for further delay.

## AXEL SPRINGER PUBLISHING HOUSE

The golden glass-and-concrete skyscraper of the **Axel Springer Verlag** ("Axel Springer Publishing House") is special to Berlin because it was built in West Berlin exactly on the border—smack against the Wall—in a direct confrontation with East Berlin at Kochstraße and Lindenstraße. On the roof Springer placed a huge sign with running text giving the news, day and night. East Germans could read it as far away as Unter den Linden, a half-mile (800 meters) away. It so angered the DDR authorities that they built the tall blue-white apartment houses on the Leipzigerstraße to obscure the view of the Springer news bulletins.

This version is disputed by the East Germans, who claim they built the tall apartment buildings as a demonstration to the West of their booming economy and their building skills. At the dedication of Europe's largest and most modern publishing house on October 6, 1966, Willy Brandt said, "My wish is that this house will one day stand at the center of an undivided city." Springer is dead, but his CDU-oriented, conservative publishing empire controls about 80 percent of all newspapers purchased in Berlin and includes the tabloid *Bild* magazine, the serious *Die Welt* Hamburg weekly newspaper, and the *Berliner Morgenpost,* the well-edited source filled with local information. In the '90s, the firm added its 19-story "silver" wing.

## STAUFFENBERG MEMORIAL

Towards the end of the War, parts of the High Command of the German Armed Forces and the Army High Command were housed in the War Ministry on Bendlerstraße (now Stauffenbergstraße) on the banks of the Landwehr Canal. They included the German General Army Office, headed by General Friedrich Olbricht (whose chief of staff was Col. Count Klaus von Stauffenberg), and the Office of the Commander-in-Chief of the Home Army, Colonel-General Friedrich Fromm. It was there that the leaders of the military resistance worked out plans for overthrowing the Nazi dictatorship and headed the unsuccessful assassination attempt against Hitler on July 20, 1944. In the same night, in what is now the Honor Courtyard, Colonel Count Stauffenberg and four of the other main conspirators were executed by firing squad for their participation in the assassination plans. Stauffenberg died crying, "Long live our sacred Germany." Other suspected conspirators were rounded up quickly by the Gestapo, taken to the Gestapo dungeons on Prinz-Albrecht-Straße, sentenced by kangaroo civilian courts, and hanged with piano wire at Plötzensee Prison (see below).

The **Gedenkstätte Deutscher Widerstand/Ehrenmal für die Opfer des 20. Juli 1944** ("Memorial to German Resistance/Monument to the Victims of July 20, 1944"), Stauffenbergstraße 13-14, side entrance, Tel. 26-99-50-00, Fax 26-54-22-30, *http://www.kulturbox.de/GDW* (open Mon.- Fri. 9 A.M. to 6 P.M., Sat.-Sun. 9 A.M. to 1 P.M.; entrance free), was opened on July 20, 1968, in the Bendlerblock. On the second floor you review over 5,000 photos and documents confirming German resistance to Nazi terror. Use bus 129 or 148.

## SOVIET MEMORIAL

Before the Wende, the **Sowjetischer Ehrenmal** ("Soviet Memorial") was the highlight of any sightseeing tour through East Berlin. Pilots use it for navigation. In an area equal to a dozen football fields, the statue of a Red Army soldier makes New York's Statue of Liberty look like a replica in a souvenir shop. It is far removed from the hub of contemporary excitement, but it never fails to stagger. Treptower Park, with its great English gardens, has been popular as a recreation area for Berliners since its design in 1876-88 and has a history of Communist opposition to power. On September 3, 1911, 200,000 Berliners assembled under red flags to hear August Bebel and Karl Liebknecht criticize the warlike moves of the kaiser. As many as three-quarters of a million assembled at a Spartacus demonstration in November 1918. Of the more than 20,000 Red Army soldiers who lost their lives in the Battle of Berlin at the close of the Second World War, more than 5,000 were laid to rest in Treptower Park (most of the others were buried in the Schönholzer Woods in Pankow).

The memorial was designed by Soviet architect Jewgeni W. Wutschetitsch using Swedish granite that the Nazis had earmarked for a victory monument. It was built on such a grandiose scale that it is difficult not to be moved by the result. After three years' work by 1,200 laborers, the memorial was dedicated on Liberation Day, May 8, 1949. The stone gateway on Puschkinallee leads directly to the grieving Mother Russia statue, carved from a 50-ton block of granite. From here a series of striking white stone tombs stretches to the hill at the center of the memorial, where a 38-foot (11.6 meters) bronze Soviet soldier stands at the summit. On his left arm he holds a German child, in his right hand the sword with which he has shattered the Nazi swastika. Inside the pedestal of the giant soldier, the crypt decorated with gold mosaics from the various former Soviet republics is filled with flowers. The total length of the memorial is 550 yards (500 meters).

Overlooking the political statement of the memorial, the park makes a moving impression. After the Wende the West Berlin government was in no mood to overlook the political statement. In the fall of 1993, the Berlin Parks Department issued a report for the "maintenance" of the park stating that the park would be returned to historic use, meaning that the Russian statements would be torn down and live animals and plants growing would be taken away probably according to the model of the ruination of Alexanderplatz. When or if this will happen is anyone's guess. The citizens of Treptow like the park as it stands. It is well maintained. Weeds are kept pulled. It is the first place they take their out-of-town visitors. Perhaps the reactions against the Red architecture will die before action is taken. Use S-Bhf Plänterwald, then take bus 166 or 167, three stops along the one-way highway. On departure use bus 166 or 167 to S-Bhf Treptower Park—or use the White Fleet's Treptower Park landing on the Spree. Up the road, one stop before bus 166 or 167 drops you at the Soviet Memorial, you see two small domes, like the shells of overgrown turtles, in a wild field. This is the **Archenhold-Sternwarte** ("Archenhold Observatory"), Alt-Treptow 1, Tel. 5-34-80-80, *http://www.snafu.de/~astw*, admission DM 4. Here Albert Einstein delivered his first public lecture about his Theory of Relativity. When the telescope with a 21-meter focal length was unveiled in 1896, it was a sensation, but the days of German astronomical excellence have been passed by men walking on the moon, probes on Mars and Jupiter, and telescope in space. The 50-centimeter reflecting telescope is no longer cutting edge. This is a people's planetarium/observatory. The price for the German-language planetarium show is a bargain, but Jupiter is broken.

## PLÖTZENSEE MEMORIAL

**Gedenkstätte Plötzensee**, Hüttigpfad, Tel. 344-3226 (open Mar.-Sept. 8:30 A.M. to 6 P.M., Oct.-Feb. to 4 P.M.; admission free) is in northwest Berlin where the districts of Charlottenburg and Wedding meet. The prison was required by Kaiser Wilhelm II "in case the city of Berlin should ever break down and rise once more in impudent intemperance against its sovereign." Down the cobbled Hüttigpfad (path), the squat red brick bungalow within the high walls was used as an execution chamber between 1933 and 1945. After Brandenburg Penitentiary, *"Plöze,"* as it was known, was the largest in northern Germany. With the exception of the extermination camps, no place was more bloody. In the whitewashed stone execution room, some 2,500 men, women, and teenagers were guillotined or hanged. (The guillotine was taken away by the Russians at the end of the War.) Prior to Hitler's seizure of power, death sentences were carried out only by beheading. On March 29, 1933, six days after the passing of Hitler's Enabling Act, execution by hanging was also introduced. On Hitler's orders, the death sentences of 89 men of the Stauffenberg July Plot were carried out by hanging them from six meat hooks with piano wire to prolong their agony. "They must all be hanged like cattle," Hitler ordered, and they were. It was Hitler's express wish that films be made so he might view their last twitchings afterwards. In a single night, September 7-8, 1943, between 7:30 P.M. and 8:30 A.M., 186 people were hanged in groups of eight, faster than the corpses could be transported to the Anatomical Institute for experiments.

THE BERLIN OF FASCISM AND COLD WAR

In 1952, the Berlin Senate erected here the Memorial to the Victims of the Hitler dictatorship. You visit the dank execution room and see the butchers' hooks used to support the nooses of the hanged political prisoners. On one side is an urn filled with earth from several Nazi concentration camps. The inner courtyard of the complex is surrounded by a high concrete wall reminding you of a prison yard or of a concentration camp.

Not far from the memorial site in Plötzensee, at Heckerdamm 230, the Catholic church, **Maria Regina Martyrum** (Tel. 3-82-60-11), was erected in 1963 by Hans Schädel and Friedrich Ebert as a memorial to victims who shed their blood for freedom of religion and conscience during Nazi times. The gray walls of the courtyard evoke concentration camps. The crypt is almost completely dark. On the right, below a simple pietà, three tombs represent those who died. Use U-Bhf Mierendorffplatz, bus 123, 126 or from S-Bhf Tiergarten use bus 123 to Saatwinkler Damm, the end of the line.

## SACHSENHAUSEN MEMORIAL

The city of Oranienburg bordering Berlin on the north received city rights in 1232. In the 17th century, Luise Henriette, wife of the elector and a princess from the house of Orange, built there a baroque palace that gave the city and county its name. The chemical factory built in 1814 was where Friedrich Ferdinand Runge discovered aniline in 1833, caffeine and atropine in 1834.

In 1933, the Nazis built Germany's first concentration camp in a closed brewery, **Sachsenhausen** by Oranienburg. They made no secret of the existence of their camps; rather they traded on the fear of being sent there. Fear kept most Germans quiet. In Sachsenhausen, the mass murder installation, more than 100,000 political prisoners, Jews, homosexuals, and undesirables were slaughtered. Now you can visit the **Gedenkstätte und Museum Sachsenhausen** ("Memorial and Museum Sachsenhausen"), Straße der Nationen, 22, Tel. 803-715 (open 8:30 A.M. to 6 P.M.; Oct. to Mar., to 4:30 P.M.). An enlarged **Jüdische Museum** ("Jewish Museum") and exhibition was open in rebuilt Barracks 39 in November 1997. Use S-Bhf Oranienburg, the end of the S-Bahn line, or regional trains RE2, RB12, or RB19.

When the Red Army administered the Soviet Zone of Germany, German liberals and prisoners were imprisoned by Stalin's KGB in Sachsenhausen and Berlin-Hohenschönhausen between 1945 and 1950. In the chaotic conditions of 1945-46, it was enough to be seen wearing some discarded

Nazi clothing, to be heard talking about Hitler, or simply to be in the wrong place at the wrong time. At a time when the civilian population did not have enough to eat, the prisoners starved. Every third prisoner died.

Stalinist terror was superimposed upon Nazi terror. More than 20,000 German prisoners were killed and buried in mass graves in the woods of Schmachtenhagen near the Sachsenhausen camp where Jews had been annihilated. A memorial chiseled in a sandstone boulder in the woods marks the burial of the German victims of Stalinism from **KGB Special Camp No. 7**. On Oct. 24, 1997, an eight-foot (2.5 meters) high, four-ton, angular Swedish stone memorial was placed on a small hill in the Gärtnerstraße cemetery where the skeletons of 127 nameless victims of **Special Camp No. 3** had been transferred. The victims were discovered in 1995 in a simple, ivy-covered mass grave where, in 1945/46 their bodies had been tossed like animals into a bomb crater and covered by mud. The memorial stone was created by sculptor Roland Luchmann and designer Elke Fehring.

In Berlin-Hohenschönhausen, **Special Camp No. 4** was erected on Freienwalder Straße in the middle of 1945 on the site of a former mess hall which was soon enlarged. Behind high walls and barbed wire, it was a special workshop of the Red Army where among other things stolen American automobiles were stripped. **Camp No. 1** served as the central interrogation prison for the KGB until it was turned over to the East Berlin secret police in 1951. **Camp No. 2** was used for a time as a Stasi-prisoner work camp.

## FORMER STASI HEADQUARTERS

The **Ministerium für Staatsicherheit** ("Ministry for State Security") was the official name for *Stasi,* the word everyone knows and Berliners hate, the ominous surveillance organization that was the backbone of East Germany's Police State.

At the Stasi headquarters on Normannenstraße in the Lichtenberg district, faceless gray office blocks stretched for hundreds of yards. Its 85,000 full-time staff worked or took orders from here; 1,052 specialists taped telephone calls, 2,100 steamed open letters, and 5,000 followed suspects. Stasi also paid 109,000 secret informers so that in a population of about 16 million, about one in 80 worked for the Stasi. They opened mail, tapped telephone lines, filmed, recorded, burgled, and blackmailed. They placed human or electronic eyes and ears everywhere, thus creating a poisonous atmosphere that kept a mistrusting population suspicious of their neighbors, working associates, drinking buddies, brothers, and sisters. So many East Germans informed on each other that there are files on about one of every three East Germans accounting for 50 miles of Stasi files in Berlin alone.

After a prolonged political debate, the files were opened to the public on January 2, 1992. Advocates of the law allowing individuals to see their own files argued that such a step would be a vital part of confronting the past while opponents feared it would unleash waves of hatred and revenge as people learned who among them were Stasi informers. Despite cautions to think carefully before applying, more than 3,000 individuals filled out applications to see their files on the first day. Applications continued running at about 20,000 a month.

One of the important turning points in the reunification process occurred at Stasi headquarters on January 15, 1990. A crowd of about 100,000 protesters broke open a door, smashed furniture, ransacked files, and left a trail of graffiti. Damage was far less than the million Marks announced by the DDR. The important damage was psychological.

The site has been now honored with the title **Forschungs- und Gedenkstätte Normannenstraße** ("Research and Memorial Site Normannen Street"), Ruschestraße 59, House 1 (Lichtenberg), Tel. 553-6854 (open Tue.-Fri. 11 A.M. to 6 P.M., Sat.-Sun. 2 P.M. to 6 P.M.). It is filled with ugly fragments of people control. There are microphones hidden in tree trunks; cameras buried in watering cans. Use U-Bhf Magdalenenstraße.

When you don't want to go all the way into the suburbs for a sight of the Stasi, just look to one of the nicest buildings in East Berlin, the 1988-restored, Gründerzeit turn-of-the-century building on the corner of Behrenstraße and Glinkastraße just down the street from the Comedic Opera. It has arched windows framed by delicate fluted columns, a stone eagle peering out of its rounded cornice, and a coat of thick, cream paint that sets it off from the gray stone buildings around it. Its restoration was the best thing the Stasi did for the neighborhood. It was spy headquarters for the missions and embassies in the neighborhood.

# WEISSENSEE

Many of the more than 112,000 graves in Europe's largest Jewish cemetery show how many people, and particularly young people, died between 1933 and 1945. Under many of the tombstones there are fewer graves than names, signifying that some of the dead actually died somewhere else—in the case of writer Kurt Tucholsky's mother, in a concentration camp.

**Jüdischer Friedhof Weißensee**, ("Jewish Cemetery") Herbert-Baum-Straße 45, Tel. 925-33-30 (open Sun.-Thur. 10 A.M. to 5 P.M., Fri. 8 A.M. to 3 P.M.;

admission free; men should wear a hat or borrow a skullcap from the caretaker). The largest Jewish cemetery in Europe, in the (now) East Berlin district of Weißensee, was founded together with the community in 1880. It differs from other Berlin Jewish cemeteries because of its great size—100 acres (40 hectares)—and because its relatively short time period coincides with a time when Berlin Jews had received full civil rights and achieved unprecedented prosperity. The tranquillity of the oak- and beech-covered grounds evokes the early 20th-century Jewish community of Berlin, which was the most affluent, most emancipated, and most prominent in Europe. Most of the inscriptions are in German only showing that most of these Berlin Jews felt themselves to be very German, but most identify a birthplace somewhere else, usually to the east of Berlin.

Just inside the entrance, to the right behind the brick memorial temple you find the graves of distinguished rabbis, educators, lawyers, scientists, artists, and musicians, including composer Louis Lewandowski, chemist Max Jaffe, and painter Lesser Ury. Although prominent Jews were traditionally buried in the smaller Jewish cemetery at 23 Schönhauser Allee (Tel. 441-98-24), you see huge mausoleums farther into the cemetery from the late 19th century showing the wealth of some Berlin Jews of the time. Here you find Emil Rathenau, the founder of AEG, the electrical concern, and Hermann Tietz, the department store pioneer. That the cemetery is also the resting place of pro-Russian hero Herbert Baum is partially responsible for the support given by the East German government after the War. Use S-Bhf Greifswalder Straße, then streetcar.

## HAUS OF THE WANNSEE CONFERENCE

For entrance, press the bell: "Bitte 1x klingeln." Beside the idyllic Wannsee far from the center of Berlin, on a secluded site at the seventh bus stop, stands a mansion of significance. On January 20, 1942, Reinhard Heydrich, the ruthless head of the Nazi's *Reichssicherheitshauptamt* ("Reich Security Main Office"), convened a Wannsee Conference of 14 high-ranking civil servants in the Villa Minoux. The decision to exterminate European Jews had been made earlier. The Wannsee Conference concerned itself with the organization and implementation of the "The Final Solution." In the gray administrative headquarters for the German branch of Interpol, Nazi leaders framed the plans for mobilizing their extermination camps in Poland and Czechoslovakia (which had been set up in 1941) into factories of mass murder. The Jews remaining throughout Nazi-occupied Europe, including the Reich itself, would be eliminated. Europe would become *Judenfrei*.

Fifty years later, on January 20, 1992, the suburban villa down the road from painter Max Liebermann's former summer residence at Am Großen Wannsee 42, is now the **Gedenkstätte Haus der Wannsee-Konferenz**, Am Großen Wannsee 56-58, Tel. 441-98-24, (open Tue.-Fri. 10 A.M. to 6 P.M.; Sat.-Sun. from 2 P.M., admission free) officials and rabbis opened Germany's first permanent memorial to the six million Jews who were put to death. The museum houses photographs of mass graves and quotations describing the calculated roundups and systematic murders of the planned Final Solution. The photos are titled in English, eloquent, and powerfully arranged, but the texts are in German only. English-language brochures are free. Use S-Bhf Wannsee, then bus 114.

Jews were persecuted from the start of the Hitler government in 1933. Nazi leaders repeated for more than a decade their intention to annihilate the Jews, but the bureaucratic decisions establishing the deportation systems and organizing the death camps were not approved until the Wannsee meeting. It was a 90-minute session that concluded with pleasant chatter and a round of cognac. In 1947, the minutes of the conference, recorded by Adolf Eichmann, were found in the files of the German Foreign Office.

When the Nazis came to power, about 500,000 Jews lived in Germany. Today the government recognizes 35,000 members of the Jewish community. Unofficial estimates put the number closer to 50,000, and growing, with recent immigrants from the former Soviet Union.

## TRACK NO. 17, BAHNHOF GRUNEWALD

In the Grunewald train station you will notice the memorial to deported Jews at the train station where Berlin Jews were herded into cattle cars for brutal transportation to concentration and extermination camps. Nazis deported 55,699 Berlin Jews from Bahnhof Grunewald and other train stations. Most of them were murdered. Track No. 17, where the deportation trains loaded, is framed with a steel band. The horrible dates and numbers of those Jews sent to their deaths are recorded at 186 places on the edge of the platform.

## 5. Sports

The areas described in this section are not amenable to sports activities. Boys sometimes kick around a soccer ball on the field left empty by the destruction of the Anhalter Bahnhof, but not for much longer, because this field is slated for construction of a new entertainment stadium.

## 6. Shopping

In Kreuzberg (Chapter 8), south of the former Nazi headquarters region, you find flea markets and secondhand shops.

## 7. Nightlife and Entertainment

You wouldn't expect to find nightlife and entertainment near ugly surroundings, but walk a few blocks south of the former Nazi headquarters to the Kreuzberg district (Chapter 8) and there you find nightlife, walk a few blocks north to the historic center of Berlin (Chapter 4) to find opera and theater, the Tiergarten's (Chapter 6) Cultural Forum is a short trip west via Potsdamer Platz and the Gendarmenmarkt's Schauspielhaus beckons only blocks to the East.

# 8

# Kreuzberg

## 1. Orientation

Kreuzberg literally means "Mountain of the Cross," referring to the highest mountain in Berlin with a height of 216 feet (66 meters). The makeup of the district surrounding the rise isn't what it used to be. It used to be Berlin's antiestablishment embarrassment—rebellious and naughty. But Kreuzberg has reformed, or disintegrated, depending on your viewpoint.

No one has ever been able to figure out what to do with Kreuzberg. It didn't even have an official name until it was created from heterogeneous communities upon the formation of Greater Berlin in 1920. The historical city sections of South Friedrichstadt, Luisenstadt, and Tempelhofer Vorstadt were tossed together to form Greater Berlin's Sixth District. At that time there were 380,000 inhabitants. Now there are 150,000, of which about one-third are foreigners, and 20,278 are unemployed, and it is a youthful district—only 8.4% are older than 65 (Berlin's average is 13.9%)—yet it is still Berlin's most densely populated district with the highest density of dogs (next to an Eastern residential area).

Kreuzberg still differs so widely across its boundaries that there are, for all practical purposes, two Kreuzbergs, each identified by its separate former postal zip code, 61 and 36. The working class neighborhood is still called "SO 36" because of its former Berlin postal zip code: "SüdOst 36." It was known respectfully throughout Berlin for its four "A's": *Alternative, Arbeitslose, Anarchisten,* and *Altbauten* ("alternative living, unemployment, anarchism, and ancient buildings"). It was one of Berlin's most beloved communities because of the spicy **Kreuzberger Mischung** ("Kreuzberg Mixture"). Hourly workers and laborers lived in the street-facing front houses and in the first back courtyard. When you wandered into the second and third back courtyards, you would find factories. Kreuzberg 61 is residential, but SO 36 residents once put up their own wall to keep foreigners out unless they bought a Kreuzberger passport.

In 1734, King Friedrich Wilhelm I's taxation wall (in part a high wooden fence) ran through the quarter that is now Kreuzberg. The wall wasn't for military purposes, but for a taxation boundary and a barrier to keep soldiers from deserting from the drill field. You can trace the route of the Wall by the raised U-Bahn right-of-way. Two of the gates through the wall still remain: Kottbusser Tor and Schlesisches Tor. Hallesches Tor is gone, marked only by a U-Bahn station. These gates are regarded as the most representative of the old taxation wall—except for the 200-year-old Brandenburg Gate.

## 2. The Hotel Scene

**Hotel Riehmers Hofgarten** (Yorckstraße 83, Kreuzberg 61) opened in 1985 in the historic Riehmers Hofgarten and closed in 1997, a million Marks in debt. Kreuzberg is depressed compared to the booming new areas of Berlin, so hoteliers are putting their investments into more profitable areas of Berlin.

**Hotel Transit** (Hagelberger Straße 53-54, Tel. 789-047-0, Fax 789-047-77), US$50, single; US$58, double, including breakfast, provides 49 rooms with shower. Use U-Bhf Mehringdamm, S-Bhf Yorckstraße, bus 119, 219, or N19.

## 3. Restaurants and Cafés

**Altes Zollhaus**, Carl-Herz-Ufer 30, Tel. 692-3300 (open for dinners only Tue.-Sat.) is a paradise for gourmets in SO61. Located at the steamer landing on the Landwehr Canal, the price levels are at high tide. Reservations required. Use U-Bhf Prinzenstraße, bus 140.

The **Atlantic Café**, Bergmannstraße 100, Tel. 691-92-92 (open daily 10 A.M. to 2 A.M.) is inexpensive, with good German food, a long bar, sidewalk tables, a billiard table, and good, inexpensive breakfasts until 5 P.M., but don't plan to meet someone here. It's too crowded. Use U-Bhf Gneisenaustraße.

**Barcomi's**, Bergmannstraße 21, Tel. 694-81-38 (open Mon.-Sat. 9 A.M. to midnight, Sun. from 10 A.M.), on the corner of Marheinekeplatz, you can get real American-flavored coffee, bagels, brownies, and other bakery items that make Amis homesick. At night you can expect readings and lectures. Use U-Bhf Gneisenaustraße.

**Café am Ufer**, Paul-Lincke-Ufer 42-43, Tel. 612-28-27 (open 10 A.M. to midnight) is beautifully situated on the bank of the Landwehr Canal. The café has tables outside and art on the walls inside. Great for breakfasts from 10 A.M.

**Café Stresemann**, Stresemannstraße 90, Tel. 261-17-60 (open 9 A.M. to 1 A.M.) attracts a young crowd with breakfasts to 4 P.M. Use S-Bhf Anhalter Bahnhof.

**Golgotha** im Viktoriapark, Dudenstraße 48-64, Tel. 785-24-53 (open from 11 A.M. to 6 A.M.), has an authentic beer garden atmosphere. If you don't mind sitting on uncomfortable benches, standing in line for beer, and shouting just to be heard, you quickly absorb the feeling of the *Kiez.* Just follow the crowds next to the Katzbach stadium. It's also perfect for breakfast beside the waterfall during the summer. Use U- or S-Bhf Yorckstraße.

**Großbeerenkeller**, Großbeerenstraße 90, Tel. 251-30-64 (open Mon.-Fri. 4 P.M. to 2 A.M., Sat. from 6 P.M.), is a typical Kreuzberg Kneipe with beer, grilled potatoes, Silesian specialties, smoke, Kreuzberg *Mischung,* actors, and groupies.

Outside the Technology Museum you can enjoy the coffee, beer, and snacks of the **Gaststätte für Verkehr und Technik,** Tel. 2-62-68 (open 11 A.M. to 6 P.M.).

## 4. Sightseeing

### KREUZBERG 61

Kreuzberg is a typical neighborhood for Berlin. The main thoroughfare is Yorckstraße which is only 25 feet (7 meters) narrower than Unter den Linden. The SPD political party has just built their high-rise Berlin headquarters here, at the intersection of Wilhelmstraße and Stresemannstraße, the *Willy-Brandt-Haus.*

When you pass beneath the two stone figures through the gateway arches across the street from the Kreuzberg city hall on shabby Yorckstraße, you step back 100 years. You discover a fantasy of green courtyards, tall trees, wrought-iron gates, balconies, lanterns, stucco-decorated houses, and narrow cobblestone paths. **Riehmers Hofgarten** ("Riehmer's Court Garden") is a dreamlike ensemble of 24 Renaissance houses that architect Wilhelm Riehmer built to defy the advocates of Gründerzeit architecture of the time. The establishment felt that his 1881-92 buildings were wasteful and reprehensible, but with the passing years the 17,000-square-foot (1,600 square meters) Riehmer's Court has become recognized as one of the most beautiful residence blocks in all of Berlin. It was landmarked in 1964. The city noise is far outside through the three entrances. One is an iron gate between Großbeerenstraße 56 and 57. Another is through the arch decorated with huge figures of two sea gods—Atlantises—holding a lion's face on Yorckstraße. The third is from Hagelberger Straße. The Hofgarten contains bistros, cafés, a movie house, Kneipen, and a disco. There's always something going on here. One spot, that was once rented by officers of the Prussian mounted infantry stationed nearby, for better or worse has been taken by the Kreuzberg taxation office. Several successful artists with established reputations live here, but the lesser-known artists of Kreuzberg have drifted away because of rising rents in the prized location.

A few doors from Riehmers Hofgarten, the brick church at Yorckstraße 88-89 is unusual as well. The 1903 **St. Bonifatious** was built sideways so that its narrow side faces the street, it fronts directly on Kreuzberg's busiest street, and it doesn't stand alone on a hill but adjoins such commerce as the Burger King restaurant. Catholic religious services are performed in a Lutheran community, and it contains a delightful courtyard supporting several rental properties.

**Mehringplatz** is an example of an old, beautiful, very busy traffic hub of the late 19th century that has been ruined by a novel circular housing development with a statue of *Winged Victory* by Christian Daniel Rauch in the center. At the north end is Rainer Kriester's 1975 aluminum work of art titled *Where do we come from where are we going?* showing two disembodied legs, both with left feet.

The **Willy-Brandt-Haus**, Wilhelmstraße 140 (open Mon.-Sat. 10 A.M. to 6 P.M.; Sun. 11 A.M. to 5 P.M.) is Berlin's 1996 headquarters building for the SPD political party, but it didn't really assume full importance until its Bonn contingent lumbered in during summer 1999. The striking structure is ecological friendly regarding energy consumption, heating, and air-conditioning. Drop into the bistro/restaurant **Espede** ("SPD") for a snack. Use U-Bhf Hallesches Tor—near the Martin Gropius Building.

The **Kreuzberg mountain**, 216 feet (66 meters) high, is Berlin's highest natural mountain. Berlin Schnauze calls it the "Berlin Zugspitze" (the Zugspitze is the tallest Alp in Germany) and confirms that it is the only one in Berlin to have an altitude of 6,600—in this case, 6,600 centimeters. It is covered with one of Berlin's most genuinely likable green spaces, **Viktoriapark,** which is better known to Kreuzbergers as *Kreuzbergpark* for the cross at the top of the National Memorial. It is one of four large *Volksgärten* that were laid out by Berlin planners in the last half of the 19th century. It was named for Crown Princess Victoria, the wife of later Kaiser Friedrich III who took the throne in 1888, ruled for 99 days, and died the same year. Hermann Mächtig laid out his plans in 1879-80. Work began in 1888 and was completed in 1894. It was expanded westward by Albert Brodersen in 1912-14. During the Second World War, the park was badly damaged but retained its general character. It was placed under national preservation in 1980 and touched up in 1986. Mächtig's great artificial waterfall, which first flowed in October 1893, is flanked by flights of steps. It trickles into a small pond where you see Ernst Hertel's 1910 erotic bronze sculpture *Ein seltener Fang* ("A Rare Catch") showing a muscular fisher pulling a sensuous mermaid from the waters. Operation of the waterfall is made possible by three sponsors with Axel Springer Publications paying the lion's share.

Kreuzberg hill is dominated by one of Schinkel's few Gothic works. His **Nationaldenkmal** ("National Memorial"), a war memorial, marks the Wars of Liberation against Napoleon. It has the form of a slim, 65-foot-high (20 meters), carved-stone and wrought-iron spire copied from the Cologne cathedral topped with the iron cross designed by King Friedrich Wilhelm III in 1813. A succession of plaques around the base mark Prussia's victories from Leipzig in 1813 to Waterloo (Belle Alliance) in 1815. The statues by Christian Daniel Rauch and others show the faces of contemporary generals and members of the royal family. The cornerstone was laid on September 19, 1818, in the presence of the king and Russian Czar Alexander I. Originally the 62-foot (19 meters) high memorial stood on a platform with only 11 steps, but it was severely criticized for not being impressive enough, so in 1878 the memorial was raised 26 feet (8 meters) and rotated 21 degrees. During its restoration in 1980-86, the rusted-through spire was virtually replaced. From the platform you see a decent, but distant, panorama as far as the television Tower in East Berlin. At the foot of the hill, on Kreuzbergstraße, take a look at the antique green-patina preserved former urinal so typical for the neighborhood. Berlin Schnauze has labeled it *Café Achteck*, ("Café Octagon"). You won't be able to order coffee here. At one time there were more than 100 in Berlin. In 1951, there were 75. At last count there were 21 and the end was in sight. The city claims it is too expensive to maintain this street furniture.

Behind the Schinkel monument you can make out the former brick **Schultheiss brewery**, dating from 1830. Although Schultheiss moved to

Weißensee in 1995, they remained true to their roots when they left behind the old foundry for concerts and the **Brauereimuseum** ("Brewery Museum"), Methfesselstraße 24-48, Tel. 960-90. Use U-Bhf Platz der Luftbrücke, bus 104, 119, 184, 340, or 341. In the park, a wooden cross marks the revolution in East Berlin on June 17, 1953.

In the 1996-98 remodeled **Berlin-Museum,** Lindenstraße 61, Tel. 23-80-90-30 behind the yellow neoclassical 1735 facade of Philipp Gerlach in Berlin's first purpose-built administrative building, you discover an eclectic collection of some delightful Berlin memorabilia from before, during, and after the Nazi period. This is a pleasing visit once you become familiar with Berlin and can associate the items you find. Here you can see at last an authentic graffiti-painted section of the actual Wall. There are also fascinating scale models of two sections of the Wall, one near Kreuzberg and one through a rural wooded area, that were built on the orders of former DDR President Honecker.

A curious piece of luck for anyone interested in Berlin's history has been displayed in the museum since 1982. It seems that an artist, whose name has been lost, took his pen and palette down to Under den Linden in 1820 and spent weeks on the dividing strip drawing every building on the north and south sides of the avenue between the Brandenburg Gate and the Berlin City Palace. His panorama, almost 25 feet long, shows a complete progression of Linden's houses, church, opera house, and adjoining structures. You see the strollers, lovers, debating students, children with drums and flags, mothers with children, a funeral procession, a fire truck, soldiers, and coaches of the time. On the second floor of the museum, a good collection of Zille's caricatures are on display. Use bus 240 from U-Bhf Hallesches Tor.

The precious Berlin Museum building with its wrought-iron balconies and gilded crests (and Christian crown) is overshadowed next door by the immense, multi-sharp-angled, aluminum-skin **Jüdische Museum** ("Jewish Museum") that's shaped like a lightning bolt at Lindenstraße 14. Designed by Swiss architect, Daniel Libeskind, this is one of the most significant and hotly debated cultural buildings of the post-war period. With the *zick-zack* shaped, 23-sided shell beside the conventional, late baroque building of the Berlin Museum, even the building's design is tense. Libeskind drew inspiration from his own scribblings, as well as from the many erasures that Berlin has endured. Strangely inaccessible spaces intrude on the maze of massive galleries, which form a distorted Star of David when viewed from above. In its labyrinthine interior there is always light and shadow. It opened in November 1998, containing the exhibition-collection from the

Jewish Section of the Martin Gropius Building (Chapter 7). Use bus 240 from U-Bhf Hallesches Tor.

The **Deutsches Technikmuseum Berlin** ("German Technical Museum in Berlin") was formerly known as the **Museum für Verkehr und Technik** ("Transportation and Technical Museum"), Trebbiner Straße 9, Tel. 254-84-0 (open Tue.-Fri. 9 A.M. to 5:30 P.M., Sat.-Sun. 10 A.M. to 6 P.M.; entrance adults DM 5, students DM 2). It is a favorite for Berliners and a delight for the technically minded, but those in search of art treasures or political history can better spend their time elsewhere. Partially set in the converted, overgrown freight yard of the former Anhalter Bahnhof (a gateway has been preserved), it's crowded with families with children on Sundays, so it is a good idea to avoid going on this day. The signs are in German and occasionally English.

Use U-Bhf Möckernbrücke, U-Bhf Gleisdreieck, which means "Rail Triangle," bus 129 or 248. U-Bhf Gleisdreieck is unusual because two U-Bahn lines are linked together by ramps. As you exit a U-Bahn station, look for the direction sign. The museum was opened in 1983. The public visited the central traffic hall for the first time in 1985. In 1987, the hall for railroad, bridge, and ship building opened. The second locomotive arrived in 1988. Inside the museum you see many classic automobiles; the copper-and-cast-iron 1904 fire engine; a 1922 Brennabor automobile, which could reach 45 mph (70 km/hr); a bizarre, finned 1921 Rumpler; and Germany's best-selling small car in 1924, the Grattawagen. There are radial air-cooled, six-cylinder in-line, water-cooled, and all designs of motors including a room-sized V-12 liquid-cooled motor used on a seaplane.

On the first floor there is a technical exhibit of computers and calculators. The ancient bicycle exhibit featuring a wooden 1820 model will amuse anyone who has ever ridden a bicycle: two-wheelers with leather seats and carvings of horses on the front; bicycles made out of wood with removable, candlelit headlights; a **Wanderhochrad** ("touring high bicycle") from 1886; and an original 1818 hobbyhorse.

Filling the main hall is the greatest steam locomotive display of great Prussian locomotives of various kinds, small and large, in the world. Side-by-side examples include a mammoth freight steam locomotive of the Austrian Südbahn built in 1860, small 1903 colonial field locomotives, and an enormous ("gigantic" is not too tame a word) 1914 Prussian traffic locomotive P-8. All show years of hard usage. A Prussian S-10 **Schnellzug** ("Fast Train") has been arc-torch-separated away to display the steam-driven inner workings with each part marked in German explaining its function. You can walk in a clean trench below one train to study the undercarriage to get a feeling for the oil and grease that accumulates during service.

Outside in the courtyard you see an original round table and a steam-driven snowplow locomotive. Included is an original arch salvaged from the Anhalter Bahnhof after its destruction. A vast exterior wall painting showing various modes of transportation is now hidden by the construction of the new DM 140 million high-rise extension of the museum to showcase the shipping and air travel collections. The cornerstone was laid on March 27, 1996, but it won't be completed until the year 2000. Berlin architects Helga Pitz and Ulrich Wolf have devised a low-energy building in which daylight and solar energy will be used to optimum effect.

## ANHALTER TRAIN STATION

Sally Bowles made her grand entry into Berlin here in Isherwood's *Goodbye to Berlin.* Kaiser Wilhelm II had his own private waiting room and welcomed King Umberto I of Italy and Czar Nicholas II of Russia. Hitler used the station for his triumphal return to Berlin after Germany's annexation of Austria in 1938 and victory over France in 1940.

**Anhalter Bahnhof,** Europe's largest and tallest covered train station, was built from 1875 to 1880. It was 112 feet (34.25 meters) high, 558 feet (170 meters) long, and 200 feet (61 meters) wide. It could have contained the complete St. Marks' square in Venice with room to spare for the pigeons. The rail yards stretched for three miles (five kilometers) through Kreuzberg. Each day saw 120 trains speeding to destinations like Constantinople, Brindisi, and Nice.

The station was severely damaged during World War II, but despite gaping holes in the roof, the walls remained sound and it was thought at the time that it would make an excellent museum. Trains continued running until May 18, 1952, when the surviving remains were destroyed by a surprise terrorist bombing for unknown reasons.

Except for the portico, which luckily survived the explosion, the station was razed in 1960-61. Now you see merely the preserved brown-brick facade consisting of four columns and four circular windows, but it is worth seeing because of the decoration and detail such as Corinthian columns, and you can imagine the station stretching across the huge green field where children are playing soccer.

Anhalter Bahnhof was designed by Franz Schwechten (1841-1924), the same architect as the Kaiser-Wilhelm-Gedächtniskirche. (Considering the fate of these two works, he was a very unlucky architect indeed.) It was opened in 1880 by Kaiser Wilhelm II at the time Schwechten headed the high-rise building section of the Berliner Anhalter Railroad (from

1871 to 1882). Schwechten also built the factories of AEG in Berlin, Haus Vaterland, the Palace in Posnan, and the Hohenzollern Bridge over the Rhine River in Cologne.

Use S-Bhf Anhalter Bahnhof to visit remnants of the Anhalter Bahnhof international station. The S-Bahn station is excellently restored with escalators, white and green enameled tiles, Art Deco lights over the platforms, and oaken benches. On the walls you see color and black-and-white historical photos of the Bahnhof. The biggest, in color, shows a French tricolor flying above the gigantic station, steam locomotives exiting the structure, and the fountain in front.

The empty area left by the demolition of Anhalter Bahnhof is slated to accommodate, when funds are found, the new **Tempodrom,** which was the mammoth tent used for rock concerts in the Tiergarten which had to give way for construction of the new home of the German **Bundesrat** ("Federal Court").

"End of the line. Station Gleisdreieck. Everybody out," a woman's voice announced over the loudspeaker. July 31, 1991, was the end of the line for Berlin's *Magnetbahn* after carrying 2.5 million passengers over 71,400 miles (115,000 kilometers) in two years.

U-Bhf Gleisdreieck was the former terminus for the one-mile (1.6 kilometers) demonstration Maglev (magnetic levitation) train line M-1 to Kemperplatz that was built by the German electrical firm, AEG. The smooth-riding cars were outfitted like any U- or S-Bahn train; scientific interest was in the propulsion (although brake failures sometimes smashed up the stations). The Maglev stations were dismantled at a cost of DM 10 million to allow reconstruction of U-Bahn lines U2 and U15 connecting East and West Berlin. AEG's seed money was well spent, it led to financing the controversial Transrapid high-speed Maglev line between Berlin and Hamburg, but along the way AEG was swallowed by a bigger corporate fish.

## SO 36

So far you've seen the highlights of respectable Kreuzberg 61. Now men can put on their nose rings and women can strip to show their tattoos so they won't feel out of place in SO 36, which is the neighborhood between Oranienplatz, the Landwehrkanal, and the Spree River.

So many foreigners, students, dropouts, and believers in alternative lifestyles lived in SO 36 that they created a new word to describe it: the **Szene,** which dates from the Flower Power days of the '60s. Not only visitors but also Berlin residents respected and boasted about this area for its individuality.

# KREUZBERG SO 36

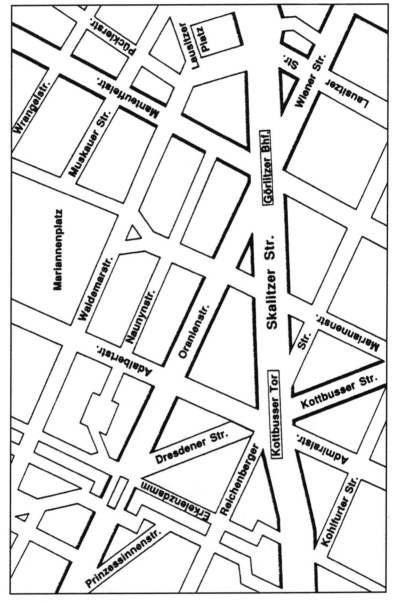

Young people were exempt from military duty in Berlin, so Kreuzberg filled with passivists from all over West Germany avoiding the draft and collecting subsidies, like allowances from home. When President Reagan visited Berlin in 1987, Kreuzberg was sealed off with barbed wire. Kreuzberg was formerly isolated by the Wall in an out-of-the-way pocket of the divided city. The nearby Wall protected them. The press called Berlin an island, the politicians called Berlin a fortress, but to the residents of SO 36, Berlin was a party. Artists from all over the world came here. They established almost 300 theaters, shows, galleries, stages, film houses, and other imaginative cultural arrangements.

The fall of the Wall on November 9, 1989, was a catastrophe for SO 36. In a few months Kreuzberg changed from exotic Wallflower, with plumes and spangles, to unwilling neighbor of boring, dormant district Mitte in East Berlin. SO 36 was no longer on the fringe of West Berlin. It was back in the middle, a thoroughfare between East and West. All at once investors began knocking, not only from West Germany but from all over Europe, the U.S., and Japan. Nikon settled on Kochstraße; a Bavarian firm on Moritzplatz. A high-rise office building rose on the Yorckbrücke. Boutiques and fine shops sprang up with entrepreneurs hoping to profit from the new through traffic. Rents exploded—up 800 percent.

If it weren't for the presence of Turkish residents, SO 36 would have resembled the radical areas of many large U.S. university cities, such as Berkeley, but it's incorrect, as you may have heard, that Berlin is the world's second largest Turkish city. In 1961, West Berlin had 20,000 non-German residents. By 1975, there were 190,000. By the end of 1989, there were at least 297,000. Now, of 3.4 million Berlin residents, there are some 420,000 foreigners (about 12 percent), of which 40 percent are Turks. With 168,000 Turks (40,000 in Kreuzberg), the size of the Turkish population in Berlin hardly counts statistically. Istanbul's population is 5,800,000, Ankara's is 1,700,000, Izmir's is 2,300,000, Adana's is 1,700,000, etc. If you come to Kreuzberg to see Oriental bazaars and souks, you are going to be disappointed, but in late afternoon and early evening you will see the occasional woman decked in beautiful Turkish finery. By and large you will find a very Westernized neighborhood, occasional Turkish and Greek delis and takeouts, occasional Turkish and Greek restaurants, and apartment houses with flowers in the window boxes.

The hub of SO 36 is Kottbusser Tor, which everyone calls **Kotti.** It is sort of a run-down Piccadilly Circus, Times Square, or Sather Gate. In fact, it was a gate in the former Prussian tax wall, but only the name remains. Much of the housing is too-large apartment dwellings—many with balconies and flower boxes. Graffiti is the main form of decoration: "Fight the city planners—this is our town." For SO 36, use U-Bhf Kottbusser Tor.

Shortly up Adalbertstraße from the Kotti is the small **Kreuzberg Museum**, Adalbertstraße 95/96, open daily 2-6 P.M., but the pleasure of SO 36 comes from wandering curiously to find out what's up. There's an excellent, representative graffiti mural on the wall of an apartment building on Admiralstraße across from the Grillhaus Klein-Istanbul. It is signed: "Berlin, one love, hip hop." A second cute sight is Ludmila Seefried-Matejkova's **Denkmal des Admirals** ("Memorial of the Admirals"), a contemporary bronze showing two Kreuzberg youths in the fashions of 1985. It is down funky Admiralstraße off the Kotti. You smile at the contrast between old and new by comparing the stoned youth with two bronze admirals back-to-back standing on an hourglass above them, looking for the good old times with telescopes.

One of the few things worth sightseeing is the **Künstlerhaus Bethanien** ("Artist's House Bethanien") at Mariannenplatz 2, Tel. 616-9030, that you reach (bus 140) from Kottbusser Tor via Adalbertstraße. The 1845-47 yellow-brick hospital with two neo-Gothic towers that was to be torn town in 1984 was one of the first buildings occupied by young people in Berlin. After fierce arguing and strung-out discussions, a practical solution was finally found: Bethanien was established as Kreuzberg's Artists' Center providing artists' working spaces, ateliers, display rooms, and theater halls. Exhibitions are held (open daily 2 to 7 P.M.; admission free).

The **Bundesdruckerei** ("Federal Printing Office") between Oranien- and Kommandantenstraße is busy turning out notes of Europe's new currency, the Euro so that on January 1, 2002, every Berliner can have a wallet bulging with 5-, 10-, 20-, 50-, 100-, 200-, and 500-Euro notes.

Kreuzbergers call the length of Line U-1 running overhead above the Kotti, **Orient Express.** It connects Kotti with U-Bhf Schlesisches Tor, which is known as "Little Istanbul." *Line One*, the very popular movie about this line, is enjoyed by everyone.

## 5. Sports

**Sommerbad Kreuzberg,** Gitschiner Straße 18-31, Tel. 2588-5412/16 (open daily 8 A.M. to 6:30/8 P.M.). Swimming. Use U-Bhf Prinzenstraße.

**Sportjugendclub (SJC) Kreuzberg**, Admiralstraße 36/37, Tel. 615-79-75. Sports center for youth offers billiards, skateboarding, table tennis, basketball, and a gymnasium as well as aerobic and dance classes. Organizes weekend trips and bicycle tours. Use U-Bhf Kottbusser Tor.

**Schwimmhalle Kreuzberg**, Baerwaldstraße 64, Tel. 25-88-31-24.

# KOTTI TO U-SCHLESISCHES TOR—"THE ORIENT EXPRESS"

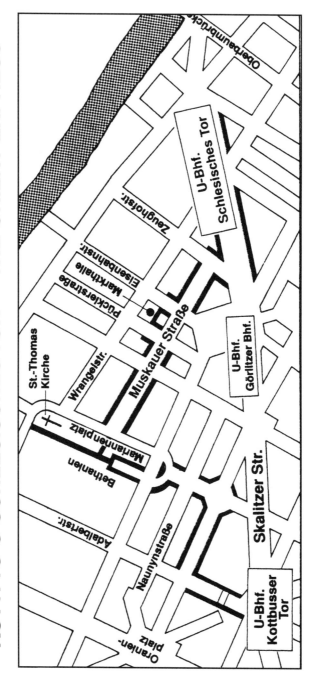

**Schwimmhalle Kreuzberg 61**, Wiener Straße 591, Tel. 25-88-58-15 (open Tue.-Sun. 8 A.M. to 10 P.M., Mon. from 5 P.M.).

## 6. Shopping

**Türkischer Basar** ("Turkish Bazaar"), Maybachufer (Tue. and Fri., noon to 6:30 P.M.) was started in 1882 beside the canal and became the largest and cheapest weekly market in Berlin following the Second World War. The Turkish market has a fascinating Oriental flair where you can buy low-priced vegetables and exotic spices. Use U-Bhf Schönleinstraße.

**Öko-Markt am Chamissoplatz** ("Ecological Market") (open Sat. 8 A.M. to 2 P.M.) is a weekly market near Tempelhof. Use U-Bhf Platz der Luftbrücke.

**Mauerspecht's Staatsauflösung** ("Wall Woodpecker's Going-Out-of-Business State"), Haus am Checkpoint Charlie, Friedrichstraße 44, Tel. 253-72-50 (open daily 9 A.M. to 10 P.M.). If it really has to be a piece of the Wall, then this is the place most likely to stock authentic ones. The motto for store owners Ulrike Wolf and Alwain Nachtweh is "history in your hand." Accordingly, they have a large selection of metals, military insignia, and other debris left floating by soldiers of former East Germany and Soviet Union.

You can find a couple of shops for magic freaks in the area. The **Zauberkönig** ("Magic King"), Hermannstraße 84-90, Neukölln, has all the equipment necessary to make champagne glasses disappear or to pull rabbits out of a hat. Use U-Bhf Leinestraße, bus 144. **Zauberzentrale** ("Magic Center"), on Friedrichstraße, offers professional advice to the apprentice magician on how to saw his assistant in half without creating a bloodbath.

## 7. Nightlife and Entertainment

The Kreuzberg Szene focuses on Oranienstraße. It's not like what it was before the opening of the Wall, but you find Turkish stores and many Kneipen. Kreuzberg is also home to a number of small theaters:

Kreuzberg 61's neoclassical **Riehmers Hofgarten**, Yorckstraße 83, Tel. 78-10-11, makes a fun place to spend an evening.

The **Schmiedehof** ("Blacksmith's Square") in the former Schultheiss brewery in Viktoriapark is one of the most attractive ensembles of Berlin's Gründerzeit architecture. During July and August, the artistic square is home to open-air jazz concerts on Friday evenings and classical works on Saturday nights at **Kreuzberger Hofkonzerte,** Methfesselstraße 28-48,

Tel. 247-49-777 (entrance fee varies with work presented). Use U-Bhf Mehringdamm or U-Bhf Platz der Luftbrücke.

The **Hebbel-Theater**, Stresemannstraße 29, Tel. 25-90-04-27, Fax 25-90-04-49, *http://www.hebbel-theater.de*, designed by Oskar Kaufmann, opened in 1908 with a performance of Friedrich Hebbel's *Maria Magdalena.* The theater was restored in 1987 for Berlin's 750th anniversary. Behind the massive limestone facade you will find a luxurious interior. Today it presents avantgarde dance, music, and drama. It is a high point of the Berlin cultural landscape. Use U-Bhf Hallesches Tor.

**Theater am Halleschen Ufer**, Hallesches Ufer 32, Tel. 2-51-06-56, Fax 2-51-27-16, is Berlin's main venue for independent theater, mostly contemporary dance and avant garde theater. Use U-Bhf Möckernbrücke or U-Bhf Hallesches Tor.

**Freilichtkino Kreuzberg**, Mariannenplatz 2, Tel. 24-31-30-30, is the 500-seat open-air movie house in the inner courtyard of the Künstlerhaus Bethanien. It shows classic films in the original language with German subtitles. Use U-Bhf Kottbusser Tor.

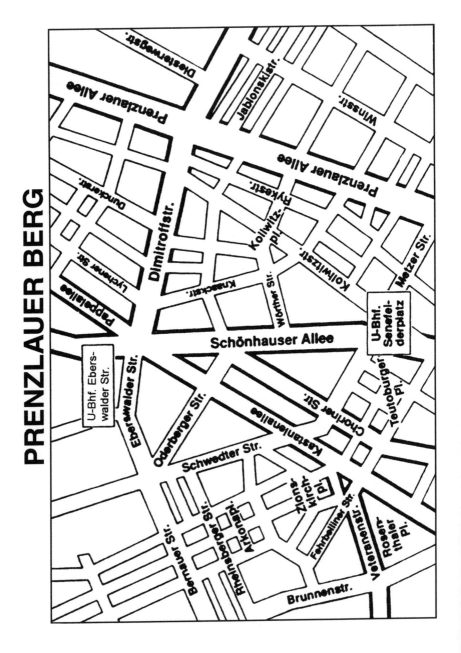

PRENZLAUER BERG

# 9

# Prenzlauer Berg

## 1. Orientation

Because "*Berg*" means "mountain," anyone who goes to Prenzlauer Berg of course wonders where the mountain is. The mountain is a hill so small right across from U-Bhf Senefelderplatz that you might overlook it. Prenzlauer Berg got its name because it lay outside the Prenzlauer Tor ("gate") in the early city wall leading to the city of Prenzlau. Prenzlauer Berg was Berlin's most densely populated city section—an anthill of tenements not far northeast from Berlin's center—so thickly built that for years there was no space for memorials. They had to prize space for the Alois Senefelder memorial. Space for the Käthe Kollwitz memorial was found only after Wartime bombing destroyed her former home. Still, the desolate Jewish Cemetery is a memorial. The Water Tower on Knaackstraße is a monument of technical achievement as well as a memorial of anti-Fascist resistance. Well worth seeing is the Peace Temple on Rykestraße and the preserved brewery between Knaackstraße and Schönhauser Allee. You are likely to cross under the *Magistratsschirm,* or "Town Council's Umbrella."

During the Ice Age glaciers leveled almost everything in the Spree basin, but left rises in Prenzlauer Berg and Kreuzberg, the highest natural hills in Berlin. Berliners exaggerate. In Berlin, any slight rise automatically becomes a mountain. Bicycle riders seem to agree.

Farmers tilled their wheat fields here 150 years ago and windmills were common, especially on Prenzlauer Berg hill, where farmers crowded more than 30 spinning windmills. It was no wonder that 150 years ago the region was called "Mühlenberg" (*Mühle* meaning "mill").

Since the area lay outside Berlin's tax wall, construction didn't begin until about 1860, but when it began, it began with a furor of land speculation. With the industrialization of Berlin and the naming of Berlin as Germany's capital city in 1871, droves of workers moved to Berlin. They tried to find work and places to live. In a very short time planners laid out residential quarters around the former center of Berlin for the industrial workers. Industry, and especially breweries, moved into Prenzlauer Berg. Streets were given French names because the quarter was built after the German-French War in which Germany had annexed Alsace-Lorraine.

**Mietskasernen** ("Rental Barracks"/"Tenements") replaced windmills. Land speculation and exorbitant land prices led to owners crowding as many people as possible into a small area. They considered that day workers didn't need much air or greenery. Prenzlauer Berg had the least green area of any Berlin district. It still has no forest land or water for recreation. Behind the facades of the Mietkasernen there were usually three or four crowded back courtyards. It was very claustrophobic. The large entrances were sized by the fire department to allow their fire engines to enter. Everything looked fine from the street, but most people lived in the back courtyards.

The courtyards were usually dark, or relatively dark, with the sun hidden by the high walls. When someone played music, everyone heard it. When someone smoked, all smelled it. When a newly married couple squabbled, everyone listened. One said that the typical Berlin courtyard had a characteristic odor: "Sauerkraut," the food of the poor people. Many people lived here; not so many these days. Many rooms are empty now.

The heights of the buildings were limited to three stories by the water pressure available to put out fires. That means that if a building is three stories tall, it is probably very old. Most buildings here are three stories high. Before the Wende, the residents frequently had rooftop parties because private residential parties were not allowed. When the police came, because the buildings are all 72 feet (22 meters) high, the merrymakers would just move from roof to roof without end and without difficulty to carry on their partying. Because there are no trees or greenery, noise in the buildings is a problem.

Prevailing winds come from the west, so city planners placed the industrial sections in the eastern part of Berlin. The four old quarters taken by workers were Kreuzberg, Friedrichshain, Prenzlauer Berg, and Wedding. Laborers lived in the east and white-collar workers lived in the west—Zehlendorf, Schöneberg, Wilmersdorf, and Charlottenburg—where they wouldn't be exposed to pollution and industrial exhausts. Between Schönhauser and Prenzlauer Allee was found one of the most unhealthy neighborhoods, especially in fall and winter when the air was filled with the stink of burning lignite.

In the Second World War Prenzlauer Berg was relatively spared from damage because it was a residential quarter and had no strategic importance. You can still see old structures, even if they are in terrible condition.

Now Prenzlauer Berg is popular with the many young people who came to Berlin (long before the Wende) seeking an apartment. They looked into the back courtyards, picked out one with a dirty window, saw that the apartment was empty, broke into the apartment, renovated it, and applied to the city saying, "I have painted and renovated the apartment and now I would like to have it." Because the apartment was state-owned, they usually received permission.

During the DDR regime there were no statistics collected, but after the Wende, statistics showed that one-tenth of all apartments in Prenzlauer Berg were empty. The empty apartments were not cared for and in bad condition: dank, with many things broken. There were about 80,000 apartments in Prenzlauer Berg; 8,000 were unoccupied. It is said that Prenzlauer Berg was one of the greatest rehabilitation areas of Europe.

Many of the young people who lived here were nonconformists. Prenzlauer Berg was known as a paradise for dropouts in the DDR. With residents such as these, Prenzlauer Berg developed its unique culture known as the **Szene,** which became even stronger after the Wende. Young people fleeing from Kreuzberg's sudden exposure to the world after the Wende squatted in Prenzlauer Berg almost as soon as the Wall came down. The word was that the scene was "purer" and "more authentic" in Prenzlauer Berg. Living costs were low, so it might have been similar, but there was an important difference: there were until recently almost no foreigners in Prenzlauer Berg. There were about 1,000 in 145,000 in DDR times, now there are almost nine times as many.

Three roads called *Allees* lead from three former city gates through the district: Schönhauser, Prenzlauer, and Greifswalder Allee. Bornholmer Straße serves as the northern boundary to this entirely residential area which is considered to be the most typical in East Berlin. You don't see any historical buildings or palaces, and despite this, Prenzlauer Berg has a special ambience—*Kneipen*, artists' centers, anarchy. Residents go late to bed and get out of bed only reluctantly before noon. Expect to find the cafés and restaurants closed in the mornings and open late at night.

Times have changed. Prenzlauer Berg is on the way to becoming a yuppie neighborhood. The new rich are coming to this neighborhood because it is so comfortable. Kollwitzplatz is an "in" neighborhood. Speculators have carved out luxurious apartments with extravagant rents in Gründerzeit houses. Contrast this with the neighborhood where Kollwitz lived: tenements with outdoor toilets. The Kneipe on the corner of Husemannstraße and Wörther Straße is pleasant and many residents come here, but now there are more and more tourists. The owner tore out the back courtyard and planted greenery within to attract tourists and yuppies. The makeup of the singular neighborhood has become less radical. **Franz Garten/Café** and the **Franz Club** at the corner of Schönhauser Allee in the brewery comprised one of the largest and best known youth clubs in Berlin. Formerly it was DDR-supported, but then it was privatized and very busy, holding events every night such as rock, jazz, movies, theater, and small art exhibits in a lively atmosphere. It contained various shops including a recorded music shop. Families took their children in the afternoon. After 10 P.M. it became very lively until 5-6 A.M. It closed in 1997. Many of the former patrons had moved elsewhere.

## 2. The Hotel Scene

Prenzlauer Berg is a district ripe for new hotels. The best is the **Sorat Hotel Gustavo** (Prenzlauer Allee 169, Tel. 446-610, Fax 446-61661), with glass facade, which was opened in June 1994, with an interior designed by the Spanish artist Gustavo. US$103-50, single; US$128-72, double; breakfast buffet included.

**Ibis Hotel Berlin Mitte** (Prenzlauer Allee 4, Tel. 44-333-0, Fax 44-333-111), US$72-102, double or single, breakfast included, is in Prenzlauer Berg, despite its misleading name. In the U.S., Tel. Accor at 800-221-4542.

**Bornholmer Hof** (Bornholmer Straße 92, Tel./Fax 4-44-05-73) is an 18-room pension in outer Prenzlauer Berg. US$47, single; US$67, double; breakfast buffet included. Use S-Bhf Bornholmer Straße.

## 3. Restaurants and Cafés

With more than 50 bars in the area of Kollwitzplatz and a solid line of outdoor cafés along Knaackstraße across from the Water Tower that are crammed on warm evenings with happy locals dining and drinking, Berlin has an ordinance requiring outdoor beer gardens to observe a 10 P.M. curfew so that residents who must keep office hours can get some sleep. How can you get around this ordinance?

**Café Anita Wronski**, Knaackstraße 26-28, Tel. 442-84-83 (open 10 A.M. to 3 A.M.) serves breakfast until 3 P.M. on weekends and the best Café Olé across from the Water Tower. Use U-Bhf Senefelderplatz.

**Gugelhof**, Knaackstraße 37, Tel. 0177/250-19-20 (open 9 A.M. to 1 A.M.), has the best Alsatian food and the neatest personnel in the area. It's not cheap. Try the cheese fondue. Use U-Bhf Senefelderplatz.

**Kommandantur**, Knaackstraße 20/Rykestraße, Tel. 442-77-25 (open from 6 P.M.), is small, loud, and a good place to meet people. It's a legendary Szene institution with a Russian touch. Use U-Bhf Senefelderplatz.

**Pasternak**, Knaackstraße 22-24, Tel. 441-33-99 (open noon to 2 A.M.). Facing the Water Tower, it's one of Berlin's best-known traditional literature cafés. It's more of a Kneipe in turn-of-the-century surroundings than a Russian restaurant. Use U-Bhf Senefelderplatz.

**Mao Thai**, Wörther Straße 30, Tel. 441-92-61 (open Mon.-Fri. noon to 3 P.M. and 6 to 11:30 P.M., Sunday noon to midnight). Crowds rush to one of the top Thai restaurants in Berlin. Use U-Bhf Senefelderplatz.

**Santiago**, Wörther Straße 36, Tel. 441-25-55 (open from 6 P.M.). Small, bright cocktail bar with simple daily menus and a large summer patio. Use U-Bhf Senefelderplatz.

**Krähe**, Kollwitzstraße 84, Tel. 442-82-91 (open Mon.-Fri. 5:30 P.M. to 1 A.M., Sat.-Sun. from 10 A.M.) has international, inexpensive food. The menu changes daily. Use U-Bhf Senefelderplatz.

**November**, Husemannstraße. 15, Tel. 442-84-25 (open 10 A.M. to 3 A.M.). Its location on Husemannstraße makes in recommendable. Use U-Bhf Senefelderplatz.

**Konnopkes Imbiß**, under the U-Bhf Eberswalder Straße (Mon.-Fri. 5 A.M. to 7 P.M., Sat.-Sun. 6 A.M. to 6 P.M.). Be sure to try the Currywurst. Everyone agrees that it's the best in Berlin.

**Offenbach-Stuben,** Stubenkammerstraße 8, Tel. 445-85-02 (open daily 6 P.M. to 2 A.M.). Restaurant with German home cooking. Use S-Bhf Prenzlauer Allee, tram 1.

**Rosenbaum**, Oderberger Straße 61 (at Choriner Straße), Tel. 448-4610 (open from 6 P.M.), located in scruffy Prenzlauer Berg, looks like a scruffy bistro, but it is one of the best restaurants in East Berlin. Waiters serve fine French food for the guest with the fine wallet. Use U-Bhf Eberswalder Straße.

**Café Dodge** Dunckerstraße 80a, Tel. 445-95-34 (open daily 9 A.M. to 2 A.M.), as in Dodge City. So you come all the way to Berlin for a California

BorderBurger or an Austin-TexasBurger or maybe Eggs Benedict? Use U-Bhf Eberswalder Straße.

## 4. Sightseeing

### SENEFELDERPLATZ

Alois Senefelder invented lithography. At U-Bhf Senefelderplatz, when Rudolf Pohle chiseled Senefelder's name on the pedestal of his 1892 marble sculpture, he chiseled it in mirror image as an appropriate tribute to the man who changed the 19th-century printing world.

The first house right from the exit of the Senefelderplatz U-Bhf Bahn station—the damaged house covered with graffiti, with broken windows and the red and black flag, the flag of anarchy, hanging from the top window—is the first house that was "captured" in its entirety in November 1989, during the Wende. It had been empty, a former Jewish old-age home that the police wanted to make into a new complex. Then came the Wende and anarchists moved into the building. The house is a curiosity.

After the Wende, the East Berlin police (who were—and are—concerned for their jobs) tried to curry favor by forming a security partnership with the radical-left residents. Nearby is a soccer stadium. After a game skinheads tried to storm the building. The police protected the house, but the windows were broken and metal bars were installed over them.

Across the street from U-Bhf Senefelderplatz was the Pfeffer Brauerei, which has been converted into an unconventional beer garden/music center with events, Techno-parties, you name it. From 1945 until the Wende it housed *Neues Deutschland*, the party organ of the Communist regime. The building is still state-owned, so rents are high. Farther down the street you see (in German) the written story of Senefelderplatz.

### WATER TOWER

The **Wasserturm** ("Water Tower") at the corner of Kolmarerstraße and Knaackstraße is the logo for the community. Before an English firm began to build the water supply in 1855-56, this was a popular location for windmills. Then a slim, high observation tower and an adjacent, open (later covered) deep basin was built. Finally the massive tower was built in 1877. The entire complex was used until 1915 when it was transformed into housing, which it remains today. Water pumped from the Spree into the water tower was adequate to supply all of Berlin at the time; now there are other sources.

These two towers became the symbol of Prenzlauer Berg. These two towers, one thin and one fat without windows, atop the Prenzlauer Berg functioned as a Nazi torture chamber when Hitler came to power. Storm troopers broke into homes, businesses, and bars and hauled their victims to makeshift concentration camps. One of the most notorious was this misused eight-story brick water tower. Workers from all over Berlin were imprisoned in the water works. A memorial stone in front recalls the victims.

Most people in Prenzlauer Berg cook with gas, but generally heat with *Braunkohl* ("lignite"), one of the great ecological disasters of Berlin. Even the gas presents a major problem because the 120-year-old gas lines are no longer pressure-tight. They are porous, and leak, and the gas is killing the trees along many of the streets.

## SYNAGOGUE

North of the Water Tower, at the beginning of Rykestraße, a **Synagoge** exists in the courtyard of #53 (Tel. 442-59-31). Despite looting by the Nazis and SA stormtroopers using it for a horse stall, it remains in good condition. It was reconsecrated in 1953. The House of God carried the nickname **Friedenstempel** ("Temple of Peace" or "Peace Temple"). It seats 2,000—more than the number of those in 1945 who survived Nazi extermination. At that time, the rabbi had difficulty securing the necessary 10 men for services. Every second Sunday a butcher flew from Budapest to slaughter on Monday kosher beef and lamb. The kosher meat market is on Eberswalder Straße.

The synagogue and Jewish businesses were burned during the *Kristall-nacht,* but not the ones in the courtyards, because of the danger of fire to the surrounding tenement blocks which were so densely occupied. During the War the courtyards were used as horse stalls. Sometimes they are now used for concerts and memorial services to remember the *Kristallnacht.*

The red building in the front was once used as a Jewish school with about 150 children attending in 1926. On January 30, 1933, the Jewish community decided to abandon the Jewish school in order to encourage assimilation in the community. Not long afterwards Hitler was elected chancellor and the school had to be enlarged to accommodate Jewish teachers who had been fired from other schools. The curriculum of the school changed drastically in order to prepare children for life abroad. English began to be taught. They had to offer a separate recreation area and playground because Jewish children were ostracized. After Jewish children were forbidden to attend German schools, hundreds more flooded the school. Despite impossible circumstances, the school survived until 1942.

## KOLLWITZ SQUARE

Over Knaackstraße you come to **Kollwitzplatz** ("Wörther Platz," until 1945). Kollwitzplatz is the heart and center of Prenzlauer Berg. Käthe Kollwitz was a painter and sculptor, a prominent member of the Sezession Movement. She came from Königsberg in East Prussia to study art in Berlin, where she met and married a medical student, Karl Kollwitz, to become a doctor's wife in working-class Prenzlauer Berg. Her powerful charcoal drawings, woodcuts, and sculptures of hollow-eyed women and children gained attention. Kollwitz's art was labeled "Gutter art" by Joseph Goebbels because it was too abstract. The Nazis banned any exhibition of her work and dismissed her from her teaching post at the Academy. Her present-day museum is located in the West at Fasanenstraße 24 (Chapter 3) in an upscale area in stark contrast to the Prenzlauer Berg neighborhood where she worked.

She lived for 50 years at 25 Weißenbergerstraße (renamed Kollwitzstraße) before it was destroyed by British bombs in 1943 and she had to leave for Dresden, where she died in 1945.

In the garden of the Prenzlauer Berg district offices at Fröbelstraße 17, you can see the historically landmarked sculpture *Protecting Mother*, which Fritz Diedrich made in 1951 according to a plaster cast from Kollwitz (some claim it was actually sculpted by Kollwitz herself). It shows a hunched, sad but proud woman. This is its third location. Until 1960 it stood in the center of Kollwitzplatz. Then it moved to the corner of Kollwitz- and Knaackstraße before it was displaced by new construction. It was relocated to the district offices on July 8, 1997, the 130th birthday of the artist and sculptor.

In the center of Kollwitzplatz there is a 1958 bronze Käthe Kollwitz memorial by Hamburg sculptor Gustav Seitz showing the social critic/artist larger than life, but based on a self-portrait from 1938. Because it is bronze, one can see which part is bright from frequent rubbing by passers-by. In this case it is her hand.

New arrivals from Kreuzberg now have art galleries, good bookstores, and punk cafés featuring black leather and vegetarian sandwiches. Across the square you can see ateliers of artists. The theater here was the first independent theater in DDR Berlin. It is listed in the theater guides as "Theater ohne Namen" ("No-name Theater"). There is always much activity here. The area around the square is the gathering point of the Szene—in the new cafés or simply on the street. In the middle of the 1980s, about 50 novelists and 300 painters lived here.

Before the Wende residents attempted unofficial festivals (*Fête*) on the Kollwitzplatz. They were forbidden. They were called *Fête bei Käte*. While the official festival for the unification of Germany was going on at the Reichstag on the night of October 2, 1990, there was a *Fête bei Käte* to celebrate the formation of the new "Autonomous Republic of Utopia" with many thousands of people, "for all who," according to the Utopian declaration of independence, "want to look reality in the eye." When residents went through the streets they spray-painted the street signs black, because on that night the administration of the East Berlin police force was transferred to the West Berlin police. Residents feared that West Berlin police would meddle in their quarter. West Berlin police didn't know East Berlin; they had to go around with a city map to find their way. To make it difficult for the new Western police to learn the neighborhood, the residents blacked out the street signs.

Parents bring their children to Kollwitzplatz to play in the very beautiful green playground fields—on swings made out of automobile tires. It is a communication center. In the evening many cafés and Kneipen set tables outside—something new for the former DDR—and life is very active. It is said that one goes to bed late in Prenzlauer Berg and gets up late because it is so quiet until noon.

In Prenzlauer Berg there is much enterprise. After the Wende many children's playgrounds were built. On the wall by the Jewish Cemetery the children can do their own creating. There is a "Playmobile," an old trailer on streets or squares allowing children to play and paint, and improvise theater. Children are lent video cameras to make their own films, and they call it "Kollywood," because of its location on Kollwitzplatz.

## HUSEMANNSTRASSE

From Kollwitzplatz branches Husemannstraße, the most representative street of Prenzlauer Berg. On the 750th anniversary of Berlin, to impress tourists, DDR authorities reconstructed the Nikolaiviertel near Alexanderplatz, Sophienstraße in the Scheunenviertel, and in Prenzlauer Berg: Husemannstraße, with a lot of kitsch. Older spellings of words that had disappeared over the years were dug up and reused. The buildings were repainted in that greeny-buff color of turn-of-the-century Berlin.

The DDR rebuilt entire basement apartments where handwork such as weaving was done formerly. You can enter these new shops to watch weaving demonstrations. Everything is new: the street signs and the historic water pumps. They reconstructed the street to look as it did at the turn of the century. The residents call it "Disneyland." Despite the Schnauze, this block is such an attractive piece of nostalgia that it is worth walking here from the Water Tower.

At Husemannstraße 8 you see the sign for the entrance to the **Friseur-Museum** ("Barber's Museum"). One man made a witty, small, private Barber's Museum. The owner has a small collection of barber equipment. In the Middle Ages, barbers also pulled teeth. All such things are shown here. At Husemannstraße 12, there is a small museum with an exhibit from the Märkisches Museum (see Chapter 4) showing how Berlin workers lived at the turn of the century with photos and documents of the living style of the proletariat. It includes a coffee shop. Next door to it is a wash boutique without any washing machines. There is an old-fashioned shoemaker's shop. A beer *Lokal* is very pleasant. Residents have painted out the signs on the first block down Husemannstraße.

The **Prenzlauer Berg Museum für Heimatgeschichte und Stadtkultur** ("Prenzlauer Berg Museum of Local History and Culture"), Prenzlauer Allee 75, Tel. 42-40-1097 (open Tue.-Wed. 10 A.M.-noon and 1 to 5 P.M., Thur. 10 A.M.-noon and 1 to 7 P.M., Sat. 1 to 5 P.M.), presents a glimpse of local and Jewish history in Prenzlauer Berg. Use S-Bhf Prenzlauer Allee, tram 1.

## CULTURAL BREWERY

On the corner of Sredzkistrasße and Schönhauser Allee you see one of the few large industrial buildings remaining from the last century in the inner city. The large brown brick building complex of the old Schultheiss brewery was located here on the high ground because brewmasters could sink deeper cellars where temperatures could be more accurately controlled. There were several breweries in the area. This one still stands. It is a very handsome huge complex that once included production and storage facilities, a beer restaurant, and stables for the beer-wagon horses.

The brewery is the most attractive building in Prenzlauer Berg, and now it is a preserved building. It is an interesting story. It has towers built strictly for decoration in the so-called Gründerzeit style, almost like a castle. The later additions were totally functional. On one corner is a tower like a castle's; in the back is a blond-brick (with inlays of red brick) smokestack. It looks like the buildings of the Industrial Revolution in England.

Many such old breweries have been converted to other uses—furniture warehouses, for example—but in Prenzlauer Berg artists took the initiative to try to make the entire complex into a cultural and entertainment center with European standing. **Kulturbrauerei** ("Cultural Brewery"), Knaackstraße 97, Tel. 441-92-69/70/71, it is called. In 1997, they received a grant of DM 100 million from the successor to Treuhand (see Chapter 7) to improve the 6.2 acre (270,000 square meters) space with parking and giant multiplex movie palaces, but immediately ran into objections from the owner of the

*Colosseum* multiplex on Schönhauser Allee. Lawyers are drawing overtime. Use U-Bhf Eberswald Straße.

## NEIGHBORHOOD BATHS

On Oderburger Straße, which is pretty shabby compared to some of the other streets in Prenzlauer Berg, the **Stadtbad Prenzlauer-Berg** ("City Baths") is a preserved location. During the post-War days residents without bathing facilities at their home had to use such facilities, but patrons with facial hair had to exercise great caution when exiting in winter to keep ice from forming instantly in their beards. The baths cost almost nothing. The sign shows a happy bear being bathed by two women. The main entrance is closed, but there is a decrepit side entrance to a sauna (open 9:30 A.M. to 8 P.M.; women only Mon. and Thur.; men only Tue., Fri., and Sun. 8-11 A.M.; families Wed. and Sat. 8 A.M. to 3:30 P.M.). Inside is a small swimming pool in Jugendstil. Theater groups present productions there.

## TOWN COUNCIL'S UMBRELLA

As Berlin grew faster and faster after 1870, the ever-expanding new suburbs had to be connected by public transportation. By the end of the 19th century, horse-drawn carriages were trotting down Kastanienallee where streetcar tracks now run between Schönhauser Tor and Pankow. On July 25, 1913, the U-Bahn was completed from Alexanderplatz to Schönhauser Allee, where it climbed above ground and became an elevated railroad. Prenzlauer Berg residents were happy to call the section covering the central dividing strip of Schönhauser Allee, the **Magistratsschirm** ("Town Council's Umbrella"), where they could stand sheltered from the rain. It remains substantially the same today as when it was opened 80 years ago.

## PRATER GARDENS

Where the remaining chestnut trees stretch to heaven lies the cultural oasis of Prenzlauer Berg, the **Kreiskulturhaus Prater** ("District Cultural House Prater"), Kastanienallee 7-9, Tel. 4-48-56-88, Fax 4-41-88-52 (open Mon.-Fri. 6 P.M. to 2 A.M., Sat.-Sun. from noon), a Berlin institution. Berlin's oldest and largest beer garden is idyllic. Long wooden tables and benches reach through the shadows of the high chestnuts. It is the last existing beer garden in Prenzlauer Berg. Even in bad weather it serves down-to-earth, delicious food.

In 1852 a beer outlet was opened here in the suburbs. In 1881, when horse carriages trotted past on Kastanienallee, the **Prater Gardens** became a favorite getaway from the city. You can imagine in the middle of the last century, Uncle Fritz saying to Aunt Grete, "Come, we'll have a beer in the Prater." They had a summer theater, garden concerts, and operetta evenings. As the tenements creeped around the Prater, it became a meeting place for laborers. August Bebel, Clara Zetkin, and Rosa Luxemburg addressed gathered crowds. Fritz and Grete went West with the bombing and the Cold War, replaced by the proletariat.

There used to be many beer gardens in East Berlin. Even now in the summer months you can enjoy the *Sauerkraut-Polka* every Wednesday when the actors from the "Neutral Taste Zone" take the stage. Perfumed clouds from gray-haired women (men of this generation are in the minority) lead you to the tea-dance every Saturday from 3 to 6 P.M. to swirl and glide to big band sounds. Use U-Bhf Eberswalder Straße.

## JEWISH CEMETERY

Composer Giacomo Meyerbeer (d. 1864), publisher Leopold Ullstein (d. 1899), and painter Max Liebermann (d. 1935), whose family had a plot here, were buried at Schönhauser Allee 23-25 in the **Alte Jüdische Friedhof** ("Old Jewish Cemetery"). The cemetery was completely torn apart and desecrated by the Nazis. It was used, together with the Jewish old-age home, for an assembly point for the deportation of Jews to extermination camps. Plaques and a memorial stone for Moses Mendelssohn recall the ugly past. Admission is free. The gates are open Mon.-Thur. 8 A.M. to 4 P.M., Fri. to 1 P.M.

## WALL PARK

The most representative length of the notorious Berlin Wall still standing is located on the Prenzlauer Berg/Wedding (East/West) border in the **Mauerpark am Friedrich-Ludwig-Jahn-Park** ("Wall Park in the Friedrich Ludwig Jahn Park"). There is no need to remove it as a residential eyesore because it is located across from a scrap metal shop in the shadow of DDR's Max Schmeling sports arena. This makes a decent photo to bring home (afternoons are better). Because the Wall is available to anyone with a spray can, and there is no legal prohibition, the graffiti is constantly being updated. Use U-Bhf Eberswalder Straße and/or bus 190.

## 5. Sports

The red-enameled **Max Schmeling Sports Arena**, Cantianstraße 24, Tel. 827-83-0, Fax 827-83-111, in Friedrich-Ludwig-Jahn-Park provides

Prenzlauer Berg with a 8,500-seat stadium that is home court for the Berlin Albatross basketball team. Tennis courts are nearby. Use U-Bhf Eberswalder Straße.

Jahn was a teacher, known as the *Turnvater*, the founder of modern gymnastics. His nationalism glorified strength. He denounced mental and physical softness such as drinking coffee or alcohol, smoking tobacco, and eating sweets.

**Radsporthalle** ("Bicycle Sports Hall"), Fritz-Riedel-Straße 53, Tel. 827-83-0, Fax 827-83-111, is located in an apple orchard.

**Sportjugendclub (SJC) Prenzlauer Berg**, Kollwitzstraße 8, Tel. 442-13-70. Sports center for youth offers billiards, skateboarding, table tennis, basketball, and a gymnasium as well as aerobic and dance classes. Organizes weekend trips and bicycle tours. Use U-Bhf Senefelderplatz.

**Schwimmhalle Prenzlauer Berg**, Anton-Saefkow-Platz 1, Tel. 972-91-69 (open every weekday morning except Wed. 6:30 to 9 A.M., plus Mon. and Wed. 3 to 9 P.M., Tue. and Thur. 6 to 9:30 P.M., Fri. 4:30 to 9:30 P.M., Sat. 9 A.M. to 8 P.M., Sun. 8 A.M. to 8 P.M.).

**Schwimmhalle Lilli Henoch**, Lilli-Henoch-Straße 20, Tel. 425-84-07 (open Mon. 4:30 to 9:30 P.M., Tue. 6:30 to 8:45 A.M. and 4:30 to 9:30 P.M., Wed. 4 to 9:30 P.M., Sat. 9 A.M. to 5 P.M., Sun. 8 A.M. to 1 P.M.).

**Schwimmhalle Hans Eisler**, Hans-Eisler-Straße 1, Tel. 423-07-55 (open Mon.-Fri. 6:30 to 8:45 A.M., plus Tue. and Fri. 4 to 9:30 P.M., Sat. 9 A.M. to 5 P.M., Sun. 8 A.M. to 1 P.M.).

## 6. Shopping

Organized shopping in the usual sense is rare in Prenzlauer Berg, but you will often be able to find bargains in scattered small shops run by free-market entrepreneurs.

**Große Marktfreiheit**, Schönhauser Allee 36-39, is the flea market in the courtyard of the Kulturbrauerei. Use U-Bhf Eberswalder Straße.

## 7. Nightlife and Entertainment

The *Szene* in Prenzlauer Berg is centered on Kollwitzplatz. Here life is faster, with an artistic orientation. Prices are lower. Check out Pfefferberg, Knaack-Club, and the Kulturbrauerei.

**Pfefferberg**, Schönhauser Allee 176, Tel. 449-6534. Beer garden venue offers disco evenings as well as frequent multi-cultural, artistic, ecological, and avant garde projects. Use U-Bhf Senefelderplatz.

**Knaack-Club**, Greifswalder Straße 224, Tel. 44-270-60 (disco Wed.-Sat. 10 P.M. to 6 A.M.; concerts Sun.-Thur. 9 P.M., Fri.-Sat. 10 P.M.). On Fridays and

Saturdays choose from three discos with different styles. Visit five different bars or a VIP lounge and an American pool table. The scurrilous cellar disco *Darmwäsche* ("Intestinal Washing") is flashy. Use S-Bhf Greifswalder Straße.

**Kulturbrauerei**, Knaackstraße 97, Tel. 441-9269. The multi-cultural center on the location of a former brewery offers concerts, readings, and quarters for promising artists and musicians. Use U-Bhf Eberswalder Straße.

**Café Nord,** Schönhauser Allee 83, Tel. 448-2683 (open Tue.-Fri. 9 P.M. to 5 A.M., Sat. 8 P.M. to 4 A.M., Sun. 6 P.M. to midnight). Young crowd. Dancing.

**AKBA Lounge**, Sredzkisstraße 64, entertains you with House and dancing. Use U-Bhf Eberswalder Straße.

**Duncker Club**, Dunckerstraße 64, was trashy earlier. Now you have a bar and changing concerts. Use U-Bhf Eberswalder Straße.

**Junction-Bar**, Gneisenaustraße 18 (open 11 P.M.), gemütliche Jazzkneipe where you always find a concert. The second set is at 12:30 A.M. Admission usually DM 5. Use U-Bhf Eberswalder Straße.

**Zeiss-Großplanetarium Berlin** im Ernst-Thälmann-Park, Prenzlauer Allee 80, Tel. 421-84-50, Fax 425-12-52, *http://www.snafu.de/~astw/zgp* (open Mon.-Fri. 10 to 12 A.M., Wed. & Sat. 1:30 to 9 P.M., Fri. 6 to 9 P.M., Sun. 1:30 to 6 P.M.; admission DM 8). Visit Europe's largest planetarium for a trip to Berlin in Space, Sirius, or the Grand Tour. Use S-Bhf Prenzlauer Allee.

# 10

# Residential Berlin

## 1. Orientation

The districts of Schöneberg, Zehlendorf, Steglitz, Tempelhof, and Spandau occupy the southern and western regions of Greater Berlin. They stretch from centrally located Kurfürstendamm to Berlin's southern boundary and west to the border with Potsdam. The districts are generally vanilla, primarily middle-class bedroom communities that offer shopping, dining, beer drinking, and sleeping. They seem relaxed after the hectic pace of Kurfürstendamm but they are home to the average Berliner and comprise an important part of the Berlin experience because they contain worthwhile sightseeing locales, particularly the Dahlem museums and Schöneberg Town Hall. Spandau by contrast retains a certain feeling of centuries past, and is the site of the historic Citadel.

Before incorporation into Greater Berlin in 1920, Spandau was a city in its own right, far removed from downtown. First mentioned in 1198 (1998 was its 800th anniversary), Spandau received city rights in 1230, making it even older than Berlin. Its sister city is Boca Raton.

Spandauers brag about their location. They point out that on about 185 days of the year, westerly winds skim across their 11-mile (18 kilometers) by

7.2-mile (12 kilometers) green band of forests, fields, parks, and lakes and supply oxygen to the more thickly populated inner city. Spandau is now Berlin's second largest district, 35.5 square miles (9,191 hectares) on the far western fringe of Greater Berlin, with one of Berlin's lowest population (223,000) densities because of the Havel River and the *Tegelersee* ("Lake Tegel"). It is an interesting quarter. Take a good look at the Citadel, the Old City, and so forth. Instead of heading into the heart of the busy metropolis, you can find a very pleasant hotel here. It is connected to downtown by three stops on the U-7 Line: U-Bhf Rathaus-Spandau, U-Bhf Altstadt-Spandau, and U-Bhf Zitadelle. Mainline, regional, and S-Bahn trains serve the new train station.

Schöneberg, a sophisticated, mid-sized district (4.75 square miles—1,229 hectares) with a population of 151,400, lies directly south of Tiergarten district. It is served by U-Bahn line 4 through the Rathaus Schöneberg station to U-Bhf Innsbrucker Platz. Larger Steglitz, 12.3 square miles (3,196 hectares), adjacent to Schöneberg, is a middle-class community with a suburban, busy feeling to it. Steglitz was the last residence of Bauhaus when Miës van der Rohe moved the remnants of the Bauhaus school into an abandoned telephone factory. Within weeks of seizing power, Hitler set his storm trooper thugs in action against it. It closed four months later. Miës van der Rohe moved to London. The second highest fraction of women in Berlin (54.6 percent) do their shopping on Schloßstraße. You can reach it easily by either S- or U-Bahn to the Rathaus Steglitz junction. Connections between the two transportation systems are good.

Tempelhof, a 10,082-acre (4,080 hectares) woodland area enclosed by the Great Elector in 1678 for breeding rabbits, was incorporated into Berlin in 1860. Adjacent to Steglitz, it is a residential district notable principally for its airfield and associated Airlift Memorial. Women comprise 53.6 percent (third highest in Berlin) of its 191,000 residents. It was Hitler's idea to link Tempelhof to the Reichstag by a three-mile-long grand avenue inspired by Paris' Champs Elysées, but two and a half times as long.

The 100,000 residents of the district of Zehlendorf celebrated its 750th anniversary in 1992. At the southwestern corner of Berlin, Zehlendorf provides a pool of greenery for all of Berlin to enjoy. Geographically large, 27.2 square miles (7,053 hectares), it is 15 percent water and 34 percent forest, including the Grunewald, Schlachtensee, Wannsee, and Nikolassee, where you indulge yourself in Chapter 11, Green Berlin. The Dahlem neighborhood lies on the district's border with Wilmersdorf. Hectic university life runs rampant. Dahlem houses the 59,000-student **Freie Universität** (FU) ("Free University"), Berlin's largest, and attracts visitors to the Dahlem collections of the **Staatlichen Museen zu Berlin**. Also in Dahlem you find the American Way of Life, former home of the U.S. forces in Berlin.

## 2. The Hotel Scene

Those arriving in Berlin by automobile can avoid the difficulties of driving in the congested heart of Berlin or the ubiquitous construction detours in the historic district by staying in a quieter residential neighborhood. The excellent public transportation system lets you get around easily while leaving your automobile safely parked at your hotel. Hotels in the northern part of Schöneberg near Ku'damm are listed in Chapter 3, the Heart of the City. Those in the green of Zehlendorf are given in Chapter 11. Others, including some convenient places to stay, in Spandau, Tempelhof, and Steglitz, can provide you lodging in quieter surroundings with places to park.

Across from the dark-red brick Steglitz city hall stands the enormous, modern **Steglitz International Hotel,** or simply "S.I." (Albrechtstraße 2, Tel. 790-05-0, Fax 790-05-521, *http://www.utell.com*), anchoring the *Steglitzer Kreisel,* a large shopping center. US$89-100, single; US$111-28, double; breakfast buffet included. Connections are easy at U- and S-Bhf Steglitz Rathaus. In the U.S., Tel. Utell at 800-207-6900.

**Hotel Achat** (Heiderreuterstraße 37-38, Spandau, Tel. 330-72-0, Fax 330-72-455). Living in a green dimension. US$67-167, single; US$89-194; breakfast buffet included. Use RB-Bhf Spandau.

**Hotel Herbst** (Moritzstraße 20, Spandau, Tel. 53-37-000, Fax 3-33-73-65) is convenient for those not wanting to go into the center of Berlin. It has 21 rooms, no restaurant. US$75-77, single; US$106-08, double; breakfast buffet included.

**Holiday Inn Berlin-Esplanade** (Rohrdamm 80, Tel. 38-38-9-0, Fax 38-38-9-900, *http://www.holiday-inn.com*), a modern hotel in the Siemensstadt section of Spandau, lies not far from Charlottenburg district and only two miles from Tegel Airport. US$128-78, single; US$150-200, double; breakfast buffet US$14 extra. Use U-Bhf Rohrdamm. In the U.S., call Holiday Inn, Tel. 800-465-4329.

**Hotel Alt-Tempelhof** (Luise-Henriette-Straße 4, Tempelhof, Tel. 75-685-0, Fax 75-685-100) is a modern hotel in a pleasant residential surrounding less than two minutes walk from U-Bhf Alt-Tempelhof. It is not especially close to Tempelhof Airport. US$100-33, single; US$125-53, double; breakfast buffet included. Weekend special: US$89, single; US$106, double.

## 3. Restaurants and Cafés

In Zehlendorf, you find the

**Alter Krug Dahlem**, Königin-Luise-Straße 52, Tel. 8-32-50-89 (open Tue.-Sat. 1 P.M. to midnight., Sun. noon to 5 P.M.). Located in a preserved farmhouse, here you enjoy outstanding German food and wine. The fish is recommended. Garden terrace in Dahlem.

**Cristallo**, Teltower Damm 52, Tel. 815-66-09 (open noon-11:30 P.M.) features Italian cooking. Here you are served the best pasta instead of spaghetti, excellent meat creations instead of pizza, and enjoy a pastel dining room decorated with good art instead of plastic dining quarters. Reservations recommended.

In Schöneberg, how about "Roo" burgers from Australia? At the **Outback**, Cranachstraße 1, Tel. 855-67-09 (open Mon.-Sat. 6 P.M.-2 A.M., Sun. from 10 A.M.), relax in wicker chairs, under palm trees, and eat kangaroo meat and other "Quickies."

**Aroma**, Hochkirchstraße 8, Tel. 782-5821 (open daily 4 P.M.-2 A.M., Sun. from noon). Where do you find the best pizza in Berlin in an extremely informal atmosphere? Try Aroma, but their fresh Italian menu doesn't end there. Use U- or S-Bhf Yorckstraße.

**Leydicke**, Mansteinstraße 4, Tel. 2-16-29-73 (open 4 P.M.-1 A.M.), is a traditional distillery. This Kneipe has been in the same family for a hundred years, the most original pub that Berlin has produced. Fruit wines made in-house are the specialty. It is just across the line from Kreuzberg. Use U- or S-Bhf Yorckstraße.

**Blumenladen**, Bahnhofstraße 4a, Tel. 852-09-09 (open 6 P.M.-1 A.M.), occupies the former flower shop in the S-Bahnhof Friedenau, but more important, serves excellent Italian cuisine.

**Café M**, Goltzstraße 33, Tel. 216-70-92 (open 24 hours). Don't be shocked by the interior. It is one of the talked about Szene meeting points in Schöneberg. Former punks are growing old like the café. It is loud, hectic, and always full. Lots of nice people drop in. Across the street on Höhe Frankenstraße you can find one of the best hot dogs in Berlin. Use U-Eisenacher Straße or bus 187.

In Tempelhof, drop into the **Café Olé** in the UFA-Fabrik (see text).

In Spandau, the **Zitadelle Schänke** ("Citadel Pub Room") in the Citadel's Julius Tower, Tel. 334-21-06 (open Tue.-Sun. 11 A.M. to 4 P.M., à la carte, medieval menu after 7 P.M.), features medieval fantasy banquets: hearty meals—preferably eaten with your fingers—accompanied by minstrels. The Citadel's medieval atmosphere makes it possible.

**Brauhaus Spandau**, Im Kolk, Neuendorfer Straße 1, Tel. 35-39-07-0, Fax 35-39-07-11 (open Fri.-Sat. 11 A.M. to 2 A.M., Tue.-Thur. to 1 A.M., Mon. from 4 p.m, Sun. 10 A.M. to midnight). Spacious beerhall with Bavarian buffet between copper beer kettles. On Sunday mornings, drink your breakfast with live music. From April to September, slurp your beer in the garden with a view of the Havel, locks, and the Citadel.

Across from Spandau's Nikolai Church, on the square named "Markt," is an old-fashioned Viennese coffeehouse. **Konditorei Altstadt-Café** which

serves breakfast from 8 A.M., Sundays from 10 A.M. It features tables set out
into the square itself. Some of the buildings are still *Fachwerk* (half-timbered
farmers' houses) dating from the Middle Ages.
Also on Markt in Spandau, **Konditorei Fester**, Markt 4, Tel. 333-58-72
(open Mon.-Sat. 8 A.M. to 6 P.M., Sun. from 1 P.M.) is a café with tradition.
Its tradition features an excellent breakfast buffet on Saturdays only, 8 A.M.
to noon, and wonderful homemade cakes, tortes, and pralines.
**Restaurant Stube und Küche**, Lindenufer 17 (Spandau), Tel. 333-73-73
(open 6 P.M.) is a rustic restaurant between Havel and Spree.
**Café Lutetia**, Kinkelstraße 54, Tel. 353-021-77 (open 9 A.M. to midnight)
lies a few steps from the Spandau city hall. The changing art exhibits give
the gemütlich café a decent, modern flair. Snacking on nachos and
baguettes in all variations inside and out makes this a meeting point for
the young and youthful. Use U-Bhf Rathaus Spandau.
**Spandau Weißbierstube**, Kinkelstraße 51, Tel. 333-37-35 (open Tue.-Sat.
from 5 P.M., Sun. noon to 10 P.M.). One block from the Spandau town hall
north on Altstädter-Ring. Sitting in the courtyard beside the brick wall in
summer is especially fine.
Restaurant **Vladi am Kolk,** Hoher Steinweg 5, Tel. 333-61-85 (open
Tue.-Sat. 3:30 to 11:30 P.M., Sun. 11:30 A.M. to 10 P.M.). Bohemian cooking
across from Spandau's city wall. After dinner be sure to have a shot of
Becherovka schnapps. Use U-Bhf Altstadt-Spandau.
Steglitz offers you **Hoppegarten**, Schloßstraße 56, Tel. 791-83-78 (open
Sun.-Thur. 9 A.M. to 3 A.M., Fri.-Sat. to 4 A.M.). The menu here looks like a
small thick book. You can order anything German that you might like. Do
you like pig's neck steak? Or do you prefer leg of rabbit? Goose?
**Zenit**, Liebenswalder Straße 2 (Wedding), Tel. 456-82-72, Fax 456-24-32
(open Mon.-Thur. 10 A.M. to 11:30 P.M., Fri.-Sat. from 6 P.M., Sun. brunch 10
A.M. to 3 P.M.), has a summer garden restaurant in a preserved blacksmith
shop. You won't find a better vegetarian restaurant. Try the Käsespätzl
(cheese noodles) or stuffed mushrooms. Use U-Bhf Nauener Platz.

## 4. Sightseeing

### SCHÖNEBERG

**Rathaus Schöneberg** ("Schöneberg Town Hall"), Tel. 78-76-23-04, Fax
78-76-33-08, is located on present John-F.-Kennedy-Platz. It was the venue
selected by President Kennedy for his "Ich bin ein Berliner" rallying call in
July 1963, at the height of the Cold War. Berlin Schnauze has that because
of the success of his speech, when Chancellor Helmut Kohl visited Beijing,

he said, "Ich bin ein Pekinese." It happens that "Berliner" is a colloquial term in many cities such as Wien (Vienna) and Zürich for a jelly donut (never mind that jelly donuts were not popular in Berlin). As a result of Kennedy's speech, plastic jelly donuts began to be sold in Berlin souvenir shops with the inscription: "Ich bin ein Berliner."

Schöneberg Town Hall was the home for the mayor of all Berlin while the Red Rathaus in Mitte was being remodeled. Now he and his staff have occupied their new quarters. The Berlin City Council remained berthed in the Schöneberg Town Hall until its new quarters in Kreuzberg (Chapter 8) were ready in 1994. The Schöneberg mayor is trying to figure out how to make up the loss of rent.

The town hall offers an exhibition honoring former Berlin mayor Willy Brandt, *Um die Freiheit Kämpfen*, ("Fight for freedom"). Tel. 787-707-0 (open 10 A.M.-6 P.M.). Use U-Bhf Rathaus Schöneberg.

The **Freiheitsglocke** ("Freedom Bell") in the town hall, a replica of the liberty bell subscribed to by 17 million Americans, was presented to Berliners by General Clay on October 24, 1950, United Nations Day. It rings every day at noon. The 230-foot (70 meters) tower is open on Sundays and Wednesdays.

Adjacent to the transportation authorities' administrative headquarters at Potsdamer Straße 188, you find the neglected **Königskolonnaden** ("King's Colonnades") and a group of statuary entitled *The Horse Tamers* which form an extraordinary collection of classical architecture. In 1910, two years after the site was converted from the botanical garden that had been first planted by the Great Elector in 1679, the columns were moved from their former place on Alexanderplatz to make room for a department store there. They were built between 1777 and 1780 by Karl von Gontard. Two of the figures in the niches are copies, while the originals (Mercury and the River Goddess) stand in the Glienicke Palace Park (see Chapter 11).

Past the King's Colonnades, you approach the 550-room building on **Kleistpark** which was begun in 1909 to give larger quarters to the Berlin Supreme Court, who found their old offices on Unter den Linden too cramped. During Hitler's time, the Supreme Court became more or less worthless except when, on July 20, 1944, the judges were summoned to sentence the participants in the assassination attempt on *der Führer*. Scarcely an hour later the rebels were hanged at Plötzensee.

At the end of the War, the victorious powers commandeered the slightly damaged building and upgraded it for the Four-Power Headquarters for all Germany. You no longer saw judges' robes here; you saw uniforms. Europe was in ruins but here were four precisely placed tables—one for each of the victorious countries. The doors were marked in three languages. The menus were printed in three languages. Four flags flew outside. In 1954 the Berlin Conference of Foreign Ministers was convened here. With the Wende, the Four Powers returned the building. In December 1991, the Berlin Supreme Court resumed their duties in this building. Use U-Bhf Kleistpark.

For an evening with the stars, **Wilhelm-Foerster-Sternwarte mit Zeiss-Planetarium am Insulaner** ("Wilhelm Foerster Observatory with Zeiss Planetarium"), Musterdamm 90 (am Insulaner), Tel. 79-00-93-0, Fax 79-00-93-12, *http://www.be.schule.de/schulen/wfs*, provides shows that the young love. Most start at 8 P.M. Adults, DM 7.50; school children and students, DM 5.

# STEGLITZ

When **Rathaus Steglitz** ("Steglitz Town Hall"), Schloßstraße 37, which was designed by the same architect as the Charlottenburg and Spandau town halls, was built, at 130 feet (40 meters), it was the tallest building in Steglitz. And the most important. Now the landmarked building is about average height, and over 100 years old. On March 22, 1898, the brick building became headquarters for Steglitz with a population of 20,000—but growing. The 1901 Ratskeller gave way to U-Bahn construction in 1972. Across from Rathaus Steglitz, you see West Berlin's tallest building, the **Steglitzer Kreisel**, Schloßstraße 80. Most of Steglitz' district administration is housed here. Exhibitions, open during normal office hours, are mounted on the 16th floor. Use U- or S-Bhf Rathaus Steglitz.

The **Botanischer Garten** ("Botanical Gardens"), Königin-Luise-Straße 6-8, Tel. 830-06-0 (open daily 9 A.M. to 8 P.M., Apr., Aug., and Sept., to 9 P.M., May-July; admission DM 6), is the 106-acre (43 hectares) site of 20,000 species of tidily arranged and well-marked specimens from palms to orchids that you skim past aboard the S-Bahn in Steglitz. Elector Friedrich Wilhelm originated Berlin's first botanical garden in 1646, when he noticed that monks of the times were planting medicinal plants in their monastery gardens. He decided that his palace was an ideal place for his private, healthful plot of land. The present site, laid out in 1897-1903 on a potato field, is Germany's largest and one of Europe's richest. The gardens are organized in three parts: the arboretum, the gardens, and the 15 hothouses all under the care of the Free University since 1995. The architecturally interesting *Tropical House* dominates the garden with its 92-foot (28 meters) high roof. It is 200 feet (60 meters) long and 100 feet (30 meters) wide, almost the size of an aircraft hangar. It's worth seeing the rare species on artificial hills, the numerous exhibition houses, and the large cacti and the orchid collections. It's kept at a constant 76 degrees Fahrenheit (24 degrees

Celsius) like your dream vacation. In 80 minutes by foot you visit the Italian gardens, the Asian central mountains, the German beaches, and the cacti of the desert. Admission to the **Botanisches Museum** is free (open Tue.-Sun. 10 A.M. to 5 P.M.). For the Königin-Luise-Straße entrance, use bus 101 or 183; for the Unter den Eichen entrance, use S-Bhf Botanischer Garten or bus 148.

## ZEHLENDORF

The **Brücke-Museum,** Bussardsteig 9, Tel. 831-20-29, Fax 8-31-59-61 (open daily except Tue. 11 A.M. to 5 P.M.), is a small, modern house in a sober, one-story box, that seems the perfect size. It opened in 1967 on the fringe of the Grunewald Forest. Here you discover a compelling collection of explosive and hectic oil cityscapes, glass painting, sculptures, watercolors, and graphic prints of expressionists, based on 74 canvases donated by Karl Schmidt-Rottluff (he took his name from his birthplace in Rottluff near Chemnitz), plus temporary exhibits. The *Brücke* ("Bridge") was the founding movement of Expressionism. The movement began in Dresden in 1905 where Ernst Ludwig Kirchner joined forces with other young painters. In 1906, Emil Nolde and Max Pechstein came aboard. Five years later the movement spread to Berlin under the name of the "The New Secession." Karl Schmidt-Rottluff, who gave the group its name and also designed the cheerful, friendly Weimar eagle, and his colleagues crossed from old commercial and academic styles to new, abstract techniques. They staged exhibitions in Berlin train stations so that workers might benefit from their canvases on their way to their jobs. From Berlin, they continued much of their painting in the harsh climates of the North Sea. Their style, a cry of anguish, included all varieties of subject matter in a simplified style that stressed bold outlines and gaudy colors inspired by van Gogh. They sought nature instead of plush ateliers. Although the Brücke group broke up in 1913, Expressionism continued, conflicting with the realities of the day and the stirrings of Hitlerism until 1933 when the Nazis declared such work degenerate. Use bus 115 or use U-Bhf Dahlem-Dorf, walk to Clay Allee, then left on Pücklerstraße—follow the signs.

Zehlendorf lay in the American sector of the divided city. While the presence of the French and British military in their sectors was seldom seen, the Americans made their existence very clear. In Zehlendorf they established the independent little area which Berliners called **"Little America"** on Clayallee (Gen. Lucius Clay was one of the fathers of the Berlin airlift—see Tempelhof, below). Americans formed their own settlement and brought their American Way of Life with them. Some of the houses of the living area of Little America were erected in the 1930s by architect Bruno Taut in Bauhaus style. Use U-Bhf Onkel-Toms-Hütte ("Uncle Tom's Cabin").

The last remaining American troops officially withdrew from Berlin when American military lowered the flag on Clayallee for the last time on September 7, 1994, and on September 8, a detachment of some 200 American, British, and French troops lay a wreath at Tempelhof Airport in remembrance of the 1948-49 Berlin Airlift and paraded at the Brandenburg Gate by torchlight. The Allied departure from Berlin, stipulated by the 1990 treaty which permitted German reunification and the restoration of full German sovereignty, came eight days after the last Russian occupation troops left Germany. The 20-acre (80,000 square meters) former U.S. headquarters in Zehlendorf has been allocated between Berlin's Free University and the German Secret Service. The German spies will get one of the seven former U.S. buildings on Clayallee, the university will get five, and the seventh will be used for federal research projects. The Bauhaus residences have been occupied by federal bureaucrats moving from Bonn.

The **Alliiertenmuseum** ("Allied Museum"), Clayallee in Zehlendorf (open Mon.-Sun. 10 A.M. to 6 P.M.) was officially opened on Thursday, June 25, 1998, by German Defense Minister Volker Rühr with a parade of military bands from U-Bhf Oskar-Helene-Heim to the new museum. Berlin Mayor Eberhard Diepgen thanked the 500 invited veterans for decades of service to guarantee freedom and democracy in Berlin.

The museum is divided into three phases covering the period 1945 to 1994. In the main building (a former library), you find an introduction to the museum's themes. Especially striking is a short section of the "Appendix of the Cold War," a 1,500-foot (450 meters) spy tunnel than was discovered in 1997 running between Rudow (West) and Treptow (East). In the former Outpost Theater you see uniforms and equipment and exhibits. Finally, you see Care packages and typical airlift examples. In the open spaces between the two exhibit areas you find a Royal Air Force "Hastings" that brought coal to Berlin. The French presented a wagon from a military train. America sent Jeeps. Here it is: the famous control shack from the legendary Checkpoint Charlie, a watchtower, and a length of the Berlin Wall from Potsdamer Platz that was redecorated for the museum in 1998.

Berliners find the name of the museum confusing because the museum is about events in Berlin and limited to those involving the three powers. Berliners keep in mind that there is a 1994 museum of the Red Army in the Karlshorst district of Berlin.

The annual **Deutsch-Amerikanischen-Volksfest** on Hüttenweg, open to Germans, typically with Germans dressed as Native Americans, continues every August. In 1997, you saw black-and-white cows from Wisconsin.

In 1943, when British and American bombers began destroying Berlin with tons of explosives, Nazi authorities hurried to tuck away their prized paintings and historical objects in remote salt mines in Thüringen and bunkers below the Zoo train station. It was lucky they did. When American troops arrived, one of their priorities was to send these German treasures (many of which had been displayed in galleries on Museum Island and in the Märkisches Museum that fell into the Russian sector) back to the National Gallery in Washington, D.C., for evaluation. After the Cold-War situation crystallized it was decided to return these treasures to West Berlin, but not to their original locations which by then were in East Berlin. An alternate **museum complex** was created on a War-damaged stretch in **Dahlem,** close to American defenses, to overshadow the Communist museum center on the Spree. Architects expanded the uninspired neoclassical facade of what had been an Asiatic Museum before the War. They couldn't rival the great neoclassical and baroque buildings created by brilliant Prussian architects, but the interior was a paradise.

At present the Dahlem museums are reaping the rewards of recombinations of collections. Some of the collection are being combined with similar ones on Museum Island and some Dahlem museums are closed for enlargement and redesign. The **Museum für Indische Kunst** ("Indian Art") was closed for remodeling of the Dahlem complex on May 4, 1998. When it reopens, you will see the most important collection of Indian art in Germany. The Turfan collection, with its famous fresco paintings from the sixth to the 10th century portraying Buddhist legends, is especially worth seeing. Use U-Bhf Dahlem-Dorf, which was built as a thatched-roof *Fachwerk* ("half-timbered") farmer's house, and follow the signs.

The **Museum für Völkerkunde** ("Ethnology Museum"), at Lansstraße 8 (Tue.-Fri. 10 A.M. to 6 P.M., Sat.-Sun. from 11 A.M.; admission DM 4, day card for all SMB museums DM 8), has one of the world's largest collections of anthropological objects divided into five sections: Pre-Columbian America, Africa, South Seas, South Asia, and East Asia. Children are especially fascinated with the giant hall filled with wooden boats from the Pacific islands.

The **Museum für Ostasiatische Kunst** ("Museum of Far Eastern Art"), at Lansstraße 8, reopening in 1999, shows Chinese, Korean, and Japanese art from 3000 B.C. until the present. It includes paintings, woodcuts, bronzes, ceramics, sculptures, metalworks, lacquerworks, and a 17th-century Chinese emperor's throne made of rosewood and finished in lacquer and gold with mother-of-pearl. The museum was established in 1906 and moved to the Martin Gropius Building in 1924. It has been in Dahlem since 1970. A glance shows you why this is the highlight for Japanese tourists.

The **Museum für Volkskunde** ("Museum of Folklore") exhibits about

2,000 articles of furniture, costume and jewelry, tools, crockery, and folklore objects from German-speaking populations in Europe. It is of more interest to Germans than foreigners. During reconstruction, admission is free.

## TEMPELHOF

In June 1948, a new currency, the Deutsche Mark, was introduced unilaterally in West Berlin to replace the former Reichsmark. Russian authorities considered this a breach of the Four-Power agreements and retaliated by announcing that the rail and highway routes between West Germany and West Berlin were "closed for urgent repairs." Berlin was blockaded for the next 11 months as Stalin attempted to starve out the Western half of the city. Gen. Lucius Clay, commander of the U.S. Allied Forces in Berlin, organized the biggest airlift in history, the so-called Candy-bar Rescue, to keep Berlin alive by supplying West Berlin with all its necessities by air. On June 22, 1948, the first so-called **Rosinenbomber** ("Raisin Bomber"), an American Dakota four-engine prop plane, landed at Tempelhof Airport. During the next 322 days aircraft delivered more than 2.3 million tons of goods to Berlin in 300,000 flights, flying round the clock. Coffee became known as *Blumenkaffee* because it was so thin you could see the floral pattern on the bottom of the cup. Planes landed every 90 seconds, making a turnaround in just six minutes. Even a power plant, dismantled into its components, was flown into Berlin. The airlift continued until September 30, 1949. The blockade was then lifted and the roads and rail lines reopened with little or no evidence of any repairs.

When the blockade began, the Berliners considered the Western powers a detested occupying force. To the Western powers, the Berliners were a conquered enemy. When it was lifted, Berliners and the Allies were friends and partners. Berlin was a special city again. Eduard Ludwig's **Luftbrück-denkmal** ("Airbridge Memorial" or "Airlift Memorial") in a flower garden at the edge of a gracious green park shows three, 65-foot (20 meters) arcs shooting to the sky facing west to symbolize the three air corridors used in the airlift to break the Soviet blockade. Unfortunately the 1951, reinforced concrete monument reminds you of an ungainly serving fork. Berlin Schnauze calls it the **Hungerharke** ("Hunger Rake"). It was the site of the U. S. Army's Berlin Brigade's final farewell to Berlin parade on September 8, 1994. Use U-Bhf Platz der Luftbrücke.

Across from the memorial park is the 1962 terminal for Tempelhof Airport where Orville and Wilbur Wright achieved the first powered flight, lasting 19 minutes, in 1908. The airport is being phased out because of its location in the center of the city.

**UFA-Fabrik** ("UFA [film studios] factory") Victoriastraße 10-18, Tempelhof, Tel. 752-80-85, is not a construction site, but things are always being
built. It's not a factory, but 120 people work here. Yes, the film industry
was here at one time, but that was decades ago. Nowadays, the UFA Fabrik
is one of the oldest and largest cultural centers in Berlin. You can go
there to see variety theater, circus performances, and international guest
appearances. In addition, it is a self-help center, extended family, café,
and ecological project. It ranks as the largest ecological building site in
Berlin. You find one of the largest solar plants in Berlin, greenhouse roofs
and facades, a windmill, a decentralized energy supply, and rainwater toilets.
"Alternatives" live and work in the former UFA film studios in a cinema,
guesthouse, circus, bakery, saddle shop, pottery workshop, and other
projects. Events and informational discussions are held in the **Café Olé**, Tel.
75-50-31-20 (open Tue.-Sun. from noon, Mon. from 2 P.M.), while visitors
enjoy home-baked cornbread. The UFA-Fabrik sponsors a subsidized
neighborhood and self-help center with an emphasis on preventative
health care. Use U-Bhf Ullsteinstraße, bus 140 or 246.

**ökodorf e.V.** ("Ecological Village"), Kurfürstenstraße 14, Tempelhof,
Tel. 261-24-87, is a self-administered communication center and meeting
place for groups working in ecology. Tearoom is open every Monday
(get-acquainted day) 7 to 11 P.M.

For written information contact **Netzwerk-Selbsthilfe** ("Network Self-
Help"), Gneisenaustraße 2 [im Mehringhof], Tel. 691-30-72. Through
donations, Netzwerk finances alternative projects and regards itself as a
marketplace of ideas and experience.

## SPANDAU

So far removed from the heart of Berlin that to get there you have to take
a regional train or an S-Bahn line that took 18 years to open on December
30, 1998, Spandau seems like a separate city. And it was. Spandau was first
settled by Slavic peoples in the 7th-12th centuries and remains the most
extensively researched archaeological site in the region between the Elbe
and Oder rivers. The finds give insight into the lives of the inhabitants and
illustrate the process of German settlement east of the Elbe during the
Middle Ages. Some of the carvings in wood and antler from the 12th to the
14th centuries are exhibited at the Museum of Pre- and Early History in
Charlottenburg (see Chapter 5).

In the Kolkstraße, Behnitzstraße, and Hoher Steinweg of Spandau
**Altstadt** ("Old City") you feel as though you have gone back centuries in
a time machine. The cobbled pedestrian mall, closed to auto traffic, features

every variety of shop, a fairly large Woolworths, several modern water fountains, and bells on the storefront of an optician that chime quarter-hourly. On Behnitz 5 stands the most representative late-baroque private house in Berlin. The **Kolk** is a very old part of Spandau with relics of the city wall built in the early 14th century as well as baroque and Victorian houses. It contains a historical wine parlor.

The **Reformationsplatz** contains landmarked buildings, the **St.-Niko-lai-Kirche** ("St. Nikolai Church"), the Ackerbürgerhaus (also known as Wendenschloß), a restored Tudor building from the year 1681 on Kinkelstraße, the Bürgerhaus (today Hotel Benn), and a typical Tudor building from around 1800 on Ritterstraße. The tower of the St. Nikolai Church was restored and opened in 1991. The last Gothic church made of brick remaining in West Germany, it was built between 1410 and 1450. The baptismal font is even older (1389). The Renaissance altar comes from 1581, the chandeliers from 1651. In 1567, Elector Joachim II had the tower closed to prevent potential enemies that could pillage Spandau from having a good look over the Citadel. You now may climb the tower's spiral staircase taking you 229 steps up past the church museum, pointed Schinkel windows, nesting robins, the 1926 church bell that is so loud you must open your mouth when it rings, the observation platform at 180 feet (55 meters), and finally at the top, the bell that never rings, cast from bronze in 1705.

Use U-Bhf Altstadt-Spandau. The station is a surprise. It consists of white enameled panels and decorative columns to make it also attractive.

**Spandau Rathaus** ("Spandau Town Hall") was designed by the same architect as the Charlottenburg and Steglitz town halls. It is an attractive patrician house with an eye-catching clock tower, many windows, and a green roof. The park across the highway is one of the places inhabited by the rabbits you see on the green fields throughout Berlin. Children come here to feed the rabbits. Use U-Bhf Rathaus-Spandau, which has a very elegant interior with reflecting surfaces.

The **Zitadelle** ("Citadel"), Straße am Juliusturm 1, Tel. 339-11 (open Tue.-Fri. 9 A.M. to 5 P.M., Sat.-Sun. from 10 A.M.; entrance to the courtyard is free; to the Museum and Julius Tower, DM 4), an Italian-style water-fortress at the confluence of the Havel and Spree, is one of Berlin's famous landmarks and showpiece of the military engineering of the 16th century. Individual parts are even older. The palace comes from about 1370. The largest fortress east of the Elbe River, erected to protect Berlin, it was the site of battle with the Swedes during the Thirty Years War, the Austrians during the Seven Years War, and the French during Napoleon's campaign. Originally a moated castle from the 12th century built by Margrave Albert the Bear, it was transformed between 1560 and 1594 by Elector Joachim II into the newer Italian system of fortification based on a square with arrowhead bastions at the four corners. The round **Juliusturm** ("Julius Tower"), built around 1160, remains the original water tower from the time of the Askanians, the early ruling house of Brandenburg. The tower is 100 feet (30 meters) tall, and has 145 steps leading to a platform on top from where you have a good panorama of the city. From 1722 until 1918, Spandau was the center of Prussian weapons manufacture. After the Franco-Prussian war in 1870-71, from 1874 to 1919, Bismarck stored here the Reich's treasury amounting to 120 million gold Marks. The tower houses a local history museum and, in the vaults, a unique restaurant. Unfortunately, most of the Citadel is closed to visitors and the wooded, gravel roads around the fortress do not provide much of a view or a decent perspective of the Citadel or of the Havel River nearby. Use U-Bhf Zitadelle, which is constructed all of red brick and decorated with old maps of the historic Citadel. From the station, follow the arrows about a quarter-mile (350 meters) to the Citadel itself.

Mainline Train Station, **Bahnhof Spandau**, was inaugurated in September 1998, when the great, long ICE trains began to make their first Berlin stops approaching the center of Berlin as they slowed from their rush along their new high-speed line. Bahnhof Spandau platforms were lengthened to accommodate the long trains and covered with glass arches to protect arriving and departing passengers from the weather. Inside you find all the functions you expect in a mainline train station—new ticketing counters and an information center. Regional trains supplement the high-speed trains and, since 1998/99, S-Bahn connections to Berlin neighborhoods. In 2005, the station will be served by the planned **Transrapid** magnetic levitation line to Hamburg.

## 5. Sports

**Sommerbad am Insulaner,** Munsterdamm 80, Steglitz, Tel. 7904-2432 (open daily 8 A.M. to 6-8 P.M.). Swimming, minigolf, trampoline. Use S-Bhf Priesterweg.

**Sommerbad Lichterfelde,** Hindenburgdamm 9-10, Steglitz, Tel. 7904-2438 (open daily 8 A.M. to 6:30-8 P.M.). Swimming. Use bus 112 or 185.

**Stadtbad Spandau-Süd,** Gatower Straße 19-20, Tel. 362-10-21 (Mon. 7 A.M. to 3 P.M., Tue. 7 A.M. to 6 P.M., Wed. 7 A.M. to 9:30 P.M., Thur. 10 A.M. to 5:30 P.M., Fri. 7 A.M. to 9:30 P.M., Sat. 9 A.M. to 5 P.M., Sun. 9 A.M. to 1 P.M.). Swimming; 108,000 square feet for sunbathing in summer. Use bus 131, 134, or 135.

**Stadtbad Spandau-Nord,** Radelandstraße 1, Tel. 33-03-2555 (open Mon. 6:50 to 8 A.M. and 2:30 to 7 P.M., Tue. 6:50 to 8 A.M. and 5 to 9:30 P.M., Thur. 6:50 to 8 A.M. and 2:30 to 9:30 P.M., Fri. 6:50 to 8 A.M. and 4 to 6 P.M., Sat. 9 a.m to 3 P.M. plus 3 P.M. to 5 P.M., naked. Women only Mon. and Fri. 1 to 2:30 P.M.).

**Freibad Oberhavel,** Havelschanze 27-31, Spandau, Tel. 335-1224 (open 8 A.M. to 6 P.M.). Use bus 131, 231, or 331.

**Stadtbad Schöneberg,** Sachsendamm 11, Tel. 78-76-30-05 (open Mon.-Sat. 7 A.M. to 3 P.M.).

**Stadtbad Steglitz,** Bergstraße 90, Tel. 79-04-24-41/42 (open Mon. 2 to 10 P.M., Tue. 8 A.M. to 10 P.M., Wed. 7 A.M. to 10 P.M., Thur. 8 A.M. to 5 P.M., Fri. 7 A.M. to 5 P.M., Sat. 8 A.M. to 8 P.M., Sun. 8:30 A.M. to 8 P.M.).

**Sommerbad Mariendorf,** Rixdorfer Straße 130, Tempelhof (open 7 A.M. to 7:30 P.M.). Use U-Bhf Alt-Mariendorf.

**Stadtbad Tempelhof,** Götzstraße 14-18, Tel. 75-60-27-52 (Mon. 3 to 9 P.M., Tue. 7 A.M. to noon, Wed. 7 to 10 A.M., Thur. 3 to 9:15 P.M., Fri. 10 A.M. to 9:15 P.M., Sat. 8 A.M. to 7:30 P.M., Sun. 8 A.M. to 1 P.M.).

**Stadtbad Zehlendorf,** Clayallee 330, Tel. 807-27-77 (open Mon. 7 A.M. to 8:30 P.M., Tue. 7 to 8:30 A.M. and 1 to 2:30 P.M., Fri. noon to 8:30 P.M., Sat. 7 A.M. to 1 P.M., Sun. 8 to 10:30 A.M.).

**Sportjugendclub (SJC) Wedding,** Ungarnstraße 65, Tel. 456-78-38. Sports center for youth offers billiards, skateboarding, table tennis, basketball, and a gymnasium as well as aerobic and dance classes. Organizes weekend trips and bicycle tours. Use U-Bhf Seestraße.

**Rollschuhbahn im Gemeindepark Lankwitz,** Steglitz, Mühlenstraße. Roller-blading in community park Lankwitz. Use bus 183.

**Berliner Tennis-Club,** Paradestraße 28-32, Tempelhof, Tel. 786-40-30, Fax 786-10-19. Use U-Bhf Tempelhofer Damm.

## 6. Shopping

Marlene Dietrich is from Schöneberg. Although the Schöneberger city council was refused permission to change the name of Kaiser-Wilhelm-Platz to Marlene-Dietrich-Platz, you can buy a **Marlene Dietrich coffee mug** in the city hall for DM 10. They sit next to the J. F. Kennedy coffee mugs and show the star signing the city's Golden Book in 1960 together with Willy Brandt. Tel. 78-768-888 (open Mon.-Tue. 9 A.M. to noon and 1:30 to 3 P.M., Thur. to 6 P.M., Fri. 9 A.M. to 2 P.M. only).

If you want something showing the U- and S-Bahn network, vehicles, or mascot *Elsa,* visit the transit authority's **BVG-Shop,** Potsdamer Straße 182, Schöneberg, Tel. 256-275-65, Fax 256-277-20 (open Mon.-Fri. 9 A.M. to 3

P.M., Wed. to 6 P.M.) for coffee cups, bags, tie clips, ballpoint pens, telephone cards, T-shirts, umbrellas, and more. Use U-Bhf Kleistpark.

Schloßstraße in Steglitz (there are four streets in Berlin named Schloßstraße) is, after Ku'damm, Berlin's second largest shopping street. Along its 2.5-mile (4.1 kilometers) length, there are 270 shops and department stores. North of the towering restaurant **Bierpinsel**, you find discount stores; south, elegant boutiques. This is the shopping hub for the entire southern part of incorporated Berlin. On Walther-Schreiber-Platz, an enormous **Hertie** department store stands opposite **Forum Steglitz**. A **Peak and Cloppenburg** store and associated shops provide everything the middle-class Steglitz pocketbook can afford. Use U-Bhf Walther-Schreiber-Platz, U-Bhf Schloßstraße, or U-Bhf Rathaus Steglitz.

In Tempelhof, indulge yourself in two covered markets. One on Tempelhofer Damm was joined in 1998 by one at Friedrich-Wilhelm-Straße 17-19, when a Munich firm converted the landmarked 1925 streetcar depot into a modern market. The 39,000 square-foot (3,600 square meter) area supports 10 stores including a baker, a Mediterranean specialty shop, a supermarket, and an ice cream parlor.

Spandau's **bold city** is a delightful place to do your shopping. It is lined with every kind of boutique and shop near the Markt. Prices here seem to be lower than in downtown Berlin. Use U-Bhf Altstadt-Spandau.

You find the largest and one of the most interesting and most popular markets in Berlin at the **Winterfeldtmarkt** on Winterfeldtplatz in Schöneberg. Twice a week—Wednesdays and Saturdays from 8 A.M. to 2 P.M.—100 dealers crowd their 272 stands into double rows on the large square, and offer everything multi-cultural and bio-dynamic from baked goods to corsets to spices, fruit, vegetables, and sausage specialties. You can relax afterwards in a nearby café or kneipe. Use U-Bhf Nollendorfplatz.

**Großer Trödelmarkt am den Fehrbeliner Platz**, Wilmersdorf (Sat.-Sun. 8 A.M. to 4 P.M.), another popular second-hand market takes place on a site across from U-Bhf Fehrbeliner Platz.

**UFA-Fabrik**, Victoriastraße 10-18, Tempelhof, Tel. 75-50-30 (open Mon.-Wed. and Fri. 9 A.M. to 6 P.M.; Thur. to 8:30 P.M.; Sat. 8 A.M. to 1 P.M.). Shops offer natural items, health foods, fruit, vegetables, cosmetics, and pretty things. Use U-Bhf Ullsteinstraße, bus 140 or 246.

## 7. Nightlife and Entertainment

The *Szene* in the neighborhoods takes place in Schöneberg on Winterfeldplatz/Goltzstraße. You won't find any discotheques, but lots of good cafés and Kneipen. Sit outside in summer.

The **Kleines Theater**, Südwestkorso 64, Friedenau/Schöneberg, Tel. 821-2021 or 821-3030, offers long-running, delightful satirical reviews in German.

**Ansenal-Kino**, Welserstraße 25, is a special movie house in Schöneberg showing original versions, classical, and special films. Use U-Bhf Viktoria-Luise-Platz.

**Titania-Palast**, Schloßstraße 4-5, Steglitz. Josephine Baker, Maria Callas, Marlene Dietrich, and other celebrities made famous the stage of the Titania-Palast. The Berlin Philharmonic gave its first post-War concert here. Berlin's Freie University was founded here in 1948. In 1951 it was the venue of the first international film festival. It reopened in 1995 as a movie theater. The facade of the 1928 building is being restored for its 70th anniversary. Use U-Bhf Schloßstraße.

**Adria Filmtheater**, Schloßstraße 48, Steglitz, has been running *Berlin wie es war* since 1990. No documentary makes use of such authentic scenes of a cosmopolitan city in pre-WWII years. The hand-held-camera film was banned by the Nazis and finally premiered in 1950. Sunday matinee DM 10. Use S- or U-Bhf Rathaus Steglitz.

**Schloßpark-Theater**, Schloßstraße 48, Steglitz, Tel. 793-1515. The Schloßpark-Theater, with its four Grecian columns, was previously used as a horse stable and coach-house by the Behm manor house next door. Built in 1804, it was transformed into a theater in 1921 by the architects David Gilly and Friedrich Gentz. Between 1934 and 1945 it was also used as a movie house. Now a small, but critically acclaimed ensemble presents classical and modern theater. Use S- or U-Bhf Rathaus Steglitz.

**Eierschalle 1**, Tel. 832-53-05, in Dahlem features country, rockabilly, and old-time jazz on weekends. Use U-Bhf Podbielskiallee.

In summer the **Altstadt-Theater Spandau**, Tel. 334-3000, presents comedies on the **Freilichtbühne** ("Open-air Stage") adjacent to the Citadel in Spandau. Their German-language repertory includes Shakespeare and Molière. Use U-Bhf Zitadelle.

**Kulturhaus Spandau**, Mauerstraße 6, Tel. 333-40-22, presents plays on stage and gallery and even on the roof of Spandau's Hertie department store.

**Hangar II**, Tempelhof Airport, Columbiadamm 2-6, Tel. 771-80-82, is the 43,000 square-foot (4,000 square meters) venue for musical spectaculars. Twice a month up to 4,000 ravers gather for a hard **Techno-Disco**. Admission is DM 25. Use U-Bhf Platz der Luftbrücke, bus 104, 119, 184, 341, N4, N76.

The great erotic varieté revue show in Tempelhof Airport, **La Vie en Rose,** is the business traveler's wicked night out. Showtime is at 9 P.M., Mon. dark. Left of the main airport entrance, use U-Bhf Platz der Luftbrücke, bus 104, 119, 184, 341, N4, N76.

# 11

# Green Berlin

## 1. Orientation

Take some time to see the green side of Berlin, the woods, the little parks, the trees, and then you realize that Berlin isn't just crowds of people and respectful monuments and historical buildings. Berlin has a green countryside around it. Once you're out of the hectic city, the surprisingly verdant countryside and lakes come as a treat. Thanks to the efficient S- and U-Bahn networks, it won't take you more than three-quarters of an hour.

People live here, too, but bankers, executives, diplomats, and high government officials, in mansions hidden away behind the trees, in *Villenkolonien* ("villa colonies"). The first villa colony in Am Großen Wannsee dates from 1863. "Show me sand, gold, and water, and I'll show you paradise on earth," according to one of the first builders, who was responsible for building the Berlin-Potsdam-Magdeburg private railroad, which became the S-Bahn, to this area, for a fast commute to the city center.

Some of the trees and shrubs you see growing wild in Berlin include the silver birch (*Betula pendula*), as either a tree or shrub; false acacia (*Pseudoacacia*), either a tree or bush; and mahaleb cherry (*Prunus mahaleb*), which is usually a bush, but grows to a 30-foot (10 meters) tree in Berlin.

To reach Hagenplatz, where one can go walking, jogging, or bicycle riding, take the S-Bahn to Grunewald and then bus 186, or crosstown bus 119 from the Memorial Church.

Hagenplatz is your gateway to the cool green area of parks and lovely trees. You walk from here down Fontanastraße. Soon you are inside the Berlin-Grunewald S-Bahn station delightfully restored in nouveau Hansel-and-Gretel style with a red tile roof and bright blue-and-gold clock. This is the S-Bahn station that Hansel and Gretel would have liked to have entered.

Continue through the tunnel past the S-Bahn overpass to Waldklause Café and also the 219 bus stop to U-Bhf Zoo, which you may prefer to take to arrive here.

Nearby is the entrance to the Grunewald, where you can start your walks or bicycling through lovely greenery. There is a **Wanderkarte** ("hiking map") showing where you stand, the S-Bhf Nikolassee, etc. The S-Bahn cuts right through the heart of the Grunewald from Nikolassee.

The best transportation to this location is not by bus of any kind, but by S-Bahn. Because important people and politicians themselves lived in this area, they legislated in 1890 the construction of the S-Bahn line to connect their estates in Wannsee with Bahnhof Zoo in only 15 minutes.

## 2. The Hotel Scene

Rustic and decorator hotels offer you a rich choice of fresh air in green and by blue.

**Schloßhotel Vier Jahreszeiten** (Brahmstraße 10, Wilmersdorf, Tel. 895-84-0, Fax 895-84-800) is the most expensive place to stay in the city. This former city palace is situated in its own very quiet park within the verdant Grunewald forest. Built in 1911, its original owner Walter von Pannwitz was a close friend and legal advisor of Kaiser Wilhelm II, who stayed there frequently. The Nazi government bought the property and presented it to its ally, Croatia, for an embassy. After the War, it was turned into a British officers' mess. "Grand" is too tame a word for the 54 extravagantly decorated rooms and 12 suites which were all luxuriously furnished with interior design by Karl Lagerfeld. US$324-96, single; US$373-445, double; breakfast included. In the U.S., contact Leading Hotels, Tel. 800-223-6800.

**Ravenna Hotel** (Grunewaldstraße 8, Steglitz, Tel. 7-90-910, Fax 7-92-44-12) has no restaurant. US$69-82, single; US$86-110, double; breakfast buffet included. Weekend special: US$67, single; US$94, double. Use U- or S-Steglitz.

**Landhaus Schlachtensee** (Bogotastraße 9, Zehlendorf, Tel. 809-9470,

Fax 809-947-47). Opened as a 18-room bed-and-breakfast hotel in 1987, this 1905 villa is nicely situated on the nearby Schlachtensee and Krumme Lanke lakes. US$90-110, single; US$105-35, double; breakfast buffet included. Use U-Bhf Krumme Lanke, S-Bhf Mexikoplatz, bus 211, 112, or 115.

**Sorat Hotel Humboldt-Mühle Berlin** (An der Mühle 5-9, Reinickendorf, Tel. 439040, Fax 4390-4444) is housed in an old mill and its grain silo on the shores of Lake Tegel. The hotel provides its own boat for leisurely tours. US$94-128, single; US$111-44, double; breakfast included. U.S. reservations, Tel. 800-223-5652. Use U-Bhf Alt-Tegel, bus 122, 124, or 125.

## 3. Restaurants and Cafés

**Hemingway's**, Hagenstraße 18, Tel. 825-45-71 (open 6 P.M. to 1 A.M.) is the top restaurant in Grunewald. Its international menu is expensive. Reservations are advisable.

**La Fourchette**, Königsallee 5b, Tel. 891-7201. In Grunewald with a terrace overlooking the Halensee. The location high above the Halensee is reason enough for a visit. The food and price level argue against it.

**Blockhaus Nikolskoe**, Nikolskoer Weg, Tel. 805-29-14 (open Fri.-Wed. 10 A.M. to 10 P.M.) has a panoramic terrace overlooking Pheasant Island and the Havel, but the food is unimaginative. Use bus from S-Bhf Wannsee.

**Wirtshaus Moorlake**, Moorlakeweg 6, Tel. 805-58-09, Fax 805-25-88 (open 11 A.M. to 6 P.M.), is a historical lodge on the banks of the Havel, built in 1840 by Schinkel's student, L. Persius for Friedrich Wilhelm IV. It has been a restaurant since 1896. The food is as fattening as in Bavaria.

**Wirtshaus Schildhorn**, Straße am Schildhorn 4a, Grunewald, Tel. 305-31-11 (open summer daily 11 A.M. to 8 P.M., winter Sat.-Sun. only). The recently renovated thatched-roof, 100-year-old village inn makes a fine excursion on the Havel. Flaming courses are the specialty. Open 11 A.M. to 8 P.M., Sat-Sun. in winter; daily from March.

**Vivaldi Restaurant in Schloßhotel Vier Jahreszeiten**, Brahmsstraße 6-10, Tel. 895-840. Formal and elegant. If you have to ask the price, you don't belong here. **Le Jardin** is a Wintergarden restaurant. In summer, sit outdoors.

**Waldhaus an der Havelchausee**, Havelchausee 66, Tel. 304-05-95 (open Tue.-Sun. 10 A.M. to 10 P.M.). Game is the specialty—not only on the menus, but also stuffed on the walls.

**Grunewaldturm**, Havelchausee 61, Tel. 304-12-03 (open daily from 10 A.M.). Sweet breath of air in the green on the Havel River with garden. International menu.

## 4. Sightseeing

### GRUNEWALD

The Grunewald forest was named for Elector Joachim II's hunting lodge located here, **Zum Grünen Wald,** which means "to the green wood." (Somehow, the umlaut accent over the letter u was dropped.) The woods, nearly 745 acres (3,100 hectares), stretch south from the Olympic Stadium to the Wannsee, a distance of some 5.5 miles (8.8 kilometers). It is Berlin's largest forest, filled with birch trees and larches with peeling bark. On the west it is bounded by the Havel River and to the south and east by several smaller lakes—the Schlachtensee, Krume Lanke, and the Grunewaldsee. Some marshes and lakes are landmarked areas frequented by red deer, boars, and small game. After the War 24 million new trees were planted. Some 80,000 boat owners sail on the Havel in good weather making the river seem like a yacht harbor.

After seizing all church lands, elector Joachim II decided to use some of his gain to build for himself a fine new hunting lodge on the eastern side of the Havel Lake amid the dense pines of the Spandau Forest. **Jagdschloß Grunewald** ("Grunewald Hunting Lodge"), Hüttenweg am Grunewaldsee, Tel. 813-35-97 (open mid-May to October Tue.-Sun. 10 A.M. to 5 P.M., with a lunch break 1 to 1:30 P.M.; Sat.-Sun. 10 A.M. to 4 P.M. until mid-May). Look for the inscription *Zum Grünen Wald* carved over the door. The main section with two stories and hexagonal tower in Renaissance style was built by Caspar Thyß in 1542 . In 1593 Count Rochus von Lynar added stables and domestic offices. The two wings on the lake side were built about 1770 for Friedrich the Great. The interiors date largely from the time of King Friedrich I. King Friedrich Wilhelm II and King Friedrich Wilhelm III often resided here. It now serves as the *Waldmuseum,* presenting furniture and a collection of 20 Dutch and German old masters (including Lukas Cranach) from the 16th to 19th centuries. The armory of the hunting lodge is also open to visitors. A pleasant footpath leads from the lodge along Grunewald Lake and north through the adjoining nature preserve to the Königsallee. Use bus 115 to Clayallee.

Following the First World War, Berlin's wealthier citizens commissioned leading architects to design single homes for them in the leafy surroundings of the Grunewald.

The **Teufelsberg** ("Devil's Mountain") rises in the north of the Grunewald Forest. It is West Berlin's highest mountain, 394 feet (120 meters) tall, but the **Trümmerberg** ("Hill of Rubble") is an artificial mound, created out of 33 million cubic yards (25 million cubic meters) of war rubble, meaning shattered roofing, chunks of bedroom walls, window frames, bathtubs, and places where people lived and worked. Berliners have covered it with 10,000 trees and a vineyard. Skiers use the ski jump and race down the slopes when there is enough snow on the ground; kite fliers enjoy their creations on long, warm days. Its 226-foot (69 meters) flight-control radar antenna installed in 1997 is used to control air arrivals for a distance of 50 miles (80 kilometers). In total, "Trümmerfrauen" (rubble women) built 14 artificial mountains from Berlin's war rubble known as "Hitler's Collected Works." The highest of them is the *Bunkerberg* in Friedrichshain, in East Berlin, where it is called Mont Klamott (*Klamott* meaning "ancient rubbish"). *Die Insular* is in Schöneberg. One wonders what future archaeologists will make of the rubble artifacts they uncover.

When you have use of an auto in Berlin, the scenic drive along the **Havelchaussee** through the Havel River fringes of Grunewald will take you through the lakeland area around Berlin. From the Zoo area, drive via Hardenbergstraße to Ernst-Reuter-Platz, west on Bismarckstraße, Kaiserdamm, and Heerstraße. At Scholzplatz turn left into Am Postfenn road through the northern tip of the Grunewald to the Havel. When you prefer to see this route by public transportation, bus Line 218 runs from U-Bhf Theodor-Heuss-Platz (Line U-1), U-Bhf Neu-Westend, Steubenplatz, Olympischer Platz, Waldbühne, Passenheimer Straße, Angerburger Allee, Havelchaussee, Am Postfenn, Schildhorn, Grunewaldturm, Lindwerder, Großes Fenster, Wannseebadweg, Spanische Allee, and S-Bhf Wannsee.

Havelchaussee, 6.5 miles (10.5 kilometers) long, is the second longest street in Berlin, running parallel to the River Havel, which separates Berlin from Potsdam. Off the Havelchaussee on the Schildhorn Peninsula into the Havel, a sandstone column on a small mound indicates where Jaczo, the last Wendish prince, is supposed to have been converted to Christianity.

**Grunewaldturm** ("Grunewald Tower"), Tel. 304-12-03 (open daily 10 A.M. to 5:30 P.M.; entrance DM 1.50), is Grunewald's observation point, a platform 442 feet (135 meters) above the Havel on 250-foot (77 meters) Karlsberg hill, is an 1889 semi-Gothic red-brick tower with red-brick stone steps similar to the Rote Rathaus in East Berlin. It gives a beautiful view over the Grunewald forest, Wannsee lake, and the Havel River as far as Potsdam. It was formerly known as *Kaiser-Wilhelm-Turm.*

Following south along the Havelchaussee the road approaches the Havel again near the Lieper Bucht, and slightly farther a ferry leads to the pretty island of Lindwerder with a fine view of the Havel. The Chaussee hugs the shore as far as Große Steinlanke Bay, then crosses the woods to the **Kronprinzessinnenweg** ("Crown Princesses' Path"), and then to Nikolassee and on to Wannsee.

Past the Wannsee Lido, the road continues to Schwanenwerder Island, but just short of the causeway a footpath goes off to the right to the **Großes Fenster** ("Big Window") lookout point, where you see a fine view of the Havel as far as Spandau.

## WANNSEE

From the road, turn off on the Wannseebadweg to **Strandbad Wannsee** ("Wannsee Beach"), the largest inland beach in Europe, a mile (1.6 kilometers) long and 87 yards (80 meters) wide. The sand is very, very, white. Such sand is not found here; it was imported from the North Sea. On warm summer days, some 35,000 sunbathers gather here to try to get a tan. With so many people, not many are successful.

The stretch of sand opposite the castle is called the **Bullenwinkel** ("Bull Shop"), loosely translated as "Muscle Beach," where bathing suits are optional. In the '60s the Flower Power advocates took over the stretch and it became a nude bathing beach. And now it is a comical mixture of young and old people, fat old women and men, children running here and there, serious professors, and laborers, all trying to get a full-body tan. To reach the beautiful beach Wannsee, use S-Bhf Nikolassee, a gingerbready station on Hohenzollernplatz with many shops and a Berliner Bank. Use the exit marked "Strandbad Wannsee/Spanischevallee." Bus 513 is waiting for you. Cross over the Autobahn overpass and continue down the path to the Wannsee.

For the Wannsee steamers, take either an S-Bahn or a regional railroad train to S-Bhf Wannsee. Two S-Bahn lines converge here. Line S1 brings you from Oranienburg via Friedrichstraße Station. Line S7 comes via Zoo Station from Ostkreuz. Regional train line RB33 is one stop from Charlottenburg Bahnhof and two from Zoo. Walk down the hill to catch the lake steamers at the sign "Dampfer Anlegestelle Wannsee, Stern und Kreisschiffahrt." The lake looks like an Alpine lake. There are four piers. The sightseeing boats are double- or triple-decked with deck chairs on top and dining in the lower cabins. The *Mark Brandenburg*, the largest-capacity, carries 410 passengers.

At the Wannsee turnoff from the highway, you cross **Spinnerbrücke**, called the "Bridge of the Crazy People" because on the weekend bikers make it the motorcycle center of Berlin. You pass the neo-Gothic **Rathaus Wannsee** ("Wannsee Town Hall") on Königstraße which grabs your attention with its Gothic arches and tiles over windows.

The **S-Bahn Museum** located at S-Bhf Greibnitzsee is open about one weekend a month. For current information, access *http://www.igeb.org*.

# GLIENICKE

Darkness and fog hover over **Glienicker Brücke** ("Glienicke Bridge"). Two groups of men pace toward each other, hats pulled down, the collars of their trench coats turned high. Without discussion, individuals from each side are released across the white stripe at midpoint.

Glienicke Bridge is famous for the spy exchanges between East and West that took place here. It was an ideal location: remote and exactly at the middle of the bridge that was the border between West Berlin and the East German city of Potsdam. American U-2 spy plane pilot Gary Powers was exchanged for Soviet Rudolf Abel in 1962. Anatole Scharansky crossed to West Berlin over the Glienicke Bridge to reach the West in 1986.

The only crossing in this area, the green-painted, riveted I-beam bridge with gilded railings, was blown up by the German army in the Battle of Potsdam at the closing of the Second World War, but was rebuilt by the Communists who renamed it the Einheitsbrücke ("Bridge of Unity"). It was then closed for 28 years because of the Berlin Wall. The closing made it very complicated for East Berliners to reach Potsdam. They had to travel in a circle around West Berlin. It was even more complicated for West Berliners, who first had to obtain an entry visa for the DDR, then go into East Berlin, and then finally circle around West Berlin back to Potsdam. Many Wessis still have never visited Potsdam.

With the opening of the Wall, the 1908-9 bridge over the Havel regained its original function. Rows of automobiles cross the bridge, but it is a center for confrontation still. Half the bridge belongs to Potsdam, in the state of Brandenburg. Half belongs to Berlin, which is responsible to the federal government. Potsdam wants to restore the two lanes on its half of the bridge. Berlin wants to make the whole bridge into four lanes and let the federal government pay. Potsdam says that is "ridiculous." The road through Potsdam is only two lanes wide. Potsdam certainly can't afford— and wouldn't want—to widen the road through its lovely residential area. The state of Brandenburg says the whole thing is "totally absurd," and wants to ignore it. Haven't you heard all this before?

The view from the bridge shows Potsdam's Palace Babelsberg, built in English style with English defenses, the church directly on the water that was an early Christian basilica, Pheasant Island not far away across the water and, on the left, the telephone tower that ensured communications between West Berlin and Germany before the Wende. Thirty-three technicians worked here headed by a woman. Synanon Topferei is about one mile (1500 meters) down the river.

**Volkspark Klein-Glienicke** ("People's Park Small Glienicke") is an amazingly rich verdant-green-colored landscape garden with beautifully manicured, lovely old trees spread over 287 acres along the left bank of the Havel in Berlin, but it is part of an even bigger landscape and historical ensemble extending into Potsdam. The large ensemble of palaces and parks all belong together. The buildings and gardens were laid out very harmoniously in relationship with each other. There are palaces everywhere. They were built at various times, but most of them were built in the middle of the last century for the Prussian kings' families and their countless children. Every child (every prince) received his own palace. Here you can see the early 19th-century summer residences of the sons of King Friedrich Wilhelm III.

The park was laid out in the style of an English landscape garden in the early 19th century by Peter Josef Lenné (1789-1866), who also laid out Sanssouci in Potsdam. Later refinements are due to Elector Pückler-Muskau and the artist August Wilhelm Schirmer. The path leading through the park to Nikolskoe makes a beautiful trail for hiking.

In 1824, Prince Karl of Prussia, son of King Friedrich Wilhelm III and Queen Luise, acquired a plot that had been used for fruit and wine-growing in the late 17th century and for farming in the 18th century under various owners. After 1796 Count Lindenau and after 1814 State Chancellor Elector Hardenberg began building landscape gardens.

Carl Friedrich von Schinkel, Ludwig Persius, and Ferdinand von Arnim were commissioned to build either neoclassical palaces and park buildings or Italian villas emphasizing the southern character of the gardens and recalling ancient Greek and Roman themes. The princes' art collections carried through the theme of the classic world.

The complex of palaces and parks all lie on the Havel River, some in Berlin, some in Potsdam. During the cold war, the Havel formed part of the Berlin Wall, dividing this section of West Berlin from the DDR and separating the castles on the Berlin side and those on the Potsdam side into two camps. Their relationships with one another were spoiled by this military division. Now it is again possible for you to see them all as a unity and walk or bicycle between them.

Especially worth seeing beside palace and gardens with round summer houses with Corinthian columns imitating the Lysicrates monument in Athens are the casino, the monastery, the lion fountains, the so-called Stibadium and the Große Neugierde ("Large Curiosity") by Schinkel, and the Kleine Neugierde ("Small Curiosity") teahouse (see below).

Using Glienicke Bridge as your starting point, the Italianate **Schloß Kleine Glienicke** ("Small Glienicke Palace"), designed by Schinkel for Prince Karl, brother of the first German kaiser, lies in back of trees on the

Berlin side on the north side of Königstraße. The entrance path leads from the Mövenstraße intersection.

On the right you see the Wirtschaftshof ("Groundskeepers Court"), which consists of a group of interesting living and working houses resembling Italian villas. The 1865 tower and the high archway to the horse stables and living quarters are typical of the style of Persius, who laid out the installation in 1843-48.

You enter the palace grounds at the **Johannitertor** ("Johannit Gate"). The gilded griffins are a symbol of vigilance. Left of the main path you see the sandstone palace. The rococo house bought by Prince Karl was rebuilt by Schinkel in 1825-28 along the line of ideas the prince brought back with him from his Mediterranean travels. Everywhere you see sculptures and architecture in the Italian style. Walk past into the garden to see the **Kavalierhaus** ("Knight's House") which originally had apartments for guests and high officials above horse stalls.

Farther you find Schinkel's 1828 **Remisenhof** ("Coach Yard") with the figure of Neptune and the **Orangerie** ("Hothouse") with five wraparound windows. It was built by Persius in 1839, torn down in 1940, and reconstructed in 1980-81. On your return to Königstraße walk through the arcade to the 1840 **Stibadium** alcove. Built by Persius with an elevated platform toward Potsdam, it features a Ceres (Roman goddess of agriculture) column supporting a wooden roof and a lovely granite basin also from 1840.

Walking toward the bridge on the path inside the grounds parallel to Königstraße, you find Schinkel's 1837 **Löwenbrunnen** ("Lion's Fountain"), modeled after one in Rome's Villa Medici. Here you can take fine photos of the buildings. Farther, left of the path, facing the street, is the **Kleine Neugierde** ("Small Curiosity"), Schinkel's 1825 teahouse with a Renaissance arcade that was added later.

The path leads on to a tree-covered hill where you have a beautiful view over the palace, the tower of the Knight's House, the Orangerie, and the 1816 **Pleasureground** with its trees, bushes and oval and round flower beds that were modeled after English gardens. The rubble on the lawns are remains of columns taken from the Poseidon Temple on Cape Sounion.

On the corner of the park facing the Glienicke Bridge, you find the **Große Neugierde** ("Large Curiosity"). This striking round building with 16 Corinthian columns by Schinkel in 1835-37 was based on the Lysicrates monument in Athens. It was once the terminus for the 1830-34 Havel bridge that Schinkel designed.

Following the western edge of the park up the Havel you reach the **Casino** on a terrace overlooking the banks of the river. Built in 1824-25, it was Schinkel's first work at Glienicke. The gardens were modeled after those in Pompeii. Through the pergola you see across the Havel in the direction of the Jungfernsee ("lake") to Pfingstberg, where you see the broad towers of the striking Pfingstberg Palace. The northern pergola reveals a view of the tower of the Machine House.

Away from the Havel into the garden, passing an elevated flower bed crowned with a Diana figure, you come to the **Klosterhof** ("Cloister Court") designed by Ferdinand von Arnim in 1850. It is a mixture of Byzantine and early-Middle-Ages styles. The focus of the remarkable building is the cloister purchased from the island of Certosa, near Venice, Italy. In front of the gate is a column with copies of the lions of St. Mark's Cathedral in Venice.

Farther into the interior of the park you come to a group of buildings fashioned by Persius in 1837-38 to look like an Italian castle, the **Machinenhaus, Wasserturm, and Gärtnerhaus** ("Machine House, Water Tower, and Gardener's House"). It was the wish of Prince Karl to keep verdant the trees and lawns of the park; hence the water tower and aqueducts.

The asphalted path leads to the brown **Matrosenhaus** ("Sailor's House") with a stubby tower. The house was rebuilt by Persius from an older house in a hollow to domicile the crews of the pleasure boats on the Havel.

Farther north the left fork leads to the **Teufelsbrücke** ("Devil's Bridge"), which was built by Persius in 1838 as a romantic ruin recalling the legendary, mystical bridge of the same name over the Gotthard Pass in Switzerland, which the Swiss associated in myth with the Devil.

At the **Bastion** on the **Kanonenberg** ("Cannon Mountain") you have a beautiful view over the Havel. Still farther north you come to the group of buildings of the **Jägerhof** ("Hunter's Court") which were built in 1828 by Schinkel in the English Gothic style. Prince Karl elected this style after a hunting party in England.

The English Tudor **Jägertor** ("Hunter's Gate") is the northern entrance to the park. It was built in 1842 by Persius. On the left wall a coat of arms from 1618 remains from a Brandenburg city fortress. In front of the gate is the **Landzunge Krughorn** ("Krughorn Spit") into the Havel. Here you see Peacock Island with its fairy-tale palace and the **Heilandskirche** ("Savior's Church") on the Havel like a ship in harbor. This remarkable church resembles an early Christian Italian basilica. It was built in 1841-42, based on an idea by the overweight King Friedrich Wilhelm IV ("Onkel Dicki").

The path back along the Havel to the Glienicke Bridge was laid out in 1842.

**Jagdschloß Glienicke** ("Glienicke Hunting Lodge"), on the south side of Königstraße, has seen many alterations and extensions since it was erected in 1683 as a relatively simple construction by Dieussart for the Great Elector. Its present appearance is due to the work of Ferdinand von Arnim, who in the middle of the 19th century converted the lodge in French baroque style.

## PEACOCK ISLAND

The **Pfaueninsel** ("Peacock Island"), a 0.9-mile (1.5-kilometer) long by 1,625-feet (500-meter) wide island, is the largest in the Havel River. It was declared a special nature preserve in 1924. Since then, this perfect example of late 18th-century landscape gardening by Peter Lenné, has been virtually untouched.

Crossing the street from the Wannsee S-Bahn station is like stepping into another world—a new, greener world. The difference is like night and day. You can't believe you are still in the same country, much less in the Berlin metropolis. It's quiet, forested, isolated, natural, outdoorsy, and breezy.

In 1685, the Great Elector commissioned a laboratory for the alchemist Johannes Kunckel for him to make gold. Instead, he succeeded in improving the then highly prized ruby glass, and "Kunckel Glass" became world famous.

Prince Wilhelm, later Kaiser Wilhelm I, hid on the island during the Revolution of 1848 before cutting off his distinguished beard and fleeing clean-shaven to England for refuge with Queen Victoria and Prince Albert. The revolutionaries however were true Berliners. When they saw the two words chalked by students on the palace: *National Eigenthum* ("National Property"), their revolution wilted.

During the 1936 Olympic Games, Nazi Propaganda Minister Joseph Goebbels used his position as head of the film industry to organize on the island a huge party where more than a thousand guests at dinner were impressed with the island decorated end to end with a set that resembled the Arabian Nights. Comely girls were dressed like Renaissance pages, but there was talk when, late at night, male guests began pursuing scantily-clad pages through the undergrowth.

The highlight of the island, the curious white **Märchenschloß** ("Fairy-Tale Palace") (open Tue.-Sun. 10 A.M. to 5 P.M.) that you see on posters and postcards, lies at the southwest tip of the island. Built (1794-97) by the Potsdam master cabinetmaker Johann G. Brendel in the form of an artificial ruin, it was a gift of love from King Friedrich Wilhelm II to his mistress, Countess Lichtenau. When Friedrich Wilhelm II died, Countess Lichtenau fell into disgrace and had to abandon the palace. It was later used by Friedrich Wilhelm III and Queen Luise as a summer residence.

The Biedermeier decor of the palace's eight rooms are shown by a guide in frequent German-language-only tours (Tue.-Sun. until 3 P.M.), where you shuffle around in special slippers like those in Charlottenburg Palace, but you aren't allowed upon the cunning bridge at the top.

Walking round the oak-covered island—you can't walk on the grass except at the special fields set aside and covered with sunbathers—takes you to the ruin of Jacob's Well, the **Kavalierhaus** ("Knight's House"), the **Königin-Luise-Gedächnistempel** ("Queen Luise Memorial Temple") for the queen who died prematurely, the **Meierei** ("Dairy") that was built as a ruin with an authentic facade of a patrician house from Danzig (Gdansk), the birdhouses and greenhouses. None of these are really very interesting. The island's charm lies in its solitude and vegetation. The peacocks themselves, placed here in 1842 for the Berlin Zoo, may have gone searching for warmer climes; they remain in short supply.

A ferry runs as needed (daily 8 A.M. to 8 P.M.). A ticket includes entrance to the island but not to the palace. No meals or smoking are permitted on the Pfaueninsel, but several shops in the front alcove of S-Bhf Wannsee sell sandwiches, pastries, and canned drinks that you can carry with you. Try first the bakery for the best sandwiches.

From S-Bhf Wannsee use bus A16 (daily 9:24 A.M. to 8:24 P.M.), which takes over from early-morning bus 316. Their route takes them in a circle from S-Bhf Wannsee to the Pfaueninsel and Nikolskoe. Automobile drivers may use Nikolskoer Weg.

## NIKOLSKOE

**Nikolskoe** is Russian, and it means "belonging to Nicholas," which is the name King Friedrich Wilhelm III gave to the log house he had built in 1819 on a hill overlooking Peacock Island as a surprise for his oldest daughter, Princess Charlotte, who in 1817 had married Russian Crown Prince Nicholas (later Czar Nicholas I). When the Prussian king visited his daughter and son-in-law near St. Petersburg in 1818, he was domiciled in a Russian cabin that pleased him so much that he obtained the plans and had one built in only six weeks as a surprise for his daughter when she and her husband returned the visit the following year.

The **Blockhaus,** long on the preservation list, is now a favored country restaurant. You can't tell that the original burned down in summer 1984 and that the present structure is a copy. Copying it wasn't so easy because original woods had to be imported from Finland and Canada.

From the height of the blockhouse you have a magnificent panorama over the Havel landscape and Peacock Island. Use bus 216 from S-Bhf Wannsee running daily (9:24 A.M. to 8:24 P.M.).

Only a few steps from Nikolskoe you find the **Kirche Sankt Peter und Paul** ("Sts. Peter and Paul Church") that was built in 1834-37 by August Stüler and Albert Dietrich Schadow—also a present to Friedrich Wilhelm III's daughter Charlotte, who, with the crowning of her husband in 1825, had became Czarina Alexandra. Despite the king's personal supervision, the Russian royal couple didn't think the church looked "Russian" enough, so they topped the red-brick building with an interesting copper patina-green-and-gold onion dome, an octagonal spire, and a beautiful clock facing the Havel River. It looks much newer because it's so clean. The mosaics of St. Peter and St. Paul at the chancel were given to Friedrich the Great by Pope Clement XIII.

Sts. Peter and Paul is one of Berlin's favorite wedding churches because bridal couples can enjoy the views over the Havel and Peacock Island among the scents and greenery of pines. Chimes play on the hour between noon and 6 P.M.

## AVUS

The Avus roadway pierces the Grunewald like an arrow. The red building with the star on top is its control tower. Running straighter than a ruler parallel to the S-Bahn tracks, the Avus is more than tar, asphalt, and cement. It is a piece of Berlin history and booming ideology. The Avus now belongs to the urban freeway which passes the grandstands where hundreds of thousands of Germans rooted for car racers.

Avus has experienced many highs and lows during its 70-year history. It has been a racetrack, an Autobahn, an S-Bahn, a military route, and for 30 years it was one of two land connections between Berlin and West Germany. It was blessing and curse for millions of automobile drivers who jerked or rested along its route.

Avus began with royal displeasure. Kaiser Wilhelm II had the bitter duty to congratulate the Italian Nazarro for his victory in the 1907 Taunus race. This obviously couldn't go on. Germans needed a new racetrack. It was no sooner said than done.

Two years later a racing association was formed. It took four more years to begin the earthworks. In 1921 construction of Avus was completed. Over a quarter-million spectators swarmed on a cloudy autumn day the first race over the 5.4-mile-long and 5-mile-wide straightaway. Sports enthusiasm knew no limits; national enthusiasm neither.

The first victor on the new course was Fritz von Opel. The Opel that he drove was painted red and reached a top speed of 86 mph with an average speed of 81 mph. According to the *Berliner Morgenpost* at the time: "Foreigners shall again see German determination, German workmanship, and German industry."

Avus offered the Nazis the world's first stretch of highway free of crossings and the basis of their militarily strategic network of Autobahnen. Since the fall of the Wall, Avus is only Highway "A 15," a part of the German Autobahn network. Races there are not prearranged.

## 5. Sports

**Strandbad Wannsee,** Wannseebadweg 25, Tel. 803-5450/5612 (open 7-8 A.M. to 6-8 P.M.; adult admission DM 5, children DM 3; beach cabanas are rented for the day for DM 12; until 1 P.M., DM 7; after 1 P.M., DM 3; beach chairs are rented for the day for DM 5; until 1 P.M., DM 3; after 1 P.M., 3 DM) is one of Berlin's two great beaches. The longest lakefront beach in Europe, it stretches along a 0.6-mile (1 kilometer) sandy beach with swimming and sunning (only sunbathing in September and October). Use S-Bhf Nikolassee and connecting bus 513, or 112 or 118.

Strictly speaking, the Halensee ("Lake") is in Wilmersdorf, toward Grunewald. The sandy beach with 260- by 400-foot (80 by 120 meters) swimming area, **Freibad Halensee,** Königsallee 5 (open 8 A.M. to 8 P.M.), is Berlin's oldest beach nudist community. People wear only a smile on their face. Use S-Bhf Halensee.

**Teufelsberg** is Berlin's winter sports center with two ski jumps, ski slopes, toboggan run, snow-making machines, and beautiful view.

**Eisstadion** ("Ice Stadium"), Fritz-Wildung-Straße 9, Tel. 823-40-60, ice skating in winter, roller-blading in summer. Use S-Bhf Hohenzollerndamm.

**LTTC "Rot-Weiß"** stages the German Woman's Open tennis tournament at Hundekehle Lake in Grunewald. The lovely tournament facilities and 7,000-seat stadium make this one of the world's best and most successful women's tournaments.

## 6. Shopping

Shopping arcades and green spaces are not compatible, but you find shops clustered around S-Bahn stations and stores located in the centers of the several districts (see Chapter 10).

## 7. Nightlife and Entertainment

Concerts are occasionally held in the romantic courtyard of the **Grunewald Hunting Lodge.**

# 12

# Köpenick

## 1. Orientation

The wooden sailboats glide smoothly from the width of the Großen Müggelsee (lake) into the Müggelspree. Paddle boats, canoes, rubber boats, and adventurous home-made craft float past like ducks in a row heading southeast. The destination of this small armada that you see every sunny day in perhaps the most idyllic district of Berlin, is Neu-Venedig ("New Venice") in Rahnsdorf, on the edge of Köpenick and between the Berlin Forest and eastern shore of the Müggelsee.

Visit the Captain from Köpenick on his own playing field. Enjoy the historic flair of the Old City and broad expanses of water of the Müggelsee (lake), Dahme and Spree (rivers). There's no doubt Köpenick has rich attractions to offer. There's no doubt that Köpenick possesses a charming mixture of history and nature. Also there's no doubt that Köpenick has no tourists. Most foreign visitors consider Köpenick too far from Berlin's city centers.

Köpenick district, often called "Berlin's Green Lung," has the highest hills (the Müggelberge at 377 feet—115 meters), the largest surface area (32 percent), and is the greenest of the former East Berlin districts.

Three-quarters of its 49 square miles (12,735 hectares) is covered by forest and water and traversed by hiking paths totaling 310 miles (500 kilometers) through the Berlin city forest.

Old Köpenick city—the "City on Water"—was granted city rights some 30 years earlier than Berlin, something that 109,000 Köpenickers gloat about. That it is now part of Greater Berlin is hard for them to swallow, but they still speak their own dialect.

Köpenick was for a long time before its incorporation into Greater Berlin a favorite recreation area for Berliners wanting to get away from the hustle of the big city. The island of Altstadt Köpenick between Spree, Dahme, and Kietzer Graben (see below) attracts you for a round trip. Even now with bumper-to-bumper traffic inching down the street, Alt-Köpenick, it gives you the idea of a suburban community.

The industries of Köpenick were hard hit by the Wende. Factories closed and unemployment peaked. Rehabilitation money has only sufficed to renew the Wilhelminenhofstraße in Oberschöeweide, but only 7 percent of the city was turned to rubble during the War, so Köpenick is still worth visiting just to get a feeling for the former village and to see three things: 1) Schloß Köpenick, where the king of Sweden commanded the Thirty Years War, 2) the idyllic feeling of a city at peace with water, and 3) the town hall with the Gothic arches and leaded windows in the foyer. The Ratskeller below the city hall is at least worth a good look, and, better, a memorable, gemütlich place to dine. On the downside is the horrible traffic congestion. The narrow streets form a bottleneck which has yet to be alleviated.

You can very easily imagine Köpenick as a separate small village in medieval times, with slate-roofed brick buildings typical of northern German towns like Bremen or Lübeck—but Köpenick is much more compact. It was always an important site located on lakes. There are also some similarities to Swedish architecture or even Copenhagen.

Köpenickers claim the name of the location came about when a Köpenicker fisher took to market a catch of crabs. The crabs were afraid for their lives and shouted: "Köpp nick; köpp nick!" (Don't sell!) Therefore the settlement was called "Köppnick." More scholarly lexicographers maintain it is of Slavic origin and means "Island City."

Reach Köpenick by S-Bahn line S3 (direction: Erkner) to ocher-red S-Bhf Köpenick. As early as 1842, this station was a mainline stop on the Berlin-Frankfurt am Oder train line. Now S-Bhf Köpenick is a busy station with white tiles on walls and stairs, Asians selling clothes, a flower market with reasonably priced flowers, a fast-food Köpi-curry-station, and vendors selling ice cream and beer from trailers. Posters cover many of the walls and there is a nice map showing the Köpenick district and places to go for excursions and recreation, including Oberschönweide, Grünau, Müggelheim, Schmöckwitz, and Rahnsdorf.

When it was built, Köpenick station was located so far outside the city that clever businessmen and entrepreneurs organized a horse-drawn omnibus line into the "Island City." Today it takes less time to walk than to drive because of the furious traffic—or you can take one of the literally rattling streetcars in a few minutes, but you'll find it more rewarding to stroll south along the busy Bahnhofstraße.

The **Fremdenverhrsverein Köpenick** ("Köpenick Tourist Office"), Alt Köpenick 34, Tel. 607-30-38, Fax 657-45-98 (open Mon.-Fri. 10 A.M. to 6:30 P.M., Sat.-Sun. to 5 P.M.) provides extensive town information and also offers nature excursions and each Sunday a cultural/historical walking tour of the city at 10 A.M.

The **Heimatmuseum Köpenick** ("At-home Köpenick Museum"), Alter Markt 2, presents historical information from the district in a half-timbered house.

Take the south exit from the S-Bhf Köpenick. Bahnhofstraße leads straight south from the station toward the Spree River. It is a north/south axis of unrelenting traffic noises and the houses aren't much to see (some of them crumbling), but you receive a reprieve when you turn east on Seelenbinderstraße and walk about 200 yards to the small **Mandrellaplatz.** A branch of the West German Berliner Bank has occupied the imposing German Renaissance building (1899-1901) designed by Paul Thoerner that was once the district court. A memorial on the corner honors Rudolf Mandrella, a judge in this court, who fought the Nazis.

## 2. The Hotel Scene

**Hotel am Schloß Köpenick** (Grünauer Straße 17-21, Tel. 658-05-0, Fax 658-05-450). US$67-83, single; US$83-100, double; breakfast buffet included.

**Hotel Müggelsee** (Am Großen Müggelsee, Tel. 658-82-0, Fax 658-82-263). The lake is just beyond your balcony in this large hotel on the south shore of the Müggelsee that was once a favorite of the DDR's leaders. After its US$17 million (DM 30 million) renovation, you, too, will appreciate its air-conditioning, terrace, and the landing stage on the Mügglesee. Its 172 rooms with balcony are not luxurious, but comfortable. US$ 100-39, single; US$122-67, double; breakfast buffet included. Weekend arrangements start at $95 per person in a double room.

## 3. Restaurants and Cafés

**Ratskeller Köpenick,** Alt-Köpenick 21, Tel. 657-20-35 (open 11 A.M. to midnight). Rustic. In addition to an Italian buffet, the sanely priced, complete menu that changes daily is available about noon. The wine list includes French, German, and Italian. On Fridays and Saturdays about 8-9 P.M., you have a program with theater or music ranging from jazz to cabaret. Peek in on the Jazzkeller ("cellar").

**Altstadtcafé Cöpenick,** Alt-Köpenick 14. Here you treat yourself to Cöpenick liquor or the coffee specialties *Fliegende Teppich* ("Flying Carpet") and *Dudelsack* ("Bagpipe")

**Die Spindel,** Bölschestraße 51, Tel. 645-29-37 (open daily from 11:30 A.M.) offers you plainly excellent German cooking with Brandenburg specialties and outstanding cakes.

**Kauter,** Hämmerlingstraße 13, Tel. 657-58-96 (open 11 A.M. to 11 P.M.). Reasonably priced, good German cooking plus steaks, salads, and vegetarian meals on the edge of the Wuhlheide ("heath").

**Alt-Köpenicker Bierstube,** Alt-Köpenick 32, Tel. 657-2453 (open daily 10 A.M. to midnight). Beer hall.

**Restaurant Fioretto,** Oberspreestr. 176, Tel. 657-2605 (open Tue.-Sat. 6 P.M. to 1 A.M.). Prizewinning, homemade pasta.

**Restaurant Hauptmann von Köpenick,** Mahlsdorfer Str. 1, Tel. 657-2076 (open daily 11 A.M. to 2 A.M.). Good German food and beer.

**Kietzer Krug,** Kietz 18, Tel. 657-2860 (open Mon.-Fri. 3 P.M. to 10 P.M., Sat. 9 A.M. to 1 P.M.). A good pub in the Kietz for a beer and simple snack. Try to sit outside.

**Köpenicker Weinstuben,** Bahnhofstr. 7, Tel. 657-2993 (open daily noon to midnight). Wine café. Always good food.

## 4. Sightseeing

### KÖPENICK BLOOD WEEK

Because of major industry in the area, Köpenick's workers have always been rightist. On the day of Hitler's inauguration, a red flag flew from a brewery nearby. A few months later, in June 1933, zealous to consolidate their power, a detachment of SA thugs descended on Köpenick, seized well over 500 anti-Fascists, social democrats, and trade unionists and dragged them off to local SA barracks and the local prison, where they tortured and beat the Köpenickers. They murdered 91 and tossed their mutilated corpses into the Dahme. The Nazi terror raid became known as **Köpenicker Blutwoche** ("Köpenick Blood Week").

The square was named for one of the leaders, Rudolf Mandrella, a Catholic anti-Fascist who was forming a small place of worship in the former Zellenbau. He could not reconcile the Fascist atrocities with his religious beliefs. After the Blood Week, Mandrella was imprisoned in a Gestapo hospital until 1943, when he passed to his Maker. You can visit the **Gedenkstätte Köenicker Blutwoche** ("Memorial to the Köpenick Blood Week"), Puchanstraße 12, Tel. 657-49-01 (open Mon. 10 A.M. to 4 P.M., Tue. and Thur. to 6 P.M., and Fri. to 2 P.M.), in memory of the workers massacred by SA troops in June 1993. Use S-Bhf Köpenick, bus 269.

## MECKLENBURG VILLAGE

A thatched roof is the trademark of the **Mecklenburger Dorf** ("Mecklenburg Village"), from the Tenth World Youth Festival in summer 1973, which is now nothing but a shabby excuse for an outdoor beer hall with yellow umbrellas advertising American cigarettes over preformed aggregate tables and occasional thatching in case it rains. It may have been refreshing in 1973, but now is in disrepair. The bar serves snacks and drinks. On hot summer days you can seek a cool drink under umbrellas. In winter you can take a warm mulled wine ( *Glühwein* ).

## PLATZ DES 23. APRIL

Proceed south through quiet Puchanstraße and west on Kinzerallee back to Bahnhofstraße, and then with a little care from there into Friedrichshagener Straße and to the pleasant shores of the Alte Spree River, where countless ducks and swans like to parade along the banks. Many visitors feed them throughout the year.

In back of the little Mecklenburger Dorf, the treelined area opens onto the **Platz des 23. April.** The name recalls the date that the Red Army marched into Köpenick in 1945.

One glance at the style of the white, 20-foot (6 meters) stone monument with the fist on top tells you it was built by the DDR. It is in fact fairly interesting because it is a memorial to the victims of Köpenick Blood Week by sculptor Walter Sutkowski. Reliefs on the nearby wall show scenes from the happy workers' life in Communist Germany. How long these will be allowed to remain is anyone's guess.

Cross south over the newly built Dammbrücke. The old one lasted until 1986. This is where Old Köpenick begins. The north shore of the Spree is very idyllic; you see children pushing their rental paddle boats into the river. On the west side of the bridge the Dahme River flows into the Spree.

Over a shady riverbank promenade, parallel to Alt-Köpenick, the path follows the Dahme. There is talk that now with unification the small twisting streets of this quarter will be developed into a touristy shopping area. It was founded at the end of the 18th century and the beginning of the 19th century. Some half-timbered houses date from the 17th century.

Directly opposite the city hall you see the sign "Schloß Köpenick," denoting a landing for the White Fleet river steamers. At Luisenhain, it broadens to a tended park. A sundial shows the sunny hours.

## ST. LAURENTIUS CHURCH

Down Alt-Köpenick, formerly called Schloßstraße, you see evangelical **Laurentiuskirche,** with the Martin Luther Kapelle, very brick and very old, built between 1839 and 1841. The slate, pointed roof is topped with a little star and a patina cupola with a cross. The half-timbered houses opposite date from the 17th century.

## TOWN HALL

The midpoint of Köpenick is the **Köpenicker Rathaus** ("Town Hall"), an admirable neo-Gothic brick building (1901-4) with an elaborate staircase and, since 1996, a bronze "Captain from Köpenick" in front of the door. The sculpture not only is a favorite photo for tourists, but a good-luck charm for newlyweds. The town hall, one of the finest in Berlin, was designed by Hans Schütte and Hugo Kinzer. Its 177-foot (54 meters) tower with the great Rathaus clock dominates the Spree and Dahme rivers. In the Middle Ages, on this spot stood the "Haus der Bürger."

The Rathaus's interior is nicely designed. Wonderful Gothic brick arches and the original artwork of leaded-glass windows complement the solid wooden tables.

Wedding parties gather in front of city hall. Brides wear long white dresses and carry gigantic bouquets of roses; grooms hold spring flower bouquets; both smile for photographers. Some bridegrooms rent Captain from Köpenick costumes (see below) for photography.

A visit to the Ratskeller is recommended. Its interior reminds you of the interior of the Rathaus above. It has Gothic low ceilings with dark-red brick piping over the Gothic archways. There is a modern bar surrounded by stools. Tables are butcher-block; there are bright flowers and a wooden floor. Artists have hung paintings on the walls: Italian landscapes, and Prague old city. You could say it is "Hanseatic gemütlich."

The Ratskeller is now down the steps facing the Dahme, but once it was located on the second floor and thus the Ratskeller on the second floor was counted as one of the seven wonders satirical Köpenick offered the world: a stupid teacher, a dead doctor, a mayor named Borgmann ("borrower"), a young woman (Fräulein) of 80 years, a hospital located in a cemetery, and a jail on the city location named "Freiheit" (freedom).

## CAPTAIN FROM KÖPENICK

The famous Captain from Köpenick marched a division of Prussian soldiers into the Köpenicker Rathaus on October 16, 1906. A cobbler, named Wilhelm Voigt, who had spent half his 60 years in jail and so had a long criminal record, stumbled upon a discarded army captain's uniform in Potsdam and put it on to keep warm. When he encountered 10 Prussian infantry soldiers at the Neue Wache on Unter den Linden, to his surprise they saluted him. (Clothes make the man.) Then Voigt discovered they would obey his orders even though he was scruffy and unsoldierly. Overwhelmed with his newfound power, he marched them onto a train and then to Köpenick's city hall, where he arrested the mayor and treasurer, and appropriated 4,000 Marks of municipal cash, but ignored securities worth two million. When Voigt was eventually caught he claimed he was just trying to get a passport but that he had inadvertently released the police chief, who was the only man authorized to issue passports. After he was sentenced, Kaiser Wilhelm II surprised everyone with a touch of humor and commuted his sentence and commended the Berlin people for their attention to authority.

For years this has been one of the funniest stories about Berlin, especially to Berliners, who appreciate the unthinking Prussian allegiance to rank. Voigt, incidentally, is said to have died a pauper and been buried in a Luxembourg cemetery.

Every year visitors come to the **Köpenicker Sommer** ("Köpenick Summer"), the annual festival and parade in the city quarter during the last week of June, to meet shoemaker Voigt, who is played by a popular actor, and to buy Captain-from-Köpenick souvenir glasses, scarves, and dolls. Posters illustrate a man standing in front of the Rathaus delivering a speech, with enthusiastic onlookers, an oom-pah-pah band with members wearing silver spiked helmets, and, of course, a wagonload of blonde girls riding past in a hay wagon.

## KIETZ

Now you can see the entrance gate to Palace Island, but instead turn left on Grünstraße. Its small city houses make it look like a typical shopping street, like the next street, Kietzer Straße, where you can turn right. Crossing

the busy Müggelheimer Straße, make a detour to **Kietz,** which was a separate
fishing village until 1898 when it was incorporated into Köpenick. It was
the site of a busy fishing settlement as early as 1209. In the 19th century,
375 fishers lived in 31 houses. Kietz, with its rough pavement and the
countless low houses standing one after another on the water beside the
Frauentog inlet (some of which are 200 years old), still recalls the atmosphere
of the Middle-Age fishing village despite the colorful restoration of the
houses in 1996.

Continue now in the direction of Palace Island. On the Uferplatz, you
see the fountain containing Karl Möpert's figure of "Mutter Lustig" at
Alter Markt 4. The hardworking washerwoman's scrubbing boards and
washing once draped on the shores of the Spree. Henriette Lustig (1835)
founded the first pay laundry for "elegant houses," which gained Köpenick
the reputation as the "Laundry of Berlin." At the end of the 19th century
there were 22 independent laundries here.

Traces of the early settlement of the present Berlin area have been
found here. Living quarters in the Stone Age. The convenient location
on the island at the confluence of the Dahme and Spree offered good
possibilities for catching fish. Archaeological finds show written evidence
of the development of this area in the 12th century.

Walk to Schloßplatz filled with streetcars from lines 26, 27, and 62. The
recently built wooden bridge over the Wassergraben on the river side of the
Platz between Frauentog and Dahme connects the old city with Schloßinsel.

## PALACE ISLAND

The present-day **Schloßinsel** ("Palace Island") is filled with the
palace, park, and museum, self-contained by Linden trees. It was the site
of a medieval Slav stronghold thought to have been the residence of
Prince Jaxa von Köpenick. Coins have been found with embossed script
reading "Jakza de Copnic."

**Köpenicker Schloß** ("Köpenick Palace"), one of the most important
secular buildings in the Brandenburg March, is hidden among Linden
trees on the water. It will be reopened after the remodeling of the
baroque palace is completed in year 2002.

The earthen buff-colored courtyard, enclosed by trees, with a
Friedrich of Prussia statue, gilded ornaments, and bronze sculptures has
a nice feeling. Yellow marigolds and pink geraniums add color. The first
thing you notice about the palace, which is the oldest in the Berlin area
and looks more like an impressive, fortified manor house, is the baroque
portal of Johann Arnold Nering (1682). The palace was commissioned in

its present Dutch baroque style by Elector Prince Friedrich according to plans of Dutchman Rutger von Langefeld (1677-84). Originally it was supposed to be a palace copied from Versailles, with three wings, but the elector ran out of money, so that the planned Garden Wing was abandoned and the already completed side wing became the present-day castle. It is asymmetric—its left wing has never been built. It replaced the 1572 Renaissance hunting lodge built by Elector Joachim III. During the Thirty Years War, King Gustavus Adolphus of Sweden took up quarters here.

Richly decorated rooms and ceilings lighten the interior. One of the gems of the interior decoration is the heraldry room. Convened in the heraldry room from October 22 to 28, 1730, by order of Friedrich Wilhelm I, a military tribunal sentenced to death Lt. Hans Herrmann von Katte, close friend of Crown Prince Friedrich, who had helped the prince attempt to escape to the Netherlands from his father's authoritarian control. On the king's orders, von Katte was beheaded in front of the crown prince. According to historians, the trauma led to the ruthless, militaristic disposition of the crown prince, later Friedrich II, the Great.

South of the palace, the **Kunstgewerbemuseum** ("Handicrafts Museum"), although it is closed for remodeling until year 2002, looks distinguished with figures on top of columns. After the Second World War, the DDR collected the artworks from the cellar of the Berlin City Palace on Unter den Linden together with other artworks from the East. They temporarily showed them in the rooms of the palace until they decided to blow it up. The collections were transferred to Schloß Köpenick in 1963 and arranged to give a chronological overview from the Renaissance to the present. In 1992, authorities wanted to close for restoration, but the local tourist office organized a sit-in—Berlin's first sit-in for a cultural purpose. With success. Until 1998, the museum was restored piece by piece so that the showrooms largely could remain open. It featured master European artwork from the 10th century and historical artistic handwork housed in 35 baroque rooms with magnificent stucco ceilings dating from the 10th century. The best pieces have been transferred to the Kunstgewerbemuseum in Tiergarten for display (see Chapter 6).

A structure in the wide-ranging park of the island is especially interesting, the baroque castle chapel. It was built from 1682 to 1685 according to designs of architect Johann Arnold Nering. Its richly decorated interior in contrast to its simple exterior comes as a surprise to visitors. Now the chapel is used as a concert room.

For Palace Island, use S-Bhf Spindlersfeld or S-Bhf Köpenick and streetcar 60 or 68 or bus 167 or 360 or you can use the Luisenhain landing for the river steamers. Both S-Bahn stations are in tariff zone "B."

## SPINDLERSFELD TRAIN STATION

Your walking path crosses the modern Lange Brücke ("Long Bridge"), where a glance back reveals the very attractive view of the yacht harbor over the water side of the palace on one side and the panorama of old Berlin rental housing on the other. This is one of the best places for you to take photographs of Köpenick. Underneath are two half-piers sticking into the Dahme. Children are using paddle boats on the river. It is a quiet relaxing place.

From here walk west about 10 minutes along the Oberspreestraße to S-Bhf Spindlersfeld. It's a divided road with streetcar tracks in the middle. Across the street you see the Alexander von Humboldt Schule, named for the brother of the founder of the university on Unter den Linden.

Berlin Spindlersfeld (a small brick station on the mainline between Berlin and Chemnitz) is the end of S-Bahn line 10 but still in tariff zone "B." Because line 10 bypasses downtown Berlin, you will change to the S-Bahn train waiting across the platform at S-Bhf Schöneweide when returning the center of Berlin. It's a dull ride.

## MÜGGELSEE

The **Müggelsee,** Berlin's largest lake, and the Müggelberge ("Muggel Hills"), the highest in Berlin, are in the district of Köpenick. The legendary **Teufelssee** ("Devil's Lake") can be found on Müggelheimerdamm. From the Teufelssee, a steep 126-step stairway takes you to the landmarked **Müggelturm** ("Müggel Tower"), the insignia for the quarter. From the tower's observation floor 100 feet (30 meters) above ground, you have a nice view of forest and water and the city as far as the Alexanderplatz television tower. The current tower was built in 1960 after the old wooden one burned down. Berliners call the Müggelsee Berlin's "larger bathtub," a comparison to the Wannsee.

**Strandbad Müggelsee,** Fürstenwalder Damm 838 (Köpenick), Tel. 6-487-777 (until Sept., open 8 A.M. to 8 P.M., after Sept. 15, to 6 P.M.; adult admission DM 5, children DM 3; beach cabanas are rented for the day for DM 12; until 1 P.M., DM 7; after 1 P.M., DM 3; beach chairs are rented for the day for DM 5; until 1 P.M., DM 3; or after 1 P.M., DM 3) is one of Berlin's two great beaches. It was laid out in 1929-30 and declared a national monument in 1977. Both dates are earlier than the Wannsee. You can enjoy swimming, nude bathing, beach volleyball, beach basketball, outdoor chess, table tennis, and/or swimming lessons on the beach of the Müggelsee. Use S-Bhf Friedrichshagen then tram 61 or S-Bhf Rahnsdorf then bus 161.

## 5. Sports

Köpenick's register claims 30 sports facilities, including four public tennis courts, but in reality, three large sports fields and four tennis courts are not operational due to lack of money.

In addition to the Strandbad Müggelsee, southeastern Berlin offers the **Strandbad Grünau,** Regattastraße, Sportpromenade 5, Tel. 681-3576 (open 8-9 A.M. to 6-7 P.M.). Swimming. Use S-Bhf Grünau then Tram 68.

**FEZ Kinder- und Jugendfreizeitzentrum** ("Children's and Youth Leisure Center"), An der Wuhlheide 250, Tel. 535-183 (open Tue.-Thur. 10 A.M. to 9 P.M., Fri. to 10 P.M., Sat. 1 to 6 P.M., Sun. 10 A.M. to 6 P.M.). One of two great sports parks in Berlin contains sports hall, computer room, movie theater, large outdoor park with frisbee, mini-golf, skate-board ramps, street ball, and simulators for young astronauts. Take your passport to rent equipment or bicycle. Take a trip on the park railroad. Includes the SJC. Use S-Bhf Wuhlheide, tram 26, 61, 67.

**Schwimmhalle Köpenick**, Pablo-Hervda-Straße 5, Tel. 654-30-04 (open Mon.-Wed. and Fri. 6 A.M. to 8 P.M., Sat. 9 A.M. to 6 P.M., Sun. 8 A.M. to 2 P.M.).

**Freibad Wendenschloß,** Möllhausenufer, Tel. 656-9731 (open 7-9 A.M. to 6-8 P.M.). Swimming. Use S-Bhf Köpenick or S-Bhf Grünau, then proceed by ferry.

**Freibad Friedrichshagen,** Müggelseedamm 216, Tel. 645-5756 (open 8 A.M. to 6-7 P.M.). On the Müggelsee, the smallest Berlin family swimming pool. Use S-Bhf Friedrichshagen.

**Freibad Gartenstraße,** Gartenstr. 46-48, Tel. 657-1958 (open 8-9 A.M. to 6-7 P.M.). Swimming for young adults; baby care. Use S-Bhf Köpenick.

**Badesee Wuhlheide,** Köpenicker Allee (Wuhlheide), Tel. 630-7668 (open 8-9 A.M. to 6-7 P.M.). Swimming. Use S-Bhf Wuhlheide.

## 6. Shopping

Shopping is spotty in blue-collar Köpenick, but determined enthusiasts might be able to ferret out some worthwhile antiques.

## 7. Nightlife and Entertainment

During summer there are countless presentations in the open-air theater in the **Schloßpark**, which was renovated in 1963-64. The Schloß Café and in summer the open-air restaurant make the island a popular destination.

**Bräustübl** Müggelseedamm 164 (Friedrichshagen), Tel. 645-57-167 (open daily noon to midnight, at least). If you want an authentic old Berlin atmosphere, visit Bürgerbräu brewery and relax in one of the wonderfully carved, wooden niches and absorb the crowd-pleasing music, song, and cabaret evenings.

**Allende,** Pablo-Neruda-Straße 4, Tel. 654-20-04, the well-known live club has maneuvered itself through the changing political climates. On Wednesdays: club evening with disco. Every other Saturday: Hip Hop with live acts. Every other Sunday: live concerts.

**WM66** Grünauer Straße 71-73. House and Techno threaten to collapse the roof. Use tram 68 from S-Bhf Köpenick or S-Bhf Grünau.

**Lindenhorst,** Dorotheenstr. 20, Tel. 656-0363 (open Tue.-Thur. 8 P.M. to 1 A.M., Fri.-Sat. 9 P.M. to 4 A.M.). Disco for Köpenickers.

**Xenon,** Elcknerplatz, Tel. 656-4939 (open Mon.-Sat. 10 P.M. to 5 A.M.). Youthful disco.

# 13

# Potsdam

## 1. Orientation

After the Berlin Wall came down, West Berliners at last could sightsee and vacation anywhere in the former DDR. The first place they went to see was Potsdam, for serious reasons. It was visually and historically exciting. It still is. The tourist office claims that when everything falls into place within the next 10 years it will be the "Salzburg of the East."

The world-famous Sanssouci Palace and gardens, strikingly similar to Louis XIV's Versailles, make Potsdam a favorite excursion for Americans and Germans alike. Johann Sebastian Bach played here. Voltaire argued here. But after the War, Potsdam became a Soviet garrison town. Westerners were allowed to visit, but only with approved advance arrangements, and never allowed to linger. An East German, Bach might have been welcome—he was unlikely to have carried a camera—but Voltaire, a Westerner, would not have been. Now you can stroll Sanssouci's halls, roam the 740 acres (300 hectares) of park, frolic at Neptune's Grotto, dally in the Sicilian Garden, and pay your respects to Friedrich the Great in the eternal home that he selected.

After the destruction of the City Palace by 490 British bombers during

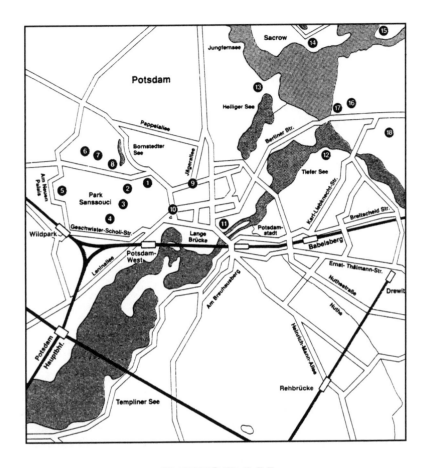

# POTSDAM

1. Sanssouci Palace
2. Chinese Teahouse
3. Roman Baths
4 Charlottenhof Palace
5. New Palace
6. Belvedere
7. Dragon House
8. Orangerie
9. Hunter Gate

10. Brandenburg Gate
11. Nikolai Church
12. Babelsberg Palace
13. Cecilienhof
14. Sacrow Holy Church
15. Peacock Island
16. Glienicke Palace
17. Glienicke Bridge
18. Böttcherberg

April 1945, some attractions have been lost forever, but it is still high on
the list of things to see because of the restorations of Schinkel's Nikolai
Church, the Dutch Quarter, Brandenburg Straße, Babelsberg Film Studio,
the Film Museum, and above all, Sanssouci Palace and Park. You can visit
Cecilienhof Lodge on the opposite side of the city, where at the Potsdam
Conference, Truman, Churchill, and Stalin reaffirmed Germany's military
occupation zones that separated Germany so decisively that the division
lasted from 1945 until 1990.

Potsdam, with a population of 140,000, is the capital city of the state of
Brandenburg. Its situation among bucolic rolling hills makes a pleasing
contrast to flat Berlin. The Havel River, which is so wide it seems like a
lake at Glienicke Bridge, flows into the Jungfernsee, the Tiefer See, the
Griebnitzsee, and the Templiner See making Potsdam seem like an island.
The Potsdam landing of Stern & Kreis shipping is in the heart of the city.

You can approach Potsdam as a diverting day excursion from Berlin by
S-Bahn or bus or—especially attractive for automobile drivers—you can
take a hotel in the more compact town before venturing into more complex
Berlin. Potsdam is an excellent destination in its own right, although Berlin
is the larger magnet.

To get to Potsdam from the west, take an ICE (InterCity Express) train
and get off at Potsdam Stadt station, the last stop before Berlin, or from
Berlin take S-Bahn line S-3 or S-7 from Berlin to Potsdam Stadt. You can
easily walk from Potsdam Stadt station across the Long Bridge toward the
landmark Nikolai Church to the historic inner city—or take a streetcar. On
the Am Alten Markt square, visit the Potsdam Information Office at
Friedrich-Ebert-Straße 5, Tel. (0331) 29-11-00 or 275-58-0 (open Apr.-Oct.,
9 A.M. to 8 P.M., Mon.-Fri.; 10 A.M. to 2 P.M., Sat.-Sun.; Nov.-Mar., 10 A.M. to
6 P.M., Mon.-Fri., 10 A.M. to 2 P.M., Sat.-Sun.). Pick up a free map, brochures,
and if you desire, book a hotel room without charge. Continue down
Friedrich-Ebert-Straße to Brandenburger Straße pedestrian mall, turning
left toward Potsdam's Brandenburg Gate. Pass through the gate to
Luisenplatz and proceed along the Allee nach Sanssouci to give yourself
the best perspective of the palace.

Air arrivals at Tegel airport take bus 109 to Berlin's Charlottenburg
train station and change there to S-Bahn. Air arrivals at Schönefeld airport
have farther to go. They must take regional train RB22 to Potsdam's
Pirschheide station or bus 602 to Potsdam Stadt, Lange Brücke. From
Templehof airport take U6 to Berlin's Friedrichstraße station and change
there to S3 or S7. Automobile drivers should exit Berliner Ring A10 at
Potsdam-Nord off-ramp, continuing on highway B273. Exiting Potsdam-Süd

off-ramp takes you to highway B2. Finally, you can use highway A115 to the Potsdam-Babelsberg exit.

Scholars trace Potsdam to 993 when the Holy Roman Emperor Otto II gave a swampy village to his aunt. A German castle appeared on the site in the 12th century. Since 1660 when the elector of Brandenburg took office, Potsdam has grown and prospered because of royalty's presence. The Great Elector and Friedrich the Great in particular dictated the town's architecture. In 1643, the Great Elector, at 23, had a modest, new palace built safely away from outbreaks of the plague and 18 miles from the noise and smells of Berlin, which was in ruins following the Thirty Years' War. In 1664, construction of a royal residence was begun. In 1685, Elector Friedrich set the stage for the growth and development of Berlin with the Potsdam Edict guaranteeing religious freedom. By 1713, Friedrich Wilhelm I, the Soldier King, had built Potsdam into a military garrison. By 1769 there were 17,000 inhabitants, of which 8,000 were soldiers.

To understand Potsdam, you have to think: "Prussia." Prussian militarism had almost everything to do with this Hohenzollern residence city. This caused the great controversy over the reburial of the Prussian kings in 1991 (see below). The royal family had two cities of residence: Berlin and Potsdam. Many of the kings felt more comfortable living in Potsdam than in Berlin because Potsdam was small, more orderly, and more easily watched, especially when soldiers in Berlin were deserting in droves. Berlin has always been a difficult city to manage. (Adolf Hitler himself was uncomfortable in Berlin; he much preferred his safe houses in Bavaria and former East Prussia.) There was no opposition to the Hohenzollerns in Potsdam. They built a splendid City Palace in Potsdam just as in Berlin. The Sanssouci installation charmed Prussian rulers exercising their fantasies.

Potsdam city begins across the Glienicke Bridge from Berlin. From the bridge you can see the border territory and a part of the Glienicke Palace, but you can't see how the parks and palaces hang together.

This is a more interesting way to approach Potsdam than by routine S-Bahn to Potsdam Stadt station. Get off the S-Bahn train at S-Bhf Wannsee and there transfer to Berlin bus 116 across Glienicke Bridge where you change to Potsdam streetcar #93 down Berliner Straße to "Am Alten Markt" stop next to the Nikolai Church.

The new green streetcar stop for Line 93 at the Potsdam end of the Glienicke Bridge was built as result of the opening of the border. Potsdam's low-rise electric streetcars run by the *Verkehrsbetrieb Potsdam*, ViP, are coupled together, two in a row, articulated, and different colors with advertising on the sides and high red pantographs on top. Berlin tickets are valid in Potsdam, as well.

## 2. The Hotel Scene

**Schloßhotel Cecilienhof** (Im Neuen Garten, Tel. (0331) 37050, Fax (0331) 292498) has marvelous, half-timbered architecture. Site of the Potsdam Conference and home of the crown prince's family on Lake Jungfern, it has a magnificent view. It is out of the way for users of public transportation, but perfect for automobile drivers. The road is well marked. US$90-135, single; US$156-94, double; breakfast buffet included.

**Arkona Hotel Voltaire** (Friedrich-Ebert-Straße 88, Tel. (0331) 2317-0, Fax (0331) 2317-100), a quiet, modern hotel, is smartly located directly in the middle of Potsdam across from the Dutch Quarter. US$110-30, single; US$130-55, double; breakfast buffet included.

**Best Western Residence-Hotel Potsdam** (Saarmunder Straße 60, Tel. (0331) 8830-0, Fax (0331) 8830511) is a large, modern hotel in a quiet location minutes from the historical center of Potsdam, with prices from US$55, single; from US$80, double; breakfast buffet included. U.S. reservations, Tel. 800-528-1234.

**Hotel Mercure** (Lange Brücke, Tel. (0331) 2722, Fax (0331) 293496), the luxury 16-story high-rise former DDR InterHotel, stands on the site of the former City Palace, so you can be sure it is right in the heart of Potsdam and near the ship landing. Visitors especially admire the view of the city from the upper stories. US$85-110, single or double; breakfast buffet US$12. U.S. Reservations, Tel. 800-221-4542.

**Dorint Kongress Hotel Potsdam** (Voltaireweg/Jägerallee), a large, low-rise, very modern, attractive hotel was opened at the end of 1997 near the Nauen Gate and the Russian Colony Alexandrowka. US$94-172, single; US$94-250, double; breakfast buffet included.

**Steigenberger MAXX Hotel Sanssouci** (Allee nach Sanssouci 1, opened March 1998) was built in the Anglo-American style of the '30s to '50s in the middle of Potsdam near the Peace Church in Sanssouci. Singles from US$56; doubles from US$133; including breakfast. U.S. reservations, Tel. 800-223-5652.

**Hotel Am Jägertor** (Hegelallee 11, Tel. 030-424396-50, Fax 030-424396-96, *http://www.utell.com*, opened August 1997) is modern and comfortable in the heart of Potsdam. US$90-110, single; US$106-139, double; breakfast buffet included. In the U.S., Tel. Utell at 800-207-6900.

**"Apart." Pension Babelsberg** (August-Bier-Straße 9, Tel. (0331) 747570, Fax (0331) 7475766) is a smaller, comfortable house in the outskirts with bicycles available. US$47-65, single; US$61-78, double; breakfast included.

**art'otel potsdam** (Zeppelinstraße 136, Tel. (0331) 9815-0, Fax (0331) 9815555, *http://www.utell.com*), in a historical building built in 1840 by

Ludwig Persius, formerly used as a granary, it is now part of a unique architectural ensemble of historic and modern styles located on the Havel River near Sanssouci Park. US$106-22, single; US$128-44, double; breakfast buffet included. In the U.S., Tel. Utell at 800-207-6900.

**Hotel Babelsberg** (Stahnsdorfer Straße 68, Tel. (0331) 749010, Fax (0331) 707668) has 42 beds located in a villa five minutes by foot from the film studios. US$36-56, single; US$50-72, double; breakfast included.

**Hotel Bayrisches Haus** (Im Wildpark 1, Tel. (0331) 963790, Fax (0331) 972329) contains 42 beds in a farmhouse-style building on the edge of Potsdam with good bus connections. US$115, single; US$72-100, double; breakfast included.

**Apartment-Hotel Bornimer Hof** (Rückertstraße 31, Tel. (0331) 549660, Fax (0331) 5496615, out of town) contains 30 apartments, some with kitchenettes. US$61-111; breakfast service, US$10.

**Filmhotel "Lili Marleen"** (Großbeerenstraße 75, Tel. (0331) 743200, Fax (0331) 74320-18) is a 1996 hotel near Babelsberg Studio decorated in the fantasy world of film. US$53, single; US$70-80, double; breakfast buffet included.

**Hotel Griebnitzsee** (Rudolf-Breitscheid-Straße 190-192, Tel. (0331) 7091-0, Fax (0331) 7091-11) provides a view of Lake Griebnitz in Babelsberg. It is close to Griebnitzsee S-Bahn station and boat landing. US$100-22, single; US$139-56, double; breakfast buffet included.

**Holländerhaus** (Kurfürstenstraße 15; Tel. (0331) 27911-0, Fax (0331) 27911-1) contains a few rooms in a Dutch-architecture building near the historical Holländischen Quarter in the center of Potsdam. US$56-106, single; US$117-61, double; breakfast included.

**Inselhotel Potsdam-Hermannswerder** (no street address; Tel. (0331) 23200, Fax (0331) 2320100) is an impressive hotel surrounded by woods on Lake Templin. US$83-106, single; US$83-133, double; breakfast included.

**Hotel-Café Reinhold** (Dortustraße 10, Tel. (0331) 284990, Fax (0331) 2849930) provides 22 beds in the center of Potsdam. US$83, single; US$83-106, double; breakfast included.

**Seminaris SeeHotel Potsdam** (An der Pirschheide, Tel. (0331) 9090-0) is a first-class hotel opened in December 1997, in Pirschheide Woods with private beach on Lake Templin. Drivers should exit "Potsdam Nord." Train travelers must use regional train station "Pirschheide." US$72-100, single; US$111-139, double; breakfast included.

**Schloßgarten Hotel** (Geschwister-Scholl-Straße 41a, Tel. (0331) 792254, Fax (0331) 901592), a small hotel across from Sanssouci Park, opened in March 1997. Use regional train to Wildpark station. US$55-70, single; US$70-90, double; breakfast included.

**Hotel Garni Vivaldi** (Karl-Liebknecht-Straße 24, Tel. (0331) 749060, Fax (0331) 7490616), a 20-bed hotel opened in May 1997, is located in the center of Babelsberg between the old city hall and historic Weberplatz. US$55, single; US$67-78, double; breakfast included.

**Hotel-Restaurant Zum Hummer** (Park Babelsberg 2, Tel. (0331) 619549, Fax (0331) 742101) provides 24 beds at Babelsberg Park. US$47, single; US$61, double.

**Zur Alten Rennbahn Hotel** (Reuterstraße, Tel. (0331) 747980, Fax (0331) 7479818) is a small hotel/restaurant in Babelsberg not far from the Babelsberg Film Studios. US$ 65, single; US$100-122, double; breakfast included.

**Parkhotel Potsdam** (Forststraße 80, Tel. (0331) 98120, Fax (0331) 9812100) is located directly at Sanssouci park in a newly built three-story building. Walk only 10 minutes to the New Palace. Use regional train station Wildpark. US$94, single; US$106, double; breakfast buffet included.

**Pension "Auf dem Kiewitt"** (Auf dem Kiewitt 8, Tel./Fax (0331) 903678) provides 25 beds. US$44, single; US$67-83, double; breakfast included.

**Froschkasten Hotel & Restaurant** (Kiezstraße 3-4, Tel./Fax (0331) 291315) includes 14 hotel rooms. US$31, single; US$50, double; breakfast included.

**Hotel-Pension Kranich** (Kirschallee 57; Tel. (0331) 28050-78/79, Fax (0331) 28050-80) above Park Sanssouci is a modest pension with bath or shower. US$68, single; US$80-85, double; breakfast included.

**Pension Landhaus Onkel Emil** (Kaiser-Friedrich-Straße 2; Tel. (0331) 500499, Fax (0331) 500683) in the countryside contains only eight beds. US$50, single, US$67, double; breakfast included.

**Pension Mark Brandenburg** (Heinrich-Mann-Allee 71, Tel. (0331) 888230, Fax (0331) 8882344). US$47, single; US$78-99, double; breakfast included.

## 3. Restaurants and Cafés

After years of suffering gastronomic neglect in Potsdam, now you can hardly turn a corner without running into an interesting menu—Nouveau Cuisine, Armenian, Thai, or multi-cultural. On Brandenburger Straße, east of Potsdam's Brandenburg Gate, you will find many cafés and small restaurants.

**Juliette**, Jägerstraße 39, Tel. (0331) 2701791 (open daily 12:30-11:30 P.M., credit cards accepted), is like a sunbeam through an overcast sky. Located on three levels with old-wood balconies, white walls and tablecloths, fresh flowers, candles, and an open fireplace, Juliette specializes in French cuisine. Expensive.

**Waage**, Am Neuen Markt 12, Tel. (0331) 2709675 (open Mon.-Fri. from 4 P.M.; Sat.-Sun. from noon), gives you a good feeling. The location of the Potsdam Ratswaage since 1836, the house fell into disrepair, but was reopened by new owners in 1996. The front is dominated by a huge bar. The back room features good food, good service. Expensive.

**Hofgarten-Restaurant im Voltaire Hotel**, Friedrich-Ebert-Straße 68 (open daily noon to 3 P.M. and 6 P.M. to midnight), has been installed in the courtyard of the hotel on the edge of the Dutch Quarter. The furnishings are modern and very attractive. The facade is beautiful. Menu features remarkably spiced and flavored Italian dishes, but the service is so slow as to be practically undetectable. Prices are reasonable.

Right where the cultural heart of Potsdam beats, right next to the Philharmonie and Hans-Otto-Theater, you find the **Café Restaurant Filmmuseum**, Schloßstraße 1, Tel. (0331) 270-20-41 (open daily noon to midnight). You can enjoy meals (pasta about DM 14, vegetarian about DM 12), or coffee and cake.

On Gutenbergstraße you find the 18th century **200 Taler Haus**, which serves Berlin-Potsdam cuisine (heavy on meat and potatoes). **Madeleine** has very good crêpes. The waiters and waitresses are French.

**Palace Restaurant** in the Cecilienhof Schloßhotel, Im Neuen Garten, Tel. (0331) 37050, Fax (0331) 292498, has entrees on the menu identical to ones of the summer of 1945 when Truman, Churchill, and Stalin ate here. The exclusive restaurant decked with circular flower arrangements features local and international cuisine. Expensive. Reservations are recommended; credit cards accepted.

Right in the freshly restored Nauen Gate you discover **aroo**, Friedrich-Ebert-Straße im Nauener Tor, Tel. (0331) 270-16-90, which opened in April 1997. An Italian Trattoria with Italian ice cream and coffee specialties, it serves breakfast, lunch, dinner, and Sunday brunch.

**Hafthorn**, Friedrich-Ebert-Straße 90 (open Mon.-Fri., 6 P.M.-4 A.M., Sat.-Sun., from 3 P.M.), offers good and inexpensive Jamaican cooking in a pleasant atmosphere.

## 4. Sightseeing

### SANSSOUCI

Friedrich Wilhelm I purchased for a hunting preserve a vast piece of land next to the small garrison town where he had installed his Guard of Giants. When Friedrich the Great inherited the throne in 1740, he declined to use his grandfather's Charlottenburg Palace, but chose to build his own, on his father's hunting preserve, farther away from Berlin. As he was strolling on the terrace of his new site with the Marquis d'Argens (1704-71) discussing among other things the construction of his palace and garden (which until then included only a wine terrace), d'Argens suggested the name "Sanssouci." "Good," said the king, speaking in French. "For the first time I am here without care [*sans souci*]."

Sanssouci is a total area of many gardens and palaces that mainly were built in two periods. At the beginning, about the middle of the 18th century, under Friedrich the Great the gracious hillside area was meant to be a summer getaway where he could rest and amuse himself. Berliners like to use the English words "weekend house." He drew the first sketches of Sanssouci Palace and oversaw its building, together with the New Palace, the Art Gallery, the New Chambers, and the Chinese Teahouse in late baroque, or rococo, based on Versailles near Paris. The model of Friedrich the Great was Louis XIV, the Sun King, the absolute ruler. For this reason the court in Sanssouci spoke French. English was often also spoken. Like Versailles, the area was an ensemble of garden areas and palaces.

One hundred years after Friedrich the Great, during a second period in the 19th century, it was Friedrich Wilhelm IV, "the Romantic King," who expanded the park with structures demonstrating his love for Italy. He was very interested in culture and art after a visit to Italy, which he found very beautiful, so he installed in Sanssouci his conceptions of Italy. He is responsible for Charlottenhof Palace, the Roman Baths, and the Great Orangerie. Everyone who enjoys Italy feels at home in Sanssouci. Use Potsdam streetcar Lines 94, 96, or 98.

**Schloß Sanssouci** ("Sanssouci Palace") Am Grünen Gitter 2 (open daily 9 A.M. to 5 P.M., except first and third Mondays of the month; capacity-limited entrance) was built above the six-tiered grapevine terrace (*Weinberg*) according to a sketch by Friedrich II himself. Georg von Knobelsdorff designed and built the rococo masterpiece in a relatively short time, three years, between 1745 and 1747, as a summer getaway on a single floor 318 feet (97 meters) long and 39 feet (12 meters) high with yellow-washed walls, 35 massive columns adorned with female figures, and a squat patina central dome with the name *Sanssouci* inscribed in letters of gold. It was Knobelsdorff's hope that Friedrich could open the great southern door of his dream palace and instantly become one with nature as the name Sanssouci states. He had a remarkable view. The trees are too tall now, but the royal family had a view over the city of Potsdam and the dome of the Nikolai Church. Friedrich gave free rein to his fantasies which had always been suppressed by his father.

Knobelsdorff attempted to create a grape terrace for cultivating wine grapes. Everyone knows Potsdam is too far north to produce good wine. Potsdam wine is known as "three-man wine": one man drinks while two others have to hold him down because it is so sour. The sun isn't strong enough; so windows were designed to create artificial lenses to focus the sun's rays onto the grape terrace.

There were many palaces in the area including the large Berlin City Palace on the Platz der Republik (see Chapter 4) the large Potsdam City Palace in the center of Potsdam, Charlottenburg Palace in Charlottenburg (see Chapter 5), and smaller palaces and lodges spread around Glienicke (Chapter 11). Prussia was not rich. The rulers exhausted their money fighting war after war. They needed huge sums to pay their military conscripts. Two-thirds and sometimes as much as five-sixths of the annual state revenue was expended on the army, which became, under the king, the state itself. Yet the Hohenzollerns found money to build palaces for nearly every family member. The palaces are very pretty but the poor people bled for them.

The palace itself is not massive and certainly not designed for crowds of visitors. Entrance is controlled because curators fear that too many people will increase the humidity and damage the palace. The best way to be sure of seeing its interior is to take the Potsdam-Sanssouci-Tour, in English and German, sponsored by the Potsdam Tourist Office (daily except Mondays from mid-April to the end of October, Tel. 280-0309). The tour, starting from the front of the Film Museum, costs DM 35, including the palace (three hours) or DM 27, without (hour and a half). Individual visitors are given numbers in the morning and if they are lucky they will get in by the afternoon. Tour groups go in first. Each day only a specific number of visitors are allowed inside to visit. To get an entrance ticket, you should arrive early, first get a card, see the gardens, and then return in the afternoon for the sightseeing tour from one brilliant and astonishing rococo room to another decorated with reliefs, painted walls and ceilings, and profusions of gilding and mirrors—all to Friedrich's rich personal taste— except that his nephew Friedrich Wilhelm II completely redecorated the bedroom office in which Friedrich the Great expired. Outside of Italy there is no place else with so much Carrara marble.

The most beautiful way to approach Sanssouci is from the **Parterre,** the ground level 132 steps below the palace, because you see from a distance the full expanse of the broad garden area, the grape terrace, and the palace. The Parterre is dominated by a great ornamental fountain surrounded by white marble statues. When you pass it, look up at the symmetrical, rococo Sanssouci Palace and note that, remarkably, the palace does not lie on the central sight lines of the gardens in front of it and therefore was not strictly symmetrical.

Behind the palace, there are two rows of 88 columns in a semicircle. Then, escalating up the slopes in back of the palace, is the **Ruinenberg,** a curiosity made out of artificial ruins (the Ruinenberg was one of the few things in Potsdam that wasn't ruined during the War) where engineers attempted to install a water supply and windmills to pump water from the Havel to make it look pastoral and to supply the water fountains. It worked for exactly one hour, in 1754, so when Friedrich the Great lived here, the fountains were out of order. During the last century engineers installed an 80-horsepower, steam-driven pumping station which pumped water from the Havel River to the fountain pool on the Ruinenberg until 1894. Architect Friedrich Ludwig Persius, seeking to enliven the countryside with exotic architecture, astonishingly designed the 1841-43 pumping station near Potsdam's Brandenburg Gate to look like a Muslim mosque (*Moschee*) with a chimney supposed to look like a minaret. It won't call you to prayer, but there are guided tours Sat.-Sun. 9 A.M. to noon and 1 to 5 P.M.. The architecture fascinates visitors, but in reality it looks more Italian than Islamic.

Luckily Sanssouci was not pillaged by the Red Army because the Soviet commander who had visited here before the War prohibited his troops from entering the park.

In front of Sanssouci, marked with a white Carrara marble statue of Flora, goddess of flowers, you find the **Tomb of Friedrich the Great,** Prussia's most famous leader. He militarily expanded the small Prussian territory into a European power. Under his leadership, Silesia fell to the Prussians during the Seven Years War. An absolute monarch, he maintained a strong central command. The command of Friedrich the Great (who was in fact not very big, a source of much humorous wordplay among Berliners) embodied the strong Prussian militarist tradition that led to two world wars.

In the first years of his rule and shortly after the building of Sanssouci, Friedrich the Great ordered the construction of an underground tomb between a flower bed and a bust of Julius Caesar on the morning side of the terrace in front of the palace, with a half-circle of shrubs in the background, so that he could see it at a glance from the windows of his palace. The tomb, 12 feet long, 6 feet wide, and 8 feet high, was totally plain inside with white chalk covering smooth walls.

During Friedrich's lifetime, this area around the flowers was used to bury his dogs. Each one received a sandstone marker with its name inscribed. They are still there, but you can hardly read them today. He buried 11 beloved dogs. Judging from bones found, one of the king's Italian greyhounds was buried right in the king's anticipated tomb.

At the death of Friedrich in 1786, his will was opened (but not published until 1791, in the French language, and finally in 1792 in German translation). Because he loved nature and lived as a philosopher, he wrote, he wanted to be buried without pomp, ostentation, or the slightest ceremony.

He wanted to be brought, at midnight on the third day after his death, under the light of a lantern, to Sanssouci and placed in the tomb he had prepared on the right-hand side of the terrace.

He died on August 17, 1786, at about 2:20 A.M. in a chair in his working chambers/bedroom in Sanssouci. Friedrich Wilhelm II, his nephew and heir to the throne, disliked his uncle intensely. He appeared about 3 A.M. and sealed off the chambers. The new king ordered Friedrich taken to the Potsdam City Palace at nine o'clock that night. On the next day Friedrich's coffin was decorated with yellow velvet and silver and he was dressed in his parade uniform. On the evening of the 18th he was taken to the Garnison Church and placed in the casket beside his father, Friedrich Wilhelm I (his mother was entombed in the Berlin Cathedral). The new king was absent.

On September 9, 1786, Friedrich Wilhelm II led a procession of 590 nobles, military officers, and government ministers to Garnison Church.

Friedrich's 150-year-long rest came to a rude halt when, on March 21, 1933, Hitler attempted to couple his new Nazi regime with the order, discipline, and obedience of the old Prussian military. President Hindenburg laid a wreath on Friedrich's coffin, setting in motion events that eventually led to the Second World War and the destruction of the Garnison Church.

Two years before the end of the War, on March 20, 1943, Hitler sent a telegram to General von Wulfen, city commander of Potsdam, ordering him to take the coffins of both Friedrich the Great and Friedrich Wilhelm I from the church to Wildpark, near Potsdam, the headquarters of Hermann Göring, Air Force commander.

When the soldiers arrived at the church with a truck, they found the sarcophagus was so heavy that it was impossible to get it out of the church, so they removed the cover of the sarcophagus with a cutting torch and carried both coffins in front of the altar. When they opened the marble sarcophagus of Friedrich Wilhelm I, it was so fragile that it shattered immediately, so they transferred the body to another coffin and hustled it through closed roads to the reinforced concrete bunker of Göring's headquarters, where they had to tilt it to get it down the narrow corridors. From there the coffins were sent to the Berntgerode Potash Mines near Heiligenstadt, but not until March 13, 1945, together with the coffins of Paul von Hindenburg and his wife (that had come to Potsdam in January 1945), 65 boxes with books from the library of Friedrich the Great, and other irreplaceable imperial Prussian relics.

Immediately after the shipment's arrival on March 14, 1945, the coffins and relics were buried 1,850 feet (565 meters) below ground. Because the cage used to lower them was too small, the coffins had to be laid at an angle so that one was damaged.

On April 27, Americans marched into Thüringen, found the coffins and the valuables, and took them to Marburg, where everything was organized. They first deposited the coffins in the cellar of Marburg Castle and then in February 1946, in a cellar room in the State Archives Building. After conferring with Hesse officials and the son of Hindenburg, in great secrecy on August 21, 1946, they placed them in the Marburg Elisabeth Church.

At the beginning of 1952, the head of the Hohenzollern family insisted that they be transferred to Castle Hohenzollern, three miles (five kilometers) south of Hechingen in the Black Forest. In the night of August 27, 1952, the coffins were taken in strict secrecy to the Christ Chapel of Castle Hohenzollern, tall and bristling with towers. At Elisabeth Church, they placed a memorial. Prince Louis Ferdinand stated, "On the day that Germany is again united in freedom—with God's blessing—the remains of the Prussian kings will return to Potsdam."

In May 1990, a few months after the collapse of the Wall, the prince reiterated his statement. On August 17, 1991, on the 205th anniversary of the death of Friedrich the Great, Friedrich's will was executed and his remains laid in the tomb on the upper terrace of Sanssouci.

Chancellor Helmut Kohl attended as a private citizen and not as a government representative despite blistering political attacks accusing him of fostering Prussian militarism. It somehow reminded some Germans of Hitler in his cutaway and Hindenburg attired in field-gray uniform with the grand cordon of the Black Eagles saluting Friedrich's tomb in the Garnison Church in Potsdam at the opening of the new Reichstag (after the fire, on March 21, 1933). There were about 1,000 demonstrators. Yet, 90,000 lined the streets and most television viewers were filled with nostalgia as Friedrich the Great, with his father, Friedrich Wilhelm I, the Soldier King, both Prussian militarists and heroes of Adolf Hitler, were returned to Potsdam for burial. Friedrich was placed in the tomb he had prepared for himself 250 years ago, a few hundred feet to the east of the front entrance of Sanssouci Palace. The coffin of his father, Friedrich Wilhelm I, was laid not far away, in the mausoleum of the 99-day kaiser, Friedrich III, in the Peace Church.

**Park Sanssouci**, Visitors' Center at the Historic Windmill, Tel. 969-4202, is a park with no two gardens alike. The gilded gate with a sign over it reading "Allee nach Sanssouci" is built in Italian style leading into the park. The **Historishe Mühle** ("Historic Windmill," open daily except Fridays from the beginning of April to mid-October), is a new addition to the park. It was a gift of the state of Westphalia in 1993.

The gardens from 250 years ago, such as the Dutch Garden of 1764-66 by Joachim Ludwig Heydert, were constructed in late baroque (rococo) and are very severe and symmetrical. Those planted later, 150 years ago, are lighter, styled after Italian and English gardens. The new ones are no longer severely symmetrical, no longer impersonal, but instead give you a feeling of nature, like you would discover while walking in remote woods. You cannot imagine you are in Germany—the surroundings are so atypical—because so much seems like Italy.

Germany's greatest landscape architect, Peter Josef Lenné, designed areas of Berlin, Potsdam, and Brandenburg, but the **Royal Gardens** of Sanssouci are considered his crowning achievement. Of Huguenot descent, Lenné was appointed to supervise the gardens of Potsdam. Originally Sanssouci was a practical garden—gardeners planted vegetables. Under Lenné it became a park for rest and recreation.

The **Sizilianischer Garten** ("Sicilian Garden") was built by Lenné during the second phase (1857). Friedrich Wilhelm II was so inspired by the art of Italy that he wanted to perpetuate it. During the Cold War, East Germans couldn't visit the south and it was hard for them to fantasize how it might be there, so they came here and used their imaginations. It was their first sighting of palm trees. The gardens are bright with lilies and begonias. Ponds are covered with water lilies of many colors. A wonderful thick pergola is completely covered with vines.

As a counterpoint to the serene southern motif of the Sicilian Garden, Lenné, also in 1857, constructed the nearby **Nordische Garten** ("Northern Garden"). You enter the Northern Garden through a gate of jagged rock. Instead of palms you find oaks and so many different kinds of pines that you think you are in Sweden. It is laid out totally differently than the southern garden. It is more severe and less colorful, with Ionic, templelike columns. Note especially the two gingko trees from Japan, the largest in Germany, which grow only grudgingly in the Berlin climate. Berliners consider it lucky to take along a leaf of the gingko tree, sort of an Oriental four-leaf clover. Unfortunately the leaves smell bad in the fall. The botanical gardens at Sanssouci nurture rare trees and plants from all over the world. Special botanical tours are led through Sanssouci gardens.

The **Neue Palais** ("New Palace," open daily, 9 A.M.-5 P.M., closed second and fourth Mondays of each month; admission DM 9.50) was built between 1763 and 1769 according to the plans of architects Johann Gottfried Büring and Karl von Gontard as a guest house for Friedrich the Great's princely guests in order to impress the world and cover up Prussia's effective bankruptcy following the three Silesian wars. Friedrich wanted to show the world that after a number of defeats in the Seven Years War, including occupation of Berlin by Russian soldiers, he still commanded resources sufficient for fighting and building at the same time. The 428 statues and the dome in the center of the building, which serves no functional purpose but was built because Friedrich decided a royal palace should have one, are meant to glorify the Prussian monarchy, but the money ran out and in the end the planned white-brick joints were just painted onto the red facade. It is an example of very Prussian middle-European baroque, inflated ego, and stolid design. It is topped by a statue of three nude female figures representing Friedrich's three chief enemies in the Seven Years War: Elizabeth of Russia, Maria Theresa of Austria, and Madame de Pompadour. They are shown holding up Friedrich's triumphal royal crown. It is a monumental structure, twice as big as Sanssouci Palace. The front of the two-story palace measures 700 feet (213 meters) and the dome at the center is 180 feet (55 meters) high, but ultimately, the New Palace is disappointing.

Inside the palace there are 200 sparsely furnished rooms, a grotto room of semiprecious gems, minerals, and fossils, and a rococo theater seating 300, but overall it seems hollow. Wilhelm II, the last Hohenzollern kaiser grew up using the New Palace as a playground, which his mother, Princess Victoria, considered the finest place to bring up children except her England. The future Wilhelm II kicked a football around, breaking available panes of glass in the immense attic running the whole length of the palace roof.

Walking east from the Neue Palace towards Sanssouci Palace, don't miss one of the quirky bright spots of the expanse, the recently restored, green and gold, round **Chinesisches Teehaus** ("Chinese Teahouse," open daily except Fridays from mid-May to mid-October). Built by Büring between 1754 and 1757 as a small rococo work of art, it shows the European enchantment with the East, with gilded life-size sandstone statues of tea-drinking, fruit-eating, and music-playing Chinese and a gilded mandarin holding a parasol, all by Benckert and Heymüller. One of the golden animal figures adorning the eaves is a large monkey with the features of Voltaire, the French philosopher who had a stormy stay with Friedrich in the palace between 1750 and 1753. The Teahouse was begun in the year Voltaire left Potsdam.

The **Orangerie** ("Hothouse," open daily except Thursdays 9 A.M.-5 p.m between mid-May and mid-October; admission DM 5) was built in 1851-57 for Friedrich Wilhelm II by August Stüler and Ludwig Hesse according to Ludwig Persius's Italian Renaissance designs in the style of a large Italian aristocratic country villa with subtropical vegetation. The warm blond brick makes it look very Italianate. It was winter quarters for all subtropical flowers and trees, with its glass, hothouse windows admitting the sun's heat and keeping them from freezing during the hard Berlin winters. There is a Raphael room, with statues and niches, but the heart of the building is the **Referiertsaal** ("lecture hall"). There is a beautiful view over the entire palace complex. It was used to entertain guests, including the Russian czars. All figures are military statues. You can see which kinds of heroes were prized by the Prussian rulers.

The **Bildergalerie** ("Art Gallery," open daily except Mondays between mid-May and mid-October, only) in the **östlicher Lustgarten** ("Eastern Pleasure Garden") was designed by Büring between 1755 and 1763. The grand single-story building was restored and reopened in autumn 1996, a single extremely long room with splendid ceiling fixtures and white-yellow marble floor with a central dome and rococo facade, paired columns defining the center, and tall windows admitting light from the garden. It housed Friedrich the Great's flourishing painting collection after it overflowed Sanssouci Palace. Friedrich opened the gallery to the public, thus creating the first museum of its kind in Germany. In a letter to his sister, Friedrich called it, "a new silly thing, if you will, but it helps to get the world a little further along."

During the confusion of the Second World War, the paintings vanished, but they have been replaced with paintings gathered from other palaces to provide walls plastered with many excellent paintings by Rubens, van Dyck, and other Italian and Flemish masters. Its centerpiece is Caravaggio's *Doubting Thomas*. The odd, grottolike terrace in front was designed by J. L. Heydert in 1763-66.

The **Neue Kammern** ("New Chambers," open year-round, daily except Fridays; admission DM 7.50) facing the formal **westlicher Lustgarten** ("Western Pleasure Garden") were built by Knobelsdorff in 1747 for storage of tropical trees in winter. Like all other happening aristocrats back then, Friedrich had to have an Orangerie for his citrus fruits. But later Friedrich required more rooms for visitors, so he commissioned G. C. Unger to convert the building into detached guest rooms in 1771-74. The sculpture in the facade is by Friedrich Christian Glume. Italian sculptors created the garden's allegorical figures in the 18th century. Each of the rooms was decorated differently, but kept devoid of furniture so that guests could request what they needed for their stay.

The **Spielburg** ("Play Mountain") was a royal field of war games for the children of the rulers. They had learned from their parents, so of course they played war games in a small military fort built where the children learned as they played.

In the quiet, southern part of the park, a new section was opened in 1825 designed by Lenné. In the center is Schinkel's small **Schloß Charlottenhof** ("Charlottenhof Palace," open daily except Wednesdays, mid-May to mid-October; admission DM 9) a classically simple palace in the style of an Italian villa with the facade of a Greek temple that was built for Crown

Prince Friedrich Wilhelm (later King Friedrich Wilhelm IV) between 1826 and 1828. Everything here is on a small scale, but Schinkel's imagination makes it look vast. You perceive warmth and openness, much appreciated in the Prussian climate.

The **Römische Bäder** ("Roman Baths," open daily except Thursdays, mid-May to mid-October, 9 A.M. to 5 P.M., closed 12-12:45 P.M. for lunch) were built in 1829-36 by Ludwig Persius in green marble according to the plans of Carl Friedrich von Schinkel. They consist of a gardener's house looking like an Italian villa, the baths themselves with an arcaded hall, an attendant's house, and a pavilion in the form of a Greek temple. Schinkel mixed the tower and pavilions unexpectedly so it takes a while to figure out just what is going on and what belongs with what.

The baths had no function. It was a small villa with columns, Pompeii-like frescoes, and a marble bathtub inside. It was merely a fantasy. The kings had the time and the money, so why not? During the summer, there are always exhibitions inside.

You come across many other lighthearted jewels while you walk at random through the gardens: the **Drachenhaus** ("Dragon House"), built as a house for the wine makers by Gontard in 1770, was modeled on Sir William Chambers' Chinese Pagoda at Kew; the **Antikentempel** ("Ancient Temple"), Gontard's 1768 copy of the Pantheon in Rome, since 1921 has been the mausoleum for the last German Kaiserin, Auguste Victoria; the **Belvedere,** by Unger in 1770-72, was based on Nero's Macellum in Rome; the **Freundschafts-Tempel** ("Friendship Temple") by Gontard in 1768, commissioned by Friedrich II in memory of his sister who died in 1757, features marble reliefs on eight Corinthian columns representing famous pairs of friends from ancient times; the **Meierei** ("Dairy Farm") was built in a Swiss style in 1832 to remind you of a Swiss farmhouse. A windmill was placed here to add a touch of the idyllic.

The most beautiful path through Sanssouci's gardens begins at the **Tor am Grünen Gitter** ("Gate of the Green Fence") to the Marly Garden, laid out by Lenné about 1850. The **Friedenskirche** ("Peace Church"), Am Grünen Gitter 3, Tel. (0331) 292329 (open daily mid-May to the beginning of October) is a late-neoclassical jewel, built by Hesse and Ferdinand Arnim in 1845-54 on the basis of concepts of Friedrich Wilhelm IV and plans by Persius. The basilica with three naves and a separate tower is a copy of St. Clementi in Rome. In the apse there is an original 12th-century mosaic of Christ taken from St. Cipriano Church in Venice. Under the altar lies the sarcophagus of Friedrich Wilhelm IV. Next to the church is the **Mausoleum** of Kaiser Friedrich III (kaiser for 99 days) built by Julius Raschdorf in 1892. Since 1991 it is also the repose of Friedrich Wilhelm I.

## POTSDAM'S CENTER

Potsdam's historic center stands in stark contrast to the cereal-box construction of mass housing built later but already stained and decaying. Casting a spell over it all is the deserted and unfinished concrete shell of a new cultural center, a forlorn monument to the previous regime's failure. The DDR rebuilt much of East Berlin, while the DDR ignored Potsdam. This angered the Potsdamers. In the 1960s and 1970s the DDR tore down Potsdam's old city quarter in order to build new houses, but the new buildings are sad. Potsdam has always been a beautiful city with many baroque houses under the Linden trees and it will cost very much to rebuild the old architecture, but that will have to be done to recover part of the former beauty.

The **Am Alten Markt** ("Old Market") is the center of Potsdam. This part of Potsdam was very heavily damaged shortly before the War's end, on April 14, 1945. Luckily neither Sanssouci nor the Dutch Quarter were heavily damaged. In the center, however, the monumental **Stadtschloß** ("City Palace") built by Philipp de Chieze in 1660-82 and altered by Georg von Knobelsdorff in 1745-56, was a victim of the War. The ruins were pulled down in 1959-60. The Barberini Palace was destroyed, as was the **Garnisonkirche** ("Garnison Church"), the great shrine of Prussianism and the undisturbed resting place of Friedrich the Great for 150 years, with its three-story tower by Philipp Gerlach and its famous carillon.

Architects wanted to make the plaza in front of the Nikolai Church look like the Piazza del Popolo in Rome. An obelisk on the square was erected by Knobelsdorff in 1750 with reliefs of four Prussian rulers from the Great Elector to Friedrich the Great. These didn't please the DDR governors, so in 1969 the faces were changed to faces of Potsdam's great architects.

The elegant circular baroque building with the small towers facing the square in front of the church is the **Alte Rathaus** ("Old City Hall") from 1753-55. The towers were the city jails. There is a statue of Atlas on top holding the golden earth ball on his shoulders. In 1776, the original globe, cast entirely from lead, tumbled from its weight and smashed to the ground. It was replaced by a lighter, copper one in 1777.

DDR restored the **Nikolaikirche** ("The Evangelical Church St. Nikolai" or Nikolai Church, with services Sun. 10 A.M., open Mon.-Fri. 2 P.M. to 5 P.M., Sat. from 10 A.M., Sun. from 11:30 A.M.) which had also been destroyed during the War, primarily because the architecture by Schinkel in 1831-37 was very, very famous and the silhouette had come to characterize Potsdam. It was built following the design of Christopher Wren's St. Paul's Cathedral in London with a dome rising 175 feet (53 meters) above the nave. It occupies the site of an earlier baroque church destroyed by fire in 1795. The four corner towers were added by F. A. Stüler and Ludwig Persius in 1843-50. The name has nothing to do with the Nikolai Church in Berlin's Nikolai Quarter. The interior has a soaring, glorious airy feeling to it despite the Corinthian columns that line the sides. The altar appears to have a Russian influence. The dome and ceiling have been beautifully restored. There is a display of the confrontation between Christianity and the State. After the War the rubble was cleared by 1947. By 1960 the church's dome had been rebuilt according to Schinkel's original design. Churches throughout West Germany contributed the copper required for its construction. Religious services were resumed in 1981, but the Garnison Church and the Barberini Palace were torn away. The Garnison's bell tower survived the War, and Potsdamers wanted to keep it, but the Communists blew it up in 1968 because of its association with Prussian militarism. To replace the Garnison's bells, every half hour you hear the sounds of the carillon on Dortusstraße, corner Yorckstraße, with bells donated by a West German veterans' group, a former parachute unit. They are collecting monies to rebuild the Garnison bell tower. Use all Potsdam streetcars to Lange Brücke/Hotel Potsdam; buses 692 or 694.

In the 1960s the ruins of the City Palace and two churches were cleared away in order to build an art center and create a Socialist capital city center to dwarf the older historical buildings. The Prussian buildings belonged to Prussian history and the Prussian history led to the First and Second World Wars. DDR planners wanted something modern, striking, something Socialistic.

Up went an **Europäisches Kunst Centrum** ("European Art Center"). It was an unpainted hulk of a building that soon became covered with graffiti. It was supposed to be a theater. When the Wende came, West German planners said, "Whoa!" They said that the silhouette of Potsdam is famous for the church and the city hall. This theater will destroy the image of Potsdam. The high-rise hotel already is spoiling the image. They wanted to pull down the nearly completed new building in order to reconstruct the square in front of the church to make it look as it once did—like an Italian piazza. The resulting Hans Otto theater is not quite what city planners would like, but it is marginally acceptable to complete the cobbled square in front of the Old Rathaus and church.

Working film studios sprang up in Potsdam in the 1920s and because of UFA, the pioneering movie studio, and the later DEFA, in the Babelsberg Film Studios, Potsdam became known as a famous movie city, like Hollywood at the time. The history of cinematography is recorded in the unique **Film-**

**museum,** Am Karl-Liebknecht-Forum 1, Tel. (0331) 271810, Fax (0331) 2718126 (open Tue.-Fri. 10 A.M.-5 P.M.; Sat.-Sun. to 6 P.M.) in the **Marstall** ("Royal Stable") which was built in 1685 as a hothouse, in the center of Potsdam. It is a treasure for film freaks. Like to visit with the grizzled vampire from the world's first Dracula movie? The recreated film studio is well worth visiting. Film cameras and stages have been reconstructed; classic films are shown—it is very interesting.

Horses were stabled in the restored red baroque Marstall, a work of Johannes Nering and Georg Knobelsdorff in 1746, the only thing left from the former palace.

The **Neue Markt** ("New Market") is the oldest part of Potsdam that is still standing. You can imagine how beautiful it once looked. In the back is a former *Fuhrhof* where merchants and visitors could park their horses and carriages. In order to see how much the carriages carried, a weighing house was constructed. This very beautiful, baroque **Gaststätte sur Ratswaage** is a good 300 years old.

**Brandenburger Straße** was rebuilt by the DDR. It is the main shopping street of Potsdam, now a pedestrian mall running between Potsdam's Brandenburg Gate and the St. Peter and Paul Church. Potsdamers call it "Broadway." The Potsdam Tourist Office maintains an Info-Branch on Brandenburger Straße, at number 18, for information and ticket sales (Tel. 0331 29-30-38 or 270-81-00, open Mon.-Fri. 10 A.M. to 7 P.M., Sat. to 2 P.M.). You see yellow, gabled houses everywhere. The Soldier King had them built in the 1730s and gave them away to his Potsdamers. The street's rows of houses still give the impression of a military base. The house owners of the time were required to quarter grenadiers in their attics. The government never gives you anything for nothing. In the house you had to billet two to six soldiers, you had to feed and clothe the solders, and you had to make room for two to six spinning wheels. The soldiers had to spin wool in their free time. The Soldier King didn't want them wasting their time, so it no surprise they always tried to run away. They had to stand in their windows in the evenings so they could be counted at roll call. House owners had to buy double beds for the soldiers. By royal decree, the soldiers had to sleep together in twos so that if one tried to run away the other could call out the guards. What if they tried to desert together?

At the end of the Brandenburger Strasße, on the Platz der Nationen, you see one of the city's gates, which is called, for logical reasons, the **Brandenburger Tor,** built by Carl Gontard and Georg Christian Unger in 1770 in baroque style as a Roman victory arch, making it 20 years older than the Brandenburg Gate on Unter den Linden in Berlin. It got its name from the road leading to the city of Brandenburg to the west of

Potsdam (and Berlin). It was restored for 5 million Marks and looks pretty good although its significance and size (four double columns versus six for the Berlin version) do not compare to the gate on Unter den Linden. Across the Havel, south of Long Bridge, you can identify the tower of the **Landtag** ("Brandenburg State Parliament building") by the outline of a circle where the Communist Party emblem stood until it was removed in 1990. The building was called "the Kremlin." It was Communist Party headquarters but originally a Prussian military academy.

There are two intriguing foreign quarters in Potsdam. The larger is the **Holländische Viertel** ("Dutch Quarter") bounded by Kurfürstenstraße and Bassinplatz, Hebbelstraße and Friedrich-Ebert-Straße. Potsdam was settled by French Protestants, Huguenots, but others as well. At the beginning of the 18th century Friedrich I, after a trip to Amsterdam, hatched a plan to establish a Dutch handwork quarter because the Netherlands was one of the leading handwork powers of the time and Dutch handwork was famous. On his orders Prussians under the direction of architect Johann Boumann fell to work building, between 1734 and 1752, a geometrically planned Dutch settlement in order to tempt Dutch handworkers to Potsdam and make them feel like they were still at home in Holland. Prussians built four blocks of row houses, with each of 134 houses decorated in so-called Dutch baroque with gables similar to those you see in the Netherlands. They were all built identically: red brick with yellow trim and a bell-shaped gable with a scallop placed within it. The side streets show older buildings made out of stone. The broad avenues indicate where canals have been filled in.

The scheme of Friedrich I was a flop. Fewer Dutch came than hoped. Only 22 families inhabited the project. The houses then had to be converted to military uses—but the kitsch architecture of the "Dutch" quarter remained. It is often used by German film crews requiring interesting backdrops. Only six of the houses were destroyed during the War but the quarter became dilapidated because for a long time nothing was made of it. There was a plan to tear down the whole thing and construct new high-rises, but luckily this idea was never realized. More than half of the Dutch-looking houses were restored because of their singularity and curiosity value in Germany. Oddly, many Dutch architects came to Potsdam after the War to rebuild the section. The houses don't have exactly the detail of architectural beauty that you see in the canal houses in Amsterdam or Utrecht or Enkhuizen, but at least they give the impression of the Netherlands and no one would imagine that they were Prussian residences.

The reason some of the streets are so broad is because they were formerly canals that were dug around the city to beautify it and facilitate trade along the Havel River and many lakes. The canals were filled in during the

1960s with War rubble. Looking at the entire line of baroque houses still standing beside the former canal near the Dutch Quarter you can imagine how beautiful it must have been. The Dutch Church is next to the bus stop and the open-air farmers market for vegetables. Across from the bus station you see the bus stop for bus 700 to Tegel Airport. Use bus 692 or streetcar 95 for the Dutch Quarter. The nearby baroque **Französische Kirche** ("French Church") at the end of Wilhelm-Pieck-Straße was built in 1752-53 by Johann Boumann the elder according to Georg Knobelsdorff's plans in the style of Rome's pantheon. The surrounding former French Quarter was mostly destroyed during the War.

Potsdam's second curious "foreign" quarter is the Russian colony **Alexandrowka** (Pappelallee/Am Schrage/Nedlitzer Straße). At the end of Friedrich-Ebert-Straße, at Puschkinallee, 13 ornately carved rural farmhouses designed in Russia were erected by Friedrich Wilhelm III to house 12 members of a Russian military chorus as a perpetual memorial to the friendship between Prussia and Russia. The 12 singers belonged to a choir that originally consisted of 62 soldiers captured by Napoleon but because of the Russian-Prussian alliance remained in the Prussian army. To make them feel at home Friedrich Wilhelm III also provided a little Russian Orthodox church. When the Russians occupied Potsdam during the Cold War, the Communists distanced themselves from the Russian Orthodox church, but it is now a place of worship for the Russians that remained in Potsdam after the withdrawal of the Russian military. Use Potsdam streetcar 95.

## NEUER GARTEN ("NEW GARDEN")

North of Potsdam's center and considerably newer than Sanssouci, the idyllic, 183-acre (74 hectares), English-style **Neuer Garten**, with an obelisk, pyramids, and a ruined temple sinking into the lake, overlooks the western shore of the Heilingen See ("Holy Lake"). At the end of the 18th century, to create a counterpoint to Sanssouci, Lenné was given his first commission by Friedrich Wilhelm II, the nephew and successor of Friedrich the Great, who was known as "Fat William," and was more interested in good food and his many mistresses than in politics. On William's commission, Lenné's New Garden was one of the most impressive examples of sentimental landscape gardening in Germany.

The **Marmorpalais** ("Marble Palace," open daily except Tuesdays 10 A.M.-5 p.m between mid-May and mid-October; winters, weekends only 10 A.M.-3 P.M.), a water castle surrounded on three sides by water, is a sweet and joyous pleasure palace of the early neoclassical Berlin school built in 1787 by Carl von Gontard. Ten years later, Carl Gotthard Langhans, who also designed the Brandenburg Gate in Berlin, fashioned the wings. In 1961, for the fifth anniversary of the DDR *Volksarmee* ("People's Army"), the Communists abused the Marble Palace by turning it into an Army Museum. They laid linoleum over the 18th-century parquet floors, covered the beautiful wall paintings of Italian landscape with latex, hid the decoration of the Grotto Salon with wallboard, and placed a Mig airplane and canons on the terrace.

It was closed for four years for painstaking restoration and partially reopened in July 1997, on the occasion of the 200th anniversary of Friedrich Wilhelm II's death. Even if the artworks are no longer there for you to admire, you can visit the Grotto Salon, the White Salon, the royal bedroom, and the inner courtyard and admire the classic furniture (including the *Clanwilliam-Kommode*, the beautiful writing cabinet of noble wood varieties that is considered the single most expensive piece of German furniture of all time), the facade, and the south steps.

A 10-minute walk from the Marble Palace, at the northern end of the park, Kaiser Wilhelm II, the last German monarch, built the Tudor **Cecilienhof** mansion (open daily 8 A.M.-5 P.M.), the summer residence for Crown Prince Wilhelm of Hohenzollern, who lived there only a short time, from 1913 until 1917, after which the monarchy abdicated. The property has been restored as a luxury hotel with the historic rooms used for the Potsdam Conference dedicated as a separate museum.

In the summer of 1945, the "Big Three," Harry Truman, Winston Churchill, and Joseph Stalin, met in Cecilienhof to seal the division of Germany and decide the fate of Europe. The conference was disrupted by Churchill's defeat in a British election, but Clement Attlee took his place at the conference table in the final days. Today the **Cecilenhof Museum**, Tel. (0331) 969-4200 (open all year except Mondays), dedicated to this famous meeting, displays the charts, maps, and massive round oak table where the Potsdam Declaration was signed on August 2, 1945. Actually, the conference was originally supposed to take place in Berlin. But the city had been nearly completely destroyed by the War. There were no longer any buildings appropriate for the summit of the allies in the anti-Hitler coalition. Marshall Georgi Zhukov, Supreme Commander of the Soviet Army, proposed the still-intact Schloß Cecilienhof as an alternative. Because the estate was empty at the time (the furnishings had disappeared without a trace in the spring of 1945), the Soviets quickly confiscated furniture from nearby buildings and forcibly ejected innocent residents from nearby houses to domicile the visiting prime minister and president. But the huge conference table was flown in especially from Moscow. The offices of the delegation, including Stalin's desk chair with armrests of carved dragons, and the conference room remain in the 1945 state, and can be visited today. In 1993 the exhibition was reconceived, but the red roses in the shape of a Soviet star, at the entrance to the meeting rooms, were kept. Use Potsdam bus 694.

## BABELSBERG

Next to Sanssouci Park and the New Garden, **Babelsberg Park** is the third largest park in Potsdam. The 320-acre (190 hectares) area green with beeches, oaks, birches, and maples was laid out by Lenné in 1832 and expanded by Count Pückler-Muskau (1843-49) bordering the Tiefer See. This is the quietest of Potsdam's parks because the easy approaches were closed by the Wall and it is still a good place to get away from the noise of Berlin. Here you find the Zoo that Friedrich I connected with his Glienicke Hunting Lodge (see Chapter 11).

**Schloß Babelsberg** (1843-49), a neglected jewel, occupies a commanding position in Babelsberg Park. The Schinkel-designed Tudor English neo-Gothic palace, with slitted windows, turrets, and crenelated parapets, was the summer residence of Kaiser Wilhelm I, the first German kaiser. Otto von Bismarck was named Prussian Minister President here on Sept. 22, 1862. It now houses exhibits of early history and prehistory (open all year, Tue.-Sun. 9 A.M. to 5 P.M.).

Exploring the park, you find the **Kleines Schloß** ("Small Palace") built for ladies, the **Marstall** ("Royal Stables") from 1838, and the **Matrosenhaus** ("Sailor's House") from 1842 that housed the royal gondoliers and those who manned the sailing ships. The symbol of the park is the **Flatowturm** ("Flatow Tower," open mid-May to mid-October). North of the tower is the **Gerichslaube** ("Judicial Passageway") that once stood in Berlin beside the old city hall in the space now occupied by the Red Rathaus (see Chapter 4). When the Red Rathaus was built, the Gerichslaube structure was moved here in 1871-72.

Stretching along the streets paralleling Lake Griebnitz runs the **Villa Colony of Babelsberg** that was the home of movie stars, wealthy bankers, publishers, and industrialists and where the delegations of the Big Three were housed during the Potsdam Conference. During the Potsdam Conference, Truman stayed at the house at Karl-Marx-Straße 2. He called it the "Nightmare House," a neo-Gothic monstrosity, and couldn't wait to get out of it and go home. Still named Karl-Marx-Straße, the street was previously named Straße der SA, and before that, Kaiserstraße. Stalin stayed in #28. Churchill and Attlee resided at Virchowstraße 23. The villa occupied by Joseph Stalin was the only one marked with a placard by the Communists. Churchill's rose-colored villa was one of the first architectural projects of Miës van der Rohe. You can visit these locations by walking from S-Bhf Griebnitzsee or by taking an hour-and-a-half walking tour, in English/German, offered by the Potsdam Tourist Office.

For contrast, visit the area around Weberplatz ("Weber" meaning "weaver") which is not far from where Potsdam's wealthy enjoyed their villas and adjacent to Park Babelsberg. Weberplatz is the center of the **Weavers' Colony in Babelsberg**, which was called **Nowawes**, Czech for "New Village." The Hohenzollern created two traditions: militarism and religious tolerance. Persecuted peoples from all over Europe could come, live, and worship in peace in Prussia. The Hohenzollerns didn't do it because they were nice guys. They did it because it paid. Beginning in 1751, countless weavers immigrated from Protestant Bohemia to Potsdam to escape the Hapsburg thumb of the devoutly Roman Catholic Maria Theresa. Friedrich II brought the refugees to Potsdam to increase the population of his lands and to encourage the industrialization of Prussia; especially, to create a domestic textile industry so that he would be freed of his foreign dependence on cloth for his soldiers' uniforms.

Friedrich granted the Bohemian weavers freedom from taxes, military duty, and billeting his soldiers in their upstairs rooms so that they actually could use them for sleeping. The houses supported two families with one small, shared kitchen, but the houses' main feature was a large room with two windows facing the street specifically designed for the purpose of working a clacking, mechanical spinning machine for 10-12 hours a day.

Friedrich located the weavers' settlement southeast of Potsdam on the barren, sandy soil between the Havel river and the old German farming settlement of Neuendorf. You can see the old, half-timbered weavers' houses, one after another, on Karl-Liebknecht-Straße, Karl-Gruhl-Straße, and around Weberplatz, Garnstraße and in Alt Nowawes. Friedrich built the Friedrich Church for the Bohemians. During its first decades the clergy were Bohemian. It is now the oldest standing church in Potsdam. North of Friedrich Church the memorial to the Czech reformer Jan Amos Comenius was erected at the end of 1995. Comenius Square was created triangular according to the philosophies of the reformer.

The weavers had a tough time in Potsdam. They didn't get along well with their neighbors. After the Seven Years' War, and with the industrialization of Europe and the competition of English textiles, weavers fell on hard times and some were reduced to stealing. They gained a reputation throughout Europe as thieves.

## BABELSBERG FILM STUDIOS

Motion-picture history was made in Potsdam. Film buffs and scholars associate 1911, when cameraman Guido Seeber acquired a small plot of land near the gates of Berlin that had been used to grow exotic flowers and animal feed, with the birth of the Babelsberg Film Studios, which today are among the oldest and largest film production facilities in the world. The first film was shot there in 1912. Directors such as Ernst Lubitsch, Friedrich Wilhelm Murnau, Fritz Lang, Josef von Sternberg, and the young Billy Wilder assured Babelsberg's artistic and commercial glory in the early years.

Expressionism introduced art to the life of film. The masterpiece of the era was the 1924 silent classic *Metropolis,* the first science fiction film, which made history, but not money. Fritz Lang called 36,000 actors and extras onto such a gigantic set that its size has not again been matched in Europe. With the coming of talkies, the movie-going public began to hear the talking, singing, and dancing of Greta Garbo, Heinz Rühmann, Lilian Harvey, Willy Fritsch, and perhaps above all, in 1930, Marlene Dietrich. Josef von Sternberg decided to cast Miss Dietrich in *The Blue Angel* after seeing her in the stage play *Two Neckties.* He had already screened her previous movies, which he disliked, but he proposed to her a screen test. She declined because she didn't test well—a waste of time. "That's all right," he said, "I've decided to use you anyway."

The UFA Studios in Babelsberg dominated the great era of German film, beginning with Robert Wiese's *The Cabinet of Dr. Caligari* in 1919, and running right through the decade until *The Blue Angel.* Those Golden Years were followed by harsher sounds when Joseph Goebbels' propaganda ministry cranked up full force and films became a political trumpet. Gifted directors and popular actors fled Nazi Germany. Fritz Lang, F. W. Murnau, and Ernst Lubitsch went on to distinguished careers in Hollywood. In 1935, Lubitsch even became production chief of Paramount. The names of Walter Slezak and Peter Lorre are among the star-shaped memorials along Los Angeles' Hollywood Boulevard.

During the Potsdam Conference, the studios were taken over by the U.S. Army's communications center so Truman could always be in contact with Washington. When the Russian army moved in, production resumed. Ernst Wilhelm Borchert and Hildegard Knef (Neff) then only 20 years old, starred in a film even before the Soviet military administration began, in April 1946, issuing licenses. When control passed to the DDR, over 700 feature films and 600 TV films were made, many of which were Socialist and rabidly anti-Fascist propaganda films.

With the encouragement of Treuhand's privatization initiatives, the French company Compagnie Immobilière Phenix (CIP) bought the studios in 1992 with the dream of making it a profitable theme park. Independent film companies were invited to use the 11-acre (4.5 hectares) grounds now overseen by the Babelsberg Studio managed by the director of *The Tin Drum*, Volker Schlöndorff, and Pierre Couveinhes. Still available is the world's largest collection of props (according to the *Guinness Book of Records*). Over a million items, including 150,000 original costumes, are stored in an area over 280,000 square feet (26,000 square meters).

Since the studio tours began in August 1993, the former "dream factory of the people" has turned into one of Brandenburg's most visited public attractions. Through 1996, over 1.6 million people visited Potsdam-Babelsberg to experience the German touch of Hollywood on the Havel River. New attractions that continue to draw visitors include the realistic-feeling dive in a Russian nuclear submarine which was brought to Babelsberg for shooting the film, *Hostile Waters*.

The decorative entrance arch was modeled on the Hollywood studios' entrances. Inside, enthroned on a cannonball, the sculpture of the flying, lying Baron Münchhausen, as he was played by UfA star Hans Albers in 1943, recalls Babelsberg's dark years when Joseph Goebbels mutated the studios into tools of his propaganda machinery. *Münchhausen*, one of the first color films, is considered an expression of helpless protest, especially because of the moon scene. The writer, "Berthold Bürger," was in fact none other than Erich Kästner, who was officially banned from working.

Taking the Babelsberg Studio tour is an amusing getaway. It is no match for Southern California studio tours, and the exhibits are far from grandiose, but it is fun, and visual, and the children will not mind that everything is in German. Thirty-minute shuttle rides swing by old and new production locations, film companies, and television studios. Check *http://www.medienstadt.de*. The entrance is on Großbeerenstraße, Tel. (0331) 721-27-55 (open 10 A.M. to 6 P.M., March-November). Take bus 692 from S-Bhf Babelsberg. Entrance costs DM 25, adult; DM 18, child. A family ticket for parents and two children costs DM 60. A two-hour special tour, including entrance, costs DM 28, adult; DM 26, child.

## EINSTEIN TOWER AND VILLA

The 1920 **Einstein Tower** on Telegrafenberg ("Telegraph Hill") has been declared a technical monument as a major example of expressionist architecture. The cupola at the top of the Einstein Tower serves as an observatory from which cosmic light can be reflected down into a subterranean astrophysical laboratory, but the building itself looks like an ungainly spaceship. Its squat, concrete tower, with four tiers of deeply recessed windows, rises heavily from an elongated base. "Organic," according to Einstein. Architect Erich Mendelsohn was born in 1887 in Allenstein (Olsztyn in present-day Poland), emigrated to England in 1933, acquired American citizenship in 1944, and died in San Francisco in 1953. Einstein used it for experiments to provide practical evidence of his theory of relativity and it still serves as a sun observatory today. The Albert Einstein science park is accessible to visitors only to the extent that weekend tours bring visitors here so as not to disrupt research work. (Tel. Urania tours (0331) 291741 or Stattreisen (0331) 481030.)

On the occasion of Einstein's 50th birthday in 1929, Berlin's municipal council voted to present Germany's foremost physicist with a city-owned villa, but this touched off such an embarrassing series of events that Einstein was led to despair and bought with his own money land in Caputh; there he built a handsome villa where he spent his summer months between 1929 and 1932. As he left his villa in Caputh in 1932 to teach another semester at Cal Tech, he said to his wife, "Before you leave our villa this time, take a good look at it. . . . You will never see it again." The **Einstein House** in Caputh is open to visitors on weekends and holidays 1-4 P.M., Tel. (0331) 70886.

## 5. Sports

Water sports are everywhere. Potsdam is an "island." It is surrounded by 19 lakes and two rivers that offer opportunities for water sports, swimming, and sailing. There is good swimming in the Heiligesee. Many go to the Wannsee in Berlin, which is not far. There is a clothing-optional beach near Cecilienhof. The largest indoor pool is on the Bräuhausberg ("Brewery Mountain").

Potsdam has signposted an "Alter Fritz" bicycle route to take you through Potsdam's romantic parks and cultural landscape. It gives you an excellent perspective as well as a delightful ride. You can bring your bike on the S-Bahn from Berlin or start at **City Rad Potsdam**, Tel. (0331) 619052, (open April-October) the bicycle rental stand adjacent to the Potsdam Stadt railroad station. Other bicycle rental locations include **Das Radhaus**, Ladestraße at the Rehbrücke regional train station, Tel. (0331) 29100; **Fahrrad Bels**, Röhrenstraße 4, Tel. (0331) 622113; and **"rent a bike"** at the Parkhotel Potsdam, Forststraße 80, Tel. (0331) 98120.

As in any German city, soccer is very popular. Babelsberg's semi-pro team is well known.

## 6. Shopping

Shopping centers and store fronts are flourishing in Potsdam, but for a wider selection of shopping opportunities, defer to Berlin.

## 7. Nightlife and Entertainment

Potsdam's nightlife is very bright in the summer. Take a walk through the Dutch Quarter. Go down Mittelstraße. At Mittelstraße 18 is a pub called **M18**. It is nice to spend an evening in the beer garden. Other interesting pubs all over the Dutch Quarter are open until 1 or 2 A.M.. **Waschhaus Potsdam**, Schiffbauergaße 1, Tel. (0331) 271-560, made it through its fifth year in 1997. This culture-house with alternative image is a concert (HipHop, Britpop, and Punkrock) and party (Techno and House) location. It's the largest alternative disco in Potsdam. Its open-air film program attracts film freaks on Wed., Fri., and Sat. at 10 P.M. Following every film there is a party. The large beer garden opens at 6 P.M. Wed.-Sun. There are bars on two levels. Use S-Bhf Potsdam Stadt, bus 694.

**Lindenpark**, in the neighborhood of the Defa film studios in Babelsberg, is Potsdam's second cultural house. Although somewhat more mainstream, Lindenpark's program and music (HipHop and Crossover bands) is similar to the Waschhaus'.

Blues clubs are popular in Potsdam. On Gutenbergstraße you find the **Gutenberg** blues club. At Zeppelinstraße 29, you find **Zepellin**. In Babelsberg is the **Kartoffel Club** ("Potato Club") on Großbeerenstraße.

The most popular disco in Potsdam is **Pflaumenbaum** ("Plumb Tree") on Zeppelinstraße. There is a disco on Friendship Island next to Potsdam Stadt train station called the **Die Insel**, which is also a restaurant and café. The **Spartacus** is on Bröderstraße.

Since 1992, the Theaterhaus Am Alten Markt, Berliner Straße 27a, Tel. (0331) 2800693, Fax (0331) 2800691, directly between the Nikolai Church and the Old City Hall, has served as the temporary home of the **Hans-Otto-Theater**, which presents acclaimed opera, musical, theater, and dance productions plus children's and youth theater. There are also productions in the baroque Palace Theater in the New Palace.

# Glossary

## Handy Words in Berlin

| | |
|---|---|
| Allee | Avenue |
| Apotheke | Prescription drug store |
| Ausgang | Exit |
| Auskunft | Information window |
| Ausverkauft | Sold out |
| | |
| Bhf | Abbreviation for *Bahnhof*, commonly used for U-and S-Bhf |
| BRD | German initials for *Bundesrepublik Deutschland*, formerly only West Germany, now united Germany |
| BVB | *Berliner Verkehrs-Betriebe* (Transit Authority of West Berlin) |
| BVG | *Berliner Verkehrs-Gesellschaft* (Former transit Authority of East Berlin) |
| Bahnhof | Train station (including U- and S-Bahnen) |
| Bahnsteig | Train platform |
| Berg | Mountain, hill |
| Bezirk | Administrative unit of Berlin |
| Brücke | Bridge |
| | |
| CDU | Christian Democratic Union (Conservative political party) |
| Chaussee | Highway |
| | |
| DB | *Deutsche Bahn*, Railroads of Germany *also* *Deutsche Bundesbahn*, Former West German Railroads |

| | |
|---|---|
| DDR | *Deutsche Demokratische Republik*, German Democratic Republic, former East Germany |
| DR | *Deutsche Reichsbahn*, former name of the German Railroads and in the East under the DDR |
| Damm | Road constructed over marshy land |
| Denkmal | Memorial |
| Dom | Cathedral |
| | |
| Einbahnstraße | One-way street |
| Eingang | Entrance |
| | |
| FDP | Free Democratic (political) Party |
| FRD | English initials for Federal Republic of Germany (present Germany and former West Germany) |
| Fahrkarten | Train/bus tickets |
| Feiertag | Holiday |
| Ferien | Vacation |
| Fernbahnsteig | Platform for mainline trains |
| Fernfahrkarten | Tickets for intercity trains |
| Flughafen | Airport |
| Freibad | Outdoor swimming |
| Frühstuck | Breakfast |
| | |
| GDR | German Democratic Republic (English initials for former East Germany) |
| Garni | Hotel without restaurant |
| Gasse | A secondary street |
| Gastarbeiter | A foreign laborer in Berlin |
| Gemütlichkeit | A homey presence |
| Gestapo | *Geheime Staatsplizei* (Secret Service Police) |
| Gründerzeit | Time of formation of the German Reich marked by representative architecture in Berlin from 1871 to about 1890 |
| gucken | To see, look |

| | |
|---|---|
| H | Symbol used to indicate bus or streetcar stop, *Haltestelle* |
| Hallenbad | Indoor swimming pool |
| Handy | Cellular Telephone |
| Hof | Courtyard |
| | |
| Imbiß | Snack counter or shop |
| Insel | Island |
| | |
| Jugendherberg | Youth hostel |
| Jugendstil | Art Nouveau |
| | |
| Kaiser | Emperor |
| Kasse | Cash register; ticket office |
| Kaufhaus | Department store |
| kein | Not any |
| Keller | Basement or cellar |
| Kiez | Distinctive neighborhood to which its residents are sentimentally attached |
| Kneipe | In Berlin, a pub ranging from cool neon hangout or a plush lounge, trendy disco, or stand-up snackbar, an exclusive restaurant or a plain living room *cum* beer tap |
| Kongreß | Convention |
| König | King |
| Kurfürst | Elector |
| | |
| Land | German state; country |
| Lokal | Bar, where people congregate |
| | |
| Mietskasern | Crowded rental housing tenement |
| | |
| Nazi | *National Sozialistiche Deutsche Arbeitpartei* (National Socialist German Workers' Party) |
| | |
| Ossi | East Berliner |
| Ost | East |

| PDS | Party of Democratic Socialism, former Communist political party in East Germany |
| Platz | City square |
| Postfach | Post office box |
| Punks | Anarchistic, relatively unorganized left wing similar to those in other countries (see Skinheads) |
| Rathaus | Town/city hall |
| Rathauskeller | Restaurant/saloon in cellar of town hall |
| Raver | Techno music disciple participating in Love Parade |
| Reich | Empire |
| Reinigung | Dry cleaning |
| Reisebüro | Travel bureau |
| SA | *Sturmabteilung* (storm battalion) |
| SPD | Social Democratic (Labor) Party |
| S.S. | *Schutzstaffel* (guard detachment) |
| S-Bahn | *Schnellbahn*, rapid-transit train) |
| Schloß | Palace |
| Schnauze | Typical sarcastic Berlin humor |
| See | Lake |
| Skinheads | Small, extreme right-wing, antiforeigner, racist group, dangerous primarily in Cottbus and Halle (see Punks) |
| Stadt | City |
| Stadtviertel | City quarter |
| Stasi | *Staatsicherheitsdienst* (DDR Secret Police) |
| Strandbad | Beach |
| Straße | Street |
| Szene | Alternative living style |
| T | Symbol used to indicate taxi stand |
| Tankstelle | Gasoline station |
| Tor | Gate, city gate, as *Brandenburger Tor* |

| | |
|---|---|
| Trabi | *Trabant,* the polluting, noisy, and ill-made East German automobile that is so beloved and so hated |
| Treuhand | Former German office charged with privatizing former DDR properties |
| Tschüß | Good-bye (very familiar and very common in Berlin) |
| Turm | Tower |
| | |
| U-Bahn | *Untergrundbahn* (subway) |
| Ufer | Lake or river shore |
| | |
| Verkauf | Sale, Sales window |
| Verkehrsamt | Tourist Office |
| Viertel | A quarter; city quarter |
| ViP | Potsdam Transit Authority |
| | |
| Wäsch Center | Laundromat |
| Wäscherei | Laundry (by piece) |
| Weg | Path |
| Wende | "Turning," the events of the reunification of East and West Germany |
| Wessi | West Berliner |
| | |
| Zweite Frühstück | Literally, "Second Breakfast," but served in the afternoon for Berliners keeping late hours |

# Index

# Index of Hotels

# Index of Restaurants and Cafés